Usury in Christendom

Usury in Christendom

The Mortal Sin that Was and Now Is Not

A Study of the Rise of the Money Power in the West

MICHAEL HOFFMAN

Independent History and Research

No Man Can Serve Two Masters

For either he will hate the one, and love the other; or else he will hold to the one, and despise the other. Ye cannot serve God and mammon.[i]

Matthew 6:24

---

[i] "*Mammon* is derived from the Aramaic word for riches (*mamona*) occurring in the Greek text of Matt. vi. 24 and Luke xvi. 9-13, and retained in the Vulgate. Owing to the quasi-personification in these passages, the word was taken by mediaeval writers as the proper name of the devil of covetousness....From the 16th century onwards it has been current in English, usually with more or less of personification, as a term of opprobrium for wealth regarded as an idol or as an evil influence" (*Oxford English Dictionary*).

 For information, address Independent History and Research, Post Office Box 849, Coeur d'Alene, Idaho 83816.

Third printing, December 2016

ISBN: 978-0-9703784-9-1

An index to the contents of this book is available online:
http://bit.ly/2fIfk0q

Portions of this book first appeared in *Revisionist History*, issues no. 12, 34, 46, 50, 51 and 55.

Cover illustration: Lucas Cranach the Elder, *Christ Drives the Usurers out of the Temple* (1521). "Cranach's enraged Jesus was celebrated as a 'burgher Apostle' striking out against *Fuggerei*...an epithet for the netherworld of contemporary commercial greed...a reference to the financier Jacob Fugger, who presided over an Augsburg-based trans-European banking empire" (Steven Ozment, *The Serpent and the Lamb*, p. 16). Ozment's reference is to an earlier work by Cranach, *Christ Driving the Money Changers Out of the Temple* (1510-1511). Frontispiece: Albrecht Dürer, *Dance Around the Golden Calf* (1507).

For the Kingship of Christ

Adveniat regnum tuum: fiat voluntas tua, sicut in caelo et in terra.

TABLE OF CONTENTS

Yahweh, who shall abide in thy tabernacle? Who shall dwell in thy holy hill?...He that does not ask interest on loans, and cannot be bribed to victimize the innocent.

Psalm 15: 1 and 5.

Psalm 15 is sometimes explained away by the apologists for usury as being a reference only to the "ideal person," just as some Catholic theologians since the Renaissance have established a loophole in Christ's command to "lend expecting nothing in return" by qualifying it as a "counsel of perfection" and equating it with His instruction to sell everything and give it to the poor, "if thou would be perfect." [ii] Unfortunately for the usury apologists, Christ did not connect perfection with his command to lend freely.

[ii] Matthew 19: 16-22. Even in this case the Fathers of the Church have disputed the notion that this counsel was limited in its scope or application. Cf. *On Social Justice: St. Basil the Great,* translated by C. Paul Schroeder (St. Valdimir's Seminary Press, 2009) pp. 53-58.

The upright man is law-abiding and honest...He never charges usury on loans, takes no interest, abstains from evil...It is Yahweh who speaks.

Ezekiel 18: 5; 8-9

"The natural form therefore, of the art of acquisition is always, and in all cases, acquisition from fruits and animals. That art, as we have said, has two forms: one which is connected with retail trade, and another which is connected with the management of the household. Of these two forms, the latter is necessary and laudable; the former is a method of exchange which is justly censured, because the gain in which it results is not naturally made, but is made at the expense of other men. The trade of the petty usurer is hated most, and with most reason: it makes a profit from currency itself, instead of making it from the process (i.e., of exchange) which currency was meant to serve. Currency came into existence merely as a means of exchange; usury tries to make it increase (as though it were an end in itself). This is the reason why usury is called by the word we commonly use (the word *tokos*, which in Greek also means breed or offspring); for as the offspring resembles its parent, so the interest bred by money is like the principal which breeds it and it may be called 'currency the son of currency.' Hence we can understand why, of all modes of acquisition, usury is the most unnatural."

Aristotle (350 B.C.) [iii]

[iii] *The Politics of Aristotle*, trans. Ernest Baker (Oxford: Clarendon Press, 1948), I.x.4-5. "...these immortal words...have shaped the development of Western commercial, legal, religious, and ethical institutions since their inception." —Stephen J. Grabill.

"When asked,"What is to be said of making profit by usury?' Cato replied, 'What is to be said of making profit by murder?"

Cicero (44 B.C.) [iv]

[iv] *De officiis in sine*, book ii.

"Whenever you have the intention of providing for a poor man for the Lord's sake, the same thing is both a gift and a loan, a gift because of the expectation of no repayment, but a loan because of the great gift of the Master who pays in his place, and who, receiving trifling things through a poor man, will give great things in return for them. 'He that hath mercy on the poor, lendeth to God.' Do you not wish to have the Lord of the universe answerable to you for payment?"

St. Basil, circa 370 A.D. [v]

---

[v] St. Augustine wrote: "Miserly man, why do you lend compound interest to men? Lend to God a hundred-fold you will have eternal life" ("*Homo miser, cur foenearis homini? Foenerare Deo et centuplum accipes vitam aeternam possidebis*").

"Si quis usuram accipit, rapinam facit, vita non vivit."

("If someone takes usury, he commits robbery, he shall not live")

St. Ambrose, *De bono mortis* (ca. 386 A.D.)

"Usura radix omnia malorum." [vi]

("Usury is the root of all evil")

St. Edward the Confessor, King of England

As monarch, St. Edward (circa 1003-1066), the last Saxon King of England, banished all who charged interest on loans. Usurers who remained in England were subject to the confiscation of their property and declared to be outside the protection of the law (i.e. outlaws). [vii]

A few months before his death, Edward's usury-free England, "was a rich and prosperous kingdom...Later generations did right to appeal to the good old laws of King Edward. He had become a symbol of a way of life which refused to die..." [viii] King Edward was canonized in 1161. His feast day on the traditional Roman Catholic calendar is October 13.

[vi] *Leges ecclesiasticae.*

[vii] Cf. *Leges Edwardi Confessoris* (ca. 1130), cap. 37, *De usaraiis.*

[viii] Frank Barlow, *Edward the Confessor* (University of California Press, 1984), pp. 286 and 288.

"Usurae arte nequissima ex ipso auro aurum nascitur."

("By the detestable art of usury gold
gives birth to gold").

Gratian,[ix] *Decretum* D.47, c.8

[ix] The twelfth century scholar Gratian, author of the immense compendium, *Concordantia discordantium canonum*, more commonly known as the *Decretum Gratiani*, was "the founder of the science of canon law" (*Catholic Encyclopedia* [1913]).

"Usury is generally prohibited because if it were allowed all manner of evils would ensue...It is clear that practically every evil follows from usury."

Pope Innocent IV (1200 - 1254)
Commentaria super libros quinque Decretalium[x]

---

[x] Frankfurt: Hieronymus Feyerabendt, (1570), ad X 5.19 rubr. Before rising to the papacy, Innocent IV had been a canonist and professor of canon law at the University of Bologna. His *Commentaria* is regarded as a brilliant work aimed, in part, at attempting to "coordinate the legitimate aspirations of secular power with the requirements of a Christian society" (*New Catholic Encyclopedia*, vol. 7, p. 525).

"In these days prevailed the horrible nuisance of the *Caursines* (bankers), to such a degree that there was hardly any one in all England, especially among the bishops, who was not caught in their net. Even the king himself was held indebted to them in an incalculable sum of money. For they circumvented the needy in their necessities, cloaking their usury under the show of trade, and pretending not to know that whatever is added to the principal is usury, under whatever name it may be called..."

Matthew of Paris, *English History* (1255) [xi]

[xi] Trans. by J. A. Giles, (London: H. G. Bohn, 1849), Vol. I, p. 2; reprinted in Roy C. Cave & Herbert H. Coulson, eds., *A Source Book for Medieval Economic History,* (Milwaukee: The Bruce Publishing Co., 1936; reprint ed., New York: Biblo & Tannen, 1965), pp. 179-180).

"...new orders of itinerant friars like the Franciscans and Dominicans organized preaching campaigns, traveling from town to town, village to village, threatening (usurious) moneylenders with the loss of their eternal souls if they did not make restitution to their victims."

David Graeber, *Debt: The First 5,000 Years*

"These mendicant friars supplemented the Lateran texts with their own...horrifying tales about the ghastly, agonizing fates awaiting all usurers in the eternal fires of Hell....The impact of the Franciscan and Dominican preaching orders also served to convince most secular governments of their sworn duty to enforce the anti-usury bans with harsh, pitiless vigor. Further strengthening the anti-usury campaign were the papal *Decretales* that Pope Gregory IX...issued in 1234. They commanded all Christian rulers to expel all usurers and to nullify all wills and testaments of unrepentant usurers."

John Munro [xii]

[xii] *Religione e istituzioni nell'economia europea: 1000-1800* (Firenze University Press, 2012), p. 181.

“Usury cries to the children of prodigality in the streets, ‘All you that will take up money or commodities on your land or possibilities, so as to banquet, riot and be drunk, come unto us and you shall be furnished; for gain we will help to damn both your souls and our own.”

Thomas Nashe, *Christ’s Tears Over Jerusalem* (1593)

Usurers "live in idleness: for usury, as one well saith, is gainful idleness; they walk inordinately, seeking gain by a trade of sin, even as the common thief or baud (pimp) doth: for what is a usurer but as (St.) Bernard saith, *fur legatis*, a thief...The Philosopher matches the usurer with the baud: and to the same purpose observe the coherence, Deut. 23: 18-19."

George Downame, *Lectures on XV Psalm* (1604).

“And yet in these days, if that men have riches,
Though they be hangmen, usurers or witches,
Devils-incarnate, such as have no shame
To act the thing that I shall blush to name,
Does that disgrace them one whit? Fie, no.
...There is no shame for rich men in these times,
For wealth will serve to cover any crimes...”

George Wither, *Abuses Stript and Whipt* (1613) [xiii]

[xiii] Wither’s writing “gave such offense that he was committed to the Marshalsea prison for several months.” *British Bibliographer* 1 (1810), pp. 4-5.

"Nature has established all things under the sun; a certain term and pitch, when they shall make stay of increase and when they shall be multiplying; the land, if it lacks a jubilee, will in time grow heartless; houses if not repaired will decay; trees will stop bearing and cattle breeding when they grow old. Men's labor and skill will fail with the passing of years. Only the usurer's money doth multiply infinitely. And this is not unnatural?" [xiv]

Roger Turner, *The Usurer's Plea Answered*
(London, 1634)

[xiv] In the late 1970s, during the zenith of the counter-culture, Wall Street brokerage firm Smith Barney became renowned for a series of iconic television commercials featuring the eminent British actor John Houseman offering a stern, if indirect, rebuke to the organic farmers, mechanics and carpenters who had dropped off the grid, were condemning the corruption of the System and horrifying their elders. Acting as a spokesman for the older generation, Houseman stated, concerning the house of usury known as Smith Barney, "They make money the old fashioned way. They earn it." Another Houseman advertisement made reference to Smith Barney's "good old-fashioned work." Many gray heads in the television audience no doubt nodded their assent, simultaneously conveying their disapproval of the young people who had chosen manual trades and meagre incomes over "respectable" money multiplication. Smith Barney wanted its target audience to think that usury-based investments represented something that was "earned," as part of a venerable tradition, contrasted with the supposed shiftless irresponsibility of the back-to-the-land counter-culture. (The Smith Barney name was dropped in September, 2012 after the brokerage was acquired by Morgan Stanley Wealth Management).

"There is one species of this price or reward...when money is lent on a contract to receive not only the principal sum again, but also an increase by way of compensation for the use; which generally is called *interest*...the enemies to interest...hold...any increase of money to be indefensibly usurious. And this they ground as well on the prohibition of it by the law of Moses among the Jews, as also upon what is said to be laid down by Aristotle, that money is naturally barren, and to make it breed money is preposterous, and a perversion of the end of its institution, which was only to serve the purposes of exchange and not increase. Hence the school divines (scholastic theologians) have branded the practice of taking interest as being contrary to the divine law both natural and revealed; and the canon law has proscribed the taking any, the least, increase for the loan of money, as a mortal sin."

Sir William Blackstone, *Commentaries on the Laws of England: Book the Second* [xv]

[xv] Clarendon Press (1775), chapter 30, pp. 454-455.

"Do you think Wordsworth could have written such poetry, if he had ever had dealings with money lenders?"

Percy Bysshe Shelley [xvi]

[xvi] Quoted in Claire Tomalin, *Shelley and His World* (London: Thames and Hudson, 1980). p. 48.

"Hegemony flows from the financial markets...and the whole of national and international life is increasingly organized around the model of speculation and debt."

Richard Seymour (2011)

"This is the prejudice against all heresies: that that thing is true, whatsoever was first; that is corrupt, whatsoever came after."

Concilium Nicinum

1

Introduction

This book is concerned with examining how the money-lovers entered and then occupied the Church.

After the Nativity, Last Supper, Crucifixion and Resurrection narratives in the New Testament, there is perhaps no more galvanizing or electrifying image than that of Jesus Christ driving the money-changers out of the Temple (John 2: 15-15; Matthew 21: 12-13). This confrontation is a gospel commentary on greed in general: "We see here how strong is the love of gain — the ruling passion of mankind. Not even the sacredness of the temple, the presence of God, the...ceremonials of religion, deterred them from this unholy traffic. So wicked men and hypocrites will always turn religion, if possible, into gain." [1]

The question is seldom asked, however, what was it that made the money-changing unholy? What specific form of avarice was in operation which brought down the righteous wrath of Jesus Christ?

In the first century A.D., to make an offering, pilgrims, as a matter of necessity, had to change foreign money into the half-shekel. "It is not easy to see the changing of coins (for the benefit of pilgrims to the Temple) as an abuse, unless those engaged in the practice were charging an unjust commission." [2]

According to the First Century A.D. oral traditions of the Pharisees as committed to writing in Mishna Sheqalim 1:3-6, money changers who had "set up in the Temple" exacted "surcharges" for their services.

---

[1] Albert Barnes, Commentary on John 2: *Barnes Notes on the New Testament.*

[2] Raymond Brown, *The Anchor Bible Commentary, The Gospel According to John I-XII* (Doubleday).

The battle we will examine consists, in part, of an economic theology that addressed a major moral conflict: a rising merchant class and its obligation to engage in commerce and exercise property rights in accordance with God, who is the supreme owner of all property, over which mankind has only stewardship. Here we encounter the battle with man-made philosophies of cupidity, such as libertarianism and "free market" capitalism, which assert an absolute right to use and dispose of property as the owners see fit. The Church historically ruled that no one had an absolute right to retain a surplus of wealth which others may need. Consequently, all forms of commerce and acquisition of wealth had to be conducted with due regard for the mutual needs of one's neighbors. These needs had a moral claim on the property, goods and other material resources of the property owner and merchant. This is largely incomprehensible to Christians today, for whom the right to pursue wealth is a fundamental axiom of their existence. "As long as I become affluent honestly, what is the problem?" they ask. The problem is that, in matters of money, contemporary "Christianity" represents a drastic departure from the spirit of the original Biblical, patristic and ecclesiastic foundation, out of which grew Christendom and the civilization of Europe. Call your pursuit of wealth whatever you like, but don't degrade the morals and ethics of Jesus Christ by calling it Christian.

"The evil of usury was taken for granted, because the practice was forbidden in the Scriptures. The divine commands repeatedly in the Bible sufficed for the guidance of those generations. But usury meant the taking of gain for the use of money...How then could trade be justified, for certainly trade involved selling at a profit? This was a real difficulty of conscience which was argued throughout the Middle

Ages. The normal answer was invariably the same. You may trade at a profit, you may not trade *for* profit. Your object must not be primarily to make a profit, but primarily to either earn your living or to help your fellow-men. It is...a matter of intention. This intention was essential, theologians believed, because it gave a purpose, and therefore a limitation, to the making of money. To make money for gain was wrong because there could be no limitation to it: never could there be a reason to cease making money, never, therefore, a limit to the amount of your money, whereas...once you had provided adequately for yourself and your own, whatever remained over and above was not yours at all, but belonged to the poor. It must be given to the poor. There was attached to it a *jus pauperum*.[3] The rich man might select his particular form of charity, but to some charity, divine or human, all superfluous wealth must go. To the mind of the Middle Ages this satisfied the teaching of the Scriptures: the substitution of a moral purpose for mere indefinite making of money." [4]

Christianity does not grant license to human nature. The license of the human being to sin is forbidden. Fornication is regarded as one of the most exquisite pleasures of our times and many modern people believe that only a fool would fail to take advantage of a situation where the opportunity arose with a man or woman of outstanding looks and personality. To the carnal mentality of the "natural man" it would be insane to do otherwise. Christianity is at war with this fallen human nature. This is its founding premise, from the Book of Genesis onward. What the carnal mentality often considers to be natural, practical and even necessary, constitutes the

---

[3] The rights of the poor.

[4] Bede Jarrett, *Social Theories in the Middle Ages*, pp. 167-168.

"wages of sin" for the soul that has been regenerated by the grace of Jesus Christ. Christianity is counter-cultural or it is nothing. For the better part of fifteen hundred years the Church made war on any compromise with Christ's Truth. Since then it has, in certain respects, cut a deal with the spirit of the world and the god of this world.

How do we account for beliefs that were not sold to the highest bidder, or merchandized according to a determinism that rules revolutionary change to be inevitable and irresistible, and where considerations of "practicality" and "being reasonable" did not result in obfuscations of the backbone of the Faith? According to that Faith, all charging of interest on loans of money is theft. How is it that moderns are astonished at the abhorrence of a moral allowance for theft?

It is the most serious kind of nullification to tamper with a law that comes from the Word of God and was upheld by the Church for fifteen centuries. The law against usury was gradually whittled away. The Renaissance and later era Roman Catholic Church was able to camouflage the overthrow. Permission for usury was mostly granted ad hoc, as a practical, bureaucratic and administrative matter. The more it became the custom and practice of Catholics, the more the ancient Biblical and ecclesiastic laws against usury were derogated and eventually totally nullified. A similar stratagem was used by Pope Paul VI in 1969 to eliminate the centuries-old Tridentine Mass of Pope Pius V, which had been in near-universal use throughout the Church.

Paul VI did not explicitly forbid the Tridentine Mass; he would have been hard pressed to justify such a ban on so venerable a rite. Rather, the Tridentine Mass was suppressed by means of a Machiavellian stratagem: a positive act rather than a negative one, the nearly universal promulgation of Pope Paul's New Mass. In addition to the cunning means by which the

Tridentine Mass was nearly abolished in the pontificate of Paul VI, tradition-minded Catholics are alert to the changes in doctrine concerning religious liberty which were promulgated at Vatican II:

"...souls concerned for their eternal welfare must understand as fully as possible...the (Second Vatican) Council declares that by reason of the dignity of his nature, the human person has the right to practice the religion of his choice. Accordingly society must protect religious liberty and organize the peaceful co-existence of the various religions. These are invited to take part in ecumenical dialogue, since they all possess their own part of truth....Thus the doctrine of religious liberty, as expressed in the Conciliar document *Dignitatis Humanae* no. 2, contradicts the teachings of Gregory XVI in *Mirari Vos*, of Pius IX in *Quanta Cura*, of Leo XIII in *Immortale Dei* and of Pius XI in *Quas Primas*. The doctrine expressed in the Dogmatic Constitution *Lumen Gentium* no. 8, according to which divine Providence uses non-Catholic sects as means of salvation, contradicts the teachings of Pius IX in the *Syllabus,* of Leo XIII in *Satis Cognitum* and of Pius XI in *Mortalium Animos*. These novel doctrines which along with many others contradict the formal and unanimous teachings of Popes before the Council, can only be qualified in the light of Catholic dogma as heretical." [5]

One wonders whether "souls concerned for their eternal welfare" must understand as fully as possible that local bishops from the 1500s onward, with the

---

5 *Bishop Williamson's Eleison Comments,* issue no. 250 (London, England: April 28, 2012). www.dinoscopus.org This writer does not share Bishop Williamson's understanding of the provenance of religious liberty – he traces it to the Enlightenment. Other tradition-oriented Catholics have termed it a masonic doctrine. We have another point of view which we hope to present in a book on freedom of conscience.

cooperation of the Vatican – and later, popes of the 16th, 18th, 19th and 20th centuries such as Leo X, Benedict XIV, Pius VIII and Benedict XV – redefined usury and lifted the ban on it as part of a gradual process of betrayal of Christ and His Church by heretical popes; a process initiated in 1515 by Medici Pope Leo X who permitted usury for a "good cause" (assistance to the poor), using a double contract as a thinly veiled disguise for the mortal sin which, after one thousand fifteen hundred years, suddenly was not.

There is nothing unprecedented about the overthrow of Catholic dogma at the Second Vatican Council. Catholic dogma on the abominable crime of usury was overthrown by a process of osmosis beginning in earnest in the late 15th century. The novel doctrine that interest on loans of money is not sinful contradicts the unanimous teachings of popes and councils before the Renaissance. It therefore can only be viewed as heretical.

Pope Paul VI was not the first pope guilty of heresy according to traditional reasoning. All those Renaissance popes who consented to the use of the technique of gradualism for the quiet overthrow of the ancient truth about usury, and those popes who altered the definition, teaching and understanding of usury – Benedict XIV, Pius VIII and Benedict XV – and *all subsequent popes who did not correct the egregious error of their predecessors and restore the Church to its original dogma on usury, are, it would seem, guilty of heresy*.

Even otherwise eminent popes bear this guilt since, by their inaction, they upheld a precedent for revolutionary change. In view of these suppressed facts, what happened at Vatican II and in the post-Conciliar era under Paul VI and subsequent popes is neither surprising nor strange. Having dumped God's law against usury it became open season on any other sacred dogma thenceforth.

Like the Catholic laity of Tudor England who formed the majority of the population of the England of King Edward VI and who were coerced into abandoning the Latin Mass, the vast majority of Catholic laity had next to nothing to do with the erosion and eventual abolition of the Catholic dogma on usury, or for that matter, Vatican II religious liberty, or Pope Paul VI's New Mass. Culpability falls almost entirely upon the bishops and popes. The laity are only culpable in so far as they submitted to the revolutionary changes, due to their exaggerated and inordinate concept of obedience to the hierarchy — an "obedience" which encumbered them to such an extent that they forsook their duty to sufficiently love Jesus Christ by upholding the integrity of His Gospel (John 14:15).

The money changers entered Christ's Church long ago, but for some odd reason, tradition-minded Catholics haven't been nearly as vigilant about this heresy as they have been about "religious liberty" and the New Mass. The idea that heretical popes are only a modernist phenomenon is a fairy tale, and it may be that this myth is too dear to the hearts of certain Catholics for them to abandon it. [6]

Modernism bloomed in the 20th century, but its roots are deep in the Renaissance. The results are that the Church itself now acts as Shylock through its

---

[6] Some Catholic traditionalists believe the "See is vacant" — that at present there's no valid pope to head the Church. They are known as "*sedevacantists*" because they believe that all modern popes since John XXIII, or, at the latest, Paul VI, are "material heretics." If their logic were consistent they would recognize that numerous popes of the past who permitted or advocated the practice of a mortal sin via their embrace of the Renaissance/modernist doctrine on usury, were also "material heretics" and therefore not popes and not someone to whom allegiance was owed, according to the sedevacantists' own logic.

"Vatican bank" and cognate financial operations, engaging in widespread usurious practices.

Double-Talking Encyclical

While there are documents indicating the derogation of the laws against usury, extant ones are few and far between. One such text, the cunning encyclical *Vix Pervenit,* seemingly opposed to usury, and issued by Pope Benedict XIV, was a double-talking document which is quoted by some Catholic opponents of usury to supposedly demonstrate that the papacy was completely opposed to usury as late as the year it was issued, 1745. These enthusiasts have failed to read or sufficiently note and comprehend Benedict XIV's "fine print," which established a gaping loophole for usury and more ominously, promoted a radical new definition of what usury denoted:

"We do not deny that at times together with the loan contract certain other titles — which are not intrinsic to the contract — may run parallel with it. From these other titles, entirely just and legitimate reasons arise to demand something over and above the amount due on the contract......it is essential...to avoid extremes, which are always evil. For instance, there are some who judge these matters with such severity that they hold any profit derived from money to be illegal and usurious..."

But of course "holding any profit derived from money to be illegal and usurious" had been the teaching of Holy Scripture and the Universal Church for fifteen hundred years. *Any profit* derived from a loan of money was deemed illegal and usurious. Pope Benedict XIV in his *Vix Pervenit* encyclical on loans, filled with pious exhortations to combat usury *according to his new understanding of it,* engaged in a revolutionary overthrow of the traditional definition of usury as that definition had been known. He lent his authority to the of-repeated lie which asserts that God and the Church never condemned "moderate" interest on money.

Where there is truth, there is Christ and His Church. Any church claiming to be of Christ that rejects or conceals the truth is not of His sheepfold. This book is an examination of the delusions and historical myths which have crippled our minds to such an extent that we cannot root out subversive forces in the Church because we know next to nothing about the rise and progress of those forces, even though many of us *think we know*.

Tradition-minded Catholics, for example, are alert to the dangers of ecumenism and the overthrow of *Extra Ecclesiam nulla salus*. These Catholics painstakingly trace and analyze the malefactors and the false philosophies and theological errors which inspired and directed them, yet when it comes to the revolutionary changes to usury law that arose with the connivance of certain popes, they are grossly ignorant and apathetic. In some flagrant cases, both Catholic and non-Catholic historians and commentators have misled Protestants into believing that it was the early Protestant Reformation that gave rise to usury and served as its main source of propagation.

In these pages we intend to pursue the spirit of Christ by pursuing the spirit of truth no matter where it leads or who may be offended by the shattering of cherished illusions. We cannot unmask the evil that afflicts our age without good counter-intelligence. Such good information will reach as far back as the eve of the Renaissance to track an occult conspiracy inside the Roman Catholic Church which manifested in a number of covert ways, and whose overt manifestation was the gradual relaxation and eventual abolition of the historic ban on usury, while shrewdly shifting the burden of culpability for that betrayal onto early Calvinists and Lutherans.

The notion that permission for usury sprang from the seedbed of Protestantism is a tissue of ignorance dispelled by an examination of a few of the salient facts of history which those who disseminate this buncombe have not bothered to do, yet they run their mouths and word processors with fierce conviction.

During the time of the Protectorate which administered the kingdom under England's first fully Protestant monarch, the boy-king Edward VI, the laws of England were returned to their immemorial Catholic position on usury, last implemented by the English Catholic King Henry VII in 1495. *All interest on money* was declared illegal.[7] The Protestant Edward VI's law banning usury is one of the most stirring jeremiads against this mortal sin ever legislated in Christendom.

An Act Against Usury
Edward VI

"...For as much as usury is by the word of God utterly prohibited as a vice most odious and detestable as in divers places in Holy Scriptures it is evident to be seen which thing is by no godly teaching, and persuasions can sink into the hearts of divers greedy, uncharitable and covetous persons of this realm, nor yet by any terrible threatenings of God's wrath and vengeance that justly hang over this realm for the great and open usury therein daily used and practiced,

---

7 King Henry VII's prohibition of usury in his realm was overthrown in 1545 by his son and successor, King Henry VIII. We term Edward VI as England's first fully Protestant king, rather than Henry VIII, because on the matter of the Mass, Henry VIII stubbornly refused the appeals of the Protestant divines and retained the Roman Catholic rite inviolate, much to their consternation and disapproval.

they will forsake such filthy gain and lucre, unless some temporary punishment be provided and ordained in that behalf. For reformation whereof be it enacted by the authority of this present parliament, that from the first day of May, which shall be in the year of our Lord 1552, the said act and statute concerning only usury, lucre, or gain of or for the loan, forbearing, or giving days of any sum or sums of money, be utterly abrogated, void and repealed. And furthermore be it enacted by the authority aforesaid, that from and after the first day of May next coming, no person or persons of what estate, degree, quality or condition, soever he or they be by any corrupt, colorable or deceitful conveyance, slight or engine, or by any way or mean shall lend, give, set out, deliver, or forbear any sum or sums of money to any person or persons, or to any corporation or body politic to or for any manner of usury increase, lucre gain, or interest to be had or hoped for over and above the sums so lent, given, set out, delivered or forborne, upon pain of forfeiture of the value, and well of the sum or sums so lent, given, set out, delivered or forborne, as also of the usury, increase, lucre, gain or interest thereof. And also upon pain of imprisonment of the body or bodies of every such offender or offenders, and also to make fine or ransom at the King's will and pleasure."

The Protestant supporters of King Edward VI's prohibition, termed usury "*praeter naturam*" (unnatural), "*idem ac hominem occidere*" (equivalent to manslaughter), "*proxima homicidi*" (next to homicide), "*malum in se*" (wrong in itself), and "damnable."

"Protestants like Latimer, Ponet, Lever and Crowley had no more mercy for the money-lender than had been shown by Cardinal Morton when he harangued parliament on the subject a half a century before, and they had all written or spoken against usury. The social doctrine rehearsed by Edward VI, with their emphasis on the need of controlling the operations of merchants and financiers, reflected the conventional mistrust of the monied interest; the (Protestant) clergy were demanding that usurers should be punished, as in the past by the canon law...The gentry...had no intention of undertaking a crusade to protect the moneybags of financiers who had squeezed them and the peasants impartially... (King Edward VI's) Act of 1552 as to usury...repealed (Henry VIII's) Act of 1545 (permitting usury), and forbad the taking of any interest whatever, under pain of imprisonment and fine, in addition to the forfeiture of principal and interest. Henceforward a pious nation was to live up to to the declaration of its parliament that, '...all usury is by the word of God utterly prohibited; a vice most odious and detestable, as in diverse places of Holy Scripture is evident to be seen.' The statute of 1552 did no more than re-enact principles which had been accepted for centuries..." [8]

The history of humanity's need for a raft of illusions salved by palliatives is a dismal one. A Roman Catholic Church aware of Original Sin should admit the original sin of its support for interest on money, and the constellation of evils that have evolved from it. Instead, the Church has kept usury intact while it dealt, sometimes dramatically, with symptoms. Leo XIII's 1891 encyclical *Rerum Novarum* ("On Capital and Labor"), was a brilliant and moving call for social justice for workers. It did all it could, within the empire of usury, to aid the plight of laborers. *Rerum Novarum* inspired Catholic activists from Peter Maurin to Rev. Fr. Charles Coughlin, both of whom led mass movements against the tyranny of plutocracy in

---

[8] Munro, op. cit., p. 170.

the twentieth century, and helped to align the Catholic Church in America with poor people and workers, even as the Church founded schools and hospitals such as Sacred Heart in Spokane, Washington, which for more than a century turned no one away from first class medical treatment for want of the ability to pay. *Rerum Novarum* did as much as possible to call on western society to end the oppression of working men and women, *except to abolish usury according to the original meaning:* any *interest on loans of money.* As a result, in the twenty-first century the sentiments behind *Rerum Novarum* are in retreat in the Catholic world and throughout the West. Usury and the Money Power are riding higher than ever because *usury cannot be reformed or palliated.* If we desire a Christian society, usury must be abolished. What is the use of calling for chastity while operating a prominent house of prostitution frequented by millions — and while absolving others of any sin in connection with its operation? One cannot campaign for Biblical justice for the poor and laborers while operating a house of usury, or while absolving others of sin in connection with its operation. The Roman Catholic Church has operated countless charities and philanthropies seeking to minister to what are, objectively, victims of usury. The usurers themselves relish this arrangement. They wreck people's lives and the Church picks up the pieces, ministering to the victims of debt peonage, while calling for a less oppressive rate of usury — rather like calling for a less immodest prostitute.

I salute the Catholic concern for the poor and the laborers, from the early church, through to St. Francis of Assisi and Dorothy Day. But until the root of the disease is addressed, the palliation of symptoms makes Catholics partners with Shylock in rendering the ravages of the mortal sin of usury slightly less onerous.

This failure of vision and will is exacerbated by the bait-and-switch which places the onus of the evil of usury on the Protestants. Catholics and Protestants are on both sides of the usury issue. Many prominent theorists of usury economics were and are Protestants. The same can be said for Catholics. But there are two crucial differences. 1. *Protestants first learned to accept usury from the bad example of influential Catholics.* 2. *Many notable Protestant theologians in the era of the early Reformation were steadfast opponents of usury in any form.* In addition to constituting the sin of false witness, scapegoating Protestantism or "Puritanism" for initiating usury in Christendom serves to absolve Catholics of the desperate need *to study the actual history* of the subversion of the Church, which was perpetrated, then as now, by Churchmen themselves. Only when Catholics take an axe to the *root* of the evil existing in their own ecclesia, rather than imagining that the root lies elsewhere, can they advance the restoration of the original and authentic Catholic teaching on interest on money, and seriously impede the financial monster now plaguing humanity.

Furthermore, when Protestants are relieved of the burden of the myth that usury was a founding principle of the sixteenth century Reformation, they are more likely to join with Catholics in pursuing with renewed vigor the reinstatement of the ecclesiastical category of interest on money as mortal sin.

S.C. Mooney, a leading contemporary Protestant opponent of interest on money, states, "What is being argued here is not a new idea, or a new interpretation of Scripture. It is the historic position. This is not a call to strike out in a new direction; it is a call to return to faithfulness to God. If we do not repent and return, we may expect more of God's discipline upon us, for He loves us and will discipline us to conform us to the image of Christ."

Usury is but one of many scourges wrought by the love of money and the empire of the Money Power which that ardor fosters. To understand how extreme is usury, let us recall that God did not intend that His people would be indebted for ten or twenty years *even if the loans were interest free*. Under the Biblical concept of the Jubilee, no indebtedness would last longer than the sabbatical seventh year. In the year after the last of seven such sabbatical years (7 x 7 = 49 years + 1), a Jubilee was to be declared and all debts canceled. Jesus Christ declared that He came to proclaim the Jubilee (the "acceptable year"). The key Jubilee passage from Leviticus (25:10) was engraved on the Liberty Bell in Philadelphia, Pennsylvania by the Founders of the United States of America.

What was our western world like before the debt-economy?

Thorold Rogers, Professor of Political Economy at Oxford University in the middle of the 19th century wrote: "At that time (i.e. the Middle Ages) a laborer could provide all the necessities for his family for a year by working fourteen weeks." G.N. Clark in his *The Wealth of England from 1496 to 1760,* writes of the medieval doctrine "that in all transactions a just price ought to be paid. This might be explained so as to mean very little more than that a seller committed a sin if he took more than the correct price...but it was often explained so as to condemn something more than simple cheating...it meant that the market price ought to be just and that meant that it ought to depend on the cost of production and not on unfair competition or on the power of the monopolist. There was a special sphere in which the doctrine of a just price took a form very natural in peasant society: in the sphere of finance it took the form of condemning usury...Indeed, Magna Carta had much to say about the evils of usury and sought to protect the property of the widow, the weak and the helpless from money-lenders. Thus it was that the fiery 19th century historian William Cobbett, after visiting Winchester Cathedral and marveling at its beauty, told his son: 'That building was made when there were no poor wretches in England called paupers...when every laboring man was clothed in good woolen cloth and when all had plenty of meat and bread ..."

Thus we have a picture of a well-fed, prosperous community, working commercially, or for gain, about one third of the year and with dozens of holidays a year (vacation days in honor of God or a saint, or a momentous victory). It was a time when Englishmen called their land "Merry England," when they owned their property with allodial title (irrevocably free and clear), instead of paying "rent" as property owners do now in America in the form of property taxes to the government.

It was in the Middle Ages of Europe when the magnificent Gothic cathedrals were constructed with voluntary subscription and labor, edifices of such beauty and power as to amaze the modern onlooker. Dozens were constructed, all without mortgages or debt of any kind; without usury. A society without usury is nowadays derided as inevitably backward, if not impossible. Those who visit the medieval Gothic cathedrals of Britain and Europe gaze upon massive edifices of splendor and proportion which we, with our usury and technology, have yet to equal.

It is interesting that the Protestant writer Gary North, who at one time was one of the leading false prophets of the 1999 Y2K panic ("the end of civilization as we know it"), is also on record justifying usury.[9] North regards the Old Testament's prohibition of usury against the poor (Exodus 22:22) as a justification

---

[9] Gary North, "The Moral Legitimacy of Interest and Banking," in *Biblical Economics Today,* vol. xi, no. 6.

for interest to be taken from brethren who aren't poor. Roger Fenton in his 1612 *A Treatise of Usurie* answers this error: "Immediately before this law of usury in Exod. 22:22, there is a law for widows and children: 'Thou shalt not trouble any widow or fatherless child.' Does it therefore follow that we may trouble a married woman or a child that has a father?"

The Critical Distinction Between Ger and Nokri

In a second example, Mr. North cites the permission to exact usury of foreigners in Deut. 23:20. He notes that this permission is coupled with another directive against the oppression of "strangers," and he draws the conclusion that interest-taking cannot be inherently oppressive, since oppression of strangers is prohibited in Leviticus 19:33-34 and interest-taking of strangers is permitted in Deut. 23:20.

In this case the premises of his argument are faulty, since his interpretation is built only upon the English text as found in the King James translation. *The "strangers" who are not to be oppressed in Leviticus are quite different from the "foreigners" of whom we may take usury in Deuteronomy.* In Leviticus the Hebrew term used is *ger*, and is sometimes given as "sojourners" in newer translations. In a parallel text, in Exodus 23:9 we read, "You shall not oppress a *ger*...for you were also *ger* in the land of Egypt." The *ger* were what we usually think of today as an "immigrant," i.e. someone from another country.

The key distinction is that the *ger* were not hostile to the Israelites in whose land they dwelt. As a condition of residing in another land they agreed to abide by the laws of that land. Thus, ancient Israel accommodated non-Israelites so long as they lived according to the laws of God. On the other hand, the "foreigners" spoken of in Deuteronomy were, as designated in Hebrew, *nokri*. In all usage of this term in the Old Testament, the *nokri* were wicked, detestable pagans, with whom God's people must not intermarry and whose gods they must not embrace. (Gen. 35:2; Ex. 23:23; Deu. 17:15; Josh. 24:23; I Sam. 7:3; Neh. 9:2,13:3). Israel was dedicated to unrelenting warfare against the *nokri*. Usury is a weapon of warfare.

Most Christians today would find it abhorrent even to consider mounting a holy war against enemies of our faith. Let us at least be equally horrified to consider participating in the warfare of usury against our own brethren. In his excellent book *Usury: Destroyer of Nations*, S.C. Mooney confronts the usury advocacy of Gary North and another prominent Protestant theologian, the late R.J. Rushdoony, both of whom argued the theory, which we will confront again later in these pages, that the Old Testament's usury proscriptions are qualified to protect only the poor from usury. Yet in Deuteronomy 23:19-20 there is no mention of the poor in the general prohibition:

"You shall not charge interest on loans to your brother, interest on money, interest on food, interest on anything that is lent for interest. You may charge a foreigner interest, but you may not charge your brother interest, that the Lord your God may bless you in all that you undertake in the land that you are entering to take possession of it."

For fifteen centuries this Bible passage was understood by the Church to mean exactly as it reads: zero interest on loans whether to the wealthy or the indigent. From the Renaissance onward however, modernist heretics created two loopholes in

Deuteronomy 23: that it only condemns high interest rates and that it only applies to the poor. [10]

S.C. Mooney: "Those who teach that a 'rich/poor' distinction qualifies God's law on usury commit an inconsistency, which subverts their method of qualifying the law on that basis. Deut. 15: 1-11 declares God's law on the remission of debts every seven years. This law is parallel in form to the law on usury...the statute on the remission of debts provides that, 'From a foreigner you may exact it, but your hand shall release whatever of yours is with your brother' (Deut. 15:3).

"...usury, which is generally unlawful, is especially unlawful and dangerous in the case of the poor...the poor are mentioned in these cases...in order to call attention to those most subject to oppression. The mention of a certain type of class of person does not imply that the law does not hold in the case of those not mentioned...The language involving the 'poor' in the Exodus and Leviticus texts has been noted. The statute on the remission of debts similarly exhorts: 'If there is among you a poor man of your brethren, within any of the gates in your land which the Lord your God is giving you, you shall not harden your heart nor shut your hand from your poor brother, but you shall open your hand wide to him and willingly lend him sufficient for his need, whatever he needs. Beware lest there be a wicked thought in your heart, saying, 'The seventh year, the year of release, is at hand,' and your eye be evil against your poor brother

---

10 For example, the *ESV Study Bible* (Crossway, 2008) commentary on Deut. 23: 19-20 misleadingly reads: "Cruelly high interest rates made situations worse. The prohibition of interest among Israelites protected the poor." The *ESV*'s dishonest insinuation is that Israelites were protected from *high* interest rates, not interest itself. By means of such underhanded tactics the Word of God is nullified and Christians are misdirected and deceived.

and you give him nothing, and he cry out to the Lord against you, and it become sin among you.' (Deut. 15:7-9).

"Amazingly, the very ones who claim that the mention of the poor in Exodus 22:25 and Leviticus 25:35 qualifies the usury statute, also bluntly state, without any qualification, that all debts are to be cancelled after six years...R.J. Rushdoony espouses the 'poor/rich' distinction as a qualification of the usury statute, and yet in the same volume states, '...no man is allowed to tax his own future by means of debt. The length of a debt is limited to six years (Deut. 15: 1-4). No man has a right to mortgage his future, since his life belongs to God.' [11]

"Gary North, another proponent of the 'poor/rich' distinction as a qualification of the usury law has said, '...a six year debt limitation is the maximum that is morally legitimate (given the provisions of the sabbatical years regarding the cancellation of all debts...)' [12]

"How is it that these scholars can find an inference in Exodus 22:25 and Leviticus 23:35 that usury is lawful in many cases, and yet fail to find a similar inference in Deuteronomy 15: 1-11? Why do they not hold that only the debts of 'poor' brethren are to be cancelled, and infer from this that it is lawful for one to continue to exact the debts of the 'rich'? The present writer agrees with their views concerning the remission of debts, particularly as cited above. The wonder is that they do not similarly expound on the usury statute, which is given in similar form."[13]

---

[11] Rushdoony, *The Institutes of Biblical Law*, p. 510.

[12] North, *An Introduction to Christian Economics* (1973), p. 10. Mooney also quotes from North's book, *Honest Money* (1986), p. 128, where North writes, "This too is basic to a Biblical social order: no loans to the faithful for over seven years (Deut. 15: 1-2)."

[13] S.C. Mooney, *Usury: Destroyer of Nations*, pp. 129-131.

Mr. North's theory about the non-oppressiveness of usury based on its Old Testament use on "strangers" was not original. We find it in later Calvinist publications, such as *Willison's Example of Plain Catechising Upon the Assembly's Shorter Catechism*, published in Dundee, Scotland in 1737: "*Q*. But were not the people of Israel discharged to take any usury or profit for lent money from their brethren? Deut. xxiii. 19. *A*. ...for strangers, who had another way of living, the Israelites were allowed to lend upon usury, and to share with them in their profits. Deut. xxiii. 20, which shews that the taking of interest is not oppressive in itself; for they are frequently prohibited to oppress a stranger, and yet allowed to take usury from him."

Richard Baxter, 1673: "Now I prove that such usury is not forbidden by God...It is expressly allowed to be used to strangers, Deut. xxiii. 19, 20, to whom nothing unjust or uncharitable might be done; only such a measure of charity was not required towards them as unto brethren." [14]

Baxter is regarded as one of the most learned and eminent Puritan exegetes of the latter half of the seventeenth century, yet here he is composing flimsy rationales on behalf of the Money Power, in the name of the Bible. He is preaching revolution — calling usury charitable and just — when in fact, "Usury was an act of murderous hostility, warfare by other means, licensed against the peoples who the Israelites were attempting to destroy, but unthinkable among people who had to live amicably together." [15]

Baxter's predecessor, the distinguished Puritan theologian Robert Bolton, forcefully restated the Biblical and patristic doctrine which Baxter, North

---

[14] *Christian Directory* (reprinted London, 1838), vol. 1, Part IV, chap. XIX, p. 838. His commentary, also on p. 838, on Christ's words in Luke 6:35 is egregious sophistry.

[15] David Hawkes, *The Culture of Usury*, p. 63.

and most modern thinkers who call themselves Christians have muddled, distorted and nullified: "Not so much as the least usury was lawful to a brother, whether he were rich or poor. If the Scriptures had put such a difference between the poor and the rich, as between the Israelite and the Canaanite: to the rich thou mayest, but to the poor Thou shalt not lend upon usury, then the case were clear. But Deut. 23: 19-20 God makes opposition, not between the poor and the rich, but between an Israelite and a Canaanite. For by stranger in that place, is meant the Hittites, the Gergashites, the Amorites, the Canaanites, the Perisites, the Hivites and Jebusites...these the Jews were commanded to destroy, Deut. 7:12. And usury was as teeth given them and allowed by God to eat them up withal." [16]

Charging interest on loans of money to Christians, or for that matter to any neighbor, turns the whole world into a population of strangers, which is what we have in our time; what Thomas Hobbes termed *bellum omnes contra omnia* (the war of all against all). In this market, called "free" (because it has been cut loose from the chief restraint on greed, the ban on usury), we devolve from the Lord's chosen people under the gospel dispensation, to a sub-human species defined mainly by our selfish appetites and acquisitions: we devolve into the "consumer," *homo economicus*.

Christ's Parable of the Talents

The Parable of the Talents is often taken to indicate Christ's approval for usury, [17] although for fifteen centuries the Church did not teach such a grotesque

---

[16] *A Short and Private Discourse* (1637).

[17] "Jesus's own parable of the talents...praises the existence of money lenders and condemns the failure to give them idle money as profligacy itself." —Jeffrey Tucker, "Catholics and 'Usury': A Tragic History," in *Crisis* magazine, Nov. 16, 2011.

and superficial interpretation, but plumbed the depth of the parable for the lesson Our Lord was seeking to impart: it is the *hard man* who expected his money to be put out at usury.

Luke 19:12-24: "He said therefore, A certain nobleman went into a far country to receive for himself a kingdom, and to return. And he called his ten servants, and delivered them ten pounds, and said unto them, Occupy till I come...And it came to pass, that when he was returned, having received the kingdom, then he commanded these servants to be called unto him, to whom he had given the money, that he might know how much every man had gained by trading.... And another came, saying, Lord, behold, here is thy pound, which I have kept laid up in a napkin: For I feared thee, because thou art an austere man: thou takest up that thou layedst not down, and reapest that thou didst not sow. And he saith unto him, Out of thine own mouth will I judge thee, thou wicked servant. Thou knewest that I was an austere man, taking up that I laid not down, and reaping that I did not sow: Wherefore then gavest not thou my money into the bank, that at my coming I might have required mine own with usury? And he said unto them that stood by, Take from him the pound, and give it to him that hath ten pounds."

The substantive point of the parable is that Jesus' statements are made in reply to the mentality of the servant who called him a "hard man" (in the Greek *austere*, i.e. harsh). The servant is terming his master, Jesus, a hard, ruthless man. The advice to put money at interest is based on an if/then proposition. The wicked servant had slandered his master in a feeble attempt to justify his own laziness. *If Christ is a cruel master,* then the servant is justified putting the money at interest.

The parable is not advocating usury, it is giving a lesson in the evil effects of being imprisoned by one's own bad thoughts. The key to understanding the parable may be found in Jesus' statement in Luke 19:22: "By your own words I will judge you, you worthless slave ..."

Bible scholar Ted Weiland: "...Note first that in addition to accusing the nobleman of being an austere or hard man, the wicked servant also accused him of taking up what he had not lain down, and reaping what he had not sown. In other words, he had accused his master of being a thief. Immediately following these false accusations, the master responds, 'Out of thine own mouth will I judge thee, thou wicked servant. Thou knewest that I was an austere man, taking up that I laid not down, and reaping that I did not sow. Wherefore then gavest not thou my money into the bank, that at my coming I might have required mine own with usury?'

"In other words, if as a servant, he considered his own master a thief, then as a servant of a thief, the very least he could have done was steal for his master in a way that would not have put him at any risk – by putting his money in a bank that paid usury. The Geneva Bible notes on Luke 19:23 concur: (e) 'To the bankers and money changers. Usury or loaning money at interest is strictly forbidden by the Bible (Ex 22:25-27; Deut. 23:19-20). Even a rate as low as one per cent interest was disallowed, (Nehemiah 5:11).'

"This servant had already told two lies. First he said the master was an austere or harsh man. This is a lie, for the Lord is merciful and gracious. Next he called his master a thief because he reaped where he did not sow. Finally the master said to him, why did you not add insult to injury and loan the money out at interest so you could call your master a 'usurer' too! If the servant had done this, his master would have been responsible for his servant's actions and guilty of usury.

"Geneva Bible Notes (1599) Yashua (Jesus) did not alter the law on usury, but validated it. He identified usury for exactly what it is – theft plain and simple. The parable of the talents also puts an end to the hypothesis that usurious business loans are acceptable. The word 'bank' in Luke 19:23 is translated from the Greek word *trapeza*, from which our English word 'trapeze' is derived – a circus apparatus that, at the best, is very risky. It is the same Greek word used in Matthew 21:12, translated as tables – as in the tables of the money changers that Yashua (Jesus) overthrew – which was followed by His chasing their owners with a scourge out of the Temple." [18]

Christ's Parable of the Unjust Steward and the Mammon of Unrighteousness

"And he said also unto his disciples, There was a certain rich man, which had a steward; and the same was accused unto him that he had wasted his goods. And he called him, and said unto him, How is it that I hear this of thee? give an account of thy stewardship; for thou mayest be no longer steward.

"Then the steward said within himself, What shall I do? for my lord taketh away from me the stewardship: I cannot dig; to beg I am ashamed. I am resolved what to do, that, when I am put out of the stewardship, they may receive me into their houses. So he called every one of his lord's debtors unto him, and said unto the first, How much owest thou unto my lord? And he said, An hundred measures of oil. And he said unto him, Take thy bill, and sit down quickly, and write fifty.

---

[18] Ted R. Weiland, *The Eighth Commandment: Thou Shalt Not Steal* (Scottsbluff, Nebrska: Mission to Israel, 2007). From *The Apostolic Bible,* the literal translation of Luke 19:23 from the Greek: "And therefore why did you not give my money unto the money-lenders table..."

Then said he to another, And how much owest thou? And he said, An hundred measures of wheat. And he said unto him, Take thy bill, and write fourscore.

"And the lord commended the unjust steward, because he had done wisely: for the children of this world are in their generation wiser than the children of light. And I say unto you, Make to yourselves friends of the mammon of unrighteousness; that, when ye fail, they may receive you into everlasting habitations" (Luke 16: 8-9).

"When Christ tells his followers to 'make friends of the unrighteous Mammon,' the word he uses (*Mammonas*) does not literally refer to a god or idol. It means rather 'the covetous man,' and was often rendered into Latin as *cupidus*. Christians are not asked to 'make friends' with him literally, but figuratively; they are to be like him in the sense that they should adopt the same acquisitive attitude toward figural and spiritual 'riches' as the covetous man does toward literal and earthly riches." [19]

Jesus did not commend the man's dishonesty. He calls him "unjust." He only used him as an illustration to show that even the most wicked sons of the world are shrewd enough to provide for themselves against coming troubles. Christians ought to be more shrewd because they are concerned with eternal matters.

"Proclaim liberty throughout the land to all the inhabitants thereof." Leviticus 25:10

Gary North charges that strict abstinence from all forms of usury will create a homeless people. This is true only in a nation full of mutual strangers and enemies, where no one would loan freely to his brother

---

[19] David Hawkes, *Culture of Usury*, p. 92 .

as God requires (Deut. 15:7-8; Matt. 5:42). On the other hand, how much homelessness would there be if borrowers were required to buy their houses only once, and not three times over? In the economics of the New World Order, one has a vested interest in his neighbor's perpetual need to borrow. In the economics of authentic Christianity, one loans freely to his neighbor because he has a vested interest in his neighbor's freedom and prosperity. Borrowing money can be a boon to families seeking homes to purchase and businessmen wanting to expand. But even loans without interest can become a problem if they result in long-term bondage to debt, since "the borrower is slave to the lender." (Proverbs 22:7). This is why the Bible ordained that loans were to expire within seven years, and in the Jubilee Year they were completely expunged, captives were freed and the land returned to the initial holders (not to banks, but to those with allodial title).

"You shall count off seven Sabbaths of years, seven times seven years...Then you shall make proclamation with the blast of the horn...you shall make proclamation with the horn throughout all your land. And you shall make holy the fiftieth year, and proclaim liberty throughout the land to all the inhabitants thereof. It shall be a Jubilee to you, every one of you shall return to your own ancestral holding, every one of you, to your family...You shall not sow, nor reap what grows, nor gather the grapes of the unpruned vines...And the land shall not be permanently sold, for the land is mine." Lev. 25: 8-23.

In a nation without a Jubilee, the government has ultimate title to all property, and the people have no claim to their own land. It is given away at will by usurping overlords, not just to the obedient and needy *ger,* but to the hostile and evil invader, the *nokri*.

It would be easy for modern people to dismiss the Jubilee year as an irrelevant atavism from the Stone Age of Old Testament times, were it not for the fact that some of the patriots who founded these United States believed it to be both relevant and binding. They also understood it to be more than just an every 50th year observance. They saw the year in which the success of the American Revolution was assured, as being the "acceptable year of the Lord," the Jubilee: "With the end of the American Revolution and the Treaty of Paris of Sept. 3, 1783, there was jubilation in the streets. The future looked bright...Many people even...believed that their debts had been dismissed when the war ended." [20]

Leviticus 25 was not only inscribed on the Liberty Bell, it was the campaign platform of laborers in Great Britain, led by Thomas Spence (1750-1814).[21] "Spence employs specific biblical passages to develop the concept of the Jubilee, the imagery of the old society's destruction...From Leviticus 25 Spence derived the Jubilee idea, whereby every fifty years each family recovers whatever land and property it had lost, as the entire society has a year-long sabbath or sabbatical...The land, owned by God, is subject to religious law and morality....one informing context for Spence's writing, then, is the message of social justice from the Pentateuch, prophets, and New Testament...Another of Spence's informing contexts...was the provincial radicalism of

---

[20] Michael Paulin, *The Ballad of Daniel Shays* (J.R. Greene, 1986).

[21] Spence suffered imprisonment for "seditious libel" and "high treason." Erroneously called England's first modern socialist, he was an enemy of big government and "giantism of all kinds." Even posthumously Spence was considered so threatening to the British establishment that three years after his death an Act of Parliament was passed prohibiting "all societies...calling themselves Spencean." ("Thomas Spence: The Trumpet of Jubilee," *Past and Present* [1977: vol. 76, no. 1]).

northeastern England in the period of protests against enclosures...The local squires tried to enclose the Newcastle commons (located on a moor) but protests...were able to repel these encroachments on ancient rights. This controversy formed the core of Spence's political ideology, as he based his 'plan' on parochial ownership of land and sharing of rents, a version of the very idea of a commons...Spence's land plan is 'little more than the Newcastle Town Moor Act writ large...'" [22]

Spence was a member of the Presbyterian High Bridge Chapel, led by the firebrand Rev. James Murray, whose 1768 pamphlet, *Sermons to Asses*, demanding radical social justice on Biblical principles, went through five editions and was reprinted in Philadelphia, Pennsylvania in 1774. Rev. Murray's mission was the education and organization of the British Christian people "concerning their civil and religious rights; in 1779 he lectured on the divine right of subjects to admonish their sovereigns...His *Sermons for the General Fast Day* (1781) include trenchant remarks on the corruptions of government...the right of resistance to oppressive and unjust laws and the justice of the American (revolutionary) cause." [23]

The modern liberal churches have persuaded the people that the Bible is a series of quaint parables and generic do-gooderisms with little practical application to economics or government. When government is mentioned in the more conservative churches it is in terms of supporting buccaneer capitalists and greed-is-good Right wing politicians who talk pro-life family values while they serve the Money Power, by removing all obstacles to its growth and suzerainty. This writer

---

22 Cf. Michael Scrivener, *Seditious Allegories* (Pennsylvania State University, 2001).

23 Cf. James E. Bradley, *Religion, Revolution and English Radicalism*.

resides in a region where the principal "Christian" newspaper in circulation is *The Capitalist Papers*. They have turned God into a bookkeeper who tracks their profits and merchandise and they don't see the blasphemy of their action because their shepherds are as ignorant as they are.

The authentic Biblical teaching about debt and finance, crime, punishment, imprisonment and how men are to govern, is strangely unknown or criminally falsified in this "information age" of ours, where the information is largely controlled, as our elections are, by the Money Power's ministers of Satan. The lovers of money are not prime targets of the "Religious Right." The mortal sin of greed is barely an issue for these deceitful workers. Yet, pray tell, what corrupts a nation and a people more than the love of money?

2

The Biblical, Patristic and Magisterial teaching on Usury

"Certainly, if the criterion of truth, as regards any doctrine, be that of St. Vincent of Lerins — that it has been held in the Church 'always, everywhere, and by all' — then on no point may a Christian of these days be more sure than that every savings institution, every loan and trust company, every bank, every loan of capital by an individual, every means by which accumulated capital has been lawfully lent even at the most moderate interest...is based on deadly sin..."

—Andrew Dickson White, co-founder and first President of Cornell University [24]

As we write these words everywhere Americans and Europeans toil under a mountain of usurious debt: students, parents of young families, the elderly, sick and infirm. Nationally, the *New York Times* reports that college students in the U.S. have "debt topping $1 trillion." [25]

In Idaho in 2012, a state that prides itself on its "Christian and conservative Republican ideals," an interest rate of up to 400% is permitted to "Payday" loan sharks by the Idaho legislature. Few priests or preachers in this heavily churched state have any thundering denunciations of this predation; nor do they impart the doctrine of the Word of God and His

---

[24] *History of the Warfare of Science with Theology in Christendom* (New York, 1897), chapter XIX: "From Leviticus to Political Economy."

[25] "Slowly, as Student Debt Rises, Colleges Confront Costs," *New York Times* (online edition), May 14, 2012.

Law concerning this ungodly oppression — what the Church historically termed *turpe lucrum* (shameful gain). What we have in our time among "Christians," even though they are well-versed in the laws of God and the traditions of His Church, is willful opposition to the established truth of God concerning money and interest on money, amounting to a determined and malicious hatred of His truth. We have tens of millions of "Christians" of this description and they are going to continue in their pursuit of interest on money even after this book is published and even if it should gain a vast audience, because to such people *God Himself sends spiritual blindness*. Their sin against Truth is so aggravated that God punishes it with final blindness and impenitence (II Thess. 2: 9-12). Without repentance there can be no forgiveness, and remission of sins is not obtained.

Interest on Loans of Money
The root and branch of the Money Power

Modern Protestants, Catholics, Mormons and Mennonites[26] are all guilty of this grotesque disobedience to God. Most would be appalled by a whorehouse in their midst, but live placidly among the banks and other houses of thievery which rob the people of their future through parasitic gain. Let us state from the outset that interest on money loans is the root and branch of the Money Power. This was known to the Church from its founding by Jesus Christ, until the dawn of the sixteenth century. Like many other bedrock Biblical and ecclesiastical truths held by the Church for centuries and now overthrown — the sanctity of marriage between a man and a woman and the fertility of the married couple in

---

[26] The founders of the Mennonite Church were implacably opposed to charging interest on loans of money. Over the years the Mennonites "drifted" from their founders' intentions and convictions.

bringing forth the offspring God ordained to be born — we are now taught that all the saints, councils and popes for more than 1,000 years had it wrong and misunderstood money and God's Word concerning it. By the light of modernity we are taught a new understanding and a new ethic amounting to a revolutionary heresy. It is from this revolt by heretics who invaded the Church that numerous other evils have followed in its wake. Rightly was it said that the love of money is the root of evil, yet today we chase after wraith-like symptoms and wonder why we are consistently set back, while the mutinous modernist agenda gains victory after victory for the agents of diabolic rebellion. It was prophesied of old that if interest on money became legal in society and the Church, then a plague of unnatural acts would eventually also become legal. Though most twenty-first century western people would scoff at the connection, the prophecy is being fulfilled.

Satan is an inveterate liar who abuses language for his own evil purposes. Satan's language is "Ambiguous and with double sense deluding." (*Paradise Regained*, I. 435).

The usurers are so ashamed of themselves that they have stooped to falsifying the Word of God to make it appear that God said what He did not say concerning interest on money. By this means, they excuse their usury and salve their bad consciences. The NIV (New International Version)'s false translation of Ezekiel 18:8 reads as follows: "He does not lend at usury or take *excessive* interest." [27]

The translator of the preceding passage is a mendacious counterfeiter of the very Word of God. God's Word in Ezekiel 18:8 concerning the mark of a God-fearing man actually reads in accurate

27 *Holy Bible: New International Version* (Zondervan, 1984). Emphasis supplied.

translation: "He does not charge usury on loans and takes no interest."

God does not qualify the word "interest" by preceding it with the word "excessive" but the NIV Bible falsifiers do. Who benefits from this fraud? Who will suffer eternal damnation because of it?

By deceitfully defining usury as "excessive" interest on loans of money, the Roman Catholic Church in the 21st century puts forth the image of itself as being an opponent of usury: "Although the quest for equitable profit is acceptable in economic and financial activity, the recourse to usury is to be morally condemned. 'Those whose usurious and avaricious dealings lead to the hunger and death of their brethren in the human family indirectly commit homicide, which is imputable to them...The Magisterium uses strong and clear words against this practice, which is still tragically widespread, describing usury as 'a scourge that is also a reality in our time and that has a stranglehold on many peoples' lives." —*The Compendium of the Social Doctrine of the Church*, (2005) paragraph #341.

Through covetousness shall they with feigned words make merchandise of you. —II Peter 2.

The advocates of mortal sin created an escape clause for their betrayal of the Gospel

While it is often said that the dogma of the Roman Catholic Church is unchanging, truth to tell, the Renaissance Church did overthrow the dogma on usury. This is disputed by many eminent Catholics; sad to say, they are in error. From the earliest period, the whole weight of the Church was brought to bear against *all* gain made from lending — not just on "unjust" interest. Since the Renaissance, both Protestant and Catholic usurers, to assuage their consciences, have redefined usury as a "high rate of interest." This falsification is nothing more than a ruse that has credibility due to ignorance.

By usury we are not referring to the Newspeak, mind-washed falsification of that term, redefined to assuage the conscience of the crooks, but rather we harken to how Christian patriarchs from the first century A.D. to the year 1500 understood it: *any interest* on a loan. Biblical scholar Ted Weiland:

"Usury and interest are one and the same thing...Usury is just an ingenious way of stealing. It 'creates out of nothing' (something only Yahweh can do), or with a stroke of a pen the illusion of money by which others are exploited and economically enslaved: 'The rich ruleth over the poor, and the borrower is servant to the lender.' (Proverbs 22:7)...When usury is involved, the weight of this slavery is compounded many times over...'Woe to him that increaseth that which is not his! How long? And to him that ladeth himself with thick clay! Shall they not rise up suddenly that shall bite thee, and awake that shall vex thee, and thou shalt be for booties (plunder) unto them? (Habakkuk 2:6-7).

"Thick clay tablets were what ancient Babylon used to engrave their usurious loan contracts. Borrowers were literally laden with weight. Today, the weight is worse, in that most people are laden with usury their entire lives, so much so that many, upon their deaths, pass their outstanding debts on to their children. Habakkuk 2:7 warns that usurers rise up and bite. The word 'bite' is translated from the verb form of *neshek*, which means interest on debt. Debt is bad enough. But interest-encumbered debt will rise up and bite you....Usury helps divert the wealth of a nation to the ungodly....In *Days of Praise*, John Morris claimed that Christians are prohibited from charging high interest: 'In financial matters, we must not lend money at high interest...Both *Webster's Dictionary* and *Bouvier's Law Dictionary* define 'usury' as exorbitant and excessive interest: '1. the practice of lending money at an exorbitant interest rate. 2. an exorbitant amount or rate of interest. The excess over the legal rate charged to a borrower for the use of money.'

"But whose morality are we going to follow – *Webster's* and *Bouvier's*, or Yahweh's? Who gets to decide what is exorbitant or excessive? *Bouvier* defined usury as the 'excess over the legal rate....' – but who gets to decide what the 'legal' rate is? Legal is anything that man has legitimized, whereas lawful is what Yahweh permits. Had Bouvier used the word 'lawful,' instead of 'legal,' the excess over the lawful rate charged to a borrower is any interest whatsoever!

"The Bible never says anything about exorbitant, excessive, or high interest, only interest period. A meager one percent usury was exorbitant in Nehemiah's estimation (Nehemiah 5:1-13). No doubt he would have considered even a hundredth of one percent to be excessive, as it should also be to anyone desiring to return to Yahweh's morality.

"Typically man's legislation is for the purpose of making illegal what Yahweh has made lawful, or making legal what Yahweh has made unlawful. *Bouvier* so much as admits to the same regarding usury: 'Originally, the word was applied to all interest reserved for the use of money; and in the early ages taking such interest was not allowed.'

"The 1828 edition of *Webster's American Dictionary of the English Language* attests to the same in its definition of usury: 1. Formerly, interest; or a premium paid or stipulated to be paid for the use of money. 2. In present usage, illegal interest; a premium or compensation paid or stipulated to be paid for the use of money borrowed or retained, beyond the rate of interest established by (man's) law.'

"Has Yahweh's morality changed or has man simply attempted to usurp His place as King, Judge, and Lawgiver (Isaiah 33:22)? Yahweh has not changed (Malachi 3:6) and, therefore, neither has His morality as codified in His laws. Contrast the fickle nature of man's legislation to the unfailing permanence of Yahweh's laws. Under man's law, if he chooses to change the legal rate, what might not be usury today may very well be usury tomorrow. Under Yahweh's law, any interest is usury and is condemned as theft perpetually. Yahweh's laws are fixed, whereas man's legislation is ever-changing and predisposed to the transient whims of man....The *Easton's Bible Dictionary* provides the biblical definition of usury: Usury: the sum paid for the use of money, hence interest; not, as in the modern sense, exorbitant interest." [28]

Usury is derived from the Latin word *usura,* defined as "a sum paid for the use of money." [29]

"The Fathers are unanimous in regarding all interest as usury, and, therefore, as a species of robbery." [30]

"Whatever exceeds the amount owed is usury." St. Ambrose, *De Tobia* (4th century).[31]

"Usury occurs when more is demanded back than what is given." Council of Nymwegen (9th century).

---

[28] Weiland, op. cit.

[29] P.G.W. Glare, *Oxford Latin Dictionary* (Oxford University Press, 2006), p. 2110.

[30] Rev. Frs. William E. Addis and Thomas Arnold, *The Catholic Dictionary*, (Imprimatur: Henry Cardinal Manning and John Cardinal McCloskey, 1896), p. 827. Cf. Tertullian (*Adv Marc.*, iv, 24, 25), Cyprian (*Testimon.* iii 48).

[31] St. Ambrose and his work *De Tobia* were favorites of poet Ezra Pound, for whom usury was a curse on civilization. Cf. Canto 99 in his *The Cantos*, wherein Pound recommends the study of *De Tobia*.

"...the condemnation of interest taking was part of the unanimous *consensus patrum*...It was not until the sixteenth century that 'usury' was redefined as high interest rates." [32]

"He then made a definition of usury, showing that it was the taking of any reward or sum above the due debt."—Thomas Wilson, Member of the English Parliament, 1571.[33]

In spite of these historic definitions of what constituted usury in Christendom for more than a millennium, we will see that the guilty parties who later revolted against the *consensus patrum* of Christian civilization did so on the excuse that usury never had been considered merely as interest on money but rather, usury had been defined as excessive interest. Interpretive subtleties and loopholes have carried the field and now undergird the nearly universal conception of what constitutes usury. By this imposture the advocates of permitting mortal sin created an escape clause for their betrayal of the Gospel. Interest on money is today in Christendom everywhere permitted so long as it is "not exorbitant" and modern Catholics and Protestants masquerade as campaigners against usury because they campaign against "Payday loans" and 400% interest rates.

---

32 Thomas Moser, "The Idea of usury in Patristic literature," in *The Canon in the History of Economics* (Routledge, 2000), p. 24.

33 M. Lindsay Kaplan (ed.), *The Merchant of Venice: Texts and Contexts* (2002: Bedford/St. Martin's), p. 202.

Usury and the Fathers of the Early Church

Clement of Alexandria: "The issue of usury made its first appearance in Christian literature in Clement's *Paidagogos* (circa A.D. 197), an instruction for new converts on Christian conduct in daily matters...Concerning the 'just man,' Clement quotes Ezekiel: 'His money he will not give on usury, and he will not take interest...This subject is taken up again some years later in the second book of his major work *Stromateis*." [34]

Tertullian considers the subject of interest in his treatise on the theology of the New Testament, *Adversus Marcionem*, where he teaches that the Gospel does not abolish the law of the Old Testament, *it exceeds it*. Tertullian writes of the just man, "He hath not...put out his money at interest, and will not accept any increase – meaning the excess amount due to interest, which is usury."

St. Cyprian of Carthage: Offers proofs in his *Testimoniorum (Ad Quirinum)* that interest taking is prohibited by the law of God.

In the early fourth century, Canon 20 of **the Council of Elvira** prohibited all clerics and laymen from participating in the sin of taking interest on loans, under penalty of excommunication.

St. Jerome in his *Commentaria in Ezechielem* stated that the prohibition against usury among the Israelites had been made universal by the New Testament. He affirmed that all interest on money is forbidden. "One should never receive more than the amount loaned."

---

34 Ibid., Moser, p. 34.

Hilary of Poitiers in his *Tractatus in Psalm XIV*: "If you are a Christian, why do you scheme to have your idle money (*otiosam pecuniam*) bear a return and make the need of your brother, for whom Christ died, the source of your enrichment?"

St. Basil in his second Homily on Psalm 15 (Septuagint): "This sin is denounced in many places in Scripture. Ezekiel accounts the taking of interest and receiving back more than one gave as being among the greatest evils,[35] and the Law specifically forbids this practice: 'You shall not charge interest to your relative or your neighbor.'[36] And again the Scripture says, 'Guile upon guile, and interest upon interest.'[37] A certain Psalm says, regarding a city that prospers amidst a multitude of evils, 'Interest-taking and guile are never absent from its squares.'[38] And now the prophet identifies this very thing as the characteristic of human perfection, saying, 'They do not lend money at interest.'

"...for those who set rates of interest, their money is loaned and bears interest and produces even more...*It is from this tendency to multiply that this kind of greed derives its name...loans are said to 'bear' interest on account of the great fecundity of evil*...The offspring of interest one might even call a 'brood of vipers'...you should have nothing to do with this monstrous creature."[39]

---

[35] Ezekiel 22:12.

[36] Deuteronomy 23:20.

[37] Jeremiah 9:6 (Septuagint).

[38] Psalm 55:12 (Septuagint).

[39] *On Social Justice: St. Basil the Great* (St. Vladimir's Seminary Press, 2009), pp. 89-90; 95 (emphasis supplied).

St. Basil then launches into an extended admonition against borrowing money, on the responsibility to repay a loan, and the virtues of frugality and living within one's means. He further states: "Listen, you rich people, to the kind of counsel I am giving...on account of your inhumanity...If you must seek a return on your investment, be satisfied with what comes from the Lord...You should expect the characteristics of philanthropy from the true Philanthropist. As it is, the interest you receive back shows every characteristic of extreme misanthropy...

"Do not refuse anyone who wants to borrow from you,' and 'do not lend your money at interest;' these commandments from the Old and New Testaments[40] were given so that you might learn what is for your benefit, and thus depart to the Lord with a good hope, receiving there the interest upon your good works, in Christ Jesus our Lord, to whom be glory and dominion forever and ever." [41]

St. Gregory of Nyssa in *Contra usurarios* (circa 379 A.D.) calls down on him who lends money at interest the vengeance of the Almighty. He further states, "...lending at interest can be called 'another kind of robbery or bloodshed...since there is no difference in getting someone's else's property by seizing it through covert housebreaking and acquiring what is not one's own by exacting interest." Gregory of Nyssa describes the lender at interest as a "poisonous serpent" and an evil, beast-like spirit. Referring to the words of the *Pater Noster* prayer of Jesus Christ — "Forgive us our debts, as we forgive our debtors" — Gregory asks, "How can you pray like this, oh usurer? How can you make a request from God in good

---

[40] Matthew 5: 42; Psalm 15: 5 (Septuagint).

[41] *On Social Justice: St. Basil the Great* (op. cit.), pp. 97-99.

conscience since he has everything and you do not know how to give?"

In *De beneficentia*, Gregory of Nyssa excoriates evil-doers who hypocritically practice outward acts of piety such as fasting. In doing so he employs terms associated with usurers: "Renounce dishonest profits! Starve to death your greed for Mammon! Let there be nothing in your house that has been acquired by violence or theft. What good is it to keep meat out of your mouth if you *bite* your brother with wickedness....What kind of piety teaches you to drink water while you hatch plots and and drink the blood of a man you have shamefully cheated?"

For St. Gregory of Nazianzus the usurer is a sinful parasite, "gathering where he had not sowed and reaping where he has not strawed" (*Oratio*). Cataloguing a list of mortal sins, Gregory of Nazianzus states, "One of us has oppressed the poor, and wrested from him his portion of land, and wrongly encroached upon his landmark by fraud or violence, and joined house to house, and field to field, to rob his neighbor of something, and been eager to have no neighbor, so as to dwell alone on the earth. Another has defiled the land with usury and interest, gathering where he had not sowed..." (Oration 16)

St. Ambrose in his aforementioned work *De Tobia*, written in 380 A.D., declared that the taking of interest on loans of money is equivalent to murder. He declared usury to be a mortal sin in *De officiis ministrorum* and *De Nabuthe*. In *De bono mortis* Ambrose stated that usurers will suffer eternal damnation. In *De Tobia* Ambrose described the usurer as a "monster" and "devil" even when lending at 1% interest ("the hundreth"): "Money is given, it is called a loan; it is termed money at interest, it is designated capital; it is written down as debt; this huge monster of many heads causes frequent exactions; the usurer names the bond, he speaks of the signature, he demands security, he talks of a pledge, he calls for sureties; he claims the legal obligation, he boasts of the interest, he praises the hundreth...*The devil is a usurer...the Savior owed nothing but He paid for all...The usurer of money...exacts his hundreth....the Redeemer came to save the hundreth sheep, not to destroy it.*" [42]

This "devil" epithet is etymologically justified. As we have noted, in Old Testament Hebrew *Neshek*, from the root *NShK* means to "bite" and signifies usury; *Nahash*, from the root *NkHSh* denotes serpent.

St. John Chrysostom taught that usury was shameless: "What can be more unreasonable than to sow without land, without rain, without plows? All those who give themselves up to this damnable culture shall reap only tares. Let us cut off these monstrous births of gold and silver; let us stop this execrable fecundity."

Pope St. Leo I: In his encyclical *Ut nobis gratulationem*, of 444 A.D: "Some people put out their money at usury in order to become wealthy. We have to complain of this, not only with regard to those in clerical office, but we likewise grieve to see that it holds true of lay people who wish to be called Christians. We decree that those who are found guilty of receiving this *turpe lucrum* (shameful gain) should be severely punished."

St. Augustine denounced the sin of interest on money in *De consensu evangelistarum*.

---

[42] Lois Miles Zucker (translator), *De Tobia* (Catholic University of America, 1933), pp. 51 and 57 (emphasis supplied).

In 789 A.D. **Charlemagne** in his *Admonitio Generalis* prohibited usury by all people, laymen as well as clerics, throughout the lands of the Holy Roman Empire, citing the following authorities: "(1) the Council of Nicea, (2) the above mentioned letter of Pope Leo, (3) the *Canones Apostollorum*, and (4) Scripture."[43] The Catholic Council of Aix-la-Chapelle promulgated Charlemagne's *Admonitio Generalis* as church doctrine.

In Charlemagne's Capitulary of Nijmegen of March, 806 he defines usury in clause 11 as "claiming back more than you give; for instance, if someone has given 10 *solidi* and asks for more than 10 in return, that is usury." Clause 16: "Lending (*foenus*) consists in providing something; the loan is fair and just when one demands no more than what he provided."

Charlemagne imposed heavy fines for usury.

King Alfred the Great (849-899) ordered that the charging of interest on loans of money was illegal throughout England. Those who received revenue from usurious loans were to forfeit their property. Christian burial was denied to them.

Unanimous Teaching of Popes and Councils Before 1500

This unanimity of the Early Church Fathers brought about a crystallization of hostility to interest-bearing loans into numberless decrees of popes, councils, monarchs and legislatures throughout Christendom. The Canon law was shaped in accordance with these prohibitions, which were enforced by the **the Council of Arles** in 314 and the **Council of Nicea** in 325: "Because many of the

---

[43] Moser, op. cit., p. 41.

Ecclesiastical Order, being led away by covetousness and desire of base gain, have forgotten the Holy Scripture which saith, 'He gave not his money upon usury,' do exercise usury, so as to demand every month a hundredth part of the principal, the holy synod thinks it just that if any take such use, by secret transaction, or by demanding the principal and one half of the principal for interest, or contrive any other fraud for filthy lucre's sake, let him be deposed from the clergy and struck out of the list."[44] (Council of Nicea, canon XVII).

Although it is claimed by apologists for usury that the Nicean Council only condemned usury among clerics and not the laity, canon XVII also quoted Psalm 15: "Lord, who shall dwell in thy tabernacle? He that hath not put out his money to usury." Psalm 15 does not qualify God's criterion for who shall dwell with Him. Anyone who practices usury will not be admitted. It was not by accident that the Council of Nicea referenced Psalm 15's total rejection of any usury practiced by anyone.

The 12th canon of the Council of Carthage (345) and the 36th canon of the Council of Aix (789) declared it to be sinful for anyone to charge any interest on money. Every great assembly of the Church, from **the Council of Elvira** in 306 to that of **Vienne in 1311**, condemned lending money at interest. The fount of Canon Law in the Middle Ages totally banned all interest on loans.[45]

---

44 The phrase "a hundredth part of the principal" connotes a 1% interest rate.

45 Cf. the Decree of Gratian, q. 3, c. iv and c. 4, q. 4, c. iv; and in 1. 5, t. 19 of the Decretals: cf. chapters 2, 5, 7, 9, 10, 13.

Medieval Struggle Against Interest on Money

"The greatest rulers under the sway of the Church – **Justinian**, in the Empire of the East; **Charlemagne**, in the Empire of the West; **Alfred in England**; **St. Louis in France** – yielded fully to this dogma. In the ninth century Alfred went so far as to confiscate the estates of money-lenders, denying them burial in consecrated ground; and similar decrees were made in other parts of Europe. In the twelfth century...St. Anselm proved from the Scriptures that the taking of interest is a breach of the Ten Commandments. **Peter Lombard**, in his *Sentences*, made the taking of interest purely and simply theft.[46] **St. Bernard**, reviving religious earnestness in the Church, took the same view.

Pope Urban III in his ruling on three cases of usury, reiterated the declaration that the passage in St. Luke forbade the taking of any interest: "Your devotion has sought our opinion on (1) whether he who will not lend unless he is assured of receiving in return more than he lent – although there is no explicit agreement to this effect – should be treated in the internal forum as if he was a usurer; (2) whether he is guilty of the same offense (of quasi-usury) who again, without a formal agreement – refuses to postpone settlement of a debt unless he receives some profit and likewise (3) a merchant who sells goods on credit for a much higher price than he would receive if the price were paid immediately. The truth of the matter in all three cases is clear in the gospel of Luke (6:35) where it is said 'Lend, expecting nothing in return.' Since all usury and increase is forbidden in the law, such men should be considered evil-doers on account of their

---

46 Peter's influential theologian's manual, *Sentences,* sought to collect all of the theology of the Fathers and the canonists. His doctrine of usury followed most closely that of Augustine and Anselm.

intention to profit and effectively compelled in the penitential forum to restore what they have received."

Pope Alexander III declared that the prohibition in this matter could never be suspended by dispensation.

"Infallible utterance"

"...This idea was still more firmly fastened upon the world by the two greatest thinkers of the time: first, by St. Thomas Aquinas, who knit it into the mind of the Church...and next by Dante, who pictured money-lenders in one of the worst regions of hell....**Pope Clement V** declared that if any one 'shall pertinaciously presume to affirm that the taking of interest for money is not a sin, we decree him to be a heretic, fit for punishment.' This infallible utterance bound the dogma with additional force on the conscience of the universal Church.

"...Nor was this a doctrine enforced by rulers only; the people were no less strenuous. In 1390 the city authorities of London enacted that, 'if any person shall lend or put into the hands of any person gold or silver to receive gain thereby, such person shall have the punishment for usurers.' And in the same year the Commons prayed the king that the laws of London against usury might have the force of statutes throughout the realm...In the fifteenth century the Council of the Church at Salzburg excluded from communion and burial any who took interest for money, and this was a very general rule throughout Germany...

"This theological hostility to the taking of interest was imbedded firmly in the canon law. Again and again it defined usury to be the taking of anything of value beyond the exact original amount of a loan; and under sanction of the universal Church it denounced this as a crime and declared all persons defending it to be guilty of heresy." [47]

In England "there had been a long series of enactments – the statutes of Alfred, of William the Conqueror, of Henry II, of Henry III, of Edward I, of Edward III, and of Henry VII – which were...penal enactments prohibiting the lending of money upon any interest whatever, under punishment more or less severe ranging from forfeiture of chattels, lands and Christian burial under Alfred, to a loss of all substance, whipping, exposure in the pillory, and perpetual banishment under William the Conqueror..."[48]

St. Anselm (1033-1109), Archbishop of Canterbury, in his *Homilia in Lucam* forbad interest on loans of money, declaring them tantamount to robbery.

St. Albert the Great ("Albert Magnus," "Doctor Universalis"; 1193-1280): Albert was the teacher of St. Thomas Aquinas; he wrote, "Usury is and always has been, without any doubt a mortal sin, according to the natural law as well as the written law" (III Sent. dist. xxxvii, art. 13).

St. Bonaventure (1221-1274), Professor of Theology at the University of Paris. Superior General of the Franciscan Order; bishop and cardinal. He declared the breeding of sterile money through the taking of interest, mortal sin and unnatural gain: *"Pecunia quantam est de se per seipsam non fructificat."*

---

[47] Andrew Dickson White, "A History of the Warfare of Science with Theology in Christendom," *The Popular Science Monthly* (1892), pp. 325-327.

[48] Franklin W. Ryan, *Usury and Usury Laws*, pp. 45-46.

Henry Goethals of Ghent ("Henricus Gandavensis," 1217-1293). Leading theologian and author of the treatises on economics and commerce *Mercimoniis et Negotiattionbus,* and *Quaestiones Quodlibetales*. In the latter he demonstrated from the Bible and the Fathers that the Church forbids interest on money because it is evil *per se*, and not due to any ecclesiastical declaration or canon law. The iniquity of usury is made so by divine law and is not subject to alteration.

Alexander of Alexandria (ca. 1268-1314). Superior-General of the Franciscan order and author of *Tractatus de Usuris*. A native of Lombardy in northern Italy, he had his work cut out for him since his homeland was replete with the usurious banking operations of its Italian "Lombards." (The heart of banking operations in London, England were, until very recently, headquartered for centuries on "Lombard Street"). [49] Alexander condemned interest on money from both the divine and the natural law.

History of the ecclesiastical laws of England: "Usury in a strict sense seemeth to be a contract upon the loan of money, to give the lender a certain profit for the use of it, upon all events, whether the borrower make any advantage of it, or the lender suffer any prejudice for want of it, or whether it be repaid on the day appointed or not. ...Manifest usurers are forbidden to make testaments themselves or to dispose of their goods by their last wills...unless he satisfy for the usury; so (too) they are forbidden to reap any benefit by the testament of others, or to be capable of any legacy of goods....Canon 109: If any offend their brethren by usury, the churchwardens...shall faithfully

---

[49] Cf. Walter Bagehot, *Lombard Street: A Description of the Money Market* (1873).

present every such offender, to the intent that he may be punished by the severity of the laws, according to his deserts and such notorious offenders shall not be admitted to holy communion, until they be reformed. In general it is said by the ecclesiastical laws, if a man be a manifest usurer, not only his testament is void (as hath said), but his body, after he is dead, is not to be buried amongst the bodies of other Christian men, in any church or churchyard, until there be restitution, or caution tendered, according to the value of such goods. By the laws of King Alfred it was ordained that the chattels of usurers should be forfeited to the king, their lands and inheritances should escheat to the lords the fee..." [50]

The dogmatic Third Lateran Council
(1179)

Canon 25:

"We therefore declare that notorious usurers should not be admitted to communion of the altar or receive Christian burial if they die in this sin."

This decree of the Third Lateran Council was not a man-made disciplinary law such as the Church prohibition against consuming meat on Friday. The Roman Catholic Church's law concerning charging interest on loans of money was based on the immemorial practice of the Church from its inception, rooted in the Word of God and confirmed by the unanimous teaching of the Magisterium. Any sin sufficient to prevent a Catholic from receiving Holy Communion (the Eucharist), constitutes a transgression so grave it was judged to be "mortal" –

50 *Ecclesiastical Law in Four Volumes*, transl. Richard Burn, vol. 4, pp. 39-42.

subject to eternal punishment after death if not confessed and forgiven before death. Are any twenty-first century lenders who charge interest on loans denied Communion in the Roman Catholic Church? The answer is a resounding no. The modernist Roman Catholic Church that evolved from out of the time when the Renaissance popes began to rot the Church from the inside-out with their whittling of God's law on usury, stands convicted of denying, suppressing and overthrowing one of the oldest statutes of the original and true Catholic Church, which also happens to be the law of God Himself as committed to Holy Scripture. The admirers of the occupants of the papacy from the Renaissance era onward have seldom scrupled to admit that the pontiffs' betrayal of the sacred dogma of interest on money was highly derogatory to the general merit of the papacy.

Pope "Gregory IX (1170-1241) was elected to the papacy in 1227...Gregory's pontificate was marked by a continuous battle against heresy as indicated by the constitutions inserted into the *Corpus iuris canonici*, among which was included the ruling *Naviganti de usuries*. This famous ruling condemned all known forms of usury..." [51]

The Constitution of the (Third) Lateran Council against usurers to be "inviolably observed"

In 1274, the Second Council of Lyons, at which **Pope Gregory X** presided, reaffirmed the dogma of the Third Lateran Council against all interest on

[51] Stephen J. Grabill (ed.), *Sourcebook in Late Scholastic Monetary Theory*, p. 237. In *Naviganti* Pope Gregory IX put forth a powerful and authoritative reaffirmation of the truths of Holy Scripture and the Catholic Church.

money and ordered that Council against usurers was to be "inviolably observed."

Fourteenth General Council of the Catholic Church: Lyons II

Constitution 26

"Desiring to check the canker of usury which devours souls and exhausts resources, we command that the constitution of the Lateran Council against usurers be inviolably observed under threat of divine malediction. And since the fewer the opportunities given to usurers the more easily will the practice of usury be destroyed, we decree by this constitution that no community or association, nor any individual, whatever their office, rank or status, shall permit strangers and nonresidents of their estates, who publicly practice or wish to practice usury, to rent offices for this purpose on their territory or to retain those that they already have, or permit them to dwell elsewhere, but they shall expel all known usurers from their territory within three months and shall not permit their return in the future. No one shall lease or under any other title whatsoever let them have the use of their houses for the purpose of practicing usury. Those who act otherwise, if they are churchmen, patriarchs, archbishops, or bishops incur suspension; individuals of lower rank incur excommunication, and communities and other associations arc placed under interdict. If, through obstinacy, they despise these censures for more than a month, their territories shall be placed and remain under interdict so long as the usurers remain there. If, however, they are laymen, then, notwithstanding any privilege, let their ordinaries restrain them from such excesses by ecclesiastical censure.

Constitution 27

Even though notorious usurers have made definite or general provision in their wills regarding restitution in the matter of illegally charged interest, church burial shall nevertheless be denied them till full satisfaction has been made to those to whom it is due, if they are available; in case of absence, to those who are authorized to act for them. If these also are absent, it is to be made to the ordinary of the locality, or to his vicar, or to the testator's parish priest, in the presence of witnesses residing in that parish (in this case the ordinary, vicar and rector may by the authority of this constitution receive in their name and in the presence of witnesses a pledge on which legal action may be based), or at the request of the ordinary a pledge concerning the restitution to be made may be given to a competent notary. If the amount of usury received is known, this is always to be expressed in the aforesaid pledge, otherwise the amount is to be determined by him who receives the pledge. However, he may not knowingly fix this amount at a lower figure than what he believes to be the correct one, otherwise he shall be bound to make satisfaction for the remainder.

All religious and others who dare in contravention of this constitution to admit notorious usurers to ecclesiastical burial, we decree that they incur the penalty prescribed by the Lateran Council against usurers.

No one may witness the wills of notorious usurers, and no one may hear their confession or give them absolution, unless they make full restitution or give a satisfactory pledge to that effect, in so far as their resources permit. Wills of notorious usurers that do not follow this injunction are *ipso jure* invalid. [52]

---

[52] Cf. John Gilchrist, *The Church And Economic Activity in the Middle Ages,* pp. 194-196.

By 1215 there was no question that the charging of any interest on loans of money was forbidden to Christians. Consequently, the Fourth Lateran Council, in its Canon 67, addresses usury only as it negatively affected Christians oppressed by usurious Judaic money-lenders. No one under the jurisdiction of the Church was allowed to receive interest on loans. "The original manifest usurers of Europe were the Jews, who were not subject to the jurisdiction of the Church. They were also not subject to qualms of conscience..."[53]

Judaic lenders, because they were unbaptized and therefore outside ecclesiastical jurisdiction, were permitted to charge interest to gentiles. This leniency was due in part to the recognition that the Old Testament made a provision for Israelites to charge interest to aliens.

Canon 67: "The more the Christians are restrained from the practice of usury, the more are they oppressed in this matter by the treachery of the Jews, so that in a short time they exhaust the resources of the Christians. Wishing, therefore, in this matter to protect the Christians against cruel oppression by the Jews, we ordain in this decree that if in the future under any pretext Jews extort from Christians oppressive and immoderate interest, the partnership of the Christians shall be denied them till they have made suitable satisfaction for their excesses. The Christians also, every appeal being set aside, shall, if necessary, be compelled by ecclesiastical censure to abstain from all commercial intercourse with them."

---

[53] Wood, *Medieval Economic Thought*, p. 167.

Fifteenth General Council: Vienne
(1311-1312)

Decree 29

"...if anyone falls into the error of believing and affirming that it is not a sin to practice usury, we decree that he be punished as a heretic..."

Reliable sources inform us that certain communities in violation of the law, both human and divine, approve the practice of usury. By their statutes confirmed by oath they not only permit the exaction and payment of usury, but deliberately compel debtors to pay it. They also try by heavy statutory penalties and various other means and threats to prevent recovery by individuals who demand repayment of interest. For our part, we want to put an end to these abuses and so we decree, with the approval of the council, that all civil officials of these communities, that is, magistrates, rulers, consuls, judges, lawyers and other similar officials, who in future make, write, or draw up statutes of this kind or knowingly decide that usury may be paid or in case of it having been paid may not be freely and fully restored when its return is demanded, incur the sentence of excommunication.

They shall incur the same sentence if they do not within three months remove such statutes from the books of those communities (if they have the power to do so), or if they presume in any way to observe the said statutes or customs to the same effect.

Moreover, since money-lenders frequently conclude loan-contracts in an occult or fraudulent manner, which makes it difficult to convict them on a charge of usury, we decree that they should be forced by ecclesiastical censure to produce their books on such occasions.

Finally, if anyone falls into the error of believing and affirming that it is not a sin to practice usury, we decree that he be punished as a heretic, and we strictly command the ordinaries of the localities and the inquisitors to proceed against those suspected of such errors in the same way as they would proceed against those accused publicly or suspected of heresy.

The **Council of York** in 1311 excommunicates all those who promote any statute in favor of usury.

Usury in Medieval Canon Law

The following is excerpted from T.P. McLaughlin's authoritative study, "The Teaching of the Canonists on Usury:" [54]

"The number, variety and severity of the penalties incurred by usurers is indicative of how deeply rooted, persistent and widespread was the evil... Throughout the period which is here being studied penalties are constantly being promulgated, renewed and multiplied. From decade to decade one witnesses an increasing severity as usurers become more numerous and bold in inventing new methods of obtaining usury in their attempt to circumvent the canons...

"These penalties are directed, not only against those who actually take usury, but also against their heirs and families, those who hesitate to denounce them, those who have any part in drawing up or executing their usurious contracts, notaries and judges; against those who make or enforce statutes opposed to the Canon Law on usury; against those who let houses for the purpose of money lending, and even against those in authority who allow usurers to reside within their territory; finally, against those who affirm that the

54 *Mediaeval Studies,* no. 2, pp. 1-11; 13-14; 18-20.

taking of usury is not sinful....Special penalties exist for clerics guilty of the crime of usury or who fail to enforce the canons against usury.

"...The general council held at Lyons in 1274 deals with the conduct of clerics who grant usurers ecclesiastical burial and declares that they will suffer the penalties promulgated by the Lateran Council against usurers... The Council of Lyons is referring to the canon of the Lateran Council against usurers, a canon which contains in fact two sets of penalties, one for usurers, the other for clerics who grant them Christian burial or accept their offerings. It is the second clause which Lyons orders to be applied. This is the interpretation of Joannes Andreae who adds that today this penalty is excommunication *ipso facto*. This is clear from the canons of some of the local councils. Thus the statutes of the diocese of Paris of the year 1212 declare that such clerics are *ipso facto* excommunicated, that they are suspended from office and benefice...

"In 1215 a council of Montpellier declares excommunicated and deposed clerics who administer the sacraments or grant ecclesiastical burial to usurers. By a decree of the council of Vienne inserted in the *Clementinae* it becomes the general law that clerics who give Christian burial to usurers are *ipso facto* excommunicated. This crime is listed in the work of Bérenger Frédol among the cases of excommunication where the confessor must demand special faculties from the bishop before proceeding to absolve a penitent. The same Council of Lyons threatens with severe penalties clerics of all ranks who do not co-operate in causing to be observed another of its canons concerning usurers. Ordering all foreigners who take usury to be expelled from the territory and forbidding anyone to rent them houses to carry on their business, the council declares that those who act against this decree will be suspended from office if they are patriarchs, archbishops or bishops; other ecclesiastics will be excommunicated; collegia and universitates will be placed under interdict. All of these penalties are incurred *ipso facto*. Moreover, if they remain under any of these penalties for one month and the usurers are still dwelling in their midst the whole territory falls under an interdict.

"...the Lateran Council intended to inflict new penalties upon usurers. If the penalty were only refusal of Communion this would not be new because whoever is evidently in mortal sin must be denied the Eucharist. The penalties of the Lateran Council constitute an excommunication or, more correctly, a partial excommunication. Such a penalty had already been promulgated by an earlier Lateran Council in 1139, and later synods refer to it as an excommunication to be announced by pastors several times a year, usually on all Sundays and feast days. A text of Alexander III inserted in the Decretals likewise calls it an excommunication...The penalties of this canon are first to be applied and if the usurer does not cease his money lending and make restitution he will fall under a major excommunication which will cut him off from all intercourse with the faithful.

"...A number of canons forbid priests to absolve usurers in the confessional even when they promise to make restitution. The crime of usury is a reserved case and only the bishop or one having special faculties may absolve a penitent from this sin except, of course, in danger of death. The usurer is also to be held as infamous and consequently is ineligible for the reception of dignities and honors and his testimony will not be accepted in ecclesiastical courts. The penalties for the crime of usury are not all by any means of the spiritual order. There are some which affect the usurer in his property, especially when he comes to die. In 1212 a council of Paris declares that the property of one who dies a usurer is to be confiscated by the king and distributed to the poor. At the same time it decrees that no usurer may make a last will bequeathing anything to his family, to religious establishments or to others since the fruits of rapine may not be the object of a gift.

"...It is clear from a sentence concerning Normandy, pronounced by the Parliament of Paris in 1258, that the property of a deceased usurer is held by the king only until the first assize when the affair is examined. If the claim of usury is established the property is turned over to the bishop who with the bailiff undertakes to make restitution to those who have been defrauded through usury.

"...Gregory X in the Council of Lyons in 1274 makes a general law of the canon of the Council of Paris concerning the testamentary power of a usurer. Unless certain conditions are fulfilled the last will and testament of one who is proven guilty of usury is *ipso jure* null and void. Even though by his last will a usurer orders restitution of what he has received from his business he is nevertheless to be denied Christian burial until full satisfaction has been made by his heirs or until sufficient guarantees have been given that such will be made.

"The bishop, the pastor or one delegated by either must be present at the drawing up of such a will to receive the guarantees because it often happens that the act orders restitution to be made but when the usurer has been buried the heirs find ways of preventing the execution of his last wishes. To obviate this injustice the council requires that such wills observe certain formalities and forbids all other persons, laymen or clerics, to assist at their writing unless acting as representatives of the ecclesiastical authority. It is hoped that effective restitution will result from the refusal of Christian burial to such testators who transmit to their heirs the obligation of satisfying for their unjust dealings. This canon, inserted in the *Liber Sextus*, is recalled by numerous local councils during the following century and the testaments of usurers are pronounced null and void. Every sunday pastors are to read this canon to the faithful. Notaries are forbidden to assist at the drawing up of last wills unless the parish priest be also present...

"The same penalties which are inflicted upon usurers also fall upon their heirs who oppose restitution of the ill-gotten gain and upon all others who had shared in this gain.

"A number of penalties directed against the family and servants of the usurer were aimed at bringing about the latter's conversion. The servants must leave their employ or incur the same punishment as their masters. Again they are threatened with excommunication if they remain in their service. The council held in Paris in 1212, so severe in its condemnation of the crime of usury, states that the wife of a usurer has no right to accept anything from her husband because he gives what is not his. However she is permitted to receive what is necessary while she attempts to convert him and persuades him to make restitution. When she discovers that he is incorrigible and that she can do nothing she is bound to seek a separation *quoad mensam et convivium* but not *quoad torum*. It is better that she beg than accept any support from her husband. If, however she becomes ill or is otherwise unable to beg, she may receive from him what she needs since she is reduced to the state of a beggar and is really providing him with the opportunity of making restitution to the poor in what he gives her.

"The same necessity permits children and grandchildren to receive support from their parents. A century later a council of Mainz has a similar procedure. If there is hope of correcting him, the wife is to live with her usurious husband. If not, she and her children are to leave him and live off their own property if they possess any; if they have none they are to go to relatives and friends. If the husband does not allow this they are to denounce him to the bishop. If he still remains obstinate then...they may live with him rather than become public beggars or starve. Sometimes a usurer was willing to remain a long time under sentence of excommunication, intending to arrange for restitution when he came to die. To prevent this and to forestall the new difficulty which then often arose from the opposition of the wife and family to the execution of his last will, the same council of Mainz decrees that if a usurer remain one month under sentence of excommunication the sacraments are to be refused his wife and children. An exception is made for baptism and also for the other sacraments in danger of death.

"Still other penalties are indirectly aimed at bringing about the punishment of usurers. Those who pay usury and do not within a month denounce their creditors are to be excommunicated.

"Lawyers are forbidden, not only, as we have seen, to aid in drawing up last wills of usurers, but also to defend them in court just as they are forbidden to defend heretics. One who disregards this rule will be suspended from office and if he continues to defend such cases will be excommunicated. He may, however, defend one accused of usury provided he swears to retire as soon as he is convinced that it is really a case of usury and not the case of a contract which, though charged with being usurious, is not such in fact or at least so far has not been officially branded as unjust.

"Notaries are forbidden to perform any service for usurers especially to help them in drawing up their usurious contracts or other contracts in *fraudem usurae*. Hostiensis[55] holds that a notary who acts against this canon incurs the penalty of infamy and his testimony is no longer to be accepted in a court of justice.

"...more stringent measures against usurers are promulgated by the general council of Lyons in 1274. These have force of law everywhere and are inserted in the *Liber Sextus* by Boniface VIII in 1298. No person of any rank, whether an individual or juristic person, may rent or in any way grant a house to a stranger to the district who intends to practice usury, nor allow him to continue to occupy it if it is at present being used for such purposes. All such strangers are to be expelled from the territory within three months. Those who transgress this decree will be excommunicated if they are minor clerics, suspended if they are in major orders and placed under an interdict if they are corporations. The lands of those who remain under any of these penalties for the space of a month will fall under an interdict. If laymen offend against this law the bishop will punish them by ecclesiastical censures...Beaumanoir, writing between 1279 and 1283, states that a baron who has forbidden lending at interest on his lands may seize a usurer and hold him until he has made restitution of the usury received... This canon is renewed by numerous local councils in the course of the century following...

"If one lets a house to a stranger who is not known as a usurer or lets it to him for some other purpose he is nonetheless bound to evict him as soon as he becomes aware of the true nature of his business.

"Another series of general decrees were formulated by Clement V in the Council of Vienne in 1311-1312 and incorporated in the *Clementinae*. The first part of the canon touches the question of whether the civil law

---

55 The renowned canonist, Cardinal Henry of Segusio (or "Susa"), 1200-1271.

may permit usury and declares excommunicated all secular officials of whatever rank who make, write or cause to be made or written any statute compelling debtors to pay usury which they have promised or which denies to them the right to recover usury already paid. The same penalty is incurred by those who judge according to such statutes, who enforce them or who, having the power to do so, do not within three months delete them from the statute books or suppress them if they are recognized, unwritten customs...the canonists hold that such statutes (compelling debtors to pay usury) have no binding force since they are opposed to both the divine and the ecclesiastical law.

"...Also stand condemned statutes which forbid demanding usury beyond a certain rate because they seem to implicitly approve the taking of usury provided it is not in excess of that rate.

"...The same council provides a means of more easily ascertaining the nature of the business which a man is conducting. Those accused of lending at usury are to be compelled under threat of ecclesiastical censure to show the books in which they keep an account of their transactions... One accused of the crime of usury who claims that he does not keep books must prove this claim and his own oath to that effect does not suffice to establish it... A number of councils suspend from office and benefice clerics who by assisting usurers in drawing up their contracts, by witnessing them or by keeping their accounts, lead men to believe that usury is not sinful.

"...This decree is directed not only against usurers but against all who encourage the practice of exacting usury in any way by affirming that it is not a sin. Some are teaching that there is no obligation to make restitution of usury received; others admit that the usurer is bound to make restitution but that when this is done he is not bound to do penance...

"The Church taught that the usurer was bound to make restitution and that those who had paid usury could always claim it because they had suffered an injustice. Recovery of what they had parted with in time of difficulty when they were obliged to contract a usurious debt was the incentive held out to encourage debtors to reveal the usurious practices of their creditors. Against those who openly and publicly engaged in the business of money lending at usury even such appeals were unnecessary. They were *notorii facti* and after being given a triple admonition they were excommunicated by name and the penalties of the Lateran council applied.

"For various reasons, however, debtors were often reluctant to appear as accusers and the Canon Law devised other means of bringing usurers to justice. Thus in 1212 the council of Paris commands all the faithful under threat of ecclesiastical censure to divulge to the authorities all the information they possess concerning the operations of usurers...another method was used. A letter of Innocent III addressed to the bishop of Auxerre in 1207 and later inserted in the Decretals of Gregory IX, relates that many persons are reputed usurers and yet through fear of princes and powerful men no accuser appears to denounce them or to furnish proof of the fact with the result that they escape punishment. The Pope orders the ecclesiastical judges to proceed *ex officio* against persons who enjoy such a reputation and adds that certain arguments taken in conjunction with it suffice to prove the crime of usury. Such arguments or indications, the canonists add, would be the discovery of accounts revealing the nature of their business; the fact that they sell on credit; their practice of entering into contracts which, though apparently contracts of sale, are in reality loans on security arranged in such a way that they receive the fruits of the pledge placed in their hands.

"Until the fourteenth century...the ecclesiastical courts alone are competent to try cases of usury ... ecclesiastical cases are of three kinds, spiritual, civil and criminal. Examples of criminal cases are usury, heresy and adultery where the examination and condemnation belong to the ecclesiastical judge...the examination and punishment of this crime belong to the court Christian because the usurer sins against the natural law and so principally against God Himself. Usury is forbidden by both divine and Canon Law...The prohibition of usury is from divine law and the decision which is given in the case, declaring a contract usurious or not, decides whether it is sinful or lawful. Only the Church can pronounce upon this question because it alone has the right to interpret the divine law which it does in declaring that a certain act is sinful. When, however, there is no doubt that a certain contract is usurious but there is a doubt regarding the facts of the case, when, for example it is disputed whether the usury of which the recovery is sought has actually been paid, or when it is necessary to establish other facts by means of witnesses or documents, then them secular as well as the ecclesiastical tribunal is competent to examine the case and pass sentence" *(end quote from McLaughlin)*.

The philosophy and theology of the medieval scholasticism of the "schoolmen" was typified by the work of St. Albert the Great, St. Bonaventure and St. Thomas Aquinas, among many other Catholic prodigies of erudition in this field, all of whom were adamant advocates of the immemorial Biblical and Patristic dogma against interest on money.

The English Cardinal **Robert of Courson** (also spelled "Courcon" and "Courzon"), the papal legate, was, from 1204-1210, professor at the University of Paris, the premier medieval school of theology (whose statutes he compiled in August of 1215), and the author of *Summa*, completed in 1208. He also helped prepare, and was an influence on the Church council held at Paris in 1213 as well as the Fourth Lateran Council of 1215. His *Summa* is a huge and influential work of theology consisting of chapters on penance, canon law, the regulation of clerical life, simony, robbery, usury and perjury. His treatise contra usury, *"De Usura,"* was circulated throughout medieval Europe and was in print in French late as 1902.[56]

In the preface to his *Summa*, Courson took the words of the Apostle Paul in Philippians 2:15-16 as his economics' maxim, stating that his objective was to assist the Christian, "That ye may be blameless and harmless in the midst of a crooked and perverse nation." He urged priests to encourage their parishioners to publicly denounce usurers. Cardinal Courson's influence on the Fourth Lateran Council rises to a higher magnitude of significance when we recall that it was this Council which pronounced dogmatically for transubstantiation. His great campaigns were for transubstantiation and against usury. Historian Sara Lipton draws an instructive parallel between the two:

"With the official adoption of the doctrine of transubstantiation at the Fourth Lateran Council (1215), [57] physical as well as spiritual cleanliness (of the Host, the celebrant, and the communicants) was brought into still sharper focus. So, for example,

---

56 Georges Lefévre, *Le Traité 'De Usura,' de Robert de Courcon* (l'Université de Lille, 1902).

57 Transubstantiation was first "definitively approved" by the Roman Council of 1079 (also known as the Lateran Synod) in the presence of Pope Gregory VII who was supported most notably by Lanfranc of Pavia, Prior of the Abbey of Bec in Normandy, who would become, under William the Conquerer, the Archbishop of Canterbury. 136 years after the Roman Council, transubstantiation was proclaimed as the official and authentic dogma of the Eucharistic mystery at the Fourth Lateran Council.

Alexander Nequam (1157–1217) preached on the responsibility of priests to wash their hands before handling the Body of Christ, priests were enjoined by Innocent III to wear white when celebrating the Easter Mass, and ever more elaborate measures for assuring the integrity of the consecrated wafers were adopted. Such measures did not serve just to protect the purity of the Host but also to publicly signify it. Condemnations of usurers fulfilled a similar function. Associated rhetorically and metaphorically with 'filth' in a myriad of Christian texts (to the extent that 'filthy lucre' is still a cliché), money was repeatedly linked with actual filth in the form of excrement and the 'filthy' fluid blood in those most vivid and concrete of medieval narratives, the *exempla*...Money, then, was not just an agent but a tangible sign of sin and pollution, and usurers were considered not only morally tainted (in that they were sinful) but also physically tainted (by virtue of their intimacy with 'filthy lucre'). Such associations, then, form the backdrop for both the child-pawning and other anti-usury images in the *Bible moralisée* Leviticus commentary..." [58]

"He (Cardinal Courcon) was sent to France as papal legate in 1213...during his legation (which lasted probably until November 1215) he undertook the task of reforming and streamlining the French Church and regulating the syllabus at the University of Paris. He was well prepared for his work by his academic expertise, expressed in his *Summa*, which was compiled between 1204 and 1208 and focused on the question of usury, so central to any consideration of Church benefices. This was reflected in the Church council held at Paris in 1213...Curzon was a strong

---

[58] Lipton, *Images of Intolerance: The Representation of Jews and Judaism in the Bible Moralisée*, p. 36.

proponent of general councils as an instrument of church reform and as an antidote to usury...By way of a council he advocated a return to apostolic simplicity...'Thus would be removed all usurers, all factious men and all robbers; thus would charity flourish and the fabric of the churches again be builded..." [59]

"Roberto Courcon, viro scientissimo, ecclesie Romane cardinali, adeo usuras eliminado usurarios persequebatur..." [60]

In addition to the Lateran Council's Cardinal-theologian Robert Courson, we have another leading medieval opponent of interest on money among the most illustrious of all churchmen of the age – **Archbishop of Canterbury Stephen Langton** (ca. 1155-1228), the architect of one of the West's founding documents of freedom, England's Magna Carta. Langton was a former master of theology at the University of Paris with Robert Courson (and schoolmate of the future Pope Innocent III).

The historian Matthew Paris wrote: "Archbishop Stephen rid Italy and France in great part of usurers...He preached in northern Italy, in France – especially in Arras and St. Omer – and in parts of Flanders. Aiding him in his attacks and persecutions of usury and usurers was Robert de Courcon, a most learned man and cardinal of the Roman church. Together they rooted out the practice of usury and miraculously cleansed the French kingdom of evil." [61]

---

59 Dominic Aidan Bellenger and Stella Fletcher, *Princes of the Church: A History of the English Cardinals*, pp. 11-12.

60 Matthew of Paris, quoting from the *Liber Additamentorum* at St. Albans.

61 Phyllis Barzillay Roberts, *Studies in the Sermons of Stephen Langton*, pp. 17-18.

The theologian Jacques de Vitry joined Langton and Courson in preaching a crusade against usury in western Europe, intermittently from 1213-1218. "In a passage attacking usurers in his *Historia Hierosolymitana*, Jacques likened these two preachers (Langton and Courson) to 'stars in the firmament."[62] The three preachers against interest on money are mentioned again in Matthew Paris' *Chronica Majora*. Their sermons were collected in the *Liber Additamentorum*. Langton's preaching was so intense he earned the sobriquet, *Stephanus de Lingua-Tonante* ("Stephen of the Thundering Tongue"). Archbishop Langton's primary concern as a homilist lay in exposing shady business dealings and usury, which he compared to theft. He classed usurers as creations of the devil and declared usury a mortal sin:

"Certe ner die nec nocte requiescit qui in peccato mortali est quia et ipsum facit. Sicut usura. Semper enim erescit, et nullus sapiens attingit usuram, ita est de peccato mortali."

He declared that the usurer will see cash but he will not see God: *"Si sacerdos dicit usurario, renuntia usuris; relinque multitudinem; sequere fidelium paucitatem. Cui ille. Fodere no valeo; mendicare erubesco, preterea omnes vicini mei similiter faciunt. Quasi dictat. Paucitatem non curo, multitudinem non relinquam, immo sequitur eam ad penam eternam...Usurarius videt nummum sed non videt Deum."*

The Archbishop of Canterbury stated that usurers, robbers and adulterers who call themselves Christians, vilify the name of Christ: *"Multi licet usurarii,*

---

62 Ibid., p. 18.

raptores, adulterii Christianos se nominant, in quo nomen Christi vilipendi faciunt..."

"Langton was himself a canon of Notre Dame and is credited with the composition of the sequence for the Mass of Pentecost, the *Veni, Sancte Spiritus*, a model of the austere and beautiful style he favored...His diocesan statutes of 1213-1214, similar in many respects with those promoted by the English cardinal Robert Curzon while papal legate to the French Church, set the pattern for his wider reform program promulgated at the Canterbury provincial council of Oxford in 1222, which became a model for much of the English Church." [63]

Scholasticism brought a Christian form of reasoning to the understanding of usury and its consequences, and in doing so it forged a middle course between two philosophical extremes: *rationalism* which is not subordinated to the faith, [64] and a faith-based *mysticism* that is not anchored by the God-given powers of reason. "Scholastic usury doctrine was partly based on authority in the widest sense and partly on rational arguments, either from authority or from self-evident postulate of natural reason (the 'natural law case' against usury')." [65]

---

63 Bellenger and Fletcher, op. cit., pp. 10-11.

64 William Edward Hartpole Lecky in his monumental *History of the Rise and Influence of the Spirit of Rationalism in Europe*, after acknowledging that the ban on interest on money was unanimous and created a unified "code of commercial morality" in the Church from its founding, running "through all the writings of the Fathers...in the decrees of the Councils..." terms the ban "a radical misconception, a product of dogmatic superstition," which was finally routed by the new rationalism in Europe. (Cf. volume two, pp. 250-270).

65 O.I. Langholm, *Economics in the Medieval Schools*, p. 45.

In accordance with legal terminology, Courson limits usury to the particular loan contract called a *mutuum*...Usury as an economic quantity is the increment (*res superexcrescens*) which the creditor receives in excess of the principal (*praeter sortem*) in repayment of the loan. Usury as a sin is to receive such an increment or to lend with the intention of receiving it...In a class of its own is the authority of the Lord himself exhorting his disciples in the Sermon on the Mount: "lend, hoping for nothing again" (*mutuum date nihil inde sperantes*)..." [66]

One of the most authoritative and voluminous of medieval manuals for *confessors* (priests who absolved penitents of their sins after they sorrowfully divulged them), was the 1216 *Summa confessorum* of the moral theologian Thomas of Chobham (ca. 1158 - ca. 1230), subdean of Salisbury Cathedral. Volume seven of this confessors' manual is concerned with mortal sins. Usury is classed as a subsidiary of the "seven criminal sins" of Book 3, among which is avarice. The *Summa confessorum* terms usury, *philargia,* "the love of money."

"Where there is a *mutuum*, ownership passes, whence *mutuum* means, as it were, 'yours from mine' (*de meo tuum*). Therefore if I have lent you money...immediately the money is yours...Therefore, if I receive a fee for this, I profit from what is yours, not mine. Therefore the usurer sells the debtor nothing that is his, but only time, which is God's. Therefore, since he sells a thing belonging to another, he ought not to derive any profit from it." [67] (The manual also stipulates that profit from usury must be returned before absolution can be be obtained).

"Cobham's most likely source is an early *palea* to the *Decretum*, inserted about 1180 and known from its

---

[66] Ibid., pp. 45-46.

[67] Ibid., p. 56.

incipit as *Eiciens*. Much older than Gratian, it is taken from the *Opus imperfectum in Matthaeum*, an anonymous fifth-cenury homily on Matthew, commenting on the passage which describes how Christ entered the Temple and evicted (*eiciebat*) the merchants and money-changers...'More cursed than all ...is the usurer, for he sells a thing not bought, as do the merchants, but given by God, and afterwards takes back his good, removing that of another with his own; a merchant, however, does not take back a good once sold." [68]

William of Auxerre, the Archdeacon of Beauvais, professor of theology and Pope Gregory IX's legate to the Faculty of theology at Paris, in his circa 1220 *Golden Summa ("Summa aurea")*, having defined usury ("the will to acquire something above the principal of a loan"), proceeds to declare: "Usury is directly and immediately contrary to justice which obliges us to relieve a neighbor in need, hence it is directly against the precept of the Gospel according to Luke 6, 'Lend, hoping for nothing again."

One economist has observed, "The charge of unjustly withholding what belongs to a neighbor in need is immeasurably graver than the charge of failing in charity by keeping what is rightly one's own." Here we see *the distinction between Christian justice and capitalist philanthropy*. In capitalism the philanthropist is obligated to no one. It is "his money," though from a sense of philanthropy he may, if he chooses, dispense money to those in need. Yet, if he withholds it he is not viewed as unjust, but perhaps, under certain circumstances, a little uncharitable. In Christianity, with its consciousness of the supreme overlordship of God, the Christian recognizes that the money he possesses is actually God's money, and

---

[68] Ibid., p. 58.

justice impels the Christian who possesses this money to distribute a substantial share of it to those in need.

William of Auxerre made the point of "explaining why the Church persecutes usurers more ardently than the secular powers do. To this purpose he compares usury with murder and with regular theft. A murder is an act sinful in itself (*in se*), but not according to itself (*secundum se*), says William, since it is sometimes morally permissible to take another's life for a morally overruling purpose; usury, however, being sinful both *in se* and *secundum se*, i.e. being intrinsically evil, is never permitted...The ecclesiastical judge, says William, is more subtle than the secular one. He considers the spiritual damage done by usury and persecutes usurers because they are in contempt of God." [69]

The English Dominican theologian John Bromyard (circa 1370), author of an authoritative compendium of canon law and theology, *Opus Trivium,* taught in his *Summa Praedicantium* (2, chapter 12), "The usurer is worse than the robber, because the robber usually steals at night. The usurer, however, robs by day and night, having no regard for time or solemnity, for the profit which accrues to him through a loan never sleeps, but always grows."

Manuals for Confessors Classified Usury as Mortal Sin

That usury was a mortal sin was the unanimous doctrine imparted to all confessors in the dozens of manuals compiled for their guidance and instruction by the Church up until the early modern age. We can cite example after example: the *Summa casuum* of Burchard of Strasbourg; the *Summa confessorum* of John of Freiburg; the *Summa de casibus conscientiae* of Bartolomeo of San Corcordio, the *Summa*

---

[69] Ibid., 84-85.

Confessorum of John of Saxony, the *Formula confessionis* of John Rigaud (confessor to Pope Clement V); the *Summa Astasana* of Astesanus.

The theologian Peter Lombard in his famous *Sentences,* in connection with the "fourth commandment of the second table" which forbids theft, states: "...here usury is prohibited as well, which is included under robbery" (*hic etiam usura prohibetur, quae sub rapina continetur*). The German Dominican Conrad of Höxter was professor of Canon Law at Bologna. He received the religious habit in 1220 "at the very hands of St. Dominic." His three volume manual for confessors, *Summa fratris Conradi,* condemns usury as mortal sin. "Usury is by its nature dishonest and cannot be exercised without sin...all fruits of usury are to be restored, including profit in legitimate business financed by usurious gains. If the foundation is faulty all that is built on it is faulty." Concerning the money-lending Lombards, Conrad of Höxter condemns their practice of charging usury in the guise of late fees on loan payments.

"Raymond of Penafort is remembered in the literary history of the Middle Ages for two major achievements. Besides being the author of the most influential book on penance ever written (*Summa Raymundi*), he compiled the definitive collection of decretals promulgated by Gregory IX in 1234. [70] Born near Barcelona, Raymond was nearing middle age and already a doctor of law when he entered the Dominican order in 1222. Raymond's handbook for confessors was originally composed in the 1220s...The work was printed a number of times...Usury is discussed by

---

70 *Decretales Gregor IX.* St. Raymond also edited Gratian's *Decretals*. Together these two works formed the basis of Canon law.

Raymond of Penafort in prolongation of theft, 'since usury differs little or nothing from robbery..." [71]

Four points are cited in the *Summa Raymundi* as proof of the mortal sin of usury: "the passage of ownership in a *mutuum*, the passage of risk, the non-deterioration of money and the sterility of money." These in turn are based in the decretal *Naviganti,* which was included in the final compilation by Pope Gregory IX and which originated in a letter written by the pope to Raymond of Penafort. "Hardly any work...was so frequently copied, glossed, abbreviated, adapted and imitated as the *Summa Raymundi*; European manuscript libraries abound in penitential texts deriving, in one way or another, from this source...When Vincent of Beauvais, the Dominican compiler of the largest encyclopedia of the Middle Ages, [72] cast about for suitable material on usury and commercial activity, he chose Raymond of Penafort...copying (him) more or less verbatim..." [73]

The Christian Economics of St. Thomas Aquinas

The synthesis of these works in the medieval period is found in the moral theology of St. Albert the Great and in the *De malo* and *Summa theologiae* of St. Thomas Aquinas, as well as the texts of St. Bonaventure (who, like Albert, puts forth the condemnation of interest on loans in a disquisition on the *Sentences* of Peter Lombard and, in Bonaventure's case, in his collation of the Ten Commandments).

Aquinas confronted the loophole which the money-lenders and their agents sought to sow to their advantage, a legal relativism that renders usury evil

---

[71] Ibid., p. 112.

[72] *Speculum doctrinale,* (Douay, 1624), Book 10, Chapters 102-33, cols. 956-980.

[73] Langholm (op. cit.), p. 115.

only because it is prohibited (thus leaving the door open to a future time when it will not be forbidden by the Church and therefore not evil). Aquinas replied, in *De malo*, that usury is not sinful because it is forbidden, rather, it is forbidden because it is a grave sin, *secundum se*. Historian Christopher A. Franks elaborates on the Christian economics of Aquinas:

St. "Thomas's position on usury depends, not on a particular way of configuring money, but on the very notion of abstractable exchange value that any understanding of money presupposes. Thomas argues that abstracted exchange value as such cannot have a vendible use value in addition to the exchange value it abstracts. To believe that it does indicates that a spurious 'usefulness' humans can attribute to something has been mistaken for true use value. Further, Thomas goes on to consider other possible justifications for interest on a loan, and he faults them not for misconstruing the nature of money, but for presumptively seeking a security against the future that denies the deferent receptivity necessary to humans as members of an antecedent natural order that sustains us. Thus, we can see Thomas's adherence to the usury prohibition not as evidence of his obscurantism in the face of 'economic realities,' but as his resistance to the presumption inherent in emerging economic practices...

The fruitfulness of God

"Thomas's economic teachings reflect an assumption that justice in exchange depends on commensurating the terms of exchange with the shape of the provision God unfolds for human beings. When Thomas says, 'one man cannot overbound in external riches without another man lacking them,' we are tempted to read it as a mere pious assertion to shame the rich. But it is firmly rooted in Thomas's assumptions about how God provides for human beings through fruitfulness of nature...To make a claim to wealth that outstrips that provision, as usury does, is to produce injustice.

"...Thomas's centerpiece argument attacks the very notion of usury, but he supports it with other arguments about a variety of possible titles to interest. In both cases his arguments are meant to preserve justice by rejecting inordinate claims to wealth...

"Thomas's centerpiece argument does not hinge on an antiquated understanding of money. Thomas sees in the very notion of an abstracted exchange value the possibility of economic activity that obscures the primacy of use values....

"What all of Thomas's positions on titles to income from money show is an insistence that profit can only come from nature's goods, which always requires the patience and vulnerability that waits to see what nature offers. Thomas refuses the presumption against God's providence that would seek to secure a claim to wealth that outpaces that provision.

"...to contract a price for the use of money in addition to the principal is to sell a use that does not and cannot exist...Thomas's arguments, by uncovering the most basic reason against usury (that it sells a metaphysical impossibility), confirm the rationale of the usury prohibition even in productive loans where the borrower is not needy. Thomas is concerned not only for charity, but for keeping all exchanges answerable to the contours of real wealth...

"The consumptibility argument is not meant to destroy all possible arguments for a return on one's money...The *lender at interest* presumes by staking a claim to wealth — possible future wealth — that is not disciplined by any receptivity to what God's providence may actually end up providing.

"The *investor* does not presume, but takes the risk of waiting to see what comes of it. He does not hold the title to the return of all his money, but rather makes himself vulnerable to the contingencies of how God's provision may or may not smile on the efforts of the merchant or craftsman to whom the money is entrusted...

"What if the borrower is an incompetent businessman, while the lender could quite reliably have turned a profit with his money somewhere else? This argument Thomas rejects, again because of its presumption. This is the notion of *lucrum cessans*, the notion that a lender has a title to compensation beyond the principal for forgoing the gain he might have otherwise made with his money...The reason Thomas finds it presumptive is that, unlike a risky investment, a loan involves a contract obliging the borrower in advance to compensate the lender for a potential gain the actual realization of which could only be determined by waiting to see...However reliable the alternative investment, it would involve vulnerability to the contingencies of the unfolding of God's provision, a vulnerability that *lucrum cessans* circumvents. To establish a title to such wealth irrespective of the actual possibilities and provisions the future may turn out to hold, is to set up an artificial invulnerability...One contemporary manifestation of this drive toward invulnerability is the imperative 'to convert wealth into debt in order to derive a permanent future income from it — to convert wealth that perishes, into debt that endures, debt that does not rot, costs nothing to maintain, and brings in perennial interest." [74]

---

[74] *He Became Poor: The Poverty of Christ and Aquinas's Economic Teachings*, pp. 71-83 (paragraph headings and emphasis are supplied.) Prof. Franks refutes charges by John T. Noonan (*The Scholastic Analysis of Usury*), of discrepancies in the teachings of St. Thomas Aquinas on this subject.

The Belgian theologian Giles of Lessines (ca. 1230-1304), an illustrious student of both Aquinas and Albert the Great, was the author of *De Usuris*, an important Catholic treatise on usury in the medieval age. In *De Usuris,* "Giles classifies usury as a vice of the genus of avarice, which beget cupidity, the root of all evil....Usury is sinful whether in hope or in fact (*'sive in spe sive in re'*). It is evil according to natural law and a mortal sin according to divine law...It is against the will of God." [75]

Interest on money: a pact with the devil

In the realm of historical speculation it has been conjectured that the Florentine theologian Remigio de Girolami had the venerable distinction of being both the student of St. Thomas Aquinas and the teacher of the illustrious medieval poet, Dante Alighieri. Girolami, who died in 1319, was Master of Theology at Santa Maria Novella and lecturer on theology to the papal curia in Perugia. In his *De peccato usurae*, Girolami considers usury from two perspectives: against divine law and *against nature.* Girolami equates the Satanist's pact with the devil to the taking of interest on money.

Dante Alighieri and Ezra Pound: The Stench of the Profit Motive

In Canto 11 of *The Inferno*, Dante puts the usurer together with the sodomite in the lowest reaches of hell, where they dwell *'venimmo sopra piu l'orribile stipa'* (in 'the horrible excess of stench'). In Canto 17 Dante again identifies usurers with miasma: Geryon (the personfication of fraud and usury) is "*colei che tutto 'l mondo appuzza*" ("the one who makes the whole world stink"). The sodomite reverses creation and places his genital organ not in the procreative vagina

---

[75] Langholm (op. cit.), p. 309.

of the woman but in the anal sewer of the male body, the repository of filth and stench. The sodomite takes the gift of the abundance of God's creation and perverts it into sterility. The usurer takes what is sterile (money, a mere symbol of transaction), and transforms it into the thing signified, making something out of nothing.

We may recoil in prudish dismay at the raw metaphors of the medieval poet, but Dante knew what we do not: that because the taking of interest on loans of money almost always evades being named and always calls itself by some other name, it must not be allowed to escape the complete articulation of the contours of its corruption. The mortal sin of "low" interest on money is not an issue for the modern Church. The crime of interest on money is an issue only for very few contemporary churchmen, economists, statesmen, legislators, magistrates or mandarins of western culture.

The 20th century philosopher, medievalist and poet Ezra Pound (1885-1972), who was steeped in Dante, observed: "My generation was brought up ham ignorant of economics. History was taught with omissions of the most vital facts. Every page our generation read was overshadowed by usury. *Usura* spreads her empire of forgetfulness and keeps herself under erasure...Of all usury's assaults on definition, the last and consummate is its erasure of its proper name. In *Canto* XCVI, Pound despairs of finding anyone 'whom the ooze cannot blacken,' because 'the stench of the profit motive has covered their names." [76]

In his *Canto* XLVI, Pound quotes a statement by the founder of the Bank of England, William Paterson:

---

[76] Bryan Cheyette, *Between Race and Culture* (Stanford University, 1996), p. 99.

"Hath benefit of interest on all/the monies which the bank, creates out of nothing." [77]

Dante reinforces and Pound exhumes the anathemas of the ancient Church, consigning usurers and sodomites to the same circle of the inferno, because both seek prosperity or eroticism, "without regard to production." This is a visionary discernment not only of Christian sages but of the natural law philosophers of Greek and Roman antiquity. Few insights are more foundational to the tutelary spirit of western civilization.

The Canker that Consumes the Conscience

Pound, who was in certain respects a personification of the spiritual and intellectual inheritance of the West, draws attention to usury's diabolic dimension, and adds to it the aspect of pathology which Pope Gregory X assigned to it in 1274 at the Council of Lyons II, "the canker":

The Evil is Usury, Neschek the serpent...
The canker corrupting all things, Fafnir the worm,
Syphilis of the State, of all kingdoms,
Wart of the commonweal,
Wenn-maker, corrupter of all things.

---

77 "The Bank of England and the Federal Reserve Bank in the United States stimulate the economy by pumping money into it directly. This is called 'quantitative easing.' The way the central bank does this is by buying assets – usually financial assets such as government and corporate bonds –using money it has simply created out of thin air. The institutions selling those assets (either commercial banks or other financial businesses such as insurance companies), will then have 'new' money in their accounts, which then boosts the money supply. These days the Bank doesn't have to literally print money – it is all done electronically." –BBC Business News, July 5, 2012. Many who oppose this something-from-nothing process forget that it was made possible and respectable by the legalization of interest on money, the primordial something-from-nothing alchemy that has been the norm in modern society. In a usury-free nation, "quantitative easing" would be unthinkable.

"...one of the conventional tropes of both Catholic Church councils and in early modern English denunciations of usurious moneylending. In Robert Willson's morality play *The Three Ladies of London* (1584), Conscience receives 'cankered coin' from Usury...Nicholas Breton branded the usurer in 1616 as a kind of 'canker that with the teeth of interest eats the heart of the poor.' In his 1634 treatise *The English Usurer, or Usury Condemned*, John Blaxton approvingly cites the sermon of Bishop Sands, who denounced usury as 'this canker' that 'corrupted all England.'...*In Saint George for England Allegorically Described*, Gerard Malynes praises Licurgus for banishing the 'canker worm' of usury from Sparta. Why did canker recommend itself to early modern English writers as a pathological metaphor for charging interest?...No doubt the link between canker and usury was...suggested by the longstanding convention of representing usury as a 'biting' serpent, a custom deriving from the double meaning of the Hebrew *neshech*, which, as Pound's addendum to Canto 100 assumes, means both 'usury' and 'to bite.' Indeed, in all the early modern English associations of usury with canker that I have cited, the disease is notably one that *eats,* whether the pockets of the indigent poor, the consciences of good Christians, or the nation's reserves of bullion." [78]

Shakespeare wrote of "cankered heaps of strange-achieved gold" (*2 Henry IV* act iv). In the 1602 *Geneva Bible*, in the Book of James, we read, "Your gold and silver is cankered, and the rust of them shall be a witness against you, and shall eat your flesh, as it were fire." (James 5:3.)

---

[78] Jonathan Gil Harris, *Sick Economies*, p. 84.

3

The Precursor: Usury in Florence

"...In law, a *mutuum* was a loan of fungibles, that is 'things that are fixed by weight, number or measure, such as wine, oil, grain or cash paid in copper, silver or gold.' The use of such things is identical with their consumption or destruction. Because of this trait, ownership and liability passed to the borrower, who was bound to return the equivalent of the thing borrowed rather than the thing itself. This contrasted with a *commodatum*, a loan for use — for example, the loan of a horse or a boat — in which the creditor retained both ownership and liability. Although *commodatum* was a gratuitous contract, the creditor-owner could legitimately convert it into a contract of lease and hire (*locatio et conductio*) by charging for the use of the thing. But the nature of a *mutuum* precluded charging the borrower for the use of what had become his own property. So far as the contract itself was concerned, the debtor's obligation extended only to the repayment of a thing of the same quality and quantity as the thing he was lent.

"Classical Roman law circumvented this difficulty by means of a supplementary contract called *stipulatio*, which was agreed at the same time as the *mutuum* and by which the debtor promised a separate payment called *usurae* or *fenus*. From patristic times, however, the church repudiated such agreements, forbidding the clergy to demand *usurae* and, in the west, extending the restriction to the laity..."

–Lawrin Armstrong
Usury and Public Debt
in Early Renaissance Florence

In spite of ecclesiastic and civil laws against interest on money, fallen human nature pursued greed by any means available. Laws against murder do not guarantee that there will never be a murder. This was indubitably true of usury, the instrument of the Money Power. In certain criminal cultures it persisted communally in defiance of the laws of God and government. The criminal culture in the city-state of Florence in what is today Italy, consisted in the city's deep ties to occult networks, brutal and aggressive wars, brazen legacy of crafty and ruthless loan sharking, and the fact that rather than being suppressed, sodomy was "regulated" by a Florentine bureaucracy: the *Ufficiali della'onesta*, which also "regulated" prostitution. In both cases "regulation" was a euphemism for maintaining a government monopoly on vice, and "disciplining" freelance sodomites and prostitutes who sought to engage in their activities independent of the official pimps. By the time usury was in the ascendant in Florence, sodomy was too. On the eve of the Protestant Reformation, one of the major campaigns of Girolamo Savonarola, the Dominican friar who, beginning in 1494, headed the new (and brief) anti-Medici reform government, was a string of unprecedented prosecutions for sodomy — 731 in just two years — November, 1495 to November, 1497. Savonarola was hanged and burned six months later, in May, 1498. It was reported that an elated city official declared, "Thank God, now we can sodomize!" [79]

From the fourteenth century onward a policy of aggressive capitalist acquisition by patrician oligarchs in the *Signoria* (government of Florence) was initiated, coupled with legislation that created *prestanze*, loans forcibly imposed, beginning circa 1345, on the people of Florence to service the *monte commune*, the debt of the

---

[79] Louis Crompton, *Homosexuality and Civilization*, p. 260. Also cf. Michael Rocke, *Forbidden Friendships: Homosexuality and Male Culture in Florence* (Oxford University Press, 1996).

city. The *monte* was the central instrument of the Florentine oligarchy's fiscal regime. By compelling the people to become its creditors, the government had caused its citizens to violate usury prohibitions and commit mortal sin. The principal apologist for this illegal and immoral scheme was the brilliant lay canon lawyer, Lorenzo di Antonio Ridolfi (1362-1443), a descendant of a powerful patrician family in Florence, doctor of law on the faculty of the University of Bologna, and from 1394 onward, one of the highest officials of the *Signoria*. He was consulted as an expert and judge of the civil and canon law. In February, 1404 [80]he published his *Treatise on Usury* ("*Tractus de usuris*"), [81] an early and cleverly argued erosion of traditional usury doctrine and jurisprudence, crafted to buttress the legitimacy of the commercial economy of the ruling Florentine cartel. Posing as a true Catholic he cited his motivation: "...compelled by these troubled times to explain for the spiritual good of my fellow citizens what is consistent with law and conscience in the matter of the public debt." John T. Noonan in his famous book, *The Scholastic Analysis of Usury*, fails to credit Ridolfi's canny subterfuge. Mistaking him for a writer who sought to confront the proscription against usury, Noonan did not appreciate Ridolfi's sophisticated *Realpolitik* (which would be imitated by his epigones down through the centuries). Ridolfi's shrewd thesis was that the *monte* and *the prestanze* did not deviate from the Church's ban on usury, but rather, conformed to its "spirit." Through double talk and dissembling, the assault on the immemorial dogma of the Catholic magisterium by the

---

[80] 1403 on the Florentine calendar, which began March 25.

[81] From the late Middle Ages to the Early Modern period, there are many dissertations on interest on money bearing this title, from just as many authors, such as Giambattista Lupo, Martin Bucer, Alphonso Vilagut, Gerardo Senensi, John Bolles, Alessandro Bonini, Petrus Ubaldus, Bartolomeo Ugolinus, etc.

revolutionary, canonical "policy modification" buried within Ridolfi's *Tractus de usuris*, was presented as being consistent with Catholic law and tradition, and not a substantive change. "Ridolfi's defense of the compensation paid to government creditors, like his overall emphasis on occult usury, served the interests of the rich." [82]

The unholy Trinity of Florence: The Three-for-One Monte

That a Christian veneer was needed to cover ever more brazen usury was painfully obvious. Florence's usury came about due to a mountain of fourteenth century government debt (approximately 600,000 florins in 1343), incurred from, among other causes, ceaseless warfare with neighboring city states such as Verona, Pisa and Milan, and with the pope himself. [83] By 1378 the war with the pontiff had cost Florence a million florins.

The type of usury crafted for the debtor city-state was a series of fiendishly clever arrangements producing interest-rates that made a mockery of Catholic law and would have been a source of profound scandal and outrage in Britain and central and northern Europe at the time. One of these sly mechanisms was the *monte dell'uno tre* ("three-for-one monte") of 1358, which, like other types of debt, paid 5% interest. [84] The difference being that, by means of an accounting trick, the city-state's lenders were credited with triple the amount of what they had

---

[82] Armstrong, p. 100. op.cit.

[83] From 1375 to 1378 Florence fought a war with the forces of Pope Gregory XI, the last Avignon pope (and the pontiff who restored the papacy to Rome).

[84] This is similar to the German-Catholic Nominalist *contractus trinus,* which we will consider in the next chapter.

loaned to the government, thereby increasing their interest return three-fold, to 15%.

"Between October 1365 and June 1367 there were over twenty-five hundred trades in *monte dell'uno tre* credits nominally worth almost a million florins...Gherardino di Niccolo Gherardini Giani, a member of the communal finance committee, advised a friend in Bruges, Tommaso di Piero di messer Rodolfo de' Bardi, not to sell his credits, which Gherardino was convinced would rise in value before the end of the war with the pope. He went on to suggest that Tommaso forestall an increase in his *prestanza* assessment by submitting a false declaration of assets... "[85]

The Villani family were chroniclers of the history of Florence in the early fourteenth century, as detailed in their *Cronica*, justly renowned for its eyewitness accounts of the ravages of the Black plague. In the portion penned by Matteo Villani, he wrote of the ravages of another plague in his native Florence, the *monte dell'uno tre*:

"Per questa via il comune senza altra gravezza ebbe al suo bisogno soccorso —e se bene si misura, non per carita o affezione ch'avessono i cittadini alla sua republica, ma per la cupidigia del largo profitto. Il quale fuori del buono e antico costume de' nostri maggiori molti n'ha tirati dalla mercatanzia in su l'usurae..."[86]

("By this means the commune raised the amount needed without difficulty — although it did so not because of the love or affection which the citizens felt toward their republic, but because of their cupidity when it came to large profits. This was a departure from the good old ways of our forefathers and drew many away from business into usury...").

---

85 Armstrong, op.cit., pp. 40-41.

86 *Cronica di Matteo Villani,* 8.71, Ignazio Moutier edition, 4:91.

In the 12th century, "...(w)hen asked to rule on the licitness of three transactions in which there was no express but merely an implicit agreement to repay more than the principal, Pope Urban III condemned them all, declaring the creditors 'quasi-usurers' who 'should be considered evil-doers on account of their intention to profit, and effectively compelled in the penitential forum to restore what they have received." [87]

The Usurer's Dilemma: confession & restitution or refusal of burial and eternal damnation

The mortal sin and crime of usury in Florence was committed in a context radically different from our own age — even men of great wealth and power in that time knew right from wrong and had consciences that haunted them on their deathbeds. They might make war against the pontiff himself, but the fear of God was still present in all but the most depraved:

"Indeed, as they approached their deathbeds, it seemed that usury was not just *a*, but *the* sin on the minds of wealthy men. Their illegitimate children...their...gluttony and general intemperance worried them far less. Or perhaps it was just that usury, unlike other sins, could only, according to Church law, be expiated through *full restitution* of what was sinfully gained. This was difficult if you'd spent the money...

"In the opening story of Boccaccio's *Decameron*, two usurers are terrified that their dying guest, a great and unrepentant sinner, will be refused burial and that because of their profession the local people will chase them out of town or even lynch them, in which case they too will be left unburied. The Lateran Church Council of 1179 denied Christian burial to

[87] Testament of Urban III.

usurers and the General Church Council of Lyons confirmed the ruling in 1274. 'Their bodies should be buried in ditches, together with dogs and cattle,' wrote Fra Filippo degli Agazzari. In Piacenza in 1478, when a torrential rainstorm followed the church burial of a usurer, the townsfolk dug up the corpse, paraded it in the streets, performed a mock hanging, then plunged it into the Po." [88]

"Against this sin (of interest on money) Fra Filippo (degli Agazzari) burnishes all the weapons of his armory and seeks to strike terror...by a series of dreadful 'ensamples' touching the miserable deaths of usurers...a company of fiends come for the soul of a dying usurer amid thunder, lightening, hail and rain. Now a very great multitude and innumerable, of men...dark and terrible beyond all human imagining, carry away the lost soul with fury and tempest, with inconceivable rage biting and smiting and rending and tearing him. Now all the demons of hell throng the church where a usurer...is buried...in the morning it is found that church has been cast down and hurled...into the river...the lost spirit of yet another usurer appears to his son in the form of a black smoke as it were the shadow of a man to announce to him that he is 'condemned to eternal torments, wherefrom I shall issue no more." [89]

Here is a representative account of the moral dilemma of a usurer published in the *Gli Assempri* of Fra Filippo degli Agazzari (1338-1422).[90] The *Assempri*

---

[88] Tim Parks, *Medici Money: Banking, Metaphysics, and Art in Fifteenth-Century Florence,* p. 10. (Po is the longest river in Italy).

[89] William Heywood, *The "ensamples" of Fra Filippo: A study of mediaeval Siena*, pp. 139-140.

[90] Blessed Fra Filippo was Prior of the Augustinian monastery of Lecceto in Siena. He was beatified in the year of his death.

was a collection of sermons and moral lessons preached and circulated throughout Italy. We reprint one lesson here, despite its prolixity, because it furnishes a sense of the intense pressure placed on usurers at the end of their lives, and the extent of the devotion which priests and monks exhibited in seeking to rescue souls they knew were headed for certain damnation if they did not only confess and repent, but return the riches they had gained through interest on money loans.

The Usurer's Fire

"There was a great usurer who had three sons. And it came to pass that he fell sick and that a good and skillful and wise friar (*religioso*) was sent for that he might prepare his soul. Wherefore that friar, examining him and finding that almost all that he had in the world had been gained by usury,' sought to persuade him to confess and to prepare his soul diligently, and to provide by his will for the restitution of the said usury, and in like manner to arrange all his affairs according to justice, because otherwise his soul would go to hell, and never would he find the grace of God, nor mercy, nor remission of his sins.

"The usurer answered and said that he was willing to do as the friar desired, save only that he would not make restitution of the usury because he desired not to leave his sons poor.

"The friar replied: 'Consider that if thou shalt go to hell to leave thy sons rich, they can do nothing for thy soul, but rather they will continually increase thy sufferings; and every evil use which they shall make of thy ill-gotten wealth, and the evil teaching and example which thou hast given them shall be laid at thy door.

"Moreover if they shall not amend their lives and shall not themselves restore this usury, then, since thou will have been the occasion of their wickedness, and all these things shall be brought in judgment against thy soul and shall increase thy torments.'

"Then said the usurer: 'Look you, Master Friar, such is the love that I bear for my sons that even in hell itself it would cause me great suffering if I saw them poor and in evil plight, wherefore on no wise will I ever make restitution of the usury.'

"Then said the friar: 'Behold, my son, thou art greatly deceived by the devil who causes thee to believe that in the other life, if thou shalt go to the torments of hell, thou will be able to love or to desire the welfare of any person whatsoever. For, albeit these two things are granted to thee in this life, this is so by reason of the free will which God hath given thee that thou mayest use the same to his honor and glory and reverence and to that of his Saints in as much as in thee lieth. Wherefore, if in this life thou shalt use these two things as thou should do, they will be eternally granted to thee hereafter in the glory of the life eternal, to wit always to love God and always to desire the welfare of others; and the more perfectly thou shalt have these two things in this life, the more perfectly shalt thou possess the glory of the life eternal. And, if here thou shalt have them not, be assured that thou will have hereafter other two things for ever with the devil, to wit, always to wish ill to others and always to hate God and every other thing which thou art able to think of or to imagine. So that not only wilt thou hate thy sons, but also thine own self, so that if there were neither devil nor spirit in hell to torment thee, thou thyself would torment thyself forever with all thy power.

"...God is the Highest Good, Highest Love, and Highest Charity,' and apart from him is infinite evil and infinite pride and hatred. In the time that thou hast been free to do good or evil, thou hast not desired this Highest Good, neither hast sought to do his will, nor desired to please him in anything, but hast rather chosen to please the devil in hell, and hast served and obeyed him; for this cause thou art deprived for ever of this Highest Good and Love and Charity of God; also thou shalt hold it in so great despite that thou shalt not be able to desire it either for thyself or for others. And therefore it will be a just thing that thou should be thrust with the devil into all the pains of hell. And by him shalt thou be fulfilled with four separate things, to wit with every worst and wickedest desire, and with outrageous hate against God, and against all the holy company of heaven, and against all the inhabitants of the world, and not only against thy sons but against thy own self also. And thou shalt be full of diabolic envy and of infernal pride.

"Wherefore, oh miserable man, consider what thou art doing and choose not for thy sons' sake to lose the celestial kingdom and the glory of the life eternal and the sweet company of the holy and blessed angels who eternally rejoice with Christ and with his most holy Mother in the Kingdom of the life Eternal.

"Moreover I would that thou should know that, according to that which the Saints have said, the greatest suffering which the demons in hell endure, albeit their torments are many and divers, is to be herded together and to look the one upon the blackness of the other, so terrible and horrible is that sight; and this notwithstanding that they are for ever burning in the black fire of hell. Tell me, what good can thy sons do for thee when thou shalt be cast into hell and shalt become one with the demons in such and in so many torments?...Bethink thee then...the mad and bestial love which thou hast borne thy sons will be to thee for all eternity a judgment and a torment, and their evil lives of which thou art the occasion will ever increase for thee pain upon pain in hell.

"Consider then, thou wretched man, what joy and what consolation thou shalt have in hell with thy sons, when ye shall be together and shall be filled with such infinite hatred and loathing the one against the other that like mad dogs ye shall gnaw and devour one another. Wherefore prepare thyself now while yet thou hast time, for, albeit it is late, thou still hast time to prepare thyself for death.'

"Then at the last, that friar, being filled with love and charity and seeing that he could not change the fixed resolve of the usurer, said unto him: 'Now, my son, hearken unto me and, albeit thou wilt not do that which I bid thee, at least promise me that thou will thyself pray to God that he may illuminate thy heart and mind and may give thee the wish to do right and his love and charity.' And when the friar had thus spoken he departed and he betook himself to prayer for that usurer and besought God earnestly that he would have pity upon him.

"On the following day he returned to the aforesaid usurer and found him still as obstinate as before; wherefore, being inspired by God, he said unto him: 'Behold, my son, since thou hast so much love for thy sons that for their sake thou art willing to abide forever in the fire of hell, I would, at the least, that thou should determine what love they bear to thee. Thou should do in this manner: call one of thy sons and speak to him in this way, saying: 'Behold, my son, the ill gain of usury which I have made troubles my conscience; and, if I provide not in my Will that the same shall be restored, I cannot be absolved of any sin that ever I did, and for this cause I shall go eternally to the fire of hell. Nevertheless, for the love that I bear you, and to leave you rich and independent, and to the end that ye may not come to poverty or want, I am minded rather to go to eternal torments and to burn eternally in the fire of hell, than to leave you poor.

"Now, therefore, I desire to see what love ye bear me in return for my great love for you, and what ye would be willing to do for my sake. And...because I am willing to abide eternally in the fire of hell for your sake, I wish to see if ye are willing for my sake to hold a finger over the flame of a lamp as long only as it takes to say an *Ave Maria*. And, if ye are willing to do this, I will leave you rich and will go for ever into the fire of hell which burns evermore.'

"With this counsel the usurer was content, and he promised that he would do even as the friar had said unto him. And so the friar departed and devoutly prayed to God for him.

"The usurer called one of his sons and related to him the challenge. Then the son began to sigh: but, in order that he might not seem to have so little love for his father, he put his finger over the flame of the lamp. But as soon as he felt the heat of the flame, he drew it away and wished not to hold it there for the saying of even a third part of an *Ave Maria*. He told his father that it was displeasing to God that he himself should destroy his own hand.

"Then the father called his second son, and repeated to him the aforesaid words. And the second son put his finger over the flame of the lamp, and when he felt the heat he suddenly drew it away and said to his father: 'If I myself destroyed my own hand, I should sin mortally, for no man ought for any reason whatsoever to do an injury to himself, and to offend God and his Saints. Moreover, the hurt that I should do myself would be of no benefit to you or to anyone else.'

"So the father called the third son and said to him the like words. Then the son made answer and said: 'To do this thing that you desire of me would be to tempt God, and he would be greatly displeased if I should consume my own hand. Also whosoever should hear of it would say that I was no better than a brute beast to do so mad a thing to no good end.'

"Then was the usurer touched to the heart, and his mind was illuminated by God; and he sent for the aforesaid friar and with great weeping and with much contrition confessed his sin, beseeching him to prepare his soul after such fashion as should seem best unto him, because he was ready to do everything that he should bid him do, and was minded to provide by his will for the full restitution of the usury. And he faithfully promised that if he should recover he would himself make full restitution. And he told how he had tested his sons and how they had answered. He said that he perceived that they loved him not at all, save only for the wealth which they hoped should be left unto them.

"The friar replied, saying: 'Blessing and praise and thanks be to God who hath illuminated thy heart and mind and hath given thee true repentance. And now by this thou mayest see that, when a man is dead and buried in this life, there is neither father nor mother nor wife nor children nor friends nor brethren nor kinsmen that remember him any more, save only now and again to praise or blame his actions at their good pleasure.

"Thou should know that, when thou shalt have departed this life, thou will appear before the judgment of God where no man may aid or injure thee, but only thy own good or evil deeds.'

"And, when he had said these words, the friar confessed and prepared that usurer as was convenient. And he made his Will and provided that the usury should be restored in full. And thereafter in peace he passed from this life." [91]

Cautionary sermons like the preceding were not aimed at usurers alone, but at all practitioners of greed and covetousness. Often the homiletic barbs stung the wealthy in general, as well as anyone who was viewed as a nigggardly calculator of profit.

"A continuous stream of scorn and reproof for all the current sources of pride and prestige in medieval

---

[91] Heywood, op. cit, pp. 153-159.

society poured forth from the pulpits. The ears of the people must have grown quite familiar with homiletic phrases that often sounded to them like so many threats of destruction for the powerful and the rich. Hence, for better or for worse, we must acknowledge the sermons, however little so intended, as a primary literature of secular revolt, and their authors as the heralds of political strife and future social liberties. Such persistent ventilation of the sufferings and wrongs of the poor — not exceeded, probably, by the most outspoken champions of social revolution in any age — could only end at length in one result. If the evils remained, one fine day the oppressed would take matters into their own hands..." [92]

The Usurer's Indulgence

During the illegal usury of the 1360s, the city-state of Florence had on its payroll an official known as the *Syndicus ad indulgenum,* tasked with pardoning its residents ahead of time for the crime of usury which they would commit: "...pardon, limit and remit with respect to God, conscience and the world all who have hitherto received or enjoyed, or whose predecessors received or enjoyed, or who themselves or whose predecessors will, in the course of the current year receive anything by way of gift, compensation, commission, usury or interest from the revenues of the commune for any money lent to the commune or advanced to it in any way. And make or cause to be made with regard to this pardon, limitation and remission, an instrument or instruments with all guarantees, warranties and formalities for any who desire them." [93]

Note that this pardon has nothing to do with the remission of the sin of usury. This was a lawyer's

---

[92] G.R. Owst, *Literature and Pulpit in Medieval England,* p. 236.

[93] Armstrong, op. cit., p. 54.

loophole; a release from the threat of civil and criminal prosecution, and liability for restitution, with regard to usurious proceeds from the *monte*. From 1357 through the 1370s it endeavored to ease the consciences of those who were committing mortal sin and receiving interest payments. Beginning in 1382 the Florentine regime began to issue enactments which addressed the conscience ("*conscientie*") of those citizens involved in usury, although by now it was decided that usury was too strong a word. The five percent income from the loans were placed under the category of *interesse*, under the legal fiction of "gifts, damages":

"Circa exgravationem conscientie civium Florentinorum dicti communis et maxime in denariis montis qui recipiuntur V pro centario pro aliquo dono, damno et interesse."

It was further emphasized that those receiving this income could do so without any "scruple of conscience" ("*conscientie scrupulo*") or anxiety about an obligation to make restitution ("*et sine aliquo restiutionis gravamine*").

This marks the beginning of the development of a species of brazen outlawry that in the next century would make Catholic Florence such fertile ground for Neoplatonic Kabbalism, banking and other criminal cartels. The city fathers had no authority whatsoever to relieve the consciences of the citizens who were profiting from the government's usury operations and the people knew it, but they clung to the charade as providing at least some cover for their sin. The Third Lateran Council had declared interest on money to be both mortal sin and, because it was a form of theft, a crime ("*crimen usurarum*"). This sinful crime could only be expunged by making complete restitution. In its defiance, the government of Florence had become a crime syndicate and this would be a template for Florentine power in the future Renaissance era, with ominous repercussions for the Church. Other Italian city-states were not as obstreperous as Florence. In 1382, Siena reinstated the laws against usury which had been suspended.

Florentine money bought influence in the Church but not enough to still the voices and pens of bishops and theologians who condemned as mortal sin, the "legislative subterfuges" attached to interest-bearing government loans; and their anathemas often bore fruit on an individual basis. In Florence in 1378 Giannozzo Sacchetti "repaid three hundred florins he had received in interest, pleading an uneasy conscience as his motive."[94]

The Ciompi Insurrection of 1378

For the common people of Florence, the hardest "hit were the urban poor who owned sufficient property to be assessed but could not realize the cash necessary to meet their levies...a growing proportion of the poor, particularly *sottoposti*, textile workers subject to the wool manufacturer's guild, were regularly assessed loans in the 1360s...The pressure on the poor increased sharply during the war with the pope as the number of households deemed to meet the minimum property requirements more than doubled between 1375 and 1378...the poor made use of brokers, who paid the full assessment in return for a fee and a title to the credit and the interest. During the war, eighty percent of all *prestanziati* and some ninety percent of *sottoposti*-assessed loans in Santa Maria Novella, paid "*ad perdendum*" ("to be lost") — a majority choosing to surrender their rights to speculators. The brokers to whom the *sottoposti* turned were often their employers, whose profits from speculation were thus effectively

---

94 Armstrong, p. 56.

appropriated from their employees. The burden of loans paid *ad perdendum* combined with structural inequalities built into the tax system...widen(ed) the gulf between rich and poor...for many *sottoposti* the result was a 'financial bloodletting that by the end of the impositions exceeded three hundred *soldi*, a sum equivalent to about forty days' pay for a wool-comber, and proportionately for other workers; which is to say that during the war, the *sottoposti* in effect gave their labor for free for a time period to their employers, who might thus recover a portion of their investment in a proportion corresponding to the level of *prestanze* imposed on workers'...

"The effects are illustrated in a petition poor Florentines addressed to the *Signoria* in 1369...'Lord priors of Florence: For the sake of your honor...you should do something about the taxes, the forced loans and extra levies which the poor people of Florence must pay. If you don't do something, you will discover that no one in Florence will be able to save you. There will be an uprising if these forced loans and special levies are not reduced, for there is great privation here. People are living in misery...Just think about those who have three or four or five children, and who are assessed two or three florins, and who have to live from the labor of their hands and those of their wives. How can they stay here and live?'

"...The petition the Ciompi presented to the government on 28 July 1378 included demands for the suspension of *prestanze*, the reintroduction of a wealth tax, the abolition of interest payments on the *monti* and the progressive elimination of the debt over twelve years.... The appeal proved to be prophetic, since the disparities aggravated by the *monte* system played a central role in the Ciompi insurrection of 1378." [95]

---

[95] Armstrong, pp. 42-45.

The insurrection, initiated by the wool-workers, was an armed revolt against usury. The slogan of the Florentine freedom-fighters was, "No more *monti*, no more *prestanze*!" ("No more debt, no more compulsory interest-bearing loans!"). For six weeks they held the seat of government and established three new guilds: the dyers, the doublet-makers and the wool-makers. Brutal, counter-revolutionary reprisals followed from the faithless crew who were intoxicated by money. The reaction was not entirely successful and a democratic coalition government was formed, lasting until 1382, when the full power of the regime was at last restored, the workers suppressed, and usury once again flourished under civic auspices.

In the following years, the anarchic "western schism" produced a succession of anti-popes (Clement VII, Benedict XIII and the usurious John XXIII, patron of the Medici crime syndicate of usurers), as Florence defiantly pursued its outlawed usury. The pseudo-Catholic intellectuals like Lorenzo Ridolfi sought to mask the sin by transforming it into something venial or trivial, on the road to its complete nullification. The power of money is overwhelming. It corrupts everything. The harshest church laws were searched for escape clauses by lawyers of every description. The rewards for discovering loopholes were immense. Where none existed, a play on words was devised, along with underhanded tricks intended to subvert the spirit of the strict prohibitions on usury.

Manifest and Occult Usury

Chief among these were the Lateran Council laws against public or "manifest" usurers. Aha, exclaimed the lawyers, what of usurers who conducted their business in private, under another name and were therefore not manifestly engaged? Usury that was not made public would, therefore, not be usury. By this stratagem it was claimed that only pawnbrokers and similar low level offenders fell under ecclesiastical jurisdiction and the moral definition of usury. Private banks, it was alleged, would be exempt. Many of the modern historians of economics almost unanimously slander the stalwart medieval Catholic campaigners against usury by claiming that the distinction between usury and *manifest* usury was a loophole deliberately concocted by the medieval Church.[96] In truth, the distinction had been made because the Church sought to take great care in branding someone a usurer. The Church sought to secure the conviction of only guilty parties who, without any possibility of ambiguity, were "manifestly" complicit in taking interest on money as an enterprise. The Church of the late Middle Ages was not a hair-splitting tyranny seeking to impugn a grandchild because, after her grandmother loaned her a silver coin she returned two silver coins to her, one as repayment and the other as a gift; that level of Bolshevik bureaucratic intrusion into the lives of ordinary Catholics was not the way of the Church in the 1300s. Clear proof was required, in the interest of due process, in the course of which guilty bankers as well as pawn brokers could be accused, tried and punished.

The modern spin on this prudent distinction concerning a category of notorious public usury, is a cynical attack on the sincerity of the saintly medieval Catholic popes and theologians who relentlessly attacked interest on money with the whole of their being, but who, we are expected to believe, created a semantic evasion for the benefit of the largest usury operations.

A "manifest" usurer was a witness against himself and undoubtedly guilty, therefore the law began with him. The law did not exclude private bankers since,

---

[96] Cf. for example, John Gilchrist, op.cit, p. 66. Gilchrist is in favor of usury. See his "simple solution" on p. 68.

when it could be proved that these bankers were certainly guilty of the "fraud of usury," then their usury was made manifest. As previously noted, the Council of Vienne, in its Decree 29 targeted secret ("occult") usurers: "Moreover, since money-lenders frequently conclude loan-contracts in an occult or fraudulent manner, which makes it difficult to convict them on a charge of usury, we decree that they should be forced by ecclesiastical censure to produce their books on such occasions."

T.P. McLaughlin demonstrates that the accusation that the "manifest" distinction was a means for cozening immunity for a special category of private banks, is without foundation:

"The Lateran Council of 1179 and other decrees referred to...declare that the penalties are incurred by *usurarii manifesti*. When is one to be considered a manifest usurer? Some of the Councils understand the word *manifestus* to mean notorious; the penalties are incurred by usurers who are notorious. Others, showing the influence of the teaching of the canonists, provide a more exact and complete explanation of the term. Those are manifest who have been convicted of the crime, who have confessed it before the judge or whose usurious business is carried on so openly that it cannot be concealed. Without being notorious one may be defamed by common report of the crime of usury. Such a one becomes manifest, say the councils, if he does not submit to the *purgatio canonica* within the time fixed by the bishop...A man is to be held as a manifest usurer if he confesses it extra-judicially before the parish priest or a notary public. Again, two Witnesses suffice to establish the fact that one is a usurer and such evidence renders him manifest.

"...Whereas Innocent IV is content to state briefly that manifest usurers are those who have been convicted by the courts, Bernard Bottoni discusses the question more thoroughly. A usurer, he says, may be notorious or not. If he is notorious, then no further proof is required; his crime is manifest and the penalties may be applied. If, however, he is not notorious, then a judicial examination is required to establish the fact of usury and so make his crime manifest....A man is *notorius facti* if, for example, he conducts a bank or place of business where he is prepared to lend at usury to all comers. In this case he suffers *ipso facto* the penalties provided in the law.

"A man is *notorius juris* when he has been publicly condemned as such by the Church. If he has merely the reputation of being a usurer, he is not a notorious or manifest usurer, nor do the penalties affect him until he has been publicly condemned. This sentence will become public when he has been called to answer the charge and either confesses his guilt or, denying it, is yet proved to be a usurer by the testimony of witnesses." [97]

Loopholes were sought for exceptions to the law. One of these exploited reverse obligations of the part of the debtor which were a survival from the law of the Roman empire, which decreed that the debtor, in addition to repayment of the principal, owed his creditor "gratitude" for lending without interest. Some token of "gratitude" in the form of a gift to the lender was encouraged, or in some cases mandated. In Catholic canon law there was no such mandate, and *bona fide* gifts (those that were truly voluntary as an expression of gratitude for having received an interest-free loan), were of course not banned. But where the "gifts" were actually a hidden form of interest arranged in advance as a *requirement* of the loan, they fell under the legal category of *fraudem usurarum*. These fraudulent transactions were difficult to detect,

---

[97] McLaughlin, op.cit., pp. 12-13.

and along with other loopholes (for example, *mora and poena*, and the distinction between voluntary loans and government-mandated *prestanze*), provided a cover for the sin of loans at interest.

Ridolfi, the double-talking Florentine canonist, stated that interest payments on loans to Florence should be seen "as a sort of reward for citizens' contributions to the common good rather than usury paid on a loan." The payments certainly were quite a "reward." The creditors with the biggest loans to Florence were the ones who set the interest rates: the city fathers themselves.[98] Rest assured that they did so "in good conscience," and at rates that were *consuetum lucrum et condecens* ("customary and fitting compensation").

Roman Catholics and the civil powers allied with them, were engaging in an astonishing departure from Catholic dogma: the regulation of mortal sin, to make it less wicked, while continuing to commit it! This fool's errand is with us still today. In the twenty-first century it permeates the Church and virtually every secular and ecclesiastical plan for the "reform" of usury. Abolition is not even on the agenda of most contemporary reformers. Yet, one cannot "reform" a deadly sin that damns one's soul. Modern reform efforts along these lines produce demoralizing confusion and further support the system of usury, because the usurers much prefer "reform" to abolition. The devil would rather have us tell ourselves that the manner in which we are committing the mortal sin is sufficiently "moderate" and "reasonable" that it justifies its continuation.

---

98 "By 1427, eighty-six percent of *monte* credits were owned by the richest ten percent of Florentine households...the poor, who paid their assessments *ad perdendum* or sold their credits to speculators, were ineligible to collect interest." Armstrong, op.cit., p. 100.

The Augustinian theologian Gregory of Rimini swept most of the early evasions of the moral law aside by ruling that if a creditor intended to profit from a loan, then he was guilty of usury, whether or not he loaned to the Republic of Florence or the lowliest peasant or cobbler. [99] Of the various usurious city-states in the Italian region at the time, such as Venice, that had made some deceptively covered forms of usury lawful, Gregory solemnly admonished them with the warning "God is not mocked." To which the Money Power of the region replied, "*Quod non est licitum lege, necessitas facit licitum*" ("Necessity makes it lawful"). We witness the extent to which two-faced, fork-tongued rhetoric predominated in the milieu of rising Italian commercial decadence in canonist Lorenzo Ridolfi's statement: "Debtors should not be forced to pay usury to which they have obligated themselves. But if they have sworn an oath to pay, they are obliged by the Lord to fulfill their oath."

As the pagan/humanist Renaissance dawned on the horizon of history, the Italians tended to revert to Roman rather than Biblical and Christian precedents. Chief among the former was the legal code of the Emperor Justinian. There were two troubling aspects to this Roman precedent which presaged the double-mind that came to predominate in Venice and Florence and later in Protestant and Catholic Europe as a whole: a vigorous philosophical condemnation of usury alongside a legally permissible category of usury. "Justinian...fixed the following rates of interest — maritime loans twelve percent; loans to ordinary persons, not in business, six percent; loans to high personages (*illustres*) and agriculturalists, four percent. While the taking of interest was thus approved or tolerated by...Roman law, it was at the same time reprobated by the philosophers...Cicero

---

[99] Armstrong, op. cit., pp. 68-69.

condemns usury as being hateful to mankind, and makes Cato say that it is on the same level of moral obliquity as murder; and Seneca makes a point that (later) became of some importance in the Middle Ages, namely that usury is wrongful because it involves the selling of time.[100] Plutarch develops the argument that money is sterile..." [101]

Usury Forbidden by Man-made or Divine Law?

This disconnect between rhetorical denunciation of interest on money and what was actually legal and implemented in Roman society, is the inevitable result of a separation-of-church-and-state economy that operates outside the statutes and judgements of God. Greek and Roman philosophers provided a secularized reaffirmation of the Word of God on usury, but in their own society the philosophers were almost completely impotent. When Aristotle condemned usury his condemnation was a noble articulation of the natural law, but it lacked *compelling* moral force. The law of the God of Israel in the Hebrew (Old) Testament did have that force and Jesus reinforced and clarified that Law in the Greek (New) Testament. His Church declared the destiny of those who defied God in this way: the destruction of their souls. With this dogmatic truth in place, the Church fought interest on money

---

[100] "The argument that usury is the illicit sale of time, which is common to all and therefore non-vendible, first appeared in the writings of the 12th century theologian Peter the Chanter and subsequently became a commonplace of usury analysis. It was adopted as a subsidiary argument against usury by Pope Innocent IV." (Armstrong, p. 95). "The instigators of capitalism were usurers...sellers of time..." (Jacques Le Goff, "The Usurer and Purgatory"). "Usury was a theft...of time, which belonged solely to God, because it made money out of the time that elapsed between the loan and its repayment." Le Goff, *Money and the Middle Ages*, p. 63. Also cf. William of Auxerre, *Summa aurea* (ca. 1220), III:21, q.1.

[101] George O'Brien, *An Essay on Mediaeval Economic Teaching*, pp. 161-163.

like a lion for more than a thousand years. Nothing short of this uncompromising adherence to divine truth will suffice to curb oppression, injustice and the kind of dog-eat-dog economic system that God hates (Isaiah 61:8). To build on the pagans is to build on sand; it is to inject a *spitzfindige* quibbling, compromising spirit of disputation that chisels away at the foundations which Yahweh, His Divine Son and the Holy Spirit established for all time. This is a matter of obedience to God versus rebellion.

The Romans rebelled against their philosophers' thundering abhorrence of usury, and why not? They were only the lucubrations of men. It is edifying to know that learned Greeks and Romans of antiquity opined about the evils of usury, yet their opinions are not the fount of Christendom's historic condemnation of this fraud and oppression. Notions of "philosophical" objections lead to the logical trap set by the situation ethicists: what man has made, man can change; what was true "in that time" is "parochial and dated" now, and therefore, no longer in force.[102] Accepting a philosophical premise for the ban on usury virtually guarantees its abrogation. *Pope Innocent IV declared that usury was prohibited not because it violated the natural law as set forth by Aristotle, but because it violated the divine law as set forth by God. Usury is banned because it is intrinsically evil.* No human being has the authority to render it moral, ethical or legal.

All subsequent pronouncements permitting usury, whether from papal, Protestant or civic authorities, are null and void. Recalling that usury is regarded as murder, or at the very least theft, we read, "In matters that are mortally sinful according to divine law, such

---

[102] Azo (1150-1230), the medieval Italian canon lawyer and expert on old Roman law stated that the rationale for the Emperor Justinian's permission for usury was "worldly necessity."

as theft...no bishop, not even the pope, can dispense from penance and restitution."[103]

Natural law arguments do have their place in corroborating God's moral law, and amplifying its nuances and characteristics. Anything prohibited by the Bible is also contrary to natural law. Many theologians like Gerard of Siena, in his *Tractatus de usuris et de praescriptionibus,* offered classic natural law arguments against interest on loans of money; mainly, that such loans cause a sterile thing to bear fruit, for example with regard to the fixed value of fungibles: a bushel of corn is always worth a bushel of corn, not two bushels of corn. A fungible is never worth more than itself. In contracting for more than the principal lent, the creditor subverts intrinsic value.

What should be said to the usurers today is what the Church declared for most of its existence, if you are engaged in taking interest on money you are transgressing the law of God and you do so at the peril of your soul. Until this truth is restored, taught and preached, there will be no significant erosion of the Money Power's dominion over our world, save by a miracle of God. All appeals to man-made law and philosophy will be met by counter-arguments based on other anthropomorphic sources. Where God's immutable law is invoked it cannot be derogated by heretical popes, tyrannical kings, simoniacal cardinals, crooked legislatures, or supposed Protestant scripture savants such as John Calvin, Richard Baxter and Samuel Willard, without committing the sin of rebellion, since the law of an inferior (man), cannot derogate the law of a superior (God). It is not only a question of rebellion, but idolatry. When interest on money is permitted, the authority of God Himself is

---

103 Cf. Hostiensis, archbishop of Ostia; and Guido de Baysio (1246-1313) in his *Rosarium*. (De Baysio was chairman of the department of canon law at the University of Bologna and a judge at the papal court).

derogated. Pope Innocent IV stated that the avarice generated by usury is a form of idolatry.

In response to the increase in escape clauses and equivocation, in 1371 the theologian Guido de Belloreguardo, who was the Augustinian Prior-General, declared that the fostering of avarice in the people was morally inexcusable in all circumstances. Piero degli Strozzi, provincial minister of the Dominican province in Rome responded to the effects on the Catholic people of Florence from the pressure on theologians and canonists to approve of the loopholes. Strozzi termed the arguments used to put forth the approval, "sophistry." The Dominican theologian made a veiled reference to the power of the purse wielded by the money men of Florence, which paid for the sophistry: "I say that the guarantee of the validity and security of the aforesaid (payments is) the will and power of ruling citizens who have money invested in the commune and seek a profit. And it would be very difficult to change this and to take money against their will from those whom God knows if they would willingly forgo both principal and *interesse*." Strozzi warned the people of Florence, "...beware lest under the sway of words good citizens be made usurers and led by avarice to desire profits from which they should be restrained." [104] The Dominican provincial would brook no loopholes. [105] The debt market in Florence was also denounced by numerous prominent

---

[104] Armstrong, pp. 75 and 77.

[105] Rev. Fr. Piero degli Strozzi did not completely rule out the possibility that an additional payment for a loan beyond the principal could be a gift from a grateful recipient of the loan rather than interest on the loan, if it passed certain tests, the most crucial of these being that it was voluntary. If a "gift" was contingent on receiving the loan, then, as we have noted, it was of course undoubtedly usury. Cf. Gregory of Rimini, *Tractatus*, art. 1 [ed. cit. fol. A7r]). (Piero degli Strozzi is not to be confused with the extended Strozzi clan of Florentine finaglers which we will encounter later in these pages).

theologians and canonists, among them Guglielmo Centueri, Gregory of Rimini, Guido de Belloreguardo and John Klenkock.

Mortal sin for a worthy cause: The "Charity Banks" – "*Monte Pietatis*"

One of the instruments for legalizing usury within Christian society was a "benevolent" loan-sharking operation created by individual Catholic clerics "for the love of the poor." Papal and other forms of ecclesiastic usury in the Renaissance were conducted through financial operations known as *monte pietatis* — alleged "charity" banks supposedly operated to give loans to the poor at supposedly low rates of interest. While some of these early associations operated without usury, funded by grants from altrusitic philanthropists, by the late fifteenth century the *monte pietatis* were often a subterfuge for operating a usurious bank under the guise of helping the poor. A true *mons pietatis* was "founded in London (England), where Bishop Michael Nothburg, in 1361, left 1,000 marks of silver for the establishment of a bank that should lend money on pawned objects, without interest." On the eve of the Renaissance, interest-earning *mons pietatis* operations were established throughout Italy in places such as Perugia and the Venetian Republic, by priests such as Bernardino da Feltre [106] and Bartolommeo da Colle.

---

[106] Da Feltre is considered a heroic and unassailable holy man by conservative Catholics, due to his public campaign against sins of the flesh and Judaic usurers. Yet, by his actions we know that Bernardino was the agent, conscious or not, who helped to lay the future foundation for a papal precedent for committing mortal sin by charging interest on money, as long as the "former" mortal sin thwarted "the Jews" and "helped the poor." This was a betrayal and abandonment of dogmatic truth, an act of modernist infiltration which came from the Right, using the pretext of thwarting "the Jews" to justify "moderate," incremental mortal sin.

In Perugia the supposed "charity" was a municipal corporation with directors, accountants and salesmen. "All were paid with either a fixed salary or with a percentage in the profits...the *monte*s did not lend money gratuitously, but on the contrary, the expressed intention of the founders was that the money should be lent at interest, varying from 4 percent to 12 percent...Bernardino da Feltre always insisted on the necessity of interest..."

There was a vigorous protest from true Catholic theologians against these usury schemes disguised as pious charities. The eminent Cardinal Giovanni Dominici (1356-1419) upheld the Church's traditional dogmatic prohibition on interest on money (termed "rigid" by modern historians): "Dominici followed the more rigid approach of the Dominicans toward usury — expressed, for example, in their disapproval of the public debt, or their objections to the later institution of the *Monte di Pietá*. [107]These "rigid" (a more accurate description would be "faithful and courageous") Dominicans declared that anyone who excused the practice of usury was a probable heretic.

The Servants of God, Nicholas Bariano and Johannes Andreae

Among the most learned of the traditional attacks on the mortal sin of usury was a treatise by the Augustinian theologian Nicholas Bariano, sarcastically titled, *De Monte Impietatis* (circa 1494), which raised the prophetic question of whether even a pope had the right to approve interest on loans for any reason, since such approval contravened divine law. Bariano made clear that the heresy was not the charity fund for the poor itself. What was revolutionary was the interest to be paid: "The opposition was not directed at the *mons*

---

[107] Nirit Ben-Aryeh Debby, *Renaissance Florence in the Rhetoric of Two Popular Preachers*, p. 189.

pietatis as such, but merely against the condition of requiring interest. It was not admitted that the use of the interest to maintain the charity justified the usury, since a good end could not justify evil means, and it was held that lending money at interest was intrinsically bad..."

Bariano's view was the view of the Church from time immemorial as expressed by Johannes Andreae (1270-1348), professor of canon law at the University of Bologna (where he was known as the "*iuris canonici fins*" — "the fount of canon law"):

> "It is forbidden to engage in usury even to redeem captives from the Saracens (Muslims). It cannot be argued that a greater evil can be avoided through usury, for usury is, in a sense, the greatest of evils..."[108]

Pope Alexander III (1105-1181) forbade anyone to borrow at interest even in order to ransom captives from the Muslims: "Since Scripture forbids Christians to lie on behalf of others, much more does it forbid them to take part in usury ("...*ne etiam pro redimenda vita captivi usurarum crimine involvatur*.") [109]

---

108 *Quaestio Peccatum*. "The object of canon law...is to guide people to God. This cannot be done without charity; mortal sin is a violation of charity...Usury is sinful in itself and therefore the canons condemn it as an impediment to the common good of the Faithful." (Johannes Andreae).

109 Decretal to the Archbishop of Palermo.

The Den of Thieves Returns to the House of God

The Catholic opposition was doomed, however. The heretics prevailed. On May 4, 1515, at Lateran Council V, Session X, in the Bull, *Concilii in decima sessione super materia Montis Pietatis*,[110] Giovanni di Lorenzo de' Medici, "Pope Leo X," overthrew the solemn dogma of the Roman Catholic Church from its founding, and, as "sovereign pontiff," declared that the interest-bearing *monte* banks were in no way sinful, and were in fact meritorious. Any person who claimed they were mortally sinful would, the Medici pope declared, be henceforth excommunicated.

"Some time ago there was carried on among theologians and jurists, not without scandal to the people, a controversy, which, as we have learned, has recently been renewed, regarding the relief of the poor by loans to be made to them by the public authorities, a system of relief commonly known as *montes pietatis*, which have been established in many cities of Italy by the officials of the cities and other outstanding Christians for the purpose of relieving the needs of the poor by loans of this kind and thus protecting them against the avarice of usurers.

"This institution has been approved by devout men and has also been praised, endorsed and confirmed by several of our predecessors, the supreme pontiffs. In regard to the legality of the institution, the opinions of theologians and jurists were divided. Some maintained that those *montes* were illicit in which something beyond or in return for the money lent was demanded by the promoters from the poor to whom the loan was given and that these promoters could not escape the crime of usury or injustice, since, as St. Luke testifies,

---

[110] *Bulla Concilii in decima sessione super materia Montis Pietatis: Lecta per Reverendum patrem dominum Bertrandum Episcopum Adriensis Oratorem Ducis* (Ferrariae) (s.l., s.d.), iv (Roman Curia, May 4, 1515).

Christ expressly forbade that we should hope for anything more than we gave in return for a loan. For usury means nothing else than gain or profit drawn from the use of a thing that is by its nature sterile, a profit that is acquired without labour, cost or risk. The same theologians and jurists maintained further that those institutions militated against commutative and distributive justice, because the expenses for their maintenance were extorted solely from the poor to whom the loans were given. Moreover, they added, they were an incentive to delinquency, incited to theft, and promoted general laxity.

"On the other hand, there were many theologians and jurists, in the Italian schools, who held the opposite opinion, and both in their writings and lectures supported such an excellent system, one that was so worthwhile to the rest of society, and which, in their view, was gratuitous and not a direct cause of the interest; the custody of the object pawned, however, and consequently the space, labor and personal responsibility involved were legitimate conditions or titles upon which a moderate interest could be demanded.

"One of the rules of law states that he who enjoys advantages ought also to carry responsibility, especially if Apostolic authority acquiesces. This opinion was approved by our predecessors, the Roman pontiffs Paul II, [111] Sixtus IV, Innocent VIII, Alexander VI and Julius II, and was defended and preached to

---

111 No previous pontiff had declared official approval for the operation of any bank, whether philanthropic or otherwise, which charged interest on loans of money. Beginning in 1462 with the dawn of the Renaissance, such operations had been put forth as temporary exigencies and occasionally tolerated on that basis by the reigning pontiff on an individual and *ad hoc* basis, *but never institutionalized or given formal approbation*. Under Leo X the exigency became a precedent, which in turn furnished the basis for his promulgation of a permanent institution.

the people by saints and men held in high esteem for their sanctity.

"Therefore, wishing to make suitable provisions in this matter and commending the exertions of both parties, one for its zeal for justice against the practice of usury, the other for its love of truth and devotion that the needs of the poor may be relieved, with the approval of the holy council we declare and define that the aforesaid *montes pietatis*, established by the civil authorities and thus far approved and confirmed by the Apostolic See, in which the loan is gratuitous, but for expenses and indemnity only a moderate rate of interest is received, are not be declared a species of evil or an incentive to sin, nor are they in any manner or form to be condemned as usurious, rather they are meritorious and ought to be approved, and their benefits and spiritual utility as well as the indulgences granted by the Apostolic See in connection with them ought to be preached to the people. Other *montes* similar to the above may be established with the approval of the Apostolic See. [112]

"It would indeed be much more perfect and holy if such *montes* were entirely free, that is, if those who establish them would provide some fund or revenues that would cover, if not all, at least half the salaries of officials and assistants, which would lighten the

---

[112] This is the Hegelian process — *Thesis*: zeal for justice and love of the truth in opposing interest on money are commendable. *Antithesis*: interest charged on loans to the poor is an "excellent" system and not a "direct cause" of usury, since the interest is "gratuitous." *Synthesis*: interest may be charged by charitable banks — not for profit, but for "expenses and indemnity," and this is "meritorious." It was also a 53-year-old innovation in a Church whose Magisterium for 1500 years had condemned *any interest on loans of money* as damnable, in submission to the Word of God as confirmed by Apostolic, Patristic, and Conciliar authority. On May 4, 1515 Giovanni di Lorenzo de' Medici created a template for the overthrow of Catholic Truth which would become a model for Paul VI, John Paul II and Benedict XVI, as well as the popes of usury who came before them and after Leo.

burden of the poor. For the establishment of such funds the faithful ought to be invited by means of greater indulgences.

"All religious and ecclesiastics, as well as secular persons, who in the future presume to preach or argue by word or in writing against the contents of this constitution incur the penalty of excommunication *latae sententiae,* privileges of any kind whatsoever notwithstanding, and this includes Apostolic constitutions and ordinances and similar contrary decrees."

— Pope Leo X

For having declared the lawfulness of interest on loans of money, overthrowing Apostolic constitutions and all contrary decrees, the revolutionary change agent Pope Leo X was now a heretic according to the Council of Vienne:

"...if anyone falls into the error of believing and affirming that it is not a sin to practice usury, we decree that he be punished as a heretic, and we strictly command the ordinaries of the localities and the inquisitors to proceed against those suspected of such errors in the same way as they would proceed against those accused publicly or suspected of heresy."

In these diabolic moves there is always a loophole for the sake of appearance. Leo X's bull is predicated on the two-contract escape clause central to the interest-charging "charity bank" scheme. As Leo himself stated in his bull concerning the loans he was approving, "the loan is gratuitous, but for expenses and indemnity only a moderate rate of interest is received." With this loophole it could be argued that no interest was charged on *the loan itself,* and consequently, the loan did not constitute usury. This ruse was at the heart of the *mons pietatis* system approved by the pope:

"The term interest was not readily admitted by the friends of the *montes*, who replied that there were in reality two contracts between the *montes* and the borrower: one that of the loan, which should be gratuitous, the other implying the custody of the object pawned – therefore, the use of space and personal responsibility, which should not be gratuitous...The loan, therefore, was regarded merely as a *conditio sine qua non*, and not as a direct cause of the interest." [113]

Not very many economists have been deceived by this two contract smokescreen, however. The historian of capitalism, Eugen V. Böhm-Bawerk, wrote: "...the result is a 'double contract' of the type famous in the history of the evasion of usury laws." [114]

Ridolfi: "I believe that...lenders...are immune from the sin and vice of usury and from any obligation to make restitution, always provided that they lend primarily from charity and not from hope of profit or increase..." [115]

The fictional– if not outright asinine – character of these "famous evasions" (interest charged in name of "charity"), made a mockery of Christ's Church,

---

113 Cf. "Monte Pietatis," in Charles George Herbermann (ed.), *The Catholic Encyclopedia: An International Work of Reference on the Constitution, Doctrine, Discipline, and History of the Catholic Church*, vol. x, pp. 534-536.

114 *Capital and Interest: A Critical History of Economical Theory* (London: Macmillan, 1890).

115 Ridolfi, Lorenzo, *Tractus de usuris* (1404), published in *Tractatus universi iuris* (Venice, 1584), vol. 7. Translated by Lawrin Armstrong. The treatise is divided into 179 *quaestiones* and *oppositiones* intended as a digest of canon law rulings on usury.

degrading it to the level of the money-changers Our Lord had expelled. Beginning with Medici Pope Leo X the den of thieves was stealthily making a comeback, shrouded in double-talk. The clever tactic employed was gradualism, which slowly and inexorably nibbles at the foundations of God's law, rather than shattering it with one blow. Gradualism will be familiar to students of how modern innovations such as communion-in-the-hand came to be legitimated in the pontificate of Pope Paul VI and the "conservative" Pope John Paul II. [116]

The net effect of the legitimacy which Pope Leo X accorded interest charged in the *mons pietatis* system, was the radical derogation of the "rigid" Christian dogma on usury and the establishment of a precedent for more "moderate" usury, extending beyond the limits of alleged philanthropic banks to banks in general, which is precisely what would occur.

Umberto Benigni, Professor of Ecclesiastical History at the Pontifical College, Rome: "...*monte pietatis*...exerted great influence upon the ideas concerning interest on loans, for the rigid views of the theologians of the Middle Ages in that connexion underwent a first modification, which prepared the way for a generalization of the principle that moderate interest might justly be charged..."

Note the phrase, "first modification." How daintily and with clinical coldness is heresy presented when it rears it head. The permission for the charging of interest on money formally promulgated by the hierarchy of the western Church under Leo X was the first in fifteen centuries. Christendom was being turned upside down. Heretics who hate the Church founded by Jesus Christ had invaded Rome's Vatican,

---

[116] Cf. Michael Davies, *On Communion in the Hand and Similar Frauds* (St. Paul: The Remnant Press, 1998).

assumed the papacy and initiated a slow motion revolution. Indeed, Leo X's legalization of usury would continue to metastasize until, in the twentieth century it reached its monstrous zenith 402 years later, in the 1917 Code of Canon Law promulgated by Pope Benedict XV. In canon 1543 of the code, it was determined that "it is not *per se* unlawful to contract for the legal rate of interest, unless that be clearly exorbitant." This outrage was exceeded by another: if the legal standard was not a sufficient interest rate, Catholics could, in good conscience "agree upon a higher rate if there is at hand a just and proportionate title."

The 1917 Code represented, *in flagranti delicto,* a formal acknowledgement of the usury that had been transpiring inside the Church *stratum super stratum,* since the Renaissance. The 1917 Code did not initiate interest-taking in the Catholic world. It put the final nail in the coffin of any Catholic impediment to the mortal sin of interest on loans, in what had been a gradual process of chiseling away at the Biblical, Patristic, medieval Conciliar, and papal foundations of Christ's ecclesia, by the type of conspirator the ancient Romans termed "*vendidit hic auro patriam.*" [117]

The qualification "exorbitant" left a loophole for naive Catholics to inveigh against this special category of "rapacious" interest and imagine they were acting as traditional Catholics would, but the qualification in the 1917 Code is of course meaningless, in that "exorbitant interest" is never defined. It enters the realm of the absurd when we observe that in the very next sentence of canon 1543 it is determined that Catholics who have "just and proportionate title" can rightfully receive an interest rate *above the legal rate.* Once again, no definition of what constitutes this "title" is forthcoming; consequently, despite the

---

117 "The man who sells his country for gold."

deceptive rhetoric, buccaneer capitalism was officially sanctioned by the Roman Catholic Church four centuries after a Medici pope had first institutionalized the revolutionary overthrow of God's Law. With Leo X, we saw the emergence of the serpent's *tail* within the Church. Before him, we could only follow its *trail* as it slithered through the bowels of Venice and Florence and, as we as shall see, within the Germany of Fugger and Eck.

Concerning any prelate who authenticates usurious contracts, the canonist Cardinal Hostiensis stated that such a prelate is thereby complicit in the usury, and doubly guilty, for he causes the laity to sin with confidence, by being misled into thinking that the Church approves of such contracts: "*...laici per hoc credentes contractus huiusmodi per ecclesiam approbari, securius peccant.*" [118]

"As long as the political situation allowed, Luther inveighed against usury in all of its various forms. In the early 1520s he wrote against the usurious traffic in annuities, or *Zinskauf*: 'The devil invented this system, and the Pope by confirming it has injured the whole world...Truly this traffic...must be a sign and a symbol that the world, for its grievous sins, has been sold to the devil..." [119]

30 pieces of silver: the Pope's gift to the Medici

"Leo never forgot that he was a Florentine and now, as pope, the patriarch of the Medici family. Having spearheaded the attempts to restore his exiled family to dominance in Florence, he hoped to use his influence to make the Medici more secure...he arranged for his young nephew Lorenzo de' Medici to

---

[118] Armstrong, op. cit., p. 294.

[119] Hawkes, op. cit. p. 87. This papal "*Zinskauf*" was *wuchrische zinskauf*. Cf. *Revisionist History* newsletter, issue no. 65.

be made *signore* of the city...The Medici 'pattern of control' required steady and careful watchfulness over all Florentine institutions...Florence's masters saw the *monte* not simply as a charitable foundation or even as a bank, but as an institution with political and economic potential. Once installed as ruler in Florence in 1530, Alessandro de' Medici turned his attention to the Florentine constitution and to those institutions that kept the city functioning, including the *monte di pieta*...

"Medici involvement in the *monte di pieta*, however, predated Alessandro's appointment. In 1500 a Medici first sat as one of the eight (directors of the *monte di pieta*). This prominent Medici was Lorenzo di Pierfrancesco, a second cousin of Lorenzo the Magnificent and, like his cousin, a great-grandson of Giovanni di Bicci and a member of the Cafaggiolo branch of the family...Lorenzo di Pierfrancesco held office in Florence...Along with Piero Guicciardini, Piero Soderini, and Bernardo Rucellai...one of a group of *ottimati,* or leading citizens.

"...the men who served on the *monte de pieta's* governing board ...along with Lorenzo di Pierfrancesco de' Medici, for example, were Alamanno eli Averardo Salviati, Piero eli Antonio Taddei, and Agnolo di Bernardo de' Bardi, all from pro-Medici families. The last two had kin with connections to the Medici bank, and the Salviati Company had survived the threat of bankruptcy in the mid-fifteenth century only when infused with Medici funds....Piero di Antonio Taddei acted as a kind of troubleshooter for the Medici bank and had been entrusted with closing out its Venetian operations..." [120]

---

120 Carol B. Menning, *Charity and State in Late Renaissance Italy,* pp. 104-108; 114; 116-117.

Pope Leo X's *monte di pieta* was a bank to be plundered by his Florentine-merchant relatives and cronies. Charity for the poor was the necessary front used to vindicate the once forbidden usury. It didn't take long for the mask to fall, however: "Never did the *monte's* officials recognize any irony in the fact that the *monte*, like the Jewish pawnbrokers it sought to replace...could sell unredeemed pawns at a profit...in the fall of 1529 the regime (in Florence) commanded the officials of the *monte di pieta* to assign it credits from the resources...this money amounted to an interest-free loan to the regime.[121] There is no record that collateral was offered." [122]

By 1533 the city (commune) of Florence itself was guaranteeing the solvency of the *monte di pieta* and offering to pay interest of five percent on its deposits. All this in the name of poor relief (profit was guaranteed to any depositor willing to subsidize the *monte's* "charitable activities"). The usury entailed by the *monte di pieta* was contagious and led to more robust capitalism in other areas of Catholic enterprise. "Men in the highest social and political echelons could find ways of making greater profits than the 5 percent offered by the *monte di pieta* on deposits. A classic example of the tie between more lucrative investments and public service may be found in the appointment, in 1539, of the eight new officials of the *monte commune* (i.e. the funded public debt). Ottaviano di Lorenzo de'

---

[121] The amount was sixteen thousand florins (gold coins).

[122] Menning, op. cit., p. 117. It would be an error to imagine that the Medici had no rivals or enemies in Rome or Florence and that their commercial operations were seamless. Other patrician families sought to muscle in on the profits and muscle the Medicis out. Among these were the Pazzi family who were bought off by Leo X, and the exceedingly wealthy Strozzi, whose *capo* was Filippo Strozzi, whose brother Lorenzo would temporarily take control of the *monte di pieta* in 1530.

Medici, Jacopo di Ulivieri Guadagni, Jacopo di Messer Bongianni Gianfigliazzi, Filippo di Alessandro Machiavelli, Raffaello di Luca Torrigiani, Luigi di Francesco Pieri, Averardo di Alessandro Salviati, and Matteo di Lorenzo Strozzi took office on the condition that they lend the commune sums ranging from one thousand to over three thousand florins..." [123] In return for these loans these eight were to receive a handsome rate of interest set at twelve percent *per annum.*

It is a faulty assumption to imagine that very many Catholics or Protestants today would find anything immoral about the *monte di pieta* bank, since almost all contemporary "Christians" take and receive interest, unless they are too penurious or frugal to do so. The immorality of interest mostly does not even enter the minds of modern Christians, unless it is of the "exorbitant loanshark" variety. In keeping with the modernist and heretical 1917 Canon Law, interest on loans *per se* is a dead issue. As the *monte di pieta* grew more sophisticated in the sixteenth century and matured as a financial institution, the profits it received from usury became more obvious, even as it adroitly maintained its philanthropic *raison d'etre.* One can see the contours of our modern, "annuity funds" retirement plans emerging from the Catholic interest-banking operation of the 1500s:

"In a typical arrangement, the widow Francesca di Mariotto Casini of Santa Maria Impruneta deposited thirty florins in the *monte*, 'which she may withdraw together with the interest at her pleasure.' When Francesca made her deposit, she expressed her desire that, in the event of her death, any money remaining in the account be paid 'to a poor and good girl' to be selected by a designated agent in consultation with the *monte di pieta's provveditore* (administrator).

---

[123] Ibid., p. 145.

Francesca knew that while she lived she could make use of the interest that accrued and withdraw the principal at her pleasure, but if she died, her soul would enjoy the grace that rebounded from an act of benevolence." [124]

This appears so pious, so benevolent. Who, other than Yahweh, Jesus, all the Fathers of the Church and all the dogmatic councils and Magisterium before the Renaissance, could object to this golden snare, which conceals the means by which the rule of Money gains ascendance over Christian society?

"Once it had amassed a huge reserve of capital after the 1530s, the *monte's* potential usefulness to the dukes grew accordingly...For the elite the *monte di pieta* was an excellent source of loans. Where else could Florentines find capital available at 5 percent, later at 6 percent (still a bargain)? By appealing to the duke for authorization of large loans, those who had the sovereign's ear could take advantage of the resources of an institution originally designed to offer loans at low cost to the poor.

"...The *monte* succeeded in building up capital only after receiving permission to pay 5 percent interest on deposits...These deposits, plus the profits made through the *monte's* charitable lending, created the basis for its big-time loans to the Medici and their clients. Of all the *monte's* activities, these loans had the broadest impact on ducal finance and on the character of the *monte* itself...It was, in fact...the continuing efforts of the Medici to establish an absolute state in early modern Tuscany that provided the real impetus for its involvement in its most important banking activity, the granting of large loans at the duke's order. The tremendous demands of ducal finance in the enlarged Medicean state, coupled with

---

124 Ibid., p. 153.

the remarkable consolidation of that state by the single-minded (Medici ruler) Cosimo I, resulted in an exhaustive, purposeful search for sources of money, a search that formed part of the greater plan to rationalize state finance. For...those who, invoking ties of friendship, kinship, loyal service, or political interests, could persuade the duke to authorize a loan, the *monte* handed over thousands of ducats at an unprofitable rate for the institution. Only in a state ruled by a prince who saw himself as above the law could the *monte di pieta* turn into a major lending institution for the *patriciate* and an arm of ducal finance...His use of the *monte di pieta* illustrates...his developing sense of political economy...One of the most important themes concerning the development of the Florentine *monte di pieta* was its relationship to the various Florentine states...Cosimo...succeeded in creating the basis for a bureaucratized, well-organized state to which he had closely tied various institutions of city and district alike, including those that predated his rule, and particularly the Tuscan *monte di pieta.*

"By the late 1560s the *monte* had become so much an organ not only of patronage but of state finance that it behaved like a ducal bank, even to the point of handling the monthly payroll and debiting the duke's accounts accordingly. As a source of loans to foreign potentates whom the ruler wished to cultivate, the institution bankrolled an important part of Tuscan foreign policy. The Florentine state in its several forms kept close control over the *monte,* exercising important powers beyond the latitude that the statutes permitted the eight officials. The eight themselves were elected, at first by the Great Council and later by other organs; as soon as Alessandro took over the city, he usurped the right to control the choice of the *monte's* eight officers. The tightened hold Cosimo placed over the choice of the eight and of important *monte* employees comprised a part of his overall pattern of control. The tightest bonds between *monte* and state were fashioned by Cosimo as the institution became important for its liquidity...." [125]

Catholics faithful to the Gospel of Jesus Christ did, on occasion, vigorously protest the usury perpetrated in the name of the poor. In 1574 an arch-episcopal synod in Florence condemned the *monte di pieta,* declaring that the interest the *monte di pieta* charged on loans and paid out on deposits was the sin of usury. In response, the grand duke of Florence visited Pope Gregory XIII and solicited an end to the condemnation and the protests, and the continued operation of the *monte.* Gregory granted his request and forced the synod to drop its condemnation. [126] "The only way to nurture public faith in the *monte* as a bank was to ensure that no papal prohibitions, indeed, no doubts or questions whatsoever, would raise the spectre of usury." [127]

As the centuries passed, the *monte di pieta* continued to devolve into a usury bank that used Jesus Christ as a front. In 1616 double contracts were devised to evade scrutiny. These involved *luoghi di monte*, shares in the bank made to look like an investment rather than a deposit. Lo and behold, each

---

[125] Ibid., pp. 256; 259-261.

[126] Pope Gregory XIII applauded the massacre of thousands of Protestant Huguenots in France in 1572, instigated by Catherine de' Medici, great-granddaughter of Lorenzo de' Medici ("Lorenzo the Magnificent") of Florence. It has been suggested that Shakespeare's reference in *King Henry IV, Part One* to "Turk Gregory" alluded to Gregory XIII, the pope who was popularly viewed by the English as one of 'three tyrants of the world.' "Anti-Catholic polemics often collapsed Turks and Catholics into a single, demonized figure of what were seen as the two great threats to the 'godly' kingdom; cf. John Bale's sardonic joke in *The Pageant of the Pope* (1574), where he refers to 'Pope Turban II." —David Scott Kastan, *King Henry IV Part 1*, p. 323.

[127] Menning, op.cit., p. 265.

"share" returned five percent interest; precisely what deposits in the bank had paid. What a coincidence. To increase the degree to which image was intended to prevail over reality, "share" certificates were issued. The cynicism knew no bounds: each certificate was printed under a display of the Passion wounds of Jesus. *Inter alia,* perhaps these were not so deceitful as imagined, since the camouflaged usury of these pious hypocrites opened the wounds of Our Lord.

By 1622 poverty had increased in Florence. Vagabonds and mendicants crowded the streets. "The elegance and riches of courtly society contrasted ever more starkly with the growing misery of the poor. The grand duke and his friends continued to divert money from the *monte di pieta* for their own political, social and economic needs just at the time when the institution's liquidity might have been put to use to help the very group for which it had been created – the poor." [128]

Almost twelve years to the day after Pope Leo X introduced the heresy of usury into the Catholic Church and misled the laity into believing that charging interest on loans for a "good cause" was not a sin, "On May 6, 1527, Rome suffered the worst assault that she had ever known, far more serious than anything befalling her at the time of the barbarian migrations. Nothing was spared, sacred or profane. (Medici Pope) Clement VII's [129] escape to and confinement within the walls of Castel Sant'Angelo until December, listening to the taunting of the German mercenaries calling for his death and

---

[128] Ibid., p. 263. "The *monte di pieta* of Rome made another contribution to modern finance: in 1788 it issued a note for 130 scudi that is apparently the first paper money printed in Italy" (p. 258).

[129] Pope Clement VII was the former Giulio di Giuliano de' Medici.

replacement by 'Pope Luther,' were the least of the indignities. Various cardinals and prelates, including one future pope, Julius III (1550-1555), were humiliated and tortured, altars were ransacked, the Sistine Chapel used as a stable, riches confiscated, patients in hospitals and children in orphanages were gratuitously butchered. Rape and rapine, exacerbated by raids of hoodlums under the direction of the abbot of the nearby monastery of Farfa, were followed by the onset of plague. Rome and the stench of death became one." [130]

Was this catastrophic pillage, which was unprecedented in the history of Rome, a coincidence, or the wrath of God for the perversion of His Church by a den of thieves?

The Ultimate Obstacle to the Ascendance of the Money Power over Christendom

The vast majority of contemporary specialist historians of economic history view the ancient prohibitions on usury to have been foolish and unworkable. For them interest on money represents a *deus ex machina* that cannot be resisted and should not have been prohibited by the Church (the will of God does not enter into their calculations). In the course of pursuing this line, they almost always argue that the Church's laws were made to be broken and that practically everyone of consequence, with notable exceptions, conspired in doing so. Hence, according to this thinking, the abolition of usury as a mortal sin was a great relief in itself, as well as representing relief from hypocrisy. By this way of reasoning it can be argued that the Church should remove mortal sin from adultery, since many people of consequence engage in it, is widespread, has never been eradicated

---

130 John Rao, *Black Legends and the Light of the World*, pp. 295-296. This sack of Rome was initiated by the forces of Roman Catholic Emperor Charles V of Spain.

and is the occasion for hypocrisy. The arguments in favor of the "normalcy" of usury according to human nature proceed from the point of view of situation ethics and the liberal disdain for the existence of immutable divine law.

Another fixture of modern economic history in this regard is the "everyone was doing it" claim. Because money corrupts and the love of money is the root of all corruption, it would be useless to gainsay the fact that in all times of the past when usury was outlawed, persons high and low within and without the Church were secretly profiting from it. One could cite the names of corrupted clerics that would fill several pages, who provided cover for these profits, from Francesco da Empoli to Oldradus de Ponte and Peter of Ancharano.

Furthermore, the Church had not been successful in shutting down the debt market in places such as Florence and Venice, partly because it was so well protected by a thicket of sophistry and legal fiction, predicated on the fact that, at law, the legitimacy of commercial credit transactions and *prestanze* were contingent on the intentions and inner dispositions of the lenders. Modern economists may say what they will about these facts, there is one more datum they seldom account for. The popes and councils of the pre-Renaissance era held the usurers to account at the bar of the highest and most fearsome of all judgements, the fate of their souls. As risible or trivial as this may seem to the modern agnostic or liberal mentality, it was a formidable restraint of last resort. As long as taking interest on money was a mortal sin, and absolution depended on making restitution, even those practiced deceivers who had kept the ecclesiastical courts and canon lawyers at bay in Venice and Florence for decades with lawyers of their own, knew they would one day have to face the unimpeachable requirement to make restitution for the receipt of all profit from interest on loans. The principle was stated thus:

"Nota quod quicquid recipitur ultra sortem: licet ex forma contractus non sit usurarius quoad ecclesiam iudicandus, propter intentionem tamen quoad Deum tanquam usurarius punietur nisi restituerit."

("Although the Church may not judge [a lender] a usurer on the basis of the contract's form, nevertheless God will punish him as a usurer by reason of intention unless he makes restitution"). [131]

"...many a banker had an uneasy conscience about his unholy deals. Overwhelming evidence is given in the numerous medieval testaments in which the testator ordered restitution of all usury and ill-gotten gains." [132]

"...even if usury could be hidden from secular authorities, it could never be hidden from God — or so most of the very devout Christian society then believed. Certainly most Christians in early-modern Europe firmly believed in and truly feared God's punishment for usury: i.e., eternal damnation in Hell...with unbearable, unremitting agony." [133]

As long as usury was a mortal sin, interest on money and the operations and institutions that fostered it, were conflicted, disreputable and guilt-ridden endeavors heavily burdened by a Church which held damnation to be the just fate of those who had

---

131 Armstrong, op. cit., pp. 85-86.

132 Raymond de Roover, *The Rise and Decline of the Medici Bank*, p. 12.

133 John Munro, "Usury, Calvinism and Credit in Protestant England," in *Religione e istituzioni nell'economia europea: 1000-1800*, p. 163.

undertaken this "business." The ultimate obstacle to the ascendance of the Money Power over Christendom, above and beyond all civil and criminal jurisdiction and punishment on earth, was the knowledge on the part of believers, of the fate awaiting the unrepentant usurer: the eternal death of his soul. When, over the course of centuries the change agents inside the Church finished with their gradual destruction of the defined and immemorial dogma, and interest on loans of money was – *voila* – somehow, by some act of prestidigitation, no longer a sin that would receive eternal punishment, then the last and most formidable restraint on the merciless barbarity of vulture capitalism was removed, the devil of covetousness grinned, and Christendom became increasingly marked by relations between people which Thomas Hobbes termed *Homo homini lupus est* (man being a wolf to man).

This is what Jesus Christ suffered and died for – That His supposed followers on earth, allegedly seeking to do the will of His Father in Heaven, would devour one other – only taking time off from their mutual predation long enough to remove their wolf skins and inhabit a church pew for an hour on Sunday, putting some of their ill-gotten gains in the collection plate, while imagining themselves to be His sheep?

4

Usury and Simony in Catholic Germany

"Legalized usury commits the human race to the unceasing pursuit of economic growth. Usury imposes an unstoppable expansion on the process of wealth creation; it sets in motion a driving force whose velocity increases exponentially along with compound interest, impelling us to transform all the world's human and natural resources into the form of financial representation. As the people of Renaissance England clearly saw and often said, usury is inherently insatiable. The history of the human race since restraints on usury began to be lifted has involved the sudden and dramatic colonization of the globe by money, the evaluation of human activity and the natural environment in terms of money, and the direction of an ever-increasing proportion of physical and psychological energy toward the production of money."

–David Hawkes

The debt slaves of the West sold themselves into financial servitude in putative Christian times ("the Renaissance") and have spiraled downward ever since. Talmudic-style loopholes that heretofore lurked on the margins, moved to the center, permitting the start of widespread indebtedness, until we arrived at the point where the Authority of Money assumed the supreme position of power in western civilization. This authority is so all-encompassing that if the masses of people in the twenty-first century were to be informed that for the first fifteen hundred years of Western Christian civilization, money did not have supreme authority over western society, most would think us fantasists. It was once the firm assumption of the commonweal that God's law and secular law should coincide. Prior to the Renaissance, economics was a branch of theology and ethics. I say *prior to the Renaissance*, whereas many traditional Catholic writers usually state, "*prior to the Reformation*."

Like the charge of "Judaizing Protestantism" [134] the claim that "Protestantism" was the central force behind usury absolves that branch of the cryptocracy which flourished inside the Catholic Church during the Renaissance. Sometimes distinctions are made about individual Protestant rulers regarded as philo-Catholic, such as Hilaire Belloc's assertion in his pseudo-history of the English King Charles I, [135] that it was the Money Power that overthrew Charles, using the Puritans against him, as pawns in the game.

As a historian Belloc is completely unreliable. The English Civil War was a revolt of the yeomanry against Charles' dictatorship and tyrannical Star Chamber; that was the cause of his downfall.

The Money Power, however, was well pleased with him: King Charles I had reaffirmed legalized usury, up to 8% interest – 3% higher than the limit set by Calvin. Belloc execrated John Calvin as a shylock and valorized King Charles I as a "victim" of the Money Power. Belloc remains the principal traditional Catholic source for "information" concerning the Puritan war with Charles.

---

[134] Cf. *Revisionist History newsletter* no. 52, "Judaizing Protestantism and Neo-Platonic Catholicism in Legend and Reality."

[135] *Charles I King of England* (J.B. Lippincott, 1933).

Renaissance Catholic-Nominalist Origin of Usury Legalization Theory

This erroneous assumption about the alleged "Protestant origin" of early modern usury leads to a misapprehension of the roots of usury in Christendom.[136] The gradual legalization of usury and the first steps toward the social kingship of Mammon began in Roman Catholic lands, pushing to loosen the moral strictures against usury. With this in mind it is important to note that no one in pre-Renaissance Catholic Europe would dare to argue that *usury itself* was other than sinful and criminal. The agents of the Money Power in that era had to be content with tinkering with definitions and calling usury by another name. Whatever could be proved to fall under the heading of *usury* —i.e. anything that the borrower was forced to add to the repayment of that which was loaned to him —was universally condemned. With the rise of a Catholic school of philosophy known as *nominalism*, [137] usury was gradually rehabilitated and with it a system of commerce centered on avarice and covetousness. The Italians had successfully promoted one school of usury disguised as a charity bank. It was German Catholics who fomented another school of usury which, in many ways, would prove to be more

---

136 Catholic economist Amintore Fanfani in his book *Catholicism, Protestantism and Capitalism* (Sheed and Ward, 1935), rightly attacks Max Weber's thesis of the Protestant origins of capitalism. Fanfani, to his credit, gives some sense of the extent to which Calvinists opposed the influence of mammon and greed: cf. in the 2003 IHS Press paperback edition, pp. 143-147; 149-150. Fanfani does not blame early Protestants for capitalism, but he does uphold the myth that they originated usury in Christendom.

137 "...the Pharisaic-rabbinical conception of the law...is a nominalist concept. It holds that the *halakha* (law) was determined by the human agent, which in the case of the Talmud consists of a group of rabbis who decide whether something is pure or impure, and this categorization does not derive from the inherent nature of the things." —Shany Littman, *Haaretz*, Oct. 4, 2012.

virulent since it advocated interest on money in transparent, profit-making *commercial* ventures.

In the fifteen century in Catholic Europe, the nominalists began to criticize the ban on usury which had been systematized by the Thomists. John Calvin and Martin Luther were born in the midst of a conflict between two warring schools of Roman Catholic theology and philosophy, medieval and Renaissance. The principal means for overthrowing the Thomistic reaffirmation of the Biblical and patristic ban on usury was to 1. change it from a contractual matter to a crime of intent; and 2. institutionalize a Talmudic type of loophole in God's law against usury. The first objective fell to the "Tübingen (university) school" of Catholic nominalism, headed by Gabriel Biel (ca. 1425-1495), Conrad Summenhart and the Fugger banking dynasty asset, Johann Eck (1486-1543). Eck was Martin Luther's theological nemesis. [138]

Biel had been appointed to the theological faculty of the newly formed Tübingen University on Nov. 22, 1484. Like certain Vatican Council II *periti* such as Joseph Ratzinger, Biel was strictly an orthodox papist in the vast majority of his writing and teaching. A small percentage of his work was ingeniously subversive of historic Christian teaching using the classic methodology of casuistry. In his early years (1442-1453) Biel associated with both the *via moderna* and the *via antiqua*. Consequently, he was both an articulate adovocate for the *via moderna* and a prudent user of the thought of the *via antiqua*. For example, in the Renaissance debate over the authority of St. Thomas Aquinas, Biel held that while it could by no means be nullified or disregarded, he considered it a sign of progress that Thomas could now be openly contradicted in the universities: "*Licet beatus thomas*

---

138 Cf. "Luther's Debate with Eck" in Bernhard Lohse, *Martin Luther's Theology in Historical and Systematic Development*, pp. 118-126.

sanctus credatur et ab ecclesia canonizatus...hodie in scholis publice sibi contradictur." [139]

Biel was working in the Neoplatonic tradition, specifically the writings of the Renaissance-Catholic Kabbalist, Giovanni Pico della Mirandola. Biel relies on Mirandola's authority in Biel's *Epithoma pariter et collectorium circa quattuor sententiarum libros* (Tübingen, 1501). Biel's disciples included another Tübingen professor, Henry Bebel, as well as Wendelin Steinbach and Johannes Altenstaig; the latter was the author of the influential dictionary of theology, *Vocabularius theologie*, in which Biel's authority is held to be of the highest degree. None other than Martin Luther's famous theological nemesis, the Catholic theologian Johannes Eck, the *apostolus mercatorum*, was a votary of Bebel and a student of Steinbach. Eck relied upon Biel's texts in glossing the theology of Peter Lombard. Together with Summenhart, Biel's teachings had a profound impact on Eck. Eck was also Summenhart's student. Prof. Summenhart (1455-1502), argued in his *De Contractibus licitis et que illicitus* that actions not intended to be evil should not be considered evil because they look evil.

Summenhart's *modus operandi* offers us another instructive example how sly fifteenth century modernists, in seeking to lift the prohibition on the crime of usury (long before any Protestant pursued a similar objective), were part of the chain of casuistry that stretches from the Renaissance to the contemporary papacy. The operating principle, employed effectively against all but the most careful investigators, is plausible denial, through heavily camouflaged statements and escape clauses. Though practiced by Roman Catholic modernists, this is a rabbinic method encountered in the sacred literature

---

[139] Biel, *Sacri canonis misse expositio resolutissima* (Basel, 1510).

of the Gemara and Mishneh Torah. We might term it the zigzag technique:

"The most radical and comprehensive examination of all the arguments showing the unnaturalness of usury is undertaken by Conrad Summenhart, and the result of this unprecedentedly thorough review is a revolutionary conclusion. He offers twenty-three natural-law reasons in favor of the usury prohibition, criticizes, modifies and rejects most of these reasons, and ends with two tenuous formal arguments against usury left standing. At the same time, he puts forward strong objections against the prohibition, which he leaves unanswered, and if these objections are taken as they stand, without interpretation, they seem to prove that usury itself is licit. His examination ends in a rejection of the past. Usury is left assailed in name alone. The early scholastic theory of usury is abandoned." [140]

"Eck remained indebted to the modern way all his life...Eck's acquaintance with the new Tübingen economic ethic is of even greater importance...Taken from Biel and with 'modern' open mindedness from Summenhart, Eck adapted these economic principles to the south German world of finance and eloquently defended them at (the) Bologna...disputation on the practice of collecting interest (July 15, 1515)...At issue was the legitimacy of profit-making commerce with capital, a practice long accepted by international banking and financial circles but still encountering resistance in Germany...Thus the practice urgently needed the protective rationale of a new theory of capital. A new interpretation of the church's prohibition of usury was required, an interpretation that would permit smooth financing of investments,

---

[140] John T. Noonan Jr., *The Scholastic Analysis of Usury* p. 340.

especially the rapidly expanding long-distance commerce without the restrictive overhead of a guilty conscience...the issue could be ignored no longer and the standard canon law solutions finally came under careful scrutiny." [141]

"...these factors demanded a new (Catholic) economic theory, an *oeconomia moderna*. A series of universities received requests for theological opinions from the Fugger capital of Augsburg. That Tübingen was included was fully predictable in view of the teaching tradition established by Biel and Summenhart...The university at the time must have been almost as much a center of liberal economics as centuries later it was to be a center of liberal theology." [142]

In 1535 Francois Rabelais, the Renaissance cleric and novelist, described the Fugger banking house of Augsburg, Germany as "the wealthiest merchants in Christendom."[143] "In Germany there were the Fuggers. This family, a mighty power in Europe, had been financing (Spanish Catholic) Habsburg policy since 1490, and continued to do so until the Schmalkald War (1546)." [144] The House of Habsburg produced the Emperor Charles V, whose ascendance to the throne of the Holy Roman Empire had been financed by the Fuggers. Charles was one of the earliest monarchial usurers outside of Italy in the Renaissance era, predating King Henry VIII of England by five years. In alliance with the *Staten General* of the Habsburg-occupied Netherlands, Charles V put forth a law, on

---

[141] Heiko Oberman, *Masters of the Reformation: The Emergence of a New Intellectual Climate in Europe*, pp.129-130.

[142] Ibid. p. 131.

[143] Menning, op. cit., p. 119.

[144] Joseph Lortz, *The Reformation in Germany*, vol. I, p. 300. Catholic Spain named a street in Madrid in honor of the Fuggers: Calle de Fúcar (between Atocha and Moratín streets).

October 4, 1540, permitting an interest rate of 12 percent on commercial loans. He declared that only commercial loans above 12 percent constituted usury.

1546 was the high water mark for the Fuggers, whose wealth in that year was estimated to be 300 million goldmarks.[145] The family patriarch, Jacob Fugger, was Eck's patron, and Eck, as Fugger's corrupt mouthpiece, was charged with justifying the Fugger bank's interest rate of 5%. "...it was important for Jakob Fugger and other large merchants to obtain the Church's official approval of an interest rate of five percent...Fugger...commissioned a memorandum on the question of interest from the theologian Johannes Eck of Ingolstadt..."[146]

In 1515 Eck dutifully produced the desired usurious economic rationale, in his *Tractatus contractu quinque de centum*, which held that the Fugger's interest rate on loans was completely legal and moral because it was "modest" and occurred as part of a "business" transaction. Eck argued that only lenders who intentionally preyed upon the needy were sinners. Lenders who contracted for interest on legitimate business proposals were innocent. Luther attacked Eck's casuistical ingenuity as the "fig leaves" which usury uses to hide its shame.

Dr. Gregory Lamparter, Fugger's bastard son-in-law (through Fugger's mistress, Mechthilt Belz), was twice rector of Tübingen University. Fugger lavished large sums of money on his illegitimate son-in-law. In turn, Lamparter, used his influence at Tübingen to support Eck. "Lamparter made no effort to conceal the

---

145 Ibid.

146 Mark Häberlein, *The Fuggers of Augsburg* (unpaginated digital book; cf. chapter 7, "The Fuggers in Sixteenth Century Urban Society").

fact that Jacob Fugger's interest was at stake and that Fugger had approached Eck for a written opinion." [147]

The significance of the new nominalist contractual theory concerning letters of credit and securities was that it rescued usurers from ancient Catholic punishments like forfeiture: "...in earlier generations ... (p)roof of prior involvement in usurious transactions...could mean that a commercial company would be forced to forfeit its entire capital. Appealing to Romans 11:16, *si radix sancta, et rami* ("if the dough offered as first fruits is holy, so is the whole lump"), the company's entire capital was declared 'infected." [148]

"...Biel also managed to reconcile a 'modern' doctrine of divine acceptation...The profile of the Tübingen school's first 'headmaster' comes into focus as we watch Biel draw on canon law in order cautiously to further that development upon which the expansion of early capitalism depended: the shift from currency to credit transactions. Detaching ownership from the possession or use of money had even more far-reaching consequences, because it snapped the hinge on which the traditional definition of usury swung. Canonists and theologians had concluded long before that a distinction must be made between usury, which the Vulgate expressly forbids (Luke 6:35), and 'profit through participation' in the *commenda* contract." [149]

In the "*commenda* proper," involving overseas ventures, "...the investing party who remains at home contributes two thirds of the capital, whereas the traveling party contributes one third, in addition to his labor. Profits are usually divided by half according to original investments; losses are born by both investors

---

[147] Oberman, op. cit., p. 142.

[148] Ibid., p. 132.

[149] Ibid., p. 133.

according to their respective contributions to the capital....the traveling party receives one fourth of the profit on the two thirds of the capital contributed by the other party plus all of the profit of the one third of the capital which he himself contributed. The sum is one half of the total profits. If there is a loss, the investor loses twice the amount of the traveling party, but the latter also loses the reward of his labor." [150]

The non-usurious *commenda* was a legitimate contract in the eyes of the Church because it entailed risk to the investors. "But where money was lent risk-free with the stipulation that the principal be repaid with interest, then, in the traditional view, ownership (*proprietas*) and the use of capital (*possessio*) had been illicitly separated...(and thereby constituted usury).

"The introduction of money 'backed' by external guarantee and the sale of securities or bonds not only meant a considerable expansion of the monetary economy but also made a redefinition of usury necessary, since money could no longer be considered a consumable model" as Aquinas clearly had asserted based on Scripture and Patristic tradition. "Biel remained extremely cautious in his formulations, careful to buttress his position with support from the canonist tradition...Biel was able to comb the various canonist conclusions and prohibitions for a theological framework that cleared the way for a commercially up-to-date verdict...The path was cleared by means of subtle argumentation: 'If someone desires to avoid all risk to his capital and yet to share in the profit...that is clearly usury...But if, in contrast, someone is willing to accept the risk of the possible loss of capital and to guarantee the sum to the investor for an agreed-upon price, it is not usury to pay for such security..." [151]

---

150 Cf. Robert Sabatino Lopez et al., *Medieval Trade in the Mediterranean World*, pp. 174-184.

151 Oberman, op.cit., p. 134.

Noonan judged Biel's economic theory to have "really removed all matter from the usury prohibition." [152]

"Conrad Summenhart had likewise taken up the problem of usury...his thinking was oriented not toward Aquinas but toward the more nominalistically inclined Scotist branch of the *via antiqua* (cf. his posthumously published (1507) *Commentaria in Summam physice Alberti Magni*)...in declaring the corporative capital investment contract to be basically legitimate, Summenhart had leaped the decisive barrier to commercial capitalism erected by traditional (Catholic) financial ethics. In his final statement he argued for removing the proscription of usury from underneath the protective sanction of divine law..." [153]

"...Eck had dealt with the charging of interest from a Scotist perspective early in 1514 when he discussed *distinctio* 15 of the fourth book of his lecture on the *Sentences*." [154]

Summenhart employed two of the elements of modernist-Catholic epistemology to overthrow fifteen hundred years of Church teaching against usury: casuistry, which emerged from a trend inside Catholicism itself, and the Renaissance Neoplatonic project of human alchemy, i.e. the covert processing of Christians for secret objectives. It was casuistry for Summerhart to assert his "thesis that the investor's pure intent preserves him from the sin of usury in charging interest," [155] accompanied by his prudent "caution against arousing public offense" with this

---

152 Noonan, op. cit., p. 230.

153 Oberman, op. cit, p. 134.

154 Ibid., p. 141.

155 Ibid., p. 136.

thesis. Oberman notes that "his caution against arousing public offense was...accepted...only to lend impetus to the task of reeducating the public...Precisely this desire to reeducate moved Johannes Eck to popularize a new definition of usury. As a third member of the 'Tübingen school,' he belonged to the modernist way...trained by both Biel and Summenhart...Eck entered the debate for the first time in 1514 with both theoretical and practical arguments in defense of a five percent investment contract. His theoretical contribution consisted of a new variant of the *contractus trinus,* a three-step procedure designed to escape the suspicion of usury. In this approach a partnership is first established by means of a basic agreement. A second contract follows, transforming the original participation into an investment made attractive by a potential but non-guaranteed profit. The third agreement sees the non-guaranteed ten percent return 'sold' for a smaller but risk-free five percent profit...the *contractus trinus* triumphed...and formed the foundation for ecclesiastical approval of the expanding capitalist financial system. Eck himself thought that his real contribution fell within the field of practical theology. Summenhart had removed a series of significant theoretical scruples and Eck continued his work by making a sharp distinction between the charging of interest and the sin of usury, reinforcing the money-lender's clear conscience." [156]

Eck used his influence with Pope Leo X to threaten and obstruct Catholic opponents of usury, such as Willibald Pirckheimer who, in 1515, in response to Eck's campaign for a five percent interest rate, had

---

[156] Ibid., pp. 136-137. Also cf. J. Schneid, "Dr. Johann Eck und das kirchliche Zinsverbot (*Historischpolitische Blätter für das katholische Deutschland* 108 (1891, 2]), pp. 241-259; 321-335; 473-496; 570-589; 659-681; 789-810.

translated and published in Nuremberg, Plutarch's denunciation of usury, *De vitando aere alieno*. In 1520 Pirckheimer wrote a pseudonymous satire on Eck, *Eccius dedolatus* ("The corner shaved down"). This satire is sometimes misrepresented as a Protestant mockery of Eck for his having opposed Martin Luther. This is not the case. The satire refers specifically to the 1514 Ingolstadt disputation. The debate at Ingolstadt was known to be one of three on the subject of the permissibility of charging interest in which Eck argued in the affirmative (the other usury debates which witnessed Eck's advocacy were held at the Fugger-patronized Carmelite monastery in Augusburg, also in 1514; and in Bologna on July 12, 1515).

There is indeed a reference to indulgences in the *Eccius dedolatus,* but only in connection with kickbacks Eck is alleged to have received for having argued on behalf of usury. "Eck responded by having Pirckheimer placed on the papal bull threatening excommunication (15 June 1520), together with Bernhard Adelmann and Lazarus Spengler — all of whom opposed Eck in the controversy over interest in 1514-1515..." [157]

Eck and Fugger and their more subtle Tübingen nominalist allies (who left it to Eck to act as the public face of their theories in favor of moneylending at interest), encountered some resistance from the Renaissance Catholic hierarchy, at least seemingly, as for example from the Archbishop of Eichstätt, Gabriel of Eyb, who banned a proposed disputation by Eck in favor of interest on money, while supporting Eck's controversy against Luther. The Eichstätt archbishop's ban did little to impede Eck's campaign for usury however, and won him considerable sympathy. In view of the fact that Eck's advocacy of the right to commit

---

[157] Oberman, ibid., p. 141; Eck's debate at Augusburg is recounted by Joseph Schlecht, "Dr. Johann Eck's Anfänge," in *Historisches Jahrbuch der Görresgesellschaft* 36, pp. 1 - 36).

the sin of usury did not cause him to forfeit Gabriel of Eyb's support in Eck's campaign against Luther, it may be that the archbishop's ban was mainly for public consumption by the Catholic peasants and proletariat.

Usury unites with Simony

The Fugger bank was implicated in more than the sin of usury. They were also at the center of the sin of simony, in the form of the notorious sale of indulgences. With Pope Leo X's curia in need of funds, Johann Tetzel received a commission from the pope for the sale of a so-called Jubilee indulgence. The curia "demanded large sums of money from Archbishop Albrecht of Mainz and Magdeburg for the privilege of uniting the benefices of two archbishoprics in his person at the same time, which was contrary to canon law. Albrecht had to incur large debts with the banking house of Fugger in order to raise this sum of money, and to help him pay back the money, the house of Fugger received a certain portion of the indulgence money which Tetzel collected from his penitent audience, and for this reason he was accompanied by agents from the bank on his journeyings." [158]

"In 1513 the twenty-three-year-old Albrecht of Brandenburg, youngest brother of the prince elector Joachim, was elected archbishop of the important diocese of Magdeburg by the cathedral chapter...in 1514, Albrecht was elected by the cathedral chapter of Mainz to be archbishop of this diocese also, and prince elector. He had undertaken to support the collegiate prebend at his own expense....Mainz was in need of cutting down its expenditure. Within the space of ten years the archepiscopal see had thrice fallen vacant, and each time the confirmation dues to Rome for the see and the pallium had amounted to 14,000 ducats. Now Albrecht had to apply to the pope not only for

---

[158] Gerhard Ritter, *Luther: His Life and Work*, pp. 68-69.

confirmation of his election to Mainz but also for permission to occupy this see while retaining that of Magdeburg and the administration of Halberstadt. Such an accumulation of benefices was unheard of, in Germany at least, and was in fact forbidden by canon law. But Leo X was not going to be hindered by canon law when political and financial advantage were at stake. With his decisive connivance, the ambassadors from Brandenburg were granted confirmation on payment of an additional 10,000 ducats.

"Moreover, it was the curia who made this proposal acceptable to the ambassadors, for they suggested a method by which Albrecht might raise all or part of the sum to be paid. They would make over to the archbishop of Mainz the sale of the St. Peter's indulgence...in the archdiocese of Mainz and in the Brandenburg territories, allowing him a half share in the proceeds. The contract was perfect; a deal was made with the Fuggers who, in return for a share in the income from the indulgence, advanced the archbishop 29,000 Rhenish guilders — and the whole shameful business was complete. That this let loose the Reformation storm is highly symbolic and an expression of historical retribution, for all the corruption in the Church of that time had its chief cause in the fiscalism of the curia, which was rotten with simony. In the case just mentioned, the curia, contrary to canon law, in return for cash, and in the hope of gaining political advantage, were allowing a young, worldly man to hold an irresponsible accumulation of benefices. In so doing they turned indulgences into a means of exchange in big business. The executive organ of this business carried on between the custodian of the merits won by Christ's blood and a worldly prince of the Church was a

(Fugger) bank. Corruption could scarcely have been more blatantly expressed." [159]

"The chest to receive the money always had two or three locks, the keys of which were in the custody of different persons, including a representative of the banking-house of Fugger. It could never be opened save in the presence of a notary. The ecclesiastical injunction was that the faithful had to deposit their contributions in person. To give it to the confessor or indulgence subcommissary invalidated the indulgence." [160]

Here was more than the growing encroachment of materialism in Christendom. Here was the demonic incarnation of mammonism in the form of a web of commerce encompassing both usury and simony, with the Fuggers deeply ensconced in the lucrative trade in both mortal sins, to the extent that Tetzel, the papally-appointed simoniac preacher, was accompanied on his rounds of selling indulgences, by agents of the Catholic banking house of Fugger, who supervised his cash box.

With the youthful archbishop of Mainz, "Cardinal Albrecht" in debt to the Fuggers, it is not especially surprising that the theology faculty of the University of Mainz subsequently did not reject the Fugger-sponsored theoretical legitimacy of investment interest. The Mainz faculty summarized their opinion as follows, "Some of us are indeed able to hold and defend this (Eck's) position *scholastice*" ("*Sunt enim apud nos qui eam scholastice et tenere et defensare possent*").

---

[159] Lortz, op. cit., pp. 225-226.

[160] *The Catholic Encyclopedia*, vol. 14, "Johann Tetzel."

The Catholic Roots of Protestant Capitalism

The modernist legacy of the sixteenth century Catholic nominalists such as Summenhart in his *De decimis,* was the derogation of traditional canon law as mere "statutory legislation" whenever it clashed with the demands of modernity for capitalist banking and finance. Through captains of capitalism like its alumnus Eck, and fledgling modernists such as Biel and Summenhart, the nominalist "Tübingen" school, together with the casuist rehabilitation of usury, was a seminal influence on the emergence of a Protestant school of capitalist praxis and, in later centuries, on the modernist movement within the Roman Church for the alteration of the liturgy, and ecumenical relations with non-Catholic and non-Christian religions.

Imperious rulers, avaricious bankers and greedy prelates insisted on a change of dogma. The casuists with their porous loopholes and duplicitous manipulation of language played a central role in this revolution, as did the founder of the Redemptorist Order, St. Alphonsus Liguori, "Doctor of the Church." The outline of the process of dissolution of the sacred dogma of the Magisterium has become visible, and with it the crepuscular hand of the situation-ethics which ruled the Vatican secretly for centuries, and openly since the 1960s.

Casuistry and Usury

"The casuists inherited the medieval synthesis but were vividly aware of the new social and economic realities that called it into question. They gradually realized that the old paradigm had become so surrounded by exceptions that it no longer provided a sound basis for analysis. The first move toward a new paradigm was the introduction of a theory of interest popularly referred to as 'the triple contract,' the 'German contract,' or the '5% contract.' It marked a notable departure from the medieval thesis and opened the way for a modern theory of profit from loans. The *summist* Angelus de Clavasio had given tentative approval to a form of insured investment; a lender might charge a fair price in view of sustaining potential losses...In 1515 John Eck, Dominican theologian of the University of Ingolstadt, who became famous five years later as Luther's debating opponent, defended de Clavasio's thesis in public. His defense won wide acclaim and, it is said, earned him a financial subsidy from the Fuggers, the international banking house in Augsburg.

"The name 'triple contract' expressed the essence of the arrangement that Eck popularized. Partners entered into three distinct contracts with each other. First there was a contract of partnership, which was considered legitimate by all commentators. Second, a contract of insurance was signed; under this the investor was insured against loss of his capital and, instead of paying a premium, agreed to accept a lesser percentage of the total profits than would otherwise come to him. Third, a contract was signed that guaranteed the investor a return at a set rate of interest, usually 5 percent. Thus the investor was a 'sort of debenture holder without industry or danger of losing his capital.' This was an attractive form of investment, which provided the active partner with considerable working capital. Commentators conceded that, if made with different parties, each of these three contracts would be legitimate, but most of them doubted the morality of the triple contract between two parties. They suspected 'usury' in the strict medieval sense: drawing profit without labor, loss, or risk. However, Eck replied that this form of investment entailed a loss by virtue of the title *lucrum cessans* since the investor could certainly have put his money to other, more profitable but less risky use.

"When the Jesuits arrived in Augsburg in 1555, they were dismayed to find the German contract in common use among the bankers and merchants of that great commercial city. Adhering to the more conservative view, they denounced the contract as usury, and withheld absolution from those who were engaged in it: notably, members of the Fugger family, who were bankers to the Holy Roman Empire and one of whose scions was studying to be a Jesuit. This stance stirred up a furor in the capital of European banking, and before long there was an excited exchange of letters between Augsburg and Rome. The Fuggers and the local bishop sought advice from Rome, while the German Jesuits sought advice from their headquarters. A special commission of Jesuits, including the distinguished theologian and casuist Cardinal Toletus, was instructed to present a report on the morality of the German contract to the Fourth General Congregation of the Society of Jesus (1580). The Pope himself submitted to the commission a *casus* given him by the Duke of Bavaria at the urging of Father Jasper Haywood, an exiled English Jesuit who was strongly opposed to the contract. This *casus* and the response to it represent a classical example of casuistical argument: Titius, a German, loans Sympronius a sum of money. Sympronius is a person of means, and the money is lent to him for no specific purpose. The conditions are that Titius is to receive annually five florins for every hundred lent, and afterwards have the whole capital back. There is no danger to the capital, and Titius must get his 5%, whether or not Sympronius makes a profit. The response of the commission first noted that this case could not be resolved until all of the actual circumstances had been carefully specified and examined. In response to the question whether knowledge of the general form of the contract was sufficient to warrant approval or disapproval, the commission answered in the negative.

"All the circumstances must be carefully specified: in particular, it must be ascertained whether the money was going to someone who could make it 'fructify.' In general, stated the commission, it would be prudent to advise someone considering such a contract to look for a morally less suspect investment. Next, Titius' profit would be legitimate only if it rested on one of the certainly moral entitlements such as *damnum emergens* or *lucrum cessans*. Finally, the profit would be clearly immoral if it were acquired merely in virtue of the loan. This response showed that the commission considered de Clavasio and Eck to have proposed a 'less probable opinion': this was not to be considered certainly immoral but at best suspect.

"On the basis of the commission's report, the General Congregation reaffirmed the decision of the Third Congregation, held seven years earlier, that the German contract was morally licit, and confessors could advise their penitents. This decision, which may appear odd to the modern reader, rested on the thesis, accepted by the Jesuits, that a probable opinion was sufficient to establish moral licitness. Subsequently three leading Jesuit theologian-casuists, Louis Molina,[161] Leonard Lessius, and John De Lugo, wrote exacting analyses of this form of investment, offering both practical and theoretical arguments to distinguish it from usury. The central theoretical argument was that the contract necessarily involved *lucrum cessans* and that this remained a legitimate title to interest, even when risk was eliminated. In

---

[161] Molina's *Treatise on Money* (arguments 396-410) was first published in an anthology of his writings in volume two of *De iustitia et iure* (1597), which was translated into English and published in 2007 in *Sourcebook in Late-Scholastic Monetary Theory,* pp. 139-237. Molina was a Jesuit economist and his arguments in favor of usury are exceedingly slippery. One must read carefully in order to perceive that he is in fact allowing for usury under certain tightly circumscribed circumstances; sometimes under the euphemism of a "stipend."

retrospect the German contract appears almost absurdly complex; yet some seventy-five years of debate about it led to radical change in the usury doctrine. By concentrating on this particular *casus,* moral theologians had recognized the dynamics of modern investment and the nature of economics in a world of production, banking, and trade...

"By the middle of the seventeenth century, then, the theory of usury had been turned on its head. Many different cases representing many different forms of financial transaction in different social and cultural circumstances had been debated and analyzed. The maxims from Old and New Testaments had lost their force because the general terms in which they were expressed could hardly cover the multiple kinds of transactions that passed for 'loans.' And a more subtle appreciation of the nature and functions of money, investment, and credit weakened the natural law arguments that had convinced the medieval scholastics.

"In light of these conceptual and factual developments, the definitions of usury changed from those that prevailed in the Middle Ages (e.g., 'where more is asked than is given' and 'whatever is demanded beyond the principal'), to the definition offered at the close of the debate by St. Alphonsus Liguori: [162] 'Usury is interest taken where there is no just title to profit.' At this point 'usury' has taken on the modern sense of 'excessive interest'...no longer does interest fall under the prohibition of theft. The new paradigm, reflecting the emerging science of economics, viewed money as a commodity, and the moral question asked how one could determine a 'just price' for its use.

"This long debate shows casuistry at work. Over five centuries there emerges a moral doctrine of

---

162 Liguori, *Theologia Moralis III*, v. 3, 7.

precise definitions and distinctions, of narrowly limited solutions and well-reasoned arguments. This doctrine was developed in a context marked by the pressure of powerful social, economic, and cultural changes. New circumstances pressed the casuists into new doctrines. From the thirteenth to the eighteenth century, the economy of Europe moved from subsistence farming to an extensive mercantile and commercial market. The thin lines of trade between Europe and the Near East expanded into wide streams of commerce between Europe, Asia, Africa, and America. Population increased; towns grew into cities; improved transportation facilitated travel and trade. The jigsaw puzzle of feudal principalities merged into powerful nation-states. Doctrinal dissonance and political incursions fractured the religious hegemony of the Roman Church. Finally, from the nascent power of nation-states and the impassioned belligerence of religion there arose continual and devastating international strife, with its voracious appetite for money. New circumstances pressed the casuists, as the economists of their time, to set new doctrines.

"...The casuists...sought, in the midst of the economic pressures, to bring to light the morally relevant circumstances that would permit meaningful moral discriminations. The cases they considered were genuine manifestations of new social, cultural and economic conditions...Doctrinal modifications did not come easily. Each new formulation was the product of extended, detailed debate among highly capable moralists and jurists often involving lengthy exchanges of petitions and decrees among rulers, prelates and businessmen...yielding only when they found a morally relevant circumstance or a conceptual clarification that justified a step away from the firm base of the ancient paradigm...This history of doctrinal change reveals not an evasion of morality but its progressive refinement..." [163]

---

[163] Albert R. Jonsen and Stephen Toulmin, *The Abuse of Casuistry: A History of Moral Reasoning*, pp. 188-190; 193-194.

5

The Protestant Reformation: Pro and Contra Usury

In general, Protestant theologians were split on usury along the same lines as Catholics but without a pope to settle the matter. The nominalist position refused to countenance any external enforcement against the crime of usury. They condemned "biting" loans, but permitted many other kinds of interest-bearing loans.

Some Protestants, whose world view was predicated in certain particulars upon medieval Catholic dogma, such as the bilious-tempered Martin Luther (1483-1546), generally supported the traditional prohibition of usury, qualified by a conceptual sophistication, or rather distinction, between interest on loans of money and income derived from a contract of mutual risk. Quite a bit of nonsense has been written about Luther and interest, mostly out of ignorance of the documentary record or a desire to taint his economic doctrine. The Marxist Professor Gerhard Brendler alleges, laughably, that Luther's hostility to usury was due to "his anti-semitism."[164] Norman Jones asserts without proof that "Both Luther and Melanchthon, however, were of the opinion that the secular magistrate could regulate interest for the good of the community, allowing it if he felt it was necessary."[165] Is this alleged permission from Luther a reference to interest on *mutuum*, or to a particular type of *zinskauf* – income from the sale of

---

164 *Martin Luther: Theology and Revolution* (Oxford, 1991).

165 *God and the Moneylenders*, p. 15. On Luther's reaction against peasant anti-usury "ultra-Mosaism" cf. *Revisionist History* no. 65.

annuities accruing from property? Jones doesn't say and offers no evidence or citations. If Luther had actually said that a magistrate could "regulate" (legalize) interest on money, he would have been as bad as Eck or Ridolfi, creating a loophole large enough to render most moral and civil laws against usury meaningless. But the fact is, there is no evidence that Luther said any such thing.

"In the economic sphere Luther was as conservative in the same sense as in the theological. In both he charged the Church of his day with innovation and summoned his contemporaries to return to the New Testament and to the early Middle Ages. The new Europe after the barbarian invasions had been agrarian, and the Church had bestowed the highest esteem on agriculture, next on handicraft, and last of all on commerce. This too was Luther's scale of values....

"When a loan was of food stuffs in a famine of the early Middle Ages, any replacement in excess of the goods consumed appeared to be extortion. But in a commercial venture for profit the case was different. St. Thomas saw this and sanctioned a sharing in profit by the lender provided there was also a sharing in loss. A contract of mutual risk was acceptable but not a contract of fixed return which would give to Shylock his ducats even though the ships of Antonio were on the rocks. In the age of the Renaissance, however, adventurers preferred a higher stake and bankers a more assured though lower return. The Church was ready to accommodate them both because she herself was so intimately involved in the whole process of the rise of capitalism, with banking, bookkeeping, credit, and loans. The Fuggers were not begrudged the services of the theologian John Eck to defend for a subsidy all the casuistic devices for evading the medieval and Thomistic restrictions on interest.

"Luther on the other hand became the champion of the precapitalist economy. How agrarian was his thinking is vividly exemplified in a cartoon on the title page of his tract on usury, in which a peasant is shown in the act of returning not only the goose which he had borrowed but also the eggs. Luther took his stand on the Deuteronomic prohibition of usury and the Aristotelian theory of the sterility of money. One gulden, said Luther, cannot produce another. The only way to make money is to work....Those who cannot protect themselves should be maintained by the community and the rest should work. There is but one exception. The aged with available funds may loan at interest not in excess of 5 percent or less, depending on the success of the enterprise. That is, Luther retained the contract of mutual risk. Otherwise loans for him came under the head of charity..." [166]

Luther was ferociously opposed to the financialization of the economies of Christian nations and to any rehabilitation of usurers or their "business" culture. But he also was an innovator, having urged a revolution — the overthrow of the monasteries — rather than a true reform of those once great engines of scholarship, agronomy, medicine and authentic Christian enterprise. (Some of this we trace to his unscriptural revulsion toward celibacy, a trait shared by some Protestants). Furthermore, Luther didn't take, as Bainton alleges, "his stand on the

---

166 Roland H. Bainton, *Here I Stand*, pp. 236-237. Bainton pandered to the trends of his day by attempting to sustain some of Max Weber's criticisms, which were very much in vogue in 1950, when *Here I Stand* was published. According to Bainton, Luther's intolerance for begging and his "exaltation of work as the imitation of God" had "unwittingly contributed" to the development of capitalism. If that is the case, then the Catholic monastic order of Benedictines, renowned for their arduous work ethic as epitomized by the eponymous adjective, *travailler à la benedictine*, were also responsible for the rise of capitalism.

Deuteronomic prohibition of usury." He couldn't. His "Law and Gospel" dichotomy wouldn't allow it. On the other hand, Luther's "one exception," however circumscribed by the fact that the exception was a commercial venture in which the lender-investor risked loss (Shylock would *not* have been paid under Luther's "exception"), lends itself to misunderstanding, out of which comes a precedent for meretricious exploitation of the "exception" in the future. His 5 percent for the aged was not a Florentine-style *monte pietatis*; it was a 5 percent return from an investment in an enterprise, in a contract of mutual risk. Nonetheless, Luther's exception pushed the envelope of Thomistic economics. His 1524 treatise on *Trade and Usury* does contain ambiguities that were later exploited by Lutherans who were of a more capitalist-orientation than their founder.[167] Luther should have foreseen this. He did make a distinction – which was consonant with Thomistic teaching – between interest on *mutuum* (loans of money), which he implacably opposed, and income derived from financial instruments, such as the *zinskauf* (which later became synonymous with the term *rentenkauf*) — steady income from property, the rights to which could be sold for a profit or negotiated as the basis of annuity income. [168]

Other Protestant founding fathers were influenced by the nominalists' arguments. Among the latter, the most important was the French Protestant lawyer turned theologian, Jean Cauvin ("John Calvin," 1509-1564), who drew inspiration from the French

---

167 Cf. "Trade and Usury" in *Luther's Works,* (Muhlenberg Press, 1962), vol. 45, p. 305.

168 For an explanation of *zinskauf* transactions, cf. Walther I. Brandt's introduction to "Trade and Usury," in *Luther's Works,* vol. 45, pp. 235-239.

Catholic jurist Charles du Moulin (1500-1556) and Moulin's popularizer, Francois Hottman. Moulin was influenced in turn by Tübingen's Conrad Summenhart. Moulin derived from Summenhart the belief that all loans at interest were not wrong; rather they were to be judged by the circumstances of the borrower. As long as the interest charged was "reasonable" there was nothing immoral about lending for purposes of increasing productivity. The Catholic Moulin went so far as to completely reverse the law, stating that the borrower who does not pay interest on productive capital is stealing from the lender! [169]

It was from within this Catholic milieu that Calvin formulated his doctrine. This supposed premier scripturalist, who relentlessly attacked and mocked Catholics for holding tradition on par with the Bible, based his economic teaching on the traditions of lawyer's equity theory, which nullified the Old Testament proscriptions against usury. Calvin declared that Old Testament laws were not binding on Christians in terms of an absolute prohibition on interest on money to fellow believers. He could not do the same with Christ's words on the subject in the Gospel of Luke, so he seized on the nominalists' distinction, which we confronted earlier in these pages, between interest and "biting" interest.

While Calvin had formulated a condonation of usury hedged by strict qualifications, it was observed by R.H. Tawney that "mission drift" was bound to occur: "Mankind finds in the arguments of theorists what it looks for. Calvin's indulgence to moderate interest...was remembered when the qualifications surrounding it were forgotten..."

A teacher of Calvin, the Protestant theologian Martin Bucer (1491-1551), in his *Tractatus de Usuris* enlarged on the nominalists' argument by proclaiming

---

[169] Moulin, *Tractatus contractum et usurarum* (1547).

that the Hebrew word *neshek*, translated as usury, signified that only interest on loans that were so extortionate they "bit" the borrower, were the type of interest that was forbidden. Following Bucer, Protestant theologian Henry (Heinrich) Bullinger (1504-1575) stated, "Usury is forbidden in the word of God so far as it bites his neighbor."

Bucer and Bullinger were parroting the evasions of the rabbis in this matter, as John Edwards demonstrated: "The Jewish rabbins (rabbis) distinguish between *neshec* and *tarbith*; the one, they tell us, is derived from a word that signifies to bite...and therefore they understand *neshec* concerning immoderate usury, such as is truly biting and devouring, and this they acknowledge is forbidden by the Law...But the other word, say they, which barely denotes increase, i.e. some overplus besides the principal, expresses the moderate and tolerable sort of usury...But this is a mere fancy, and hath no foundation at all in the Holy Scriptures, for these condemn not only *neshec,* but *tarbith*...As for that word *neshec*, it is apparent that it is a general term for all usury; it is a common word or name whereby that practice is expressed in Hebrew: and it imports the greatness of the sin, not any distinction of the kinds of usury." [170]

Bucer and Bullinger's Talmudic-like escape clause permits evasion of God's Law, through the argument on behalf of the notion of what Kermode terms "the different degrees of usury (depending on who was lending to whom, for what purpose and at what rate), or whether all usury was equally damnable; this question also raises the issue of differentiating between legitimate interest and illegal usury..."

---

170 John Edwards, D.D., *Theologia Reformata* (London, 1713), volume 2, pp. 547-548.

Overlooked in this rationalization was the traditional Christian belief that *all interest,* in and of itself, *took a "bite"* out of the borrower. An English Protestant critic of Bucer and Bullinger wittily took them to task, stating, "This hath been the general judgment of the church for about fifteen hundred years, without opposition in this point. Poor, silly Church of Christ, that could never find a lawful usury, before this age wherein we live."

As we have seen in the sweeping usury abolitionist legislation in the reign of Edward VI, the early Anglican Church remained faithful to the Biblical, patristic and medieval Catholic condemnation. Anglican Bishop Lancelot Andrewes rightly observed that "All usury is biting...There is no form of usury that is toothless." Andrewes believed that the etymological *neshek* distinction "...contravenes the principle of the Law itself that 'Thou shalt love they neighbor as thyself.' For it is an evil rule that decrees, 'let it be done provided it does not bite.' Evil I say, and Pharasaic. This is Christian: let it be done provided it benefits. For whether it bites or not, does not matter, if we are looking for true justice; what matters is whether it benefits or not."

The Puritan Miles Mosse responded to the new question of what constitutes "biting" interest: "There is a great difference between the biting of a flea, and the biting of a dog, and the biting of a lion: yet all are bitings, and the least will draw blood. So, there is a difference between him that takes five (percent interest) and him that takes ten and him that takes twenty...yet all is biting, and the least will consume a man in continuance." [171]

One Catholic faction, the nominalists, and one faction among the Protestants, provided King Henry

---

[171] The sermons of Mosse against usury, preached 1592-1593 at the church of St. Edmunds in Suffolk, were collected and published in London in 1595 as *The Arraignment and Conviction of Usurie*.

VIII the rationale for his deceitfully worded law of 1545, "A Bill Against Usury" (37 Hen. 8, c. 9). This statute inaugurated the legal fiction that usury no longer meant all interest whatsoever, but only *excessive* interest. This was the first law in the history of England to give connivance to the practice of lending at interest. A high rate of 10% was set as the legal limit.

Roger Fenton Contra *Usura*

The Protestant theologian Roger Fenton (1565-1615) was a Fellow of Pembroke Hall, Cambridge University, and rector of St. Stephen's, Walbrook, in London. In 1609 he succeeded Lancelot Andrewes as prebendary (canon) of St. Pancras in St. Paul's Cathedral. Rev. Fenton's lucidity and facility with the English language caused him to be chosen as one of the translators of the 1611 King James Bible. He proclaimed, "Not until sixteen hundred years after Christ did interest find any defenders."

It may be argued with a certain plausibility, that Fenton's insight into usury, which he detested with a detestation that knew no bounds, represents one of the most stirring and eloquent jeremiads ever penned concerning this sin:

"...many Christians of reformed Churches being urged to flee persecution, and to convert their goods into money, yet lacking skill to employ the same in a strange country; tender hearts thought it a pity that usury in such a case were not lawful; and nimble wits began to search, if the matter might not be so handled, and qualified by cautions and limitations, that some such thing as we call usury might be practiced. For such is the subtlety of Satan, that if he cannot hinder the growth of good corn, yet tares shall grow up with it. He thought that when men were so busied about the reforming of those gross abuses of superstition; that then was the only time to begin a new seed-plot of usury, of sacrilege, of liberty and profaneness in the other extreme. Which vices, howsoever they were little feared or thought upon in those days; yet by our time we may easily perceive to what ripeness they have grown, which then were but as seeds under the ground...

"He that turns himself into an angel of light [172] can set so fair a gloss upon a work of darkness, that the iniquity of it will hardly be discerned. He can so cunningly twist good and evil together, that the appearance of usury shall be presented without a show of injustice.

"...the gain of usury is a sweet gain, without labor, without cost, without peril...it is so pleasant and profitable a sin...This advantage then has the devil gotten against us in the practice of this sin; that usury being a trade so gainful in respect to others; so easy, so cheap, so secure without all labor...being also so common...it has bewitched even the consciences of those who are most tender in other matters...

"As usury is a sin in itself...so it is branded by the Holy Ghost for a sin of that nature and degree which does make shipwreck of conscience: the continuation of which sin cannot stand with the grace and favor of God.

"...Let some of those tender consciences who are so urgent to call for warrant out of the book of God for every ceremony and form in the Church, seek a warrant for this their practice (of usury), which so nearly concerns them, and let them seek it at the oracle of God, who has not left it, as he has many other things, either to the discretion of the Church, or wisdom of Commonwealths; but has vouchsafed to determine it in his own book to our hands: to set down an express law against it in Exodus; to renew that law

---

[172] 2 Corinthians 11:14.

again and again in Leviticus and Deuteronomy; to ratify and confirm it with no other words than he himself used at the publishing of the whole moral law...

"Since it has pleased Almighty God thus fully and exactly to express his will for our resolution in this point; let us not be ready to flee from his express word to human inventions – I mean those devised distinctions which favor the service of Mammon more than the service of God; which favor the things that be of men, to wit, the profit, the ease, the security, the sweet gain of interest; a trade which flesh and blood must needs affect and be greatly inclined unto." [173]

Roger Fenton was no anomaly. Many leaders of the early Protestant movement kindled a blaze of enmity for usury which has been ignored or concealed.

"Clearly, in the sixteenth and seventeenth centuries, most followers of Luther and Calvin were more hostile to usury than were contemporary Catholics in continental Europe, and generally more hostile than Calvin himself had been. For example, as late as the 1620s, the eminent English jurist Edward Coke (1552-1634), made Elizabeth I's Solicitor General in 1592, unequivocally stated, in pure Scholastic fashion, that by former parliamentary statutes, 'all usury is damned and prohibited,' and that 'usury is not only against the law of God...but against the laws of Nature'...many or even most early Protestants, especially in England, had both inherited and fully maintained, indeed with some considerable ferocity,

---

[173] Fenton, *A Treatise of Usury* (London: 1612), pp. 2-3; 48-49.

the long-traditional Scholastic view that usury was a vile, mortal sin, one 'against Nature." [174]

After we had written our revisionist history of white labor in early America, [175] presenting a chronicle of the enslavement of whites – not white slavery in the sense of forced prostitution, but chattel bondage of whites who had been kidnapped or "transported" from Great Britain – our work was met with some incredulity concerning the existence of anything other than white indentured servitude in America. The confusion was predicated on a failure to distinguish and study white bondage in different time periods in American history. For instance, the situation of white bondage in 1640 was radically different from that of 1780. In 1640 mainly white *slaves*, not indentured servants, toiled, usually for life, under harsh conditions on sugar and tobacco plantations in the West Indies and colonial America. From 1783 onward however, almost all bonded white labor in the newly formed United States was indentured. Failing to distinguish the differing conditions and circumstances of the early seventeenth century and the late eighteenth century occludes one's ability to grasp a suppressed epoch in the history of British America.

Something similar is at work in the misapprehension of the Protestant doctrine on usury. The situation of Protestant resistance to usury in the sixteenth century was radically different from that of Protestant attitudes toward usury in the eighteenth century. The collapse of usury resistance which took place over the course of 1500 years in the Roman

---

174 John Munro, "Usury, Calvinism and Credit in Protestant England," in *Religione e istituzioni nell'economia europea: 1000-1800*, p. 168.

175 *They Were White and They Were Slaves: The Untold History of the Enslavement of Whites in Early America* (Independent History and Research, 1993).

Catholic Church was condensed in the Protestant world to a duration of some 200 years. The critical distinction rests in an objective examination of the founding era of the Protestant Reformation. Roman Catholics and others have sought to brand Protestantism as usurious *from its foundation*. This is a formidable indictment since, if the foundations were bad, the whole edifice is ruined. Hence, if the charge is true, then the Reformation is tainted with the root of evil from its inception. The fact is, the charge is false. Moreover, it is necessary to ask, on what grounds does the Roman Church, which first infected Christendom with the plague of the mortal sin of usury and an ideology that furnished theological arguments for gradual adjustment to it, presume to point a finger at alleged Protestant failures in this regard? (Matthew 7:3).

In the following pages we present the early Protestant and Puritan stand *against* usury, and then the late Puritan position *in favor* of it, which was put forth during the degenerate phase of the Puritan church as it began its descent into fractured denominationalism and eventual decline. [176]

---

[176] When speaking of the degeneracy and decline of either the Roman Catholics or the Protestants, it is necessary to acknowledge that saintly men and woman arose in both churches despite the heresy and corruption within their leadership. We think of the French Catholic St. Vincent De Paul, and the New England Puritan theologian Jonathan Edwards, both of whom lived in eras when usury was on the rise in the hierarchy of their churches, and yet they were men of great personal rectitude and godly example; this in fulfillment of Christ's words in Matthew 16:18.

The Early Years of the Protestant Campaign Against Usury

The arch-Puritan theologian William Greenhill (1598-1671) graduated from Oxford University with the degree of M.A. in 1622. He was a Puritan from his youth, and a member of the radical "Independent" (Congregationalist) faction. Rev. Greenhill was one of the Westminster Assembly of Divines (preachers to Parliament). After the English Civil War, during the Puritan Republic, he was a commissioner of education ("Tryer of Schoolmasters and Preachers"). He earned acclaim for his homiletic exegesis of the Book of Ezekiel, delivered to crowded congregations in the city of London, and first published in five quarto volumes over the years 1645 to 1662; and subsequently reprinted three times over the centuries. For much of his career he ministered to a large assembly as vicar of the Church in Stepney, where he was esteemed by the people as 'the evening star,' due to his habit of preaching in the late afternoon. Friend and foe alike regarded him as a man of high personal integrity. He wrote, "The messengers of God must deliver the mind of God, be it pleasing or provoking, be it a matter of comfort or terror...they must announce judgments to the wicked, as well as pardon to the penitent; threats to the stubborn, as well as promises to the fainting; they must not give out what pleases themselves, but what the Lord commands them."

Greenhill was one of the hundreds of Puritan ministers in the sixteenth and seventeenth century who faithfully and conscientiously upheld the Biblical, Patristic and medieval Catholic doctrine on the mortally sinful nature of interest on money. In the following homily he restates Christendom's historic case, and answers the main evasions and objections of usury's equivocators and practitioners.

The God of Heaven and Earth Commands Them Not to be Usurers [177]

"He that hath not given forth upon usury, neither hath taken any increase, that hath withdrawn his hand from iniquity, hath executed true judgment between man and man."
Ezechiel 18:8

William Greenhill, 1651

"**O**ur prophet is upon declaring who is a righteous man. Sundry characters of such a one he hath laid down before, and here proceeds to add more; and the first is, he meddles not with usury, he increases not his estate that way. It is much in practice among the sons of men, as if Scripture did rather authorize than prohibit it.

"Upon usury...to bite; yea, to bite like a serpent. It is akin to...a serpent, saith Avenar. A serpent's biting is little felt at first, but after it inflames and ruins the man; so usury is not much felt at the beginning, but in time eats up and devours a man's whole substance: or, for that it makes a man restless, sleepless, who is bitten with it, as the biting of a serpent doth; or biting, in that, like a hungry dog or wolf, by biting and devouring others, it feeds itself. Chrysostom, *super illud*, Matt. V. *volenti mutuare*, saith, The usurer's money is like the biting of the asp. A man bitten by the asp hath a delightful sleepiness upon him, and dies sleeping, because poison sweetly diffuseth itself through his whole body; so the man that takes money of the usurer, pleases himself, thinking it a kindness and benefit unto him, but it quickly eats up a great

---

[177] This is our transcription, with typographical errors corrected, of Greenhill's text, published in *An exposition of the prophet Ezekiel: with useful observations thereupon* (Edinburgh, Scotland: James Nichol, 1863). The title, and subheadings have been supplied.

part, if not his whole estate. This kind of usury many are against, but other sorts of usury they allow and practice. I shall therefore consider what usury is, and then show you whether the Scripture will warrant any usury. What usury is:

"...In usury, three things are considerable: lending, gaining, covenanting. To lend money for gain, *interposita pactione*, that is 'usury.' When men put out their money to receive more than the principal by virtue of a covenant, contract, or compact, that makes them usurers. It is gain taken merely for the lending of a thing. Herein, it is conceived, lies the formality of it, viz. the covenanting, agreeing, and contracting to have so much for what is lent. This the word points at Exod. xxii. 25, thou shalt not put usury upon him.

"Amesius saith, it is gain sought after, aimed at from what is lent, because it is lent; and he includes in the word *quaesitum*, not only real usury, which is, contracted for, but mental usury, which is intended.

"Usury thus described I find no warrant for from the word of God, but much against it: look into these places, Exod. XXll. 25; Lev. xxv. 35-3; Deut. xxiii. 19, 20. The great God of heaven and, earth commands them not to be usurers, not to lend upon, or take, usury.

The Evasion

"The answer and evasion that some have and make here, is this: True, we must not lend upon usury to the poor, who are mentioned in the two first places, and implied in the third, but to the rich we may. To take away this evasion:

"1. Consider, there are other places where no mention of the poor is made. Psalm.xv. 5, 'He that putteth not out his money to usury.' It is spoken indefinitely; they might not put it out to the poor; and who, then, were there to put it out to, but the rich? So in Jer. xv. 10; Ezek. xxii. 12, usury is censured, and yet there is no mention of the poor. Usury seemed a cursed thing.

"2. Rich men were their brethren as well as the poor; and, Deut. xxiii. 20, 'Unto thy brother thou shalt not lend upon usury....

"3. 'What countenance, warrant, or encouragement do you find in holy writ for lending money to rich and wealthy men, especially with expectation of gain? Luke vi. 34, 'If ye lend to them of whom ye hope to receive, what thank have ye? For sinners also lend to sinners, to receive as much again.' Wicked men, the worst of all, who have no fear of God in them, will do that; therefore, saith Christ, 'Lend, hoping for nothing again.' Here is shown who should lend, and to whom. Rich men are to lend, not to borrow; and to those the lending should be who are not able to maintain their charge, drive on their callings, without help; to these, rich men should lend freely; and to others that are beggars, truly poor, they should give: Matt. v, 42, 'Give to him that asketh thee, and from him that would borrow of thee turn not thou away.' It is a duty for rich men to lend, not to borrow; and because they let many families sink in these hard times, which would do well enough had they a little support from the rich, it will stand upon their account one day. This is the evil of rich men, because they see such a man decaying, therefore they will not lend to him; but because he is upon decaying, therefore they should lend to him that he may not utterly decay, Deut. xv. 7, 8.

Biting and profitable usury

"The second evasion men have is this: Usury when it is biting, hath the serpent's sting and teeth in it; prejudices, and doth not profit, or advantage a man, then in that case (they say) it is unlawful; but if a man be a gainer by it, it is not unwarrantable; and so they distinguish between biting usury and profiting usury.

"Answer: Distinctions and arguments from etymologies are insufficient and weak. (The name) Absalom signifies a father of peace, or, the father's peace; but he was a father of war, and his father's trouble. As for 'usury,' the Scripture knows no such distinction as biting and profiting usury; it is a human invention, to make way for the satisfaction of men's covetous and greedy desires. Men think they are safe if they take usury of the rich, not of the poor; but see how the Lord strangles and cuts off this distinction by the next words in the verse: 'Neither hath taken any increase. He must not be a biting usurer, which they grant; neither must he be an increasing usurer; this is forbidden by the same authority that the other is...He is a just man that takes no more than he lends. Some would have this word to be exegetical, and so think to avoid the force of it: but though the wisdom of man be inventive to promote its own interests, yet it must not null(ify) the wisdom of God.

"Let us grant it exegetical, it is of more force against them; for the latter word must expound the former, and so *any increase* is the meaning of usury. Upon this account, then, *he is a usurer who takes any increase*. But this likes not those who plead for it. By increase they would have such increase as burdens, bites, oppresses, and consumes him that gives it. This is forcing of the word *tarbith*, which notes simply any increase or multiplication; not biting, oppressing, undoing increase. As they therefore stick to the word *nesheck*, to make one sort of usury unlawful, so we may we stick to the word *tarbith*, to make that other sort of usury unlawful, because it is said, 'he that hath not given forth upon usury, neither hath taken any increase.'

"The word notes increase of victuals, as well as of money: Lev. xxv. 37: 'Thou shalt not give him thy money upon usury, nor lend him thy victuals for increase.' There must not be increase of money or victuals; it is not meant a burdensome increase of victuals, but no increase at all.

"Some plead the lawfulness of it from Deut. xxiii. 20, Unto a stranger thou mayest lend upon usury; but unto thy brother thou shalt not lend upon usury.' Hence they conclude, that usury is simply unlawful to a brother.

"Answer: ...It was to strangers they might do it; and not to all strangers, but Canaanites only, who were designed of God to destruction; so that those they might destroy with the sword, they might devour with usury. So then, where men are not appointed to death, and to be cut off by war, they may not exercise usury.

It is our sinful covetousness to take usury one of another when we are brethren

"...The distinction of strangers is now taken away; the partition-wall is broken down, and we are all brethren. A stranger that was become a proselyte, and embraced the Jewish religion, they might not take usury of, he was a brother, Lev. xx.v. 35, 36; they had all one father, Mal. ii. 10, and so have we, and are brethren. This made Jerome upon this place, say, 'In the law, usury was taken off from the brethren, in the prophets it is forbid to all; in the gospel is yet more virtue and favor; the Lord saith, Lend to them from whom ye may expect nothing. It is the blindness of the Jews, to think they may take usury of Christians, when Christ hath made of both one, Eph. ii. 14; and it is our sinful covetousness to take usury one of another when we are brethren.'

Usury makes void three great rules our Lord and Savior has given us in the Gospel

"Some ground the lawfulness, and so their practice of it (usury) upon Matthew xxv. the parable of the talents; ver. 27, 'Ought thou not to have put my money to the exchangers, and then at my coming I should have received mine own with usury.' Hence they conclude, that Christ doth not only allow, but doth justify, usury.

"Answer:...Christ here speaks, not concerning the justice of the matter, as if he approved usurious practices, whereby men of covetous minds do increase their estates; but concerning its mode, the increase that came by such practices, which he propounds to be imitated in spiritual things. You see men of this world improve their money, and so should you improve those gifts and graces which are credited and committed unto you. Christ here justifies usury no more than he justifies the unjust steward, Luke xvi. 8, where it is said, he 'commended the unjust steward, because he had done wisely.' Why, what had he done? In one account he had defrauded his master of fifty measures of oil; in another account, he cut him short of twenty measures of wheat; yet Christ saith, 'he hath done wisely.' That is, wisely for himself, though wickedly for his master. Christ's commendation of him did not legitimate the action. If men's stewards or servants should do so now, and allege his instance, they would not hold them excusable, but have the law against them. Christ saith, that he will come as a thief, Rev. xvi. 15; and that the day of the Lord so cometh 'as a thief in the night.' 1 Thess. v. 2. Does this, therefore, countenance or justify theft?

"You see, then, no footing for usury in the word of God.

"It (usury) seems to me to make void three great rules which our Lord and Savior hath given us in the gospel. The first is that, Matt. vii. 12, 'All things whatsoever ye would that men should do to you, do ye even so to them: for this is the law and the prophets.' Now, is there any man in straits, in necessities, that would not borrow freely, rather than be tied to pay so much, not knowing whether he shall gain anything, or preserve the principal: and if any should deny it, I fear their own consciences would condemn them for it. It is true, through the custom and practice of the times, men are willing to borrow upon such rates and terms, because they cannot have monies otherwise; but if men will lay aside all respects of that kind, and look at the simple nature of the thing, they cannot but confess they had rather have money freely than upon terms; and if so, then they ought to do so to others, and not lay the burden of usury upon them. 2. It is against that great rule and command, Luke vi. 35, 'Lend, hoping for nothing again.' The Greek is...men should so lend as not to hope for, much less contract for, anything again...Lend hoping for (the return of) the principal, but nothing for the loan of it...Such lending is attributed to righteous and good men: Psalm xxxvii. 26, 'He is ever merciful, and lendeth;' and, Psalm cxii. 5, 'A good man sheweth favour, and lendeth.'

A Cloud of Witnesses Against this Mortal Sin

"It (usury) is against that great rule and command, Heb. xiii. 5, "Let your conversation be without covetousness." Should poor men be without covetousness who have little, and should not rich men who have much? They (the rich) usually are the usurers, and so most covetous. Usury is the invention and practice of covetousness, and serves only to feed the appetite thereof. Covetousness is a grievous sin; it is idolatry, as you may see, Col. iii. 5; it makes the times perilous, 2 Tim. iii. 1-2; it is the root of all evil, 1 Tim. vi. 10; it makes a man unworthy of Christian society, 1 Cor. v. 11; to be abhorred of God, Psalm. x. 3; and so to be shut out of the kingdom of heaven, 1 Cor. vi. 9, 10...Psalm. xv. I, 'Lord, who shall abide in thy tabernacle? Who shall dwell in thy holy hill?' Ver. 5, 'He that putteth not out his money to usury.'

"...Many councils have condemned it as unlawful. In the first Nicene it was condemned for a mortal sin, canon 17. The first Carthaginian determined it to be base gain, cap. 13. The Lateran Council saith, Usury is not allowed to redeem captives; Council of Vienne decrees him to be punished as a heretic who says usury is no sin. The Eliberine council degraded clergymen, and cast the people out of the church, who were usurers; cap. 20.

"Not only councils, but fathers, have been against it. Augustine upon the 36th Psalm says, "*Si plum quam dedisti expectas accipere, foeneratores*;" and Bernard calls it, "*Venenum patrimonii: inter praecepta famil.*"

"...Let, men, therefore, take heed how they touch usury, seeing there is such a cloud of witnesses against it, and not trust to a distinction of man's brain by making biting usury unlawful, but other usury lawful, lest by this distinction they get money in their coffers, and lose their souls at last; for...such gain is the sepulchre of the soul; and he will not sojourn in the tabernacle of the Lord, that puts his money to usury. Sure it is an ill trade that excludes a man from heaven.

"Money at first was invented for exchange of things uneasy to be transported, not, to beget money, or a trade, without labor; for the usurer's trade is most easy and gainful...And if usury were brought to lower rates amongst us, or rather wholly taken away, it were an honor to the gospel, and to our nation." (*End quote from William Greenhill*).

Some Myths of Max

Many Catholics and other opponents of Protestantism who believe they have the competence to venture to insert themselves into the controversy over mammonism and commerce in Christendom, have so inadequate a grasp of early modern history that they have no inkling that in nations where the Protestant Church held sway in its early years, *it was Rome and the pope who were notorious for usury and mammonism in the mind of the people.*

"Although the work of Max Weber[178] has taught us to associate capitalism with Calvinism, most English authors before the eighteenth century followed Luther in emphasizing the papist nature and history of usury, and Puritans often included a tolerance for usury (as being) among the 'rags of Rome' that they believed continued to defile the Anglican church. In 1629 Matthew Sutcliffe claimed (in his 1629 book, *A True Relation of England's Happiness*), that '...Simony and usury among the Romanists is so common that as Matthew Paris says, they account the first no sin; the second a small sin'...The Pope...has ordinary banks of usury, as the world knows, and popish writers confess, where they speak of their *Monti di pieta*." [179]

"...as far as the first generation of reformers was concerned, there was no intention, among either Lutherans or Calvinists or Anglicans, of relaxing the rules of good conscience which were supposed to control economic transactions and social relations. If anything, indeed, their tendency was to interpret them with a more rigorous severity, as a protest against the moral laxity of the Renaissance, and in particular, against the avarice which was though to be peculiarly the sin of Rome...

"The passionate anti-capitalist reaction...found expression in numerous schemes of social reconstruction...In the age of the Reformation it was voiced by (Wendel) Hipler who, in his *Divine Evangelical Reformation* urged that all merchants' companies, such as those of the Fuggers, Hochstetters and Weslers, should be abolished...by Geiler von Kaiserberg, who wrote that the monopolists were more detestable than Jews... "[180]

---

[178] *The Protestant Ethic and the Spirit of Capitalism* (1930).

[179] Hawkes, op. cit., pp. 87-88.

[180] R.H. Tawney, *Religion and the Rise of Capitalism*, pp. 77, 79.

Max Weber's landmark 1904 work, *Die Protestantische Ethik, und der Geist des Kapitalismus,* translated in English in 1930 and published as *The Protestant Ethic and the Spirit of Capitalism,* became a bestseller and has left an indelible stain on the Reformation, equating its ascendance in the West with responsibility for a miserly, workaholic, Shylock way of life in predominately Protestant nations.

Weber's indictment has become part of the folklore of Catholics, secularists and latter-day Protestants. It remains as current as the recent claim that Shakespeare intended Shylock to be understood by his Elizabethan audience as the personification not of a Jew, but of a Puritan; and it is standard boilerplate in paleo-Conservative books and magazines: "That wealth-worship – and a consequent special status for the wealthy as a kind of clerisy – should have arisen in the United States is hardly surprising, given the peculiar sort of Protestantism that was planted here from the British Isles. Starting with the Puritanism of New England, there has been a long and intimate connection between the sanctification of wealth and America's economic and social relationships." [181]

This obscurantist, comic book-style history conveniently ignores three centuries of economics in which "wealth-worshipping" Catholic bankers in Italy and Germany became the greatest capitalists in the history of Christendom, before the first Puritan had been born. This was a Renaissance-Catholic mammonism so interwoven into the fabric of church and society that it combined the jingle of coins from the sale of indulgences with the charging of interest overseen by a single Catholic bank with the assets of King Midas.

---

[181] Mike Lofgren, "Revolt of the Rich," *The American Conservative,* September, 2012, p. 21.

Was it forty-seven *Puritan* popes of Rome who have been in thrall to the Money Power to such an extent that, since certain kinds of interest banks were first legalized in 1515 by Leo X – and other forms of usury gradually thereafter – not one of these pontiffs has ever been willing to restore the divine law against usury? [182]

Was it *Puritan* Conquistadors who, in an orgy of greed unprecedented in the annals of the western hemisphere, contracted a gold fever that burned so hot it plundered and enslaved the helpless indigenous nations at their mercy? "If by the capitalist spirit is meant the temper which is prepared to sacrifice all moral scruples to the pursuit of profit...it was the economic imperialism of Catholic Portugal and Spain...which impressed contemporaries down to the Armada...'Gold,' wrote Columbus, as one enunciating a truism, 'constitutes treasure, and he who possesses it has all the needs in this world, as also the means of rescuing souls from Purgatory, and restoring them to the enjoyment of Paradise." [183]

Prof. Luciano Pellicani of the Universita degli Studi Sociali in Rome, deconstructs Max Weber's thesis:

The "change from an economy of mutual protection to one of unilateral capitalist exploitation did not await, as Max Weber has unfortunately led many people to believe, the rise of sixteenth century Protestantism...The capitalist spirit is much older than Weber believed, and it grew in surroundings permeated by the Catholic faith...the whole Italian

---

182 In 1907 Pope Pius X wrote in his encyclical *Pascendi Dominici Gregis*, that the heresy of modernism was "the synthesis of all heresies." For some reason he did not know or care — or dare — to state, that the rise of the Money Power within the Church *was at the root of modernism.*

183 Tawney, op.cit., pp. 76, 80.

Renaissance from beginning to end is filled with the awareness that 'by his own activity, man could accomplish anything; through work man became creator.

"...nothing more antithetical to the modern capitalist spirit can be imagined than the obsessive preaching of the reformed sects about the horror of Mammon, which corrupts, degrades and prostitutes everything.

"Weber also erroneously attributes a modernity to the Calvinist conception of calling. In *Institutes of Christian Religion* Calvin declares: '...there is a special call which, for the most part, God bestows on believers only, when by the internal illumination of the spirit he causes the word preached to take deep root in their hearts.' Calvin states clearly what this implies in his *Commentaires sur le Nouveau Testament*: 'Each must be content with his vocation, let him follow it, let him not desire to seek a different one.' This notion of vocation – acceptance of one's state, condemnation of covetousness and ambition, rejection of the temptation to cross assigned limits, abandonment of the search for new ways – has no real affinity with the entrepreneurial mentality.

"Calvin's last lessons, *Revelations du Prophéte Ezéchial*, proclaim a full fledged anathema against the acquisitive spirit: 'In a well-ordered republic, a man who practices usury is absolutely not tolerable...Every man whose office is usury ought to be cast out from the company and society of men, because if a totally dishonest art renders odious those who practice it, certainly usury is not only evil and dishonest gain, but also unworthy of an honest Christian man. Whoever habitually profits from usury, will be a predator and will sink in his iniquity. We must always remember that it is difficult for a man who seeks profit not to wrong his brother; because of this, it would be desirable that the names of usury, profit, and interest were completely banished from the memory of men."[184]

Swiss theologian and economist André Biéler states, "...it is not possible to honestly credit Calvin with the responsibility for the evolution of capitalism...Capitalism could develop in Protestant peoples only thanks to the relaxation of Reformed doctrine and morals." [185]

It is not an exaggeration to say that early Calvinism and its offspring, Puritanism, in the first century and-a-half of its development in Britain, Europe and America, perceived the market economy as the Kingdom of Satan. Geneva under Calvin was not a place for reaping financial profits or having the seeking after such profits as a vocation. Wherever the original fanaticism of the strict Calvinist prevailed, the capitalist market economy was severely restricted, if not almost completely eliminated.

"Calvinist spiritual hegemony with its obsessive hostility toward profit or gain...hindered the formation of a modern entrepreneurial bourgeoisie...the claim that Puritan doctrine explains the economic and professional success of the capitalist bourgeoisie is a cliché without basis...the Puritans only repeated what Christianity had always taught: that salvation is difficult if not quite impossible for the rich...the theocratic principles of Calvinist Geneva...far from actually promoting capitalist growth...w(ere) restrictive and economically antiquarian. Voetius, the ferocious doyen of the Calvinist divines of Utrecht, carried on a life-long campaign against luxury, usury

---

[184] Pellicani, *The Genesis of Capitalism and the Origins of Modernity,* pp. 36-40.

[185] Biéler, *La pensée économique et sociale de Calvin*, p. 514.

and all forms of display; excommunicating a pious woman because her husband was employed in a pawnshop and encouraging in many other parishes a similar hostility toward anything savoring of usury or profit-making.

"In economic matters...adamantine Puritans' main guide was William Ames' *De Conscientia*, which chided, among other things: 'To wish to buy cheap and sell dear is common (as St. Augustine observes), but it is a common vice;' a vice that the guardians of orthodoxy held to be much more dangerous than one might imagine, since it weakened solidarity among the faithful and opened the doors to Mammon's perverse temptations...where Orthodox Puritans held power, the state became a ministry of Church police, with the institutional charge of constant vigilance over all social and economic practices...Hebrew theology and Genevan discipline cooperated to inspire a theocratic state with no room for either religious or economic liberty..." [186]

"A few decades ago it had become very much the mode to praise the Puritans for virtues they did not possess and which they would not have considered virtues at all. In the pages of liberal history...the Puritans have been...invoked in justification for an economic philosophy of free competition and laissez-faire, though they themselves believed in government regulation of business, the fixing of just prices, and the curtailing of individual profits in the interest of the welfare of the whole." [187]

---

186 Pellicani, op. cit., pp. 46; 48-49; 51-52.

187 Perry Miller, *The Puritans*, vol. 1, pp. 4-5. Miller was a distinguished historian of the ideology of early New England. Here he is revising his own previous view of Puritan economics.

Whether we are examining Protestant London or Amsterdam, those cities and their respective nations hit their stride as capitalist societies only after they had freed themselves from the totalitarianism of the original Calvinist Reform. In London this took the form of the installation of King Charles II to the English throne after the decay of the Puritan government under Cromwell. With the death of the Puritan Republic and the restoration of the "Merry Monarch" Charles II, usury banking rode higher than ever and corruption returned as business as usual. Puritan rigor gave way not only to Charles II but eventually to the misnamed "Glorious Revolution." Under both monarchies, "England gave itself a political regime that legitimated everything vital to the development of the entrepreneurial bourgeoisie, everything the Puritan revolution had opposed: autonomy of civil society with regard to the state, separation of economy from religion,...the right to buy and sell according to the laws of the market." [188]

Cromwell was unacceptable to large swaths of Puritan society and his Republic failed not because the Cavaliers overthrew it, but rather due to the Puritan majority's loss of faith in his cynical manipulation of their idealism. The early Puritan ideal was patristic and medieval (though stripped of Catholic liturgy and papalism). Opposing it was a monarchy in late seventeenth and early eighteenth century England that gravitated toward the Renaissance and humanism. In early New England we find the last bastion of the medieval ideal as it found expression among the first and second generation Puritans. The city of London became a banking center because of its departure from early Puritan ethics, not because of them.

---

[188] Pellicani, op. cit., p. 73.

As for Amsterdam, while Calvinist Orthodoxy caught on with about one-third of the population of Holland, there were many competing churches and a large Renaissance Catholic population. Calvinists never had hegemony as they did in Geneva and New England:

"Holland...institutionalized the typically bourgeois separation between the domains of business and religion; a separation that was blasphemous to the guardians of Calvinist orthodoxy...to define Holland as a Calvinist country is a considerable stretch. An extraordinarily broad religious pluralism marked the Republic of the Seven Provinces from its inception... (in) what...contemporaries called the 'Amsterdam of religions'...Calvinists to be sure, were the largest religious group, but their numbers never exceeded a third of the population..." [189]

The "spiritual policing" aspect of early Calvinism is repellant to the modern mentality and tends to evoke ecclesiastical Stalinism. The more accurate analogy would be to the Roman Catholic Inquisition and the Catholic concept that "error has no rights." If the inquisition was correct, at least philosophically, so too was the discipline in Calvin's Geneva. Catholics may argue that at least their regime was not humorless and allowed theatres and alcohol. Actually many Catholic saints and theologians regarded theatres with horror, while Calvinists dressed in bright clothing, disdained what Samuel Johnson termed "cheerless celibacy" ("godly" widows and widowers often quickly remarried), and some partook of beer, wine and liquor. The authentic differences that span the Renaissance Catholic vs. early Puritan divide, are seldom mentioned. First, there is the passionate commitment to combatting *criminal politics*, not only in its most flagrant Machiavellian-Medici trope, but as it later

---

[189] Ibid., pp. 49-50.

manifested under King Charles I and Archbishop Laud in early seventeenth century England. Some contemporary right-wing Roman Catholics and High Church Anglicans portray the reign of Charles I as an enemy of the Money Power and a kingdom of good cheer and merriment, until dour Puritan shylocks ruined the fun. In fact, the level of discontent in England circa 1640, at the degree of corruption, bribery, aristocratic entitlement, police state tyranny (the hated star chamber), imprisonment of political and religious rivals and Anglican accommodation with these vices, was at the boiling point. Fair-minded Catholics would do well to look at more than the providential circumstance of the regular offering of Charles's Catholic Queen Henrietta-Maria's Tridentine Masses. William Prynne's ears were sliced off after he wrote a book protesting the queen's slightly risque private theatricals. Prynne was an incorruptible Puritan legal scholar much admired by English folk high and low. His needless torture (he would be ordered branded on the cheek and his ears completely removed), and the sentence of imprisonment for life imposed upon him, enraged the common people and was but one symptom of a cruel and arrogant King Charles lording it, by alleged "divine right," over a population that desired a just society and equal opportunity for education and advancement. For a considerable portion of the English yeomanry, the personal rule of Charles I was riddled with criminal politics. If Charles' cavaliers dressed finely, recited lovely poetry and were more to modern taste in their debauchery, what has this to do with the cry, then as now, for an end to criminal politics?

In early Protestant England two leading churchmen demonstrated the depths of their allegiance to the Biblical, patristic, scholastic position. The first was Dr. Thomas Wilson, writing in 1572 in his *Discourse on Usury*. Wilson stated, "Treasure doth then advance greatness when the wealth of the subject be rather in many hands than few." One historian observed that the starting point of Wilson's treatise is "a society in which property is widely distributed, in which there is a large Middle Class and, outside London, a small, though growing, proletariat, in which, in short, the typical worker is not a wage-earner, but a Peasant Farmer, a Tradesman, or a small master."

Wilson's Protestant economics were consonant with the medieval Catholic view, including the pre-Renaissance popes. The fair-minded Wilson wrote, "I would not have men altogether be enemies to the Canon Law, and to condemn everything therein written, because the Pope was author of them, as though no good law could be made by them. Nay, I will say plainly, there be some such laws made by the Pope as be right godly, say others what they will."

Wilson stated further: "Men should lend freely, as the Gospel commands, sell at the price fixed by common estimation, eschew speculation and monopoly, and so conduct their trade that they may practice it without injury to their neighbor or neglect of the law of Christian charity...recall men to justice...lest the Antichrist himself be Lord of the Harvest."

The "Antichrist's harvest" in this sense is the unnatural issue of usury. "Probably the best-known dramatic address to the question of 'unnatural' usury is Shylock's joke early in *The Merchant of Venice* (1596). Shylock tells Antonio and Bassanio a parable of the time 'When Jacob grazed his uncle Laban's sheep,' and how Jacob won for himself all the parti-colored lambs, which were born as a response to the rank ewes seeing 'certain' 'peeled' 'wands' before their eyes as they were 'in the doing of the deed' (I.3.69-88).

Antonio judges that such a process is in the hands of God, not something that human beings can manipulate against nature's rules. 'Or is your gold and silver ewes and rams?' Antonio asks Shylock, falling unwittingly into the usurer's trap: 'I cannot tell,' triumphs Shylock, 'I make it breed as fast." [190]

Dr. Wilson observed that the usurers regard the churches and regular church attendance on Sundays as useful to their regime as long as the pastors uphold the legitimacy of the usury-based wealth of the plutocrats and avoid the ancient church heritage of regulating business ethics: "Thieves steal for necessity, but usurers rob and undo all men for greedy gluttony. Usurers scratch up the whole realm of England. Either they should be exterminated or the Common Law of Edward I should be revived, whereby if twelve men could prove it, the goods of the usurer should turn to the good of the prince."

Wilson's foundational theme was above all Christian love, i.e. charity: free lending was to be looked for from Christians – *Valet fides in Christo quae per charitatem operatur* ("Faith in Christ works in charity"). This is what was hated above all by usurers both Judaic and gentile. Shakespeare depicts the attitude of Shylock toward interest-free loans issued by true Christians: "I hate him for he is a Christian. But more for that he lends out money *gratis* and brings down the rate of *usance* (usury) here with us in Venice and he rails on me, my bargains and my well won thrift, which he calls interest."

Bishop John Jewel, who in some respects personified early Anglicanism, sided with Wilson; also John Blaxton in *The English Usurer, or Usury condemned by the most learned and famous Divines of the Church of England* (1634). The Anglican bishops cited by Blaxton are Jewel, Sandys, King, Babington, Downam ("the hammer of usurers"), and Lake. They

---

190 Lloyd Edward Kermode, *Three Renaissance Usury Plays (*Manchester University Press, 2009), p. 3.

repudiated both Eck's Roman Catholic nominalism and Calvin's notion that conduct condemned by Scripture as sinful in itself could become venial when practiced with judicious moderation:

"Stealing did not become lawful, merely because the sums stolen were small. God was no respecter of persons to condone, in those who financed the rich, conduct forbidden to those who lent to the poor. The direct results of a loan at moderate interest to a well-to-do merchant might seem harmless. But the merchant would pass it on in higher prices to the consumer, and in the end the whole commonwealth, including the poor, would suffer."

Lancelot Andrewes, Bishop of Winchester, was born the son of a sailor at London, in 1555, nine years before Shakespeare. Educated at Cambridge and a gifted linguist, in 1604 he was appointed as one of the translators of the King James Version (KJV) of the Bible and became responsible for most of the KJV's Old Testament. T.S. Eliot is said to have converted to Christianity in 1927 after reading Andrewes' *Seventeen sermons on the Nativity*. Eliot wrote a book, *For Lancelot Andrewes: Essays on Style and Order* (London, 1928). Eliot's 1930 poem, "The Journey of the Magi," was inspired by Andrewes. It tells of how the birth of Jesus Christ was the death of the world of magic, astrology, and paganism.

Andrewes' campaign against usury was unique. Aquinas had argued from the *nature* of money; the aforementioned 16th century English Protestant bishops and preachers argued from the *results* of usury, but Andrewes made his case straight from the New Testament: "And if ye lend to them of whom ye hope to receive, what thank have ye? Even sinners lend to sinners, to receive again as much" (Luke 6:34). Protestant Bishop Andrewes contrasted Our Savior's

Kingdom with that of the Moneylenders' Realm. We modern people reside almost completely within the latter. Few churches today exhort against interest on loans beyond the rate of inflation, even as they make a great show of continence in marriage and other personal virtues, while in the public sphere, the Money Power proceeds to tear away the foundations of Christian morality. Everything is permissible when Mammon rules the Church. After all, "business is business." The churches have derogated usury to a minor transgression barely worthy of consideration, if, indeed, it is not honored as a Christian virtue of "our American free market."

Bishop Andrewes was the enemy of usury *and* the Elizabethan enclosures, which had driven small farmers and herders into poverty by "enclosing" the previously free-to-all grazing lands or "commons," just as the open range of the American West was eventually fenced off. We sometimes forget that what we celebrate about our cowboy era was a culture created by vast stretches of unenclosed land. Andrewes taught that the spirit of usurious monopoly is the spirt of enclosure.

As we have noted, one of the toughest laws against usury ever promulgated in the sixteenth century, in any Christian nation, whether Catholic or Protestant, occurred in Protestant England. It reinstated the ancient Church's jurisprudence that all usury was "damned and prohibited." It was enacted during the ultra-Protestant reign of the boy king, Edward VI in 1552, partly due to the intervention of Robert Crowley, an early Puritan and poor man's advocate.

King Edward's usury ban lasted for some 19 years, until 1571, when it was repealed after vigorous debate in Parliament in the reign of Queen Elizabeth I. *After 1571, there would never be another law against interest on money in Britain, only a regulation of the rate of usury, and this is the universal practice in the West in our time.*

The most striking aspect of King Henry VIII's 1545 law permitting 10% interest had been the fact that all reference to God and His Law had been omitted in its enactment. When Henry's statute was reversed in 1552 in the reign of his young son Edward, the new law reinstating the centuries-old total prohibition of interest, appealed directly to God and the Bible: "For as much as usury is by the Word of God utterly prohibited, as a vice most odious and detestable, as in diverse places of the Holy Scripture it is evident to be seen..."

The 1571 Elizabethan statute allowing "moderate" usury would be altered in 1624 in ways that reflected England's increasingly degenerate attitude toward usury and the economy. Although the law of 1571 did not officially permit lending at interest, it created a loophole in which entrepreneurs could loan *de facto* at 10%, with impunity. English merchants from 1600 onward partnered with the East India Company to expand markets overseas and the demand for loans grew. Usury was becoming a part of the English monarchy's economic model.

In 1624, in the reign of King James I, the passage of 21 Jac. I. c. 17 "Against Usury" (as all such early legislation in *favor* of usury were misnamed, presaging Orwell by more than 300 years), marked the official end of medieval usury law in England. Lending at interest was now considered to be a normal and necessary part of life, to be regulated by the state for the sake of the nation's economic welfare. Newly legal usurers like Thomas Sutton, Lionel Cranfield, John "Rich" Spencer, Baptist Hicks and other infamous money-men of the London of King James I, combined speculation with money-lending at interest, to reap enormous profits. *As their fortunes increased so too did their political power.* Cranfield became the Lord

Treasurer of England; Hicks was transformed into Sir Baptist Hicks, a member of parliament; Spencer would become Lord Mayor of London. From henceforth, wealth acquired through usury would be the road to power and influence in the sceptered isle, culminating in the establishment of the Bank of England at the end of the seventeenth century, marking the complete transfer of power from Churchmen and Commons to Moneymen and plutocracy.

The son of James I, King Charles I, married a French Catholic. He is viewed by Belloc as a supposed bastion of opposition to the Money Power. How then does Mr. Belloc account for the fact that in the third year of his reign, Charles I made his father's 1624 law signifying the final extirpation of medieval Catholic usury law in England, "perpetual"?

Bigots have indulged in a considerably biased literature consisting of stereotypical adjectives such as *"Puritan dregs"* (G.K. Chesteron) and *"grasping Puritans."* When we see the latter jibe we think of the Puritan carpenter Nehemiah Wallington who was born in London in 1598. In addition to his manual labors he was a diarist of some exertion, compiling thousands of manuscript pages during his lifetime, dedicated both to the events of his life as well as rigorous self-scrutiny of the state of his conscience. The process of getting money was for the Puritan Wallington entirely subordinate to his concern for personal salvation and his arduous pilgrimage toward the heavenly city of God. At one time Wallington discovered that his apprentice had stolen a substantial sum of money from him over a two-year period. Rather than prosecuting the man, he called upon God to "bless and sanctify this my poverty unto me." If we regard Wallington as a Puritan type, we observe what it means to serve God without regard to earthly profit, and then shamefacedly eschew glib caricatures of "grasping Puritans," for there are hypocrites in every church.

Among Christ's handpicked apostles the rate was one in twelve (John 6:70). Outstanding Puritan thinkers opposed to lending at interest included Arthur Dent, Thomas Lever,[191] Richard Porder, Henry Smith, Nathaniel Holmes, Thomas Norton, George Wither, Thomas Adams, William Greenhill, John Cotton, Richard Sibbes, William Perkins, Richard Rogers, George Gifford, John Dod, Thomas Bell, Stephen Marshall and Thomas Carew, among many others.

Even Calvin cannot be accused of changing the definition of usury for the sake of pecuniary gain. Unlike the Catholic Fugger banking dynasty asset Johannes Eck, Calvin had no known ties to merchant bankers. "It is not however just to attribute to Calvin the complete justification of liberal capitalism. His views on riches and their social ends led him to insist upon a very strict control over lending at interest; he had prophetically sensed the social ravages to which pure liberalism would lead."[192]

---

[191] Lever (1509-1577) a Puritan theologian, was a famous opponent of greed, usury and covetousness; and preacher to King Edward VI and at St. John' College, Cambridge. In 1553, with the ascension of Queen Mary Tudor, Lever fled to Switzerland, staying for a time in Geneva, where he met Calvin. Lever was an implacable foe of all interest charged on loans of money. "Among all those preachers none more bravely fought the battle of the...poor; none more vigorously, even to personal hazard and danger, exposed the cruelty, covetousness and craft of the rich and the clergy than Thomas Lever..." Edward Arber, *Sermons 1550*, p. 16.

[192] Andre Biéler, *La pensée économique et sociale de Calvin,* p. 168.

Early Puritan Resistance to Economic Secularization

The name "Puritan New England" is another cuss word. By the mid-19th century authentic Puritan theology was nearly eclipsed, except among remnants of believers. Theodore Parker forsook the faith of his Puritan forbears for Unitarianism. Henry Ward Beecher was not a Puritan, but an apostate. These and tens of thousands like them were the unbelieving children and heirs of the Puritans who had turned against their heritage. Anti-Puritans, in an act of intellectual dishonesty, refuse to recognize the distinction and continue to mislabel these apostates as "Puritan." This falsehood circulates because most people know little or nothing of early New England history and theology.

The popular imagination has been seeded with the canard of money-grasping and usury as a signifier of New England Puritan ethics. Hyper-capitalism has become a default explanation of religion and commerce among New England Puritans. Puritan-haters have promoted the idea that the whole history of New England can be summarized in a simplistic equation: New England's Puritan founders = Scrooge-like capitalism. It is undoubtedly true that as Puritanism declined, one wing decayed into money-getting. To use the *decline* as supposed evidence of the corruption of the *original creed* is about as fair or accurate as claiming that the usury of the Vatican bank under Archbishop Paul Marcinkus in the 1980s, or the usury theory of the Renaissance Catholic nominalists, tacitly legalized by Pope Pius VIII, cancels all the noble Catholic social teaching and charity of St. Francis of Assisi, St. Vincent DePaul, Mother Joseph of the Providence Sisters of Spokane, Peter Maurin, or Abbé Pierre. If we are obliged to extend the benefit of the doubt to Catholics who are members of a strictly hierarchical institution with clear lines of commanding authority, how much more so to radical Protestants such as the Puritans who subscribed to a decentralized Congregationalism and who, in a variety of times and circumstances, responded to issues regarding commerce across a spectrum of differing practices and Biblical interpretations which defy generalization.

Historian Mark Valeri (who spells the word Puritan in the lower case) writes: "Many of the leading original settlers of the Massachusetts Bay, imbued with ideals from their puritan teachers in England...sought to constrain new techniques, such as usury...that they perceived to be impersonal or vicious. They intended to institute religious discipline over all forms of social interaction. They thought that their task was to teach merchants the grammar of faith, not to conform their speech to the rules of commerce."

As Puritanism decayed into liberalism from the seventeenth century to the eighteenth, the original theology of the leaders of the Congregational churches devolved into a toleration of usurious commerce. This pattern of economic liberalism is noted within the Catholic Church from the Renaissance onward. Why do New England Protestants bear a special stigma for it? For every later Puritan such as Increase Mather and Samuel Willard who attributed commercial proficiency, expansion and prosperity to providential purpose, we can cite early New England Puritans such as Massachusetts Governor John Winthrop and Pastor John Cotton for having instituted and enforced laws against usury and overpricing. "During the 1630s and 1640s, the First Church of Boston mounted a disciplinary campaign against merchants...whose commercial practices conformed to human dictates yet violated puritan proscriptions..." (Valeri).

The forces of decline and decay afflicted the Roman Catholic and Puritan faiths along a roughly similar historical continuum. In both cases, the embrace of a devilish euphemism, "economic pragmatism" subverted the best intentions of pious Catholic and Puritan businessmen. In the case of both Catholic and Puritan laymen this was not always an instance of avarice, but rather a moral perplexity and anguish in the face of a new world of banking and commerce that gradually gained legitimacy among even some of the most otherwise devout Catholics and Puritans. From Rome came pontifically-tolerated Roman Catholic usury and the merchant culture it fostered. For some reason this worldwide Catholic devolution bears no stigma for providing a tacit Catholic moral sanction for usury banking and the ascent of the spirit of capitalism. To some extent the Catholic Church successfully escaped the stigma by having the wit to maintain a veneer of social justice rhetoric opposed to "excessive" profit.

The war between Christ's Gospel and the Money Power is perpetual. Almost from the founding of New England, Gov. Winthrop had to war against the money interests. For Christians desirous of social justice and freedom from oppression, Winthrop's struggle will be a model, assuming people will take the time to discover it. It seems that the caricature of New England Puritanism as inherently money-mad from its founding, is part of a conspiracy intended to deter us from studying and learning valuable lessons from the early Puritan struggle in America against the authority of money. The history of the anti-commercial Puritan ethic which empowered this struggle is unknown to ignoramuses, who nevertheless feel qualified to disseminate sweeping generalizations about the supposed economic ethos of early New England, which overlook the effects of the imposition of British royal control over trade in New England in the 1660s, and the revocation of Massachusetts's charter in 1684.

Certain fundamentals of Puritan teaching such as the emphasis on self-discipline, sobriety, hard work and frugality, and the socially regenerative power of religious and moral education based on Biblical literacy and personal responsibility, did sometimes lead to prosperity. Since these fundamentals are New Testament virtues and do not in themselves foster usury or oppression, it is wrong to say that in cases where early Puritans prospered this was inherently a result of participation in predatory capitalism. Christian *free enterprise,* what Aquinas regarded as property-rights-based *ethical work* which acknowledges and submits to *the higher claims* of God's law in matters of business and trade (as distinct from the "free market" economy's unrestrained pursuit of *mortally sinful profit)*, can be a blessing.

In certain respects, the Puritan expectations for a disciplined and sober Christian society undoubtedly increased the abundance and prosperity of the people, and excited the envy and calumny of outsiders. The niggardly pursuit of profit was, however, always an abominable vice among the early Puritans, as we shall see when we take up the Puritan teaching of John Dod, John Field, Arthur Dent, et. al. which have pronounced parallels with medieval Catholic attitudes toward the pursuit of wealth.

More Myths of Max

As we noted earlier, Weber's influential book, *The Protestant Ethic and the Spirit of Capitalism* is seriously flawed, yet retains the status of an authoritative classic, and Weber's blunders are seldom systematically deconstructed. For instance, Weber engaged in no thorough reading of the early Puritan texts. Weber skipped over these to consider mainly latter-day English Protestant writings which represented a modernist-evolved Protestantism shorn of foundational Puritan theology. Yet Weber had the temerity to ascribe the beliefs of later Protestants to the early Puritans. He committed a serious error by omitting an analysis of the long theological journey traveled by the Puritans of New England from its founding in the early 17th century to the mid-18th century onward. Many revilers of the Puritans have accepted Weber's conflation. This is tantamount to claiming that the medieval Catholic Church is guilty of the canonization of "Blessed" Pope John Paul II, on whose watch the pandemic of priestly molestations of boys attained a pitch of sodomitical fury.

It was the coming of *humanist Protestantism,* in place of *early Puritanism,* which created the congruence between usury capitalism and religion in New England. Puritan haters fail to engage in a basic obligation incumbent on the unbiased historian: to trace the theological distance traveled from Puritan origins to late 18th and early 19th century post-Puritan New England Protestantism. Roman Catholics who undertake this study should ask themselves whether they would accept the proposition that Vatican Council II came about due to a congruence of rigid papal authoritarianism and a history of developing Catholic theology, of which the promulgation of the dogma of the Immaculate Conception is most striking. To Protestants the connection must seem patent. Consequently, before Catholics sneer that Puritanism was only a stage in a process of decay that inevitably devolved into modern buccaneer capitalism, they ought to consider whether they will entertain the likelihood that an inordinate obedience to papal authority and a history of promulgating as infallible doctrine claims for which there is no Biblical or patristic basis, fomented obedient subservience to Vatican II and post-Conciliar modernism. These hard questions are part of the epistemology of revisionist history, in opposition to partisanship disguised as history. Revisionism demands of us the constant reexamination of our preconceptions in light of newly unearthed facts, lest we mistake man-made myths for God's Truth. This is a lifetime adventure and vocation at the very heart of what it means to be a human being endowed with the God-given faculty of reason.

Certainly the heresy of prosperity as a mark of divine approval entered into Protestantism. When Thomas Gouge asserted in 1673 that generous giving is rewarded in this life, we recognize the serpent in the garden. But men like Roger Fenton and John Cotton were representative of the genuine spirit of the early Puritans when they caution us to "Remember that riches do make it harder for a man to be saved." We begin to see from the conflicting writings of Thomas Gouge and Roger Fenton that the picture is more complex than generalizers and caricaturists have been willing to concede.

The Puritan Struggle Against Usury

Historian Mark Valeri makes the point that, "Until we appreciate the significance of the transition from puritan to post-puritan Protestantism in early New England, we will not grasp the beginning of the vexed history of religion and the market in America." We intend to provide the reader with an evocation of the *founding* principles of the Puritan theology of finance as *first* practiced in England and New England. This polity is not limited to usury *per se,* but to *all* manifestations of the sin of greed, including one sin widely overlooked today: price-gouging, or the practice of charging whatever high price for a thing or service which the market will bear. In 516, the Council of Tarragona, Canon II, enacted that "whosoever will be in the clergy, let him be careful not to buy too cheap or sell too dear, or let him be removed from the clergy."

Puritan theologian Jonathan Edwards endorsed the medieval Church's economic practices, as part of the claim among conservative Protestants to being the rightful heirs of medieval Catholicism. A recent biography reveals that"Edwards deplored free enterprise as bringing out the worst in human nature. He had long condemned the self-interested avarice that permeated the society and pointedly identified inflation and price fluctuations as moral issues: 'Tis certainly no good rule,' he declared, 'that men may buy as cheap and sell as dear as they can." [193] In our time a seller would be considered a fool by Protestants and Catholics alike for not obtaining the highest possible price. The Catholic medieval theologians loathed overpricing as did the early Puritans.

When the English Puritan Robert Keane emigrated to New England in 1635, Governor Winthrop was suspicious of Keane's reputation for hard bargaining. Winthrop paid heed to information provided by other Puritans that in England Keane had engaged in the "covetous" practice of charging higher prices for his goods than those around him. Charging a "just" price was a central tenet of medieval Thomistic *and* early Puritan theology. Mark Valeri:

"Puritans condemned merchants who attempted to circumvent local price regulations by buying goods when plentiful, transporting them and selling them at a markup where there was a dearth. They criticized financiers who purchased and sold bonds or foreign notes in the emergent money market— a tactic to circumvent anti-usury laws. They opposed traders who bought goods or farmers who hoarded their stores, kept them, and waited until prices rose to sell them. They scorned the use of notaries, lawyers and brokers,

---

[193] George M. Marsden, *Jonathan Edwards: A Life* (Yale Univ. Press, 2003), pp. 303-304. Marsden's characterization of Edwards as deploring "free enterprise" is clearly wrong; Marsden should have used the word "Capitalism" and not "free enterprise" in the preceding quote.

whose 'monstrous customs,' in the words of William Jackson from Paul's Cross, made them 'vermin of the earth.'...Puritan orators did not put a fine point on their critiques...They blasted usury plain and simple, any part of it as bad as the worst, any version of it a sin...

"Puritans outside London made the same arguments. Dissenters as varied as Thomas Hooker, Thomas Shepard and Richard Greenham were of one mind on this subject: wicked Dutch financiers, shifty Italian merchants and inhumane London credit brokers tried to make a profit from credit. The godly merchant, in contrast, never made loans for a guaranteed profit...Greenham, a country parson outside Cambridge, put the issue most starkly. No godly businessman could rightly conceive of making a profit from giving loans in any sense. Revered as a folk hero for his agitation on behalf of distressed farmers, Greenham even went so far as to repeat the medieval contention that usury was an alchemical ruse, the pretension that money itself could beget more money...

"Puritan preachers at Paul's Cross...linked usury to extortion...oppression (charging uncustomarily high prices), avarice, deceit and mammonism. Usury served as a synecdoche for the abuse of nearly any form of credit. Preachers made it synonymous with oppression when goods were sold on credit at unfair prices, with rack renting when lodging was provided on credit at inflated prices, or with unfair labor practices when debtors worked off their loans at low wages...

"Associating usury especially with falsehood, lying and deceit, godly orators often described it as a complete reversal of the true meaning of commerce: communication and union with the body social. Miles Mosse claimed in 1595 that 'to cover their sin and to uphold their credit,' usurers 'have devised fair cloaks to shroud their ragged garments and have begotten a more cunning and subtle of traffic in the world,' so that there were '13,000 devices which men of evil conscience have invented' to practice their wicked art. It was 'now one thing, now another,' inflated prices or unfairly low wages, high rents or the taking of pawns, 'always being *usury*, and yet never plainly appearing to be *usury*.' [194]

"Some puritans raised the rhetoric even higher. Usurers so disgusted Nathanael Holmes that he called them 'anthropophagos,' or cannibals. From distant Norwich, William Burton portrayed usury as a demon specter, which 'walketh up and down the streets' of London 'like a merchantman,' ready to 'possess' men 'in buying and selling,' always 'the devil's huntsman.' In 1627 John Grent used the Paul's Cross pulpit to summarize a half century of puritan apprehension about usury in London: '...amidst your great dealing and traffic' there are 'Merchants most odious among you,' that is 'merchants' of 'Time, usurers,' who personified the 'deceit and misrepresentation' that threatened to undo the commonwealth. Such was 'the chief symptom of a city's sickness.'

"...Usury was the paradigmatic temptation of merchants, standing for nearly all of their crimes of greed...puritan polemicists decried fellow Protestants who fell into avarice...They drew stark dichotomies between commercial profits and Christian piety." [195]

Valeri states that "too much has been made of the technical concessions to some of forms of increase in credit" as an indictment of the alleged predatory capitalist orientation of the first Puritans, when they actually worked assiduously against the spirit of greed and by no means endorsed a prosperity gospel or laissez-faire capitalism. "Puritan John Field

---

[194] Mosse, *The Arraignment and Conviction of Usury*, pp. 58-60.

[195] Valeri, *Heavenly Merchandize: How Religion Shaped Commerce in Puritan America*, p. 29-31.

complained in 1583 that while London's market had once been a place to exchange 'earthly commodities' such as meat, grain and metals according to God's law, it had become a place where people dealt in sheer calculation: the arithmetic of 'profit.' As a result, worldly affairs and business had fallen to mere idolatry...puritan preachers...contrasted the calculating ethos of merchants with the evangelical dispositions of saints. Cotton, Wilson and Sibbes linked self-sacrifice and a providential mind-set to proper economic behavior. *Cotton warned...that believers ought to trust in God's care and obey divine commands no matter how unprofitable*, lest their desire for 'merchandise and profits choke' their 'hearts.'

"...True contentment, Richard Sibbes preached, resided in the knowledge that *economic misfortunes were divine reproofs to strengthen the soul and wean it from material affections. They were not arbitrary disasters to be avoided at all costs*...These preachers stressed humility, trust, self-denial, charity and contentment as the prime economic virtues..." [196]

A network of Puritans in England who would form the core of New England's early leadership, struggled against the authority of money: "Besides Cotton (the) most influential spiritual mentors were Wilson and Winthrop. They learned the meaning of godliness through their acquaintance with a remarkable cluster of puritans in East Anglia...Arthur Dent, Richard Rogers, George Gifford, Stephen Marshall, John Knewstub and Thomas Carew. These pastors shared a vast correspondence, preached in each other's parishes and published lectures...Noted for their intense efforts to reform society on a local level...Nearly to a man, they preached against rising interest rates, inflated prices, enclosure...They expelled profiteers from their

---

[196] Ibid., pp. 31-32; emphasis supplied.

congregations, hounded usurers out of their parishes, turned common fields to poor relief, authored town covenants that set limits to prices on common goods...and insisted that their well-to-do parishioners provide easy, even free credit to the needy."[197]

In *Plain and Familiar Exposition of the Ten Commandments* (1603), Puritan John "Decalogue" Dod contrasted the capitalist spirit with the Christian spirit. He wrote that the authentic Christian is indifferent to worldly gain and was joyful as a result, even as worldly people were forever anxious about their profits and accounts. Merchants who endlessly strived to enhance their business "fell under Dod's censure. His saints cared more for joy, love, humility and charity toward neighbor than for their accounts."

Dod's influence among Puritans in England and New England, from the late sixteenth to the mid-seventeenth century, was very considerable. *Plain and Familiar Exposition of the Ten Commandments* was a publishing phenomenon, with nineteen editions.

Other Puritan devotional handbooks that warned against "free market" capitalism include: John Field, *Godly Prayers and Meditations* (1583); Thomas Beard, *Theatre of God's Judgment* (1597); Arthur Dent, *Plaine Man's Path-way to Heaven* (1601) and Lewis Bayly, *The Practice of Piety* (1612).

In John Mayer's 1621 *English Catechism,* Puritan families were instructed on the social sins of their time: usury, rent-racking, enclosure and inflated prices. Mayer counsels young people against financial ambition. They should "be content with moderate gain." We read these words now and snicker at what we imagine is the naiveté of the writer, in view of our own era, where total immersion in the world of money-getting has become our life to such a degree that the

---

[197] Ibid., p. 32.

thought of a family man nowadays pursuing only "moderate gain" would mark him as a loser. We have allowed our world to be rigged *by* usurers, *for* usurers, to our destruction. Under the current banking system most of us run a daily rat race merely to survive. Without plenty of money we are severely limited, in part because comparatively little is done within community networks of friends and neighbors.

These and other citations from authoritative early Puritan texts make a mockery of Max Weber's almost universally accepted mythology of *"The Protestant Ethic and the Spirit of Capitalism."* Contrary to legend, the first Puritans insisted that Christian commerce serve as a vehicle for a form of holiness that "sacrificed financial success — even if profits prospered the civil order — for the sake of obedience to God's word and charity to one's neighbor."

It is an irony of history that those who mock the early Puritans as capitalist misers and prudish fanatics are often admirers of the humanists. Yet it was the Humanist Renaissance which helped to propel an end to Puritan resistance to avaricious business-dealings and criminal politics. "In England humanist writers and political advisers became impatient with the biblical literalism and moral absolutism of godly preachers." [198]

The merchants of London came to view late sixteenth and early seventeenth century Puritan economic teaching as a serious impediment to their business affairs. Enemies of the Puritans at least ought to be truthful and not allow themselves to be party to false witness and historical hoaxes. New England's first Puritan leaders such as John Winthrop and John Cotton, never believed that merchant culture, what we would today call capitalism, could be anything other than a rival to holiness. Like their

---

[198] Ibid., p. 35.

predecessors, they suspected that merchants all too easily jettisoned Biblical rules in favor of the fastest means to gaining profits.

The early Puritans were capitalism's worst nightmare; how they came to be made synonymous with its "spirit" is an act of legerdemain by way of a malignant prejudice. In Massachusetts in 1639 John Cotton contended that merchants always sinned by charging interest on loans. He argued for what were in fact, medieval Catholic price controls. He stated that Scripture condemned those merchants who set their rates merely to maximize profits. Cotton taught that merchants should establish prices according to local custom and the intrinsic value of their goods, regardless of temporary market conditions. This was not simply rhetoric. The case of William Pynchon, a major investor and luminary in the Massachusetts Bay Company, is instructive. New England's most prolific fur trader, he owned herds of cattle and vast tracts of land. Pynchon ran afoul of the Puritan civil and ecclesiastical authorities. They accused him of paying low wages, charging high prices and monopolizing trade. In 1638 he was charged in the General Court of Connecticut. Pynchon's identification with liberal antinomians and his greed led to his banishment and return to England.

In its roots, Puritan Christianity promoted trust in Providence, a vocation that was non-pecuniary in its primary focus, concern for neighbor in the most immediate sense, and deference to the local church. The ethos of merchant networks, with their calculations of long-range profits and losses, and indifference to the daily needs of neighbors, contradicted Puritan teaching and challenged the authority of the First Church of Boston. The rivalry was between the church and the merchants. "In London this rivalry pitted professional associations such as the Merchant Taylors' Company, commercial networks and royal advisers on economic policy, against Puritan preachers, authors of devotional tracts and ministers who waged localized campaigns against usury. Unlike their fellow reformers back home in England, Puritans in New England grasped the opportunity to institute and normalize their claims over merchants. From the 1630s through the 1650s, they attempted, through the preaching and oversight of a regular ministry, formal and public church trials, church synods and civil law, to hold businessmen accountable to Christian teaching and promote religious discipline over commerce." [199]

To weaken Puritan governance, New England merchants fought back by supporting antinomian activists such as Anne Hutchinson and a philosophy of humanism. Nathaniel Ward, pastor in Aggawam (Ipswich), writing in 1641 in *The Simple Cobler of Aggawam,* blasted the humanist nexus that we today have been taught to cheer as the heroes and heroines who "moderated" Puritan "fanaticism." Ward accused them of subjecting New England to the same immorality that infected the states of Venice and the Netherlands with mercantile-humanism.[200]

---

[199] Ibid., p. 38.

[200] Humanism was behind the assault on the early Puritans, who had embraced the ordering of the economy according to Biblical statutes, as upheld during the Patristic and medieval age. In a memo known to history as *Moses His Judicials* (circa 1636), which appear to be John Cotton's notes from a meeting of Massachusetts' leaders, Cotton reiterated the belief that the non-ceremonial laws of the Old Testament, such as the Ten Commandments, were perpetual, and legally binding on Christians. One line in his hand-written memo reads: "...the more any law smells of man, the more unprofitable." The Massachusetts government's "Body of Liberties" of 1638 states: "No custom or prescription shall ever prevail among us...that can be proved to be morally sinful by the Word of God." Secular-humanists cannot abide that theocratic standard, and nowadays the smell of man is everywhere on the legislation of the morally depraved, capitalist West.

"Puritan leaders taught their people, time and again, to reject common conventions that valorized the accumulation of wealth as a national program. Preachers such as Dorchester's John White, who encouraged and advised settlement in New England, weighty divines such as (Thomas) Hooker, and nearly every devotional writer among puritans, including Dent, Gifford and Richard Rogers, made the same case: if English businessmen really aspired to alleviate poverty, then they should follow the Word.

"They should slow the pursuit of profits, reduce their consumption, refrain from acquisitive habits, limit investments in commercial ventures, forgo usury and instead use their money to provide interest-free loans or, even better, alms on the spot to needy neighbors...

"Just as puritans combated price inflation, they delivered hundreds of sermons and wrote dozens of pamphlets against usury. In formal treatises...(t)hey concluded that typical loan practices, which committed borrowers to fixed fees or interest rates, nearly always violated Scripture...

"Thomas Shepard frequently evoked the cold-hearted merchant-creditor and inflexible usurer who impoverished the godly debtor who naively trusted in older, personal modes of exchange. 'Usury' and 'oppression' went hand in hand, Richard Rogers preached, and like 'witchcraft and idolatry have no place among God's people.'

"...Bezaleel Carter, a fervent preacher in rural Cavenham, denounced well-to-do parishioners who were 'gripers, grinders of the poor, extortioners, usurers,' and in many other ways 'merciless.' Puritans in Dorchester were furious with a local usurer, Matthew Chubb, an Anglican, for demanding interest on a loan to the town and impoverishing one of his debtors. This sort of cruelty so angered Hooker that he condemned all creditors as hypocritical, mendacious and covetous. The notion of a rich Christian, he claimed...was a contradiction in terms...

"Thomas Shepard's parishioners in Essex shared interest-free loans with each other so frequently that they invested relatively little in commercial ventures. In London, pious individuals such as (Puritan) Nehemiah Wallington, a wood maker who once attended nineteen (Puritan) lectures and sermons in one week, read (William) Perkins and (William) Ames, and meditated on the spiritual counsel of Greenham and Dent – shaped his small business to religious doctrine. Praying to 'see God in my buying and selling,' he...abated the accounts of poor borrowers and never sued for unpaid debts.

"He refused to raise the price of his wares beyond customary rates, more fearful of overcharging than of losing a profit... He contented himself with a modest income...Many of the godly wrote anti-usury stipulations in their wills, directing trustees to provide loans from bequests without charging interest..." [201]

The nascent Puritan movement fought a trans-Atlantic and trans-European campaign against usury banking. William Ames defended radical Protestant regents in Holland who were struggling to expel the "Lombard" (banker) faction within their church – seeking to ban them from receiving communion at the Lord's Supper. Preachers of the Word claimed that the purifying potential of the Reformation was obstructed in England because elements within the state church tolerated price gouging and usury.

---

[201] Ibid., pp. 51-53.

"The City on a Hill" and "The Model of Charity"

New England's Puritan "City on a Hill" Biblical metaphor, seized on by President Ronald Reagan, was originally conceived by its founders as a city that outlawed conspicuous consumption, usurers and price-gouging merchants. Massachusetts' colonial Governor Winthrop summed up the Puritan vision of a sanctified economy in his address, "A Model of Christian Charity," delivered to passengers about to sail aboard the *Arbella* for Massachusetts. Mr. Reagan and his hero-worshipping epigones in the Republican party, with their buccaneer capitalism, which they equate with Christianity, would have been driven out of business in early New England, where such capitalism was labeled "natural corrupt liberties." John Winthrop is indisputably one of the founders of America, spiritually and literally. In his *Arbella* oration, Winthrop observed that the Law of nature taught people to relate to one another coldly as "one man to another." He contrasted this with the Law of the Gospel, whereby people were to always relate to their fellows, in financial (and all other) dealings, as a "brother in Christ." Winthrop practiced what he preached: he lived simply and was known to provide alms on the spot to indigents he encountered. In "A Model of Christian Charity," Winthrop stated:

Question: What rule must we observe in lending?

Answer: "Thou must observe whether thy brother has present or probable means of repaying thee. If there be none of these, thou must give to him according to his necessity, rather than lend...If he hath present means of repaying thee, thou art to look at him not as an act of mercy, but by way of commerce, wherein thou art to walk by the rule of justice; but if his means of repaying thee be probable or possible, then is he an object of thy mercy, thou must lend him, though there be danger of losing it. Deuteronomy 15:7, 'If any of thy brethren be poor etc. thou shalt lend him sufficient..."

The future governor of colonial Massachusetts also spoke of a sense of what he called "enlargement" by which he meant "...less respect for ourselves and our own right. Hence it was that in the primitive church they sold all, had things in common, neither did any man say that which he possessed was his own. Likewise in their return out of the captivity, because the work was great...and the danger of enemies was common to all, Nehemiah exhorts the Jews to liberality and readiness in remitting their debts to their brethren, and disposing liberally of his own to such as wanted, and stand not upon his own due, which he might have demanded of them." [202]

To restrain commercial greed and usury in Connecticut and Massachusetts, Preachers of the Word worked to implement church censures and the sanctions of the civil law. Here is where they encountered real resistance from the forces of Mammon. It was one thing to promote anti-usury sentiment in ecclesiastic exhortations and devotional tracts, it was quite another to attempt to use the civil and ecclesiastical power to actually crush it.

As the first governor of the Massachusetts Bay Colony, Winthrop did more than condemn usury in the abstract, he was engaged in the practical sphere, with enforcement. In 1632 he brought his own deputy governor up on charges of usury before the General Court. Thomas Dudley had sold seven bushels of corn to fellow members of his church, poor men, for a

---

[202] Nehemiah rebuilt the walls of Jerusalem to great rejoicing and in service to Yahweh, in part by convincing moneylenders to place the common welfare above their own profit; cf. Nehemiah chapter 3.

payment of ten bushels at the next harvest; the deal amounted to more than 40% increase on the loan. The Court ruled that Dudley's actions against fellow Christians were intolerable and a case of "oppressing usury." He tendered his resignation, which Winthrop magnanimously would not accept. Nevertheless, Dudley began to harbor a grudge and henceforth became Winthrop's enemy. "Perhaps nothing explains the difference between the two men more than the contrasting images of Winthrop sharing his own meagre stores to aid the hungry and Dudley bargaining with poor neighbors how much they should repay him if he lent them grain." [203]

"If there was a generally recognized leader of the (early) Puritan colony it was (John) Cotton." [204] According to Cotton, New England's eminent Congregationalist theologian, *no sin was as vile as usury*.

Valeri has dug out the example of Dennis Geere, a repentant English usurer who was brought to penitence by relocating to New England and being personally convinced of the sin of usury by the preaching he encountered there. Geere confessed that he had led a dissolute life as a usurer in England. He was moved to return the profits he had gained from the 6% and 8% interest he had charged. Living in Puritan New England in the mid-1630s he came to reject even a "nominal" rate of interest.

"Elected elders and deacons, along with their pastors, confronted parishioners accused of sins such as lying, Sabbath breaking...and usury." The accused was confronted with testimony and evidence. If found culpable but unrepentant the matter was brought to

---

203 Francis J. Bremer, *John Winthrop: America's Forgotten Founding Father*, p. 214.

204 Allan Heimert and Andrew Delbanco, *The Puritans in America: A Narrative Anthology*, p. 27.

the "public congregation" (the people assembled in church). "The church then censured, administered public rebuke, suspended from Communion or, as a last resort, excommunicated obdurate sinners...As Cotton instructed church members poised to try one dishonest tailor, their judgment carried eternal consequences...The actions...revealed a relentless confrontation between disciplinary ideals and commercial autonomy (free market capitalism)...

"From 1630 to 1654, the congregation...dealt directly with economic vices...The first excommunication ever recorded, in fact, concerned one Robert Parker, who was found guilty of oppression, or overpricing his wares...When the church excommunicated William Franklin in 1646 for overcharging another resident for some tools, they noted the interconnections between his 'extortion, deceit and lying.'...

"By conflating unjust prices with clearly defined sins such as deceit, theft and violence, *puritan leaders rebuffed antinomian and civic-humanist attempts to distinguish economic behavior from spiritual and ecclesiastical life...In this moral arena, a merchant could not claim equal but separate fidelity to commercial and Christian community.* The Boston Church claimed the prerogative to intervene...New England, Winthrop opined, had different rules for moral and political thinking than did humanist jurists...(He said): New Englanders ought to reject the false wisdom and incomplete justice of 'heathen commonwealths.'

"(T)he General Court did attempt a reform of civil laws dealing with commerce. Several codes rested on Scriptural, rather than common-law decrees: specific provisions for debt relief...a limitation of servitude to seven years...and severe restrictions on usury —a relatively low ceiling on interest rates and prohibitions against interest on loans outside of those intended for commercial investment. Legislators derived other statutes indirectly from biblical principles...These and other restraints encouraged the well-off to channel their wealth to the poor, who did not have the benefit of the institutionalized poor relief of later Protestant societies...Citing Old Testament precedents, Cotton attempted to make anti-usury statutes even stricter: he held that New England would never be pure without sanctions against all forms of usury." [205]

The Massachusetts Bay Colony's famed Saugus Iron Works, the first successful iron foundry in British America and a prototype of American industry, was founded in 1642 by Governor Winthrop. It soon ran up against investors' expectations of significant profits: the iron works had been established to "supply fellow Christians, not to enhance the profits of investors beyond a modest return." The iron was to be sold mainly to the people of New England and at low prices. Stockholder avarice resulted in lawsuits that bankrupted the factory in 1688. The forces of the Money Power in New England, led by aristocrats such as Sir Richard Saltonstall, agitated against Winthrop and Cotton, calling Cotton's ecclesiastical polity "tyranny" for enforcing Biblical law against avarice. Saltonstall pleaded "freedom of conscience" and wrote to Cotton that his "rigid ways have laid you very low in the hearts of the saints." This theme of defending usury by invoking humanism was satirized by John Udall as early as 1593 in his *The State of the Church in England*, in which a usurer loves bishops for their indifference to usury and reviles "harsh" Puritans for their interference with it.

This reputation for "harshness" endures and has been embroidered upon by modern writers from Nathaniel Hawthorne to H.L. Mencken and Arthur

---

[205] Valeri, op. cit., pp. 62-63; 65-67.

Miller, who have rendered the word "Puritan" a byword for petty, bigoted, fanatical, life-hating Pharisaic legalists whose witch-hunting is their signature image in American history. This is the enduring bias, so beloved by the Money Power, which panics at the prospect of a Bible-based economy.

Note well and ponder deeply the fact that John Cotton's church system for suppressing usury was "perhaps the last time in American history that there existed a governmental authority...to hold every individual accountable for what we now believe to be the 'natural' thing— the desire, as our jargon puts it, to maximize profit." [206]

Winthrop concluded his "Model of Christian Charity" address to the Puritans who were about to embark for New England, with a prophecy that cannot fail to tingle the spines of twenty-first century Americans with the shock of recognition:

"Beloved, there is now set before us life and good, death and evil, in that we are commanded this day to love our Lord our God, and to love one another, to walk in his ways and keep his commandments and his ordinances and laws, and the articles of our covenant with him, that we may live and be multiplied, and that the Lord our God may bless us in the land wither we go to possess it. But if our hearts shall turn away, so that we will not obey, but shall be seduced, and worship other gods — our pleasures and profits — and serve them; it is propounded unto us this day, we shall surely perish out of the good land wither we pass over this vast sea..."

---

206 *The Puritans in America: A Narrative Anthology,* p. 187.

Permission for Usury in Late Stage Puritanism

This was the extraordinary legacy of the first and second generation Puritan founders of New England which would be slowly overthrown with the approach of the 18th century by men like Increase and Cotton Mather who identified with the British empire and its ideology of trade. The old New England strictures against usury and economic oppression would give way to an assent to market mechanisms as being essential to progress.

"If, as some historians have argued, the philosophy of *laissez-faire* emerged as a result of the spread of Calvinism among the middle classes, it did so, like tolerance, by a route which was indirect. It was accepted, less because it was esteemed for its own sake, than as a compromise forced upon Calvinism at a comparatively late stage in its history, as a result of its modification by the pressure of commercial interests..." [207]

Nothing in history springs from a vacuum, and we are not suggesting that there were no covetous capitalist stirrings in Puritanism prior to the eve of the eighteenth century. The love of money is the most powerful force for evil on earth. There is no escaping it among the sons of Adam and daughters of Eve. Even during the Middle Ages a handful of dissident Catholic theologians and canon lawyers had attempted to whittle away, bit by incremental bit, the strict dogma against usury by creating lawyerly windows through which exceptions could enter — exceptions which would in turn create a precedent for more latitude in the future, "on the highway to usury." [208]

---

[207] Tawney, op.cit., p. 100.

[208] One of the most common of these was *lucrum cessans*.

Fifty-nine years before Samuel Willard put forth his homily on usury as acceptable morality for New England, the Presbyterian *Westminster Shorter Cathechism* of 1646 was published. In its commentary on the Eighth Commandment, the catechism gave its support for "the lawful procuring of wealth and outward estate." This was "something of a millionaire's charter and has been so treated by some of those raised in the Presbyterian faith ever since...the *Larger Catechism* of 1646 violently and at length denounces economic enterprise directed at self-profit; and all expositions of the *catechism* down to the nineteenth century echo these reservations and safeguards against the acquisitive spirit. Nevertheless, the bald omission of such safeguards in this very influential document (*Shorter Cathechism*), may unwittingly have done something to assist the weakening hold of religion over secular enterprise." [209]

Increase Mather's patrons were Robert Thomson of the East India Company and wealthy aristocrats such as Sir Henry Ashurst and Lord Wharton. The Mathers gradually replaced the New England loyalty to the Biblical covenant with loyalty to the Whig narrative of British history. This did not happen overnight; nor did it occur in every nook and corner of New England theology. It was principally aimed at sweeping away the founding Puritan animus toward rapacious trade and economic injustice whose root was usury. Other trappings of Puritan rectitude were strictly adhered to the better to keep up appearances. Certainly, Christian virtues of personal integrity and family size determined by the will of God, would remain an integral part of the New England character into the early 19th century. Theodore Parker, a descendant of the early Massachusetts Puritan Thomas Hastings,

---

[209] Geoffrey R. Elton and Andrew Pettegree, *Reformation Europe 1517-1559,* p. 226.

was born in 1810, the eleventh child of his God-fearing 46-year-old mother and 49-year-old father.[210] He himself would abandon the faith of his fathers for a well-publicized career as a Bible-belittling Unitarian abolitionist. It is apostates like Parker who are held up as archetypal "New England Puritans" by intellectually dishonest critics, who dare not cite John Winthrop, John Cotton or Jonathan Edwards as representative Puritans, since the record of the virtuous lives of those men is too sterling to well serve the ends for which the Puritan-hating propagandists labor.

But the high standards of the pioneers decayed all too soon. Increase Mather's 1697 book, *Pietas in Patriam* ("Love to one's Fatherland"), lionized William Phips as New England's "Knight," for his commercial ambition and enterprising genius. In the waning years of the 17th century, this was now the mark of a "saint" in New England. How swiftly had the Gospel focus of the commonwealth fallen. Addressing the governing authorities of New England in 1700, Mather signified the victory, ten years before, of England's Protestant William over the Catholic James II, in terms of money: "The abolishing of popery in the English nation is worth at least eight million pounds sterling, yearly profit." The British Empire was becoming, in an increasingly decayed New England (as contrasted with its founding Biblical vision), "The Sovereign of Merchandise." Benjamin Colman of Brattle Street Church and Ebenezer Pemberton of Old South Church, and many others, echoed the Mathers. Pemberton hailed capitalist Britain as a type of world policeman, "the defender of the Common Rights of Mankind" (unless you were a Catholic). Modernizing New England Puritans created a new usury rationale

---

[210] Parker's grandfather was Capt. John Parker, commander of the farmer-militia at the battle of Lexington in 1775.

justified by sectarian warfare, as Mark Valeri describes it: "Protestantism led to wealth, funded the empire; the empire combated Catholicism; the end of Catholicism brought civil liberties; and civil liberties allowed citizens to practice Protestant and market principles." Civil liberty, as advanced by William Petty, Nicholas Barbon, Dudley North, Josiah Child and Charles Davenant, began to be closely associated with the right to practice usury ("freedom of commerce"). So degenerate were these supposed "values-based, Christian" economists, that historian Istvan Hont in his massive study, *Jealousy of Trade: International Competition and the Nation-State in Historical Perspective,* terms them "neo-Machiavellian."

John Locke taught that "statutory limits on interest rates amounted to fictions. 'The price of the hire of money...is a natural affair, because no law can hinder men skilled in the power they have over their own goods...to purchase money to be lent at any rate whatsoever." Sir Dudley North called laws against usury "nonsensical theological arguments." Child, North and Davenant raised usury to the level of a moral imperative. England's Rev. Thomas Delaune, an influence in New England, approved this thinking.

The old Puritan Biblical mores were being replaced by the imperatives of the new commerce. The legacy of this betrayal is found in the fact that almost none of the "Christian patriots" in the often Protestant church-based, Right wing populist movements today, who advocate a return to the "good old days of America's Biblical values," associate those values with the early Puritan struggle for a usury-free commonwealth. These modern "patriots" come to America's colonial history in ignorance, because they commence their study half-way through its history and mark as their inspirational starting line a point eighty or more years after the actual one.

"An extraordinary exposition of the colonial theory of usury was set forth in 1699, by the pastors of the churches adjacent to Cambridge, Massachusetts." [211]

"In 1699, the third-generation Boston pastor Cotton Mather informed New Englanders that the Puritan ministers of the Boston area no longer regarded usury as sinful. Meeting as the Cambridge Synod, they had determined that usury...was legitimated by the 'Divine Law' of the Old Testament, given 'countenance' in the New Testament, 'Justified' by economic 'Necessity and Utility,' mandated by the ethical principle of equity, required by the philosophical meaning of money itself, and congruent with the moral Law of Charity." [212]

The 1699 Cambridge Synod's judgment was published in *Thirty Important Cases Resolved with Evidence of Scripture and Reason* (Boston: Bartholomew and Green, 1699). In it we read, "...there is no manner of reason why the usury of money should be more faulty than any other thing...there can be no reasonable pretense that should bind me to lend my money for nothing, rather than any other commodity...Humane society, as now circumstanced, would sink, if all usury were impractible...The several declamations of the Ancients against usury, must be of no farther account with us."

Samuel Willard's Capitalist "Summa"

During this period, Samuel Willard (1640-1707), though lesser known in our time than his contemporary, Increase Mather, was a theologian from among the second generation of New England Puritans. He was born in Concord, Massachusetts, the sixth of seventeen children of Simon and Mary

---

[211] E.A.J. Johnson, *American Economic Thought in the Seventeenth Century* (Russell and Russell, 1961), p. 217.

[212] Mark Valeri, *Common-Place*, April, 2006.

(Sharpe) Willard – solid, middle class Puritans who had emigrated from southeastern England in 1634. Simon was for 15 years a judge of the Massachusetts General Court. Rev. Ebenezer Pemberton described Samuel Willard's patrimony as follows: "His descent was honorable, from a sage patriot in our Israel..."

Samuel Willard obtained his M.A. degree from Harvard in 1662, and in 1663 began to preach at Groton, Massachusetts. After a devastating Indian assault nearly razed Groton in 1676, Willard was promoted to assistant pastor and later pastor of the Third Church of Boston, known as Old South. He was also Vice-President and Acting President of Harvard College from 1701-1707.

Rev. Willard gave two hundred and fifty expository lectures on the *Westminster Shorter Catechism.* He delivered nearly one a month, for nineteen years, beginning in 1688. These were published posthumously in 1726 by Joseph Sewall and Thomas Prince as: *A Compleat Body of Divinity.* Extravagant claims have been made for Willard's work: "Roughly one and a half times as long as John Calvin's *Institutes of the Christian Religion,* it is the closest thing to being a *Summa Theologiae* that Puritan New England ever produced." [213]

Willard's teaching on usury certainly did not represent a "*summa*" of New England theology *at the time of his birth.* Academics often make no distinction between the early decades, and the later ones that marked the degeneration of Puritan theology in New England. For some researchers seventeenth century Massachusetts is all one convenient, alpha-to-omega construct, from which tidy conclusions may be drawn. Seymour Van Dyken of Princeton Theological Seminary lauds Willard as one "of the chief

---

213 Ernest Benson Lowrie, *The Shape of the Puritan Mind: The Thought of Samuel Willard,* p. 3.

propagators and defenders of (the) inherited (Puritan) orthodoxy in an era of social, economic, political and religious change..." Edward M. Griffin of the University of Minnesota writes of Willard: "From the outset of his ministry, he expended his considerable energies in a noble, but ultimately futile, effort to promote the values of the first settlers."

But usury was not a "value of the first settlers," it was the modernist battering ram that caused the foundations of Puritan New England to crumble, and Willard, a conservative in other areas of doctrine such as predestination, was a modernizing revolutionary in the field of eighteenth century economics: every inch the agent of the trendy, emergent, modern-Protestant doctrine on business and finance.

The position which Samuel Willard staked out on usury is not a particularly strong apologetic. He repeatedly accuses the opponents of usury who preceded him of what one might term hate speech today. Willard seems to imply that they were so rude and impolite in their invective against usury that they invalidated their polemic. Willard regards their alleged incivility to be a point against their doctrine. He makes no reference to patristic sources or the historic Christian witness against usury. His modern argument is largely promoted on an *a priori* basis and appeals to utilitarian practicality. Appeals to scripture are also made, of course, but he does so within the confines of his rationalization that God's law against usury is riddled with exceptions and escape clauses. What is striking is the degree to which he couches his extreme usury advocacy in the Medici dodge – the appeal to charity-driven usury (extreme because he places no cap on the amount of interest that is to be charged, and regards the usurer as an honorable Christian if he is a humane creditor).

Willard did not envision that when the church grants his new theology of permission for usury and thereby upholds a "charitable usurer" as a good Christian, the inevitable result will be the confiscatory Shylock interest rates we have in our time. Where there is no limit on usury, and usurers are rehabilitated from the opprobrium with which even Calvin had rightly stigmatized them, then Biblical statutes and doctrines governing business and finance are undone, no matter how much the permission for usury is couched in pious exhortations to rectitude, compassion and fair-dealing, such as the ones with which Rev. Willard decorates his argument. The notion of a "charitable usurer" makes this writer think of a notion of a "chaste harlot." The idea that one can practice and patronize usury "within bounds," invokes the image of a church-going patron of a brothel endeavoring to keep his acts in the house of ill repute "within bounds." The prohibition against usury is absolute. Usury is a weapon of war. This is why it was allowed in Old Testament times against foreign forces, and never inside Israel. Rev. Samuel Willard's scheme for usury inside Christian Israel, to be practiced in a voluntary, spiritually-regulated framework of proportion and prudence, was a usury that never was, at least not in any form of practice that became sufficiently widespread in America to attract notice.

In discoursing on Nehemiah 5, Rev. Willard almost becomes an anti-usury campaigner, setting forth strong theoretical admonitions to lend freely to the distressed. We say 'theoretical,' because given his general advocacy of a supposedly humanely-applied usury, the notion that the poor will be given interest-free loans under his system of modernizing nullification of God's law, is not likely in practice, and subsequent events have testified to the fact that where God's laws against usury are liberalized, the poor are the first and most heavily afflicted victims of interest on money.

Many Fundamentalist and "Tea Party" Christians today would consider it an act of parasitical socialist effrontery if the poor, as a matter of course, were to receive interest-free loans. If they condescended to provide such a loan it would certainly not be done out of a sense of obligation or submission to a law of God, since they recognize no such obligation. Rev. Willard's conditions and loopholes, intended to soften his usury permission, were soon seen for what they were, a type of equivocation meant to salve troubled consciences in the interval between the withering of the old Puritan rectitude and the ascendance of Willard's "New Light" on mortal sin.

As the development of usury permission evolved gradually and became ever more expansive, Christians would be ever more indoctrinated and accustomed to the revolutionary departure from the Biblical and historic Church teaching on money. In the process of modifying God's law to suit man's appetite for commerce and profit, Willard's high-sounding rhetorical limitations and conditions are cast aside, as we see today where people who regard themselves as fervent disciples of the New Testament are equally fervent ambassadors of Mammon's most contumacious usurers, from Ayn Rand to the Mises Institute.

Samuel Willard overthrew John Calvin's two substantial limitations on unbridled greed. The first, while still vexing, offered a tangible limitation: a fixed, relatively low interest rate. The second was far more important: the denigration of the usurer as a moral cretin, a stigma which troubled the Fuggers far more than a 5% limit on interest, which was what their creature Eck had advocated on their behalf. Willard, on the other hand, made usury a legitimate vocation for a Christian: "Casuists do universally make it unlawful for any to make usury a calling...But if they are either called to such employment as take up their time about them, and that for the public benefit, and they have estates that may be improved for the benefit of mankind, it is very proper..."

To Calvin we apportion blame for following the Catholic nominalists by establishing within a Protestant Reformation which was supposedly dedicated to combating abrogations of Scripture, a precedent for diddling with God's Law. Like most tamperers he believed his diddle could be contained. He denied, based on lawyer's equity logic, that he had nullified the law. Willard's sermon was prepared during a time when the power of Mammon had become too overwhelming for some early modern churchmen to resist. His modernism consists in part in appeals to an authority he terms "the Rule of Humanity." Willard was in other respects a man who strived sincerely for the kingdom of God, but in the case of furnishing grounds for the acceptance of usury in Christendom, he succumbed to the spirit of his age. Eminent New England ministers such as Samuel Willard transmuted what had once been a grave sin into – in certain circumstances – a civic virtue instrumental for achieving personal prosperity and securing the good of the commonweal. Willard put forth the very arguments for which John Cotton had reproached Robert Keayne seventy years earlier. This modernism, formerly a minority view, was, in the eighteenth century, gradually becoming a majority belief. Valeri notes:

"Willard...overturned the logic of his puritan predecessors. Previous divines took Scripture, with its strictures against oppression, to convey absolute moral imperatives...Willard and many of his contemporaries, in contrast, accepted mercantilist arguments. They treated the language of political economy as a universal certainty while discarding the original dictates of Reformed teaching. (Cotton) Mather thus conceded in 1727 that the (Reformed) churches no longer punished market practices, as they had in previous generations...

"Willard reversed the linguistic direction set by first-generation puritans such as John Cotton. Cotton applied the language of faith to economic matters, chastening the ambitions or soothing the anxieties of merchants by telling them to trust God in their affairs. Willard brought the language of the economy to matters of faith, exciting the entrepreneurial instincts of merchants by exhorting them to invest in salvation...Cotton Mather's most thorough statement on secular vocations, his 1701 *A Christian at his Calling*, correlated moral obligation, providential order, spiritual felicity, commercial knowledge and market profits. John Cotton had counseled Christians to choose a mode of business that met the needs of the local community, even if such a trade produced slim profits. Mather, in contrast, set profitability as the chief standard for vocational choice because there was by definition 'no need for any such business' that was not 'profitable.'...John Winthrop had demanded that leaders of the Great Migration lend money without question to those in need. Mather gave nearly the opposite advice: to scrutinize would-be debtors carefully and refuse poor risks." [214]

It is at this point in history, and not before, that some of what has been written about "Protestantism and the rise of capitalism" begins to become ápropos. There were still noble exceptions, such as Rev. Benjamin Wadsworth, the prominent pastor of First Church Boston who, in his 1725 work, *The Saints Prayer to Escape Temptations*, [215] described wealthy

---

214 Valeri, pp. 156, 158 and 160. Valeri takes the title of his indispensable book from Willard's own title, *Heavenly Merchandize.*

215 See in particular, pp. 15-27.

persons as being nearly inescapably prone to wickedness.

Excerpts from a Lecture on Usury

Samuel Willard
May 29, 1705

"We are considering the righteousness which is to be observed in commutative justice between the borrower and the lender...That there must be a divine rule to adjust this affair is alike evident, because in nothing more does corrupt nature take advantage of oppression, and men would soon devour one another, if God did not set limits to their exorbitance and unlimited cravings. Here it may not be amiss briefly to enquire, whether it be lawful for the lender to contract with the borrower, for a competent gain to accrue to him from the loan?

"There are many judicious and conscientious Christians who are perplexed in their minds about this. The matter has been canvased among the greatest divines pro and con, and that not without great heats and over much bitterness of spirit and opprobrious language, especially by those who defend the negative. This is evident by their writings, which seem to favor an over-heated zeal in their cutting invectives against their antagonists...

"God has given men their estate for their outward benefits. We have before observed that these things are for the support and maintenance of the bodily life; when therefore God in his Providence bestows these things upon men, they are to use their discretion in the ordering of them, so they may afford them with His blessing, revenue for the maintaining of their comfort. Hence it belongs to the character of one that fears God

— Psalm 112:5: 'A good man shows favor and lends; he will guide his affairs with discretion.' This our Savior manifestly intimates in the Parable of the Talents, that an estate ought to be occupied for an advantage. Otherwise there is no force in the comparison which He uses. We find how He censures him that hid his in the ground (Matthew 25:27). Nor indeed would men be capable of long improving part of their substance for charitable uses, if they did not thus do, but always spend on the stock (principal), which in time would be expended.

"There is therefore an honest gain to be moderately sought in the improvement of such estates. It is true, it must be honest...There are diverse ways in which men have advantage to improve their estates by commerce. Man is not bound to earn what he has only by his bodily labor, and let his gains lay by unoccupied; but this may and ought to be done in a way of mutual commerce and exchange, where men have wherewith so to do; and this for the common benefit and good of mankind, and the advancement of the public weal, as all experience assures us. This may be done by...lending of money to others...The adversaries of lending money upon interest have sought to stigmatize it with all manner of odious reflections, as if they would cry it down with noise and banter; but it is but a noise and railery, without solid reason or cogency of arguing, and it is only applicable to the abuse and not to the right use of it, and is equally applicable to other ways of commerce when abused, of which they are like capable. And this way is found on experience to be as necessary and profitable for the common benefit of mankind as any other. For the more clear demonstration of this, we may in general observe that the main difference between this and the other sorts of commerce lies in that the advance of the interest upon the principal is upon the consideration of time; as to other things which belong to it, they are common with the other, and are in them acknowledged to be lawful.

"...it is no way repugnant to, but agreeable with, the Law of Nature or right reason, that a man should make a competent gain by his money so lent...Men ought to improve their estates so as to make gain by them, provided it be not to the wrong or injury of their neighbors...and if it be otherwise it is either the borrower's fault or the unavoidable event of the governing Providence of God...And as to the rule of charity, a man's kindness may as really appear in this way of lending...Besides, a man owes charity to himself as well as to his neighbor...

"...this way of gain is nowhere absolutely forbidden in the Word of God by any law obliging mankind. This is the great clamor and urged to confute all other pleas by, whatsoever of reason and equity there may seem to be in them. And I confess, if it be so indeed, all mouths must be stopped and it is altogether in vain to set our reason against the declared will of God in His Word...

"We do indeed find such a law as is expressed, given Israel in the wilderness recorded in Exodus 22:25...Leviticus 25:35 etc...Deuteronomy 23: 19-20...And to this Law are other expressions used afterwards...Proverbs 28:8. Ezekiel 18:8 and elsewhere; concerning which there are diverse things to be observed, which I shall briefly epitomize and leave to rational consideration. This law was either purely moral or positive, and accommodated to the Israelite polity, between which a great difference must be acknowledged. That there was a moral equity on which it was to be grounded, need not be denied, viz. that all oppression was to be avoided and that we should not exact on our neighbor to his necessary damage. But that it was universally moral is disproved by the explication of the law itself, Deut. 23:20. It was therefore restrained to their brethren of their own nation. Whereas it is certain that if the thing itself had been moral, it had been universally unlawful, and might no more have been practiced to a stranger than an Israelite...Again, if this law was purely moral, this would not have been restrained to only one sort of men...Moral propositions are not universal, but limited, as is evident in the express terms of the law. This is further manifest by the exception which hath made on this account: Deut. 15:4 'Save when there shall be no poor among you.' Which intimates that it was not made to them unlawful in it itself, but only according to their circumstances. Nor is it prohibited in the gospel absolutely. The great text alleged for it (Luke 6:35) only intimates that there are cases in which it may be duty (which none will deny). All that can, in reason be argued from it, is only that when a neighbor (whether friend or enemy) is distressed with want and asks to borrow of us, our despair of having either interest or principal ought not to try our hands. And it rather signifies that the thing itself would in justice be due, were not the person an object of charity...

"We must consider the condition of the persons to whom we lend. There are the poor who are necessitated to borrow that they may not perish and starve, and it is merely for the support of their bodies. Now, not only the law of Moses but the light of nature forbids all manner of exaction of interest upon those on this account. Such was the state of many Jews after their return from captivity. Hence Nehemiah treated so severe with the usurers of that time. Neh. 5. Such persons are objects of our charity and we ought, according to our ability, to give to them for their succor, and much more to lend to them without expectation of gain...We ought not, therefore, to refuse to do a free kindness for such, because we reserve what we have for the making of gain, which is an effect of forbidden covetousness and a cruel hardening of our hearts against our poor brethren..." [216]

Willard's usury is sometimes excused by the acknowledgement of his good qualities: he was an opponent of the Salem witch trials and the pastor to whom one of the Salem judges publicly confessed his shame. [217] The father of 20 children, Willard baptized many youngsters at Old South, including, in 1706, the infant son of Josiah and Abiah Franklin, who would grow up and be known to history as Benjamin Franklin. We are certainly willing to entertain the exculpation of Rev. Willard for his public defense of "limited" usury in consideration of his other good qualities, on one condition: to wit, that ministers of the Gospel who are public defenders of "limited" forms of robbery and burglary be similarly excused, as long as they are kind-hearted in other aspects of their lives and precepts.

An Antidote to Hating the Puritans

The persistent legend that the original Calvinists and Puritans were little more than greedheads directly responsible for the capitalism which lashes us today, is subversive nonsense. Even the belief that the Puritans under Oliver Cromwell were enthusiastic murderers of the Irish, is open to correction. A significant number of Puritan soldiers would not fight in Ireland against the Irish. Who has ever heard of this noble act of conscientious objection? It is wholly suppressed.

In 1649 dissident Puritan soldiers circulated among their comrades in arms a tract, *Certain Queries Propounded to the Consideration of such as were*

---

216 Samuel Willard, *A Compleat Body of Divinity*, pp. 698-701.

217 Cf. Eve LaPlante, *Salem Witch Judge: The Life and Repentance of Samuel Sewall* (HarperCollins, 2007), pp. 199-201; and Seymour Van Dyken, *Samuel Willard*, p. 182.

Intended for the Service of Ireland, urging them to refuse go to war in Ireland. In it they argued that the Irish nation "hath for some hundreds or thousands of years enjoyed and possessed...the Land...without any others laying claim to having a more special right to the same." They asked, "Whether Julius Caesar, Alexander the Great, William, Duke of Normandy or any other (of) the great conquerors of the world, were any other than so many great and lawless thieves; and whether it be not altogether as unjust to take our (Irish) neighbor's land and liberties from them, as our neighbor's goods of our own nation?"

It is true that New England Puritans tended toward micromanagement of daily life, tiresome factional and inter-denominational squabbles and rivalry, limits on freedom of speech and, in one case, the hanging of "heretics" (four Quakers, executed 1659-1661); and of course the notorious witch trials. [218] These facts mar, but do not nullify the Puritan crusade for a just price (*justum pretium*), a living wage, and freedom from usury. That these early "Preachers of the Word" have come to be equated in history texts and popular media with fostering rapacious capitalism goes to show the extent to which we are continually lied to by shadowy forces promoting a hidden agenda. Those who call themselves Christians and look to the first generation Puritan founders of America for support for their "laissez-faire, free market," profit-supremacist system, look in vain.

We have sought to dispel the staple fiction of some Roman Catholics, later echoed by partisans of the Southern Confederacy, who claim that from the beginning, New England Puritanism was representative of the most miserly forms of economic predation; Roman Catholicism allegedly being the only

---

[218] For an account of the long-buried arcana of the Salem-witch accusers cf. *Revisionist History* no. 30, "The Myth of the Salem Witch Craze."

religious bastion against Mammonism in all of Christendom.

Are these fables about the first Puritans seeded by the Cryptocracy to keep us from studying the radical Protestant roots of resistance to the authority of money? With the virtual collapse of the credibility of popery in the 21st century – with its melangé of institutionalized child molestation and "infallible" canonization of "Blessed" John Paul II, patron saint of Voodoo in Benin and Koran-kissing in Rome – an alternative to papalolatry is intensely to be desired. [219]

How can those of us who execrate usury, whether we be Catholic, Protestant or independent, have anything but esteem for Protestant and Puritan leaders such as Andrewes, Sibbes, Jewel, Cotton and Winthrop, and others like them? They used church and state to curb this plague of plagues. Their sermons, books and legal writings stand as a template for a Christian future in which economic exchange is regulated by the mercy of the Gospel, not the pitiless power of money.

Calvin's Letter on Usury

This is an excerpt from an undated letter (circa 1545), written in French, to an unnamed Christian (possibly Claude de Sachin), who had inquired about usury. Calvin wrote:

"...I have learned from the example of others how perilous it is to respond to the question for which you seek my counsel...if we permit it (usury), then some, under this guise, would be content to act with unbridled license, unable to abide any limits...it would be desirable if usurers were chased from every

---

[219] In our protest of the *idolization* of mere human beings (Romans 3:10; Matt. 20: 25-28), we mean to take nothing away from the esteem due to faithful and saintly pre-Renaissance pontiffs who upheld the integrity and authority of the Word of God.

country...Passages in both the prophets and the Psalms display the Holy Spirit's anger against usurers...usury almost always travels with two inseparable companions: tyrannical cruelty and the art of deception. This is why the Holy Spirit elsewhere advises all holy men, who praise and fear God, to abstain from usury...This is why no one should take interest from the poor and no one, destitute by virtue of indigence or some affliction or calamity, should be forced into it...

"The situation in which God brought the Jews together, combined with other circumstances, made commerce without usury apt among them. Our situation is quite different. For that reason, I am unwilling to condemn it, so long as it is practiced with equity and charity...we ought not to judge usury according to a few passages of scripture, but in accordance with the principle of equity."

Three years after Calvin's death, his letter was publicly debated at the Huguenot synod at Verteuil, France in 1567, where its sentiments were eventually adopted.[220] Calvin was trained as a lawyer and his preference in this case for equity over Scripture derives from the Greek principle represented by the word *epyeykie* ("epiky"), denoting "reasonableness" as opposed to "rigid law," which looks suspiciously like a Talmudic loophole, or *prozbul,* such as Hillel granted to first century Jewish usurers. (In western legal iconography, a blindfolded "Goddess of Justice" holds the scales of *equity*). In Calvin's permission for limited and restricted usury, we see an appeal not to divine law but situation ethics ("Our situation is quite different)." Thus saith the U.S. Supreme Court when ruling that abortion on demand is a "right."

---

220 For the complete text cf. *Calvin's Ecclesiastical Advice.*

Before critics gloat, however, recall that Calvin inherited his version of permissible usury from the Roman Catholic nominalists who pioneered it.

Furthermore, Puritans did not make an infallible pope out of Calvin. They were free to reject his qualified approbation, and the early Puritans did so vigorously, as documented herein. In the first decades of the settlement of the Massachusetts Bay Colony, Calvin's views on interest were ignored, or interpreted in the narrowest manner most likely to obstruct usurers and harass their operations ("it would be desirable if usurers were chased from every country").

It is sobering to consider the fact that if we were to apply Calvin's views on usury now, even with his loopholes, many American banks, most Wall Street investment houses and all "payday loan" operations would be summarily shuttered, and the church-goers among the unrepentant owners and stockholders of these Christless pestholes would be excommunicated.

6

A Faithful Irishman

Persecuted for holding usury to be mortal sin

Rags Make Paper. Paper Makes Money. Money Makes Banks. Banks Make Loans. Loans Make Beggars. Beggars Make Rags.

What would the appropriately named Rev. Fr. *Jeremiah* O'Callaghan think of today's "conservative Christian" Republican party boosters? This Irish priest was suspended in south Cork in 1819 and banished by Catholic Bishop William Coppinger for his refusal of absolution to an unrepentant Roscarberry "gombeenman" (money-lender, in this case a merchant who charged interest on purchases made on credit).[221] The gombeenman would not make restitution.[222] O'Callaghan's persistent insistence on the implementation of Biblical and traditional Catholic law on usury and mammon led him to write his book, *Usury: Proof that it is Repugnant to Divine and Ecclesiastical Law and Destructive to Civil Society*.[223] This work was a favorite of the renowned Protestant historian William Cobbett, who

---

221 Other names for them in Ireland were "cormorant," and, in the local dialect, "*breiseoirí*" and "*´usairí.*"

222 Later, when contacted by a Vatican commission investigating the case, the money-lender actually thanked Fr. O'Callghan for remaining faithful to what the money-lender acknowledged was the traditional Irish teaching against usury. For scathing portraits of usurers in Ireland cf. William Carleton, *Black Prophet* (1847), Thomas Farrow, *The Money-lender Unmasked* (1895) and Liam O'Flaherty, *The House of Gold* (1929).

223 Published in 1825; reprinted 1834 and 1856.

wrote, "The Rev. Mr. O'Callaghan, in his excellent little work, which I had the honor to republish last winter, and which ought to be read by every man, and especially every young man, in the kingdom, has shown, that the ancient philosophers, the Fathers of the Church, both Testaments, the Canons of the Church, the decision of Popes and Councils, all agree, all declare, that to take money for the use of money is sinful." O'Callaghan served for a time as tutor to Cobbett's children and contributed to Cobbett's classic work, *History of the Protestant Reformation in England and Ireland.*

O'Callaghan traveled to Rome to appeal his suspension, but the "Vatican people were tired of him. His insistence on upholding the orthodox doctrine, after the Church had tacitly dropped it, was causing embarrassment in high places. They cut off his allowance and he had to leave Rome...Reconciliation with the Bishop was now out of the question. Coppinger had taken great offense at the complaints about himself published in *Usury*, and he would not even consider O'Callaghan's request to be restored to his priestly duties until he had published a full retraction and apology. Since this required the suppression and denial of facts, O'Callaghan would not do so. The Bishop's new stipulation, he said, was merely an attempt to conceal the truth of the matter, that he had been sacked for teaching the words of Christ, clearly stated in St. Luke's Gospel (6:35): 'Lend, hoping for nothing again.' But the rights and wrongs of the affair counted for nothing. Coppinger had power over his former priest and used it crushingly. True to his promise, he prevented O'Callaghan from obtaining a post in his or any other diocese..." [224]

Fr. O'Callaghan was forced into exile in faraway Vermont, USA, where it was supposed he would have few opportunities to clash with the monied elite, and where he

---

224 John Michell, *Eccentric Lives*, p. 53-54. The "complaints" about Bishop Coppinger published by Fr. O'Callaghan consisted of the charge that the bishop himself was a usurer, being "often the bearer of interest from his debtors to him."

was largely unsupervised. But O'Callaghan possessed ideals similar to those of another liberty-loving Irish-American, Matthew Lyon, a former white slave who served in Congress and bucked the Sedition Act. Fr. O'Callaghan was critical of the contrived patriotism and state worship beginning to emerge in New England. While it is supposed by critics that every Catholic priest in those days was a type of hook-nosed, Spanish-style inquisitor, the Irish Catholics, for centuries victims of a tyrannical English monarchy and a Protestant inquisition, brought with them uniquely untamed aspirations for freedom. Fr. O'Callaghan was no exception. "Deeply mistrustful of banks...He was also suspicious that Vermont's 'civil religion' was a carefully conceived...distraction from injustice. He wrote, 'Vermont law-makers, while they manufacture the yoke of slavery for the people, while they frame laws to rob and defraud them, get up celebrations of independence, abolition societies, missionary societies, Bible societies..." [225]

While ministering in Vermont, Fr. O'Callaghan published *Exposure of Vermont Banking* and built a church in Burlington which was torched by arsonists. The church was defiantly rebuilt by O'Callaghan. In 1854, at age 74, he left Vermont for Holyoke, Massachusetts. There he used his personal life savings to construct the town's first Catholic church, St. Jerome's, where he gave sermons in Gaelic. He died in Holyoke in 1861 at 81 years-of-age. A monument to his memory stands in the St. Jerome churchyard.

---

225 Paul Searls, *Two Vermonts,* (University of New Hampshire Press, 2006), p. 54.

Mortal Sin becomes no sin

Beginning in August of 1830, in the pontificate of Pope Pius VIII (Francesco Castiglioni), Christianity's millennial ban on usury was again being radically derogated,[226] making official what had been de facto in many regions of the Catholic world for centuries: "Under his influence, in the summer of 1830 both the Holy Office and the Penitentiary stipulated that the confessor who absolves a lender who has not exceeded the legal rate of interest (5 percent in France) 'must not be harassed." [227]

Pius VIII had ushered in the new age of official, *overt* banking-friendly Catholicism. (He was struck dead three months later). Two years later, "In 1832 the Rothschild bank of Paris had extended a loan to keep the papacy afloat....In July 1849...the pope (Pius IX) cast lines anew to the Rothschild bank...In January 1850 Rothschild approved a loan of 50 million francs...In 1857 (Vatican Secretary of State Giacomo) Antonelli used Peter's Pence as collateral in negotiating a new loan with Rothschild." [228]

In December 18, 1872, an interest rate of 8 percent was granted as lawful for Catholics by the Holy Office in response to an inquiry by the Bishop of Ariano. Pius VIII's successor, Pope Gregory XVI (Bartolomeo Cappellari) continued to oversee the formal establishment of the moral and ethical permission for interest on money. No subsequent pope, whatever his reputation for orthodoxy or holiness, ever moved to restore the ancient Biblical, Apostolic, Patristic, Roman Catholic dogma on interest.

---

[226] Cf. *Resp. Pii VIII ad episc. Rhedonensem datum in audientia, 18 Aug. 1830*. Denziger-Bannwart, nos. 1609 and 1610.

[227] Philippe Levillain, ed., *The Papacy: An Encyclopedia*, vol. 2, p. 1191.

[228] Jason Berry, *Render Unto Rome: The Secret Life of Money in the Catholic Church*, pp. 43-45. "Peter's Pence is the Vatican's most important collection; it is taken once a year in late June, in parishes across the developed world" (p. 36).

In 1891 Pope Leo XIII, like many well-intentioned Catholics today, wrote a jeremiad, *Rerum Novarum,* in favor of the rights of workers and offering various bromides allegedly intended, in part, to alleviate the dreadful worldwide repercussions of interest on money. The successor text to *Rerum Novarum*, Pope Pius XI's *Quadragesimo Anno* of 1931, also sought to palliate the worst excesses of the capitalist system. But since the mortal sin itself was allowed to stand in both encyclicals, Christendom sank ever further into the grip of Mammon.

In the early 19th century, "14 decisions of the Congregations of the Holy Office, the Penitentiary...stat(ed) that the faithful who lend money at moderate rates of interest 'are not to be disturbed...The Holy See now puts out its funds at interest and requires ecclesiastical administrators to do the same..." [229] Hence we observe that the Catholic Church after 1830 *required* the commission of mortal sin by its "ecclesiastical administrators"!

The earliest formal Holy Office order to leave those who took interest on loans of money undisturbed is from 1822 in response to a request for clarification by Cardinal Galeffi concerning a woman in Lyon who was refused absolution because she was a usurer. The Holy Office replied that the woman was to be absolved anyway: "...in 1822 a penitent in Lyon, Mlle. de Saint-Marcel, who had been refused absolution for receiving legal interest for invested property, appealed to Rome and had the case decided by the Holy Office against the confessor, on the proviso that the penitent express a willingness to abide by any future decision which might be made by the Holy See. This was the prelude to some thirteen similar decisions made, in response to enquiries, by the Congregations of the Holy Office, the Penitentiary, and Propaganda in the course of the nineteenth century...In these it is declared, often without reference to any special extrinsic title or even to

---

229 "Usury," *New Catholic Encylopedia* (Catholic University of America, 1967), vol. 14, p. 499.

civil law, that the faithful, even though they be clerics and religious, who lend money for a moderate rate of interest are 'not to be distrubed' (*non esse inquietandos*).

"...of the magnitude of this 'moderate rate,' the Holy See was unwilling to give any general definition...Following the decisions of the Roman Congregations in the nineteenth century, in the twentieth century fairly unanimous agreement was to be found among theologians to the proposition that any Catholic is allowed to take interest on money loans, provided the interest is not excessive and does not cause hardship to the poor...the Holy See itself puts out its funds at interest and require ecclesiastical administrators to do the same." [230]

Initial decisions in favor of interest on money were issued 18 August, 1830; 31 August, 1831; 11 February 1832, 17 January 1838; 26 March 1840; 28 February 1871, with more to come in the deluge of revolution, culminating in Canon 1543 of the *Codex Juris Canonici of 1917* (1917 Code of Canon Law): "...in lending a fungible thing it is not in itself illicit to contract for legal interest, unless this be manifestly excessive..." [231]

The Ecumenical Council of Vienne (1311-1312) decreed: "If anyone shall fall into the error, obstinately to affirm that to practice usuries be not a sin, we decree that he shall be punished as a heretic. And we strictly enjoin the Ordinaries and the Inquistitors of heresy to proceed against those who are suspected of this error, as against persons accused or suspected of heresy."

Rev. Fr. O'Callaghan: "When a pastor allows, either from ignorance, or infidelity, his wretched flock to practice

---

230 Thomas F. Divine, S.J., *Interest: An Historical and Analytical Study*), pp. 109-110; 116.

231 This is effectively a license for libertarian capitalism since no definition of "excessive" is given, and no distinction is made between *mutuum* and *locatio*.

interest...(if shepherds, not wolves, they could be called)...thus is the whole community drawn into perdition...It is asserted on behalf of the usurers, that as the State possesses a dominion over life and property, they are justified in exacting whatever rate of interest is allowed by the laws of the State. The temporal ruler would, according to the above notion, be justified for any species of tyranny for taxing in England the people to beggary, and pillaging the asylums of the poor; for erecting, as in Turkey, the harem; or for cutting off, Herod-like, the deformed babies, as they used to do in Algiers, to the end of improving the human race; each tyrant may claim, according to the foregoing notion, the right of disposing at pleasure, all the people and property within his dominions. Ye hypocritical infidels...Ye make mockery of the commands of God so as to follow the bent of your corrupt inclinations. Were the laws of man opposed to your passions, you would with equal facility throw them aside, provided you could escape worldly punishment. To what laws has the Consecration Oath, ordained from the authority of the Holy Council of Trent by Pope Pius IV bound us? To the temporal, or Ecclesiastical laws? We answer, to the Ecclesiastical: for that oath says: 'I likewise undoubtedly receive and profess all things delivered, defined, and declared by the Sacred Canons and General Councils, and particularly by the Holy Council of Trent. And I condemn, reject, and anathematize things contrary thereto.'

"That oath, taken by every prelate in communion with the See of Rome, leaves him no option; he must receive and profess *all* the Canons of all the General Councils, both ancient and modern; the Canons regarding faith and morals equally; he must receive and profess them all, not as many of them as he pleases....If a prelate, therefore, practices or silently connives at the practice of usury, in contempt of all the Sacred Canons heretofore recited, does he not, in addition to all the censures provided in the said Canons, incur the terrific guilt of perjury? I cannot conceive how he can free himself from that stigma...

"Recollect that the Gospel, not the human laws, will be the rule of judgment; and that vengeance will be given, not for disobeying the human laws, but the Gospel of our Lord Jesus Christ. Hence flows the Catholic principle, *Decretal Gratian XI*, Quasi. 3. Chap. 93: if the ruler ordains things not contrary to the Scriptures, let the servant obey the ruler; but if he ordain things contrary thereto, let him obey the Lord of the soul, rather than the lord of the body. If the emperor or ruler decrees a just matter, obey the ruler; but if he decrees a sinful thing, answer him from Acts 5, We must obey God, rather than men. The same principle applies to wives regarding their husbands; to servants regarding their masters; and to children respecting their parents. That they ought to obey their husbands, masters, and parents only in the things that are not opposed to the law of God (St. Jerome, *Epist. on Titus*). The ancient Irish certainly had their eye steadfastly fixed upon that principle. When the Protestant ruler ordered them, under pains and penalties, to abandon the priest and the altar, they obeyed God rather than men. Had they been slaves to self and to mammon, as the moderns are, could Ireland now boast of either Priest or altar?" [232]

What Pius VIII and his successors imposed on Christendom was the reinstitution of the pagan Roman Empire's practice of usury by legal subterfuge, by defining usury as "only" a certain *rate* of interest (in this case an ambiguous undefined "moderate" rate). Such lawyerly evasions in this field nearly always lead to the rise of greed-based predatory capitalism. In the young and vibrant Roman Republic, circa 342 B.C. the *Lex Genucia* banned *all* lending at interest. Centuries later, in the era of the late Roman Empire as it rapidly decayed, the law defined usury only as interest in excess of 50%. It's no coincidence that in New Jersey at present the general usury limit is 50% for corporations. According to the American Bankers

---

[232] O'Callaghan, *Usury Funds, and Banks*, pp. 219-221.

Association there are 26 states in the U.S. that have no limit on what bank credit card issuers can charge for interest rates. In a truly Christian nation this admission would be as shameful as a disclosure that someone had robbed an elderly couple or had an abortion.

Equally despicable and Christ-dishonoring is the notion that Americans are affluent when the Shylock economy is humming along; the "blessings" of capitalism etc. Yet, when the Shylock system is on the ascendant the majority of the people are in debt, because that debt is the engine of the overheated economy. Surrounded by electronic gadgets of every description and cars, boats, ATVs and snowmobiles, we think ourselves well off because our masters declare it to be so, when in fact, in terms of meaningful work, leisure time, stable marriages, lasting friendships and actual ownership (not mortgage) of land, we are but pompous paupers. Loneliness in America is a plague. Americans are friendless, loveless and adrift. Yet, for the past sixty years we have been told to be content that we live in the richest country in the world and share in the wealth. Yet, debtors are not rich. "Debt is the worst poverty" (T. Fuller, 1732). The Cryptocrats who tell us otherwise are engaged in a civic magic, performing the work of making something metaphysically real even though it is an illusion.

Jeremiah O'Callaghan and William Cobbett "lived in daily expectation that the system of loans and paper money would reach its limits and burst like a bubble...On hearing that a bank in his home town had gone bankrupt, Cobbett gave a public dinner in the streets." [233]

Imagine their jubilation if Cobbett and O'Callaghan had lived to see our own day, when the happy prospect of the collapse of Shylock's criminal financial system is at hand. There is more to this than just pointing fingers at bankers and CEOs, however. When sojourning among the Amish we discovered that many of them practiced the medieval Catholic doctrine of the *just price*, in contrast with

---

233 Michell, op. cit, p. 55.

the modern notion of a price set by "whatever the market will bear," which is considered ethical and fair by all churches of which we are aware, including modern Catholicism, excepting some Amish churches: "In the Middle Ages there was a just price for everything. It was one which enabled all those who contributed to making and selling the article to earn 'an honest living' suitable to his station in life. For them the law of supply and demand was no reason for raising the price above the sum considered just." [234]

One Amish master carpenter we knew charged only $10 per hour in the year 1995, when he could have easily commanded three times that sum. And he was not a rich man. Somehow the Amish, tenacious clingers to tradition that they are, have held on to a scrap of ecclesiastic tradition more than a thousand years old, demonstrating that the refusal of avarice is a two-way street, operating at the top and the bottom of the economic arrangement. Communism recruits by rendering avarice by the poor and the working class legitimate, and building covetous resentment against the wealthy and the owners of property and businesses. Avarice and envy are wrong in all classes of people. Christ did not advocate a Robin Hood ethic. The Bible tells us that God is no respecter of persons, rich or poor, and as Jesus said, the poor you will have with you always. For our claims on the bankers and financiers to have moral force we must use whatever is within our power to practice charity and justice in our own dealings.

The other half of the equation is the medieval standard of a *living wage,* defined as the pay which one full-time worker would need to support an entire family adequately but not luxuriously, something to which conservative Republican economists are most averse. A few years ago this writer heard one such Republican leader make the statement that the Detroit auto-makers were in trouble not because of foolish and incompetent decisions by the

---

[234] Hugh Barty-King, *The Worst Poverty,* (1997), p. 2.

corporate executives, but due to the payment of good wages and health care benefits to the workers who produced the cars! What this Republican strategist was seeking was the impoverishment of the American worker by the continued importation of cheap labor from central America and the Far East. This Republican was a type of terrorist, but the terror he wants to visit on American families is performed with a pen and a computer rather than a gun and a bomb. The fundamentalist Protestant churches are silent when Republicans openly call for a cheap labor economy wherein American husbands and wives must work two and three jobs around the clock in order to sustain their families. These labor policies do not support family values, rather they directly foster birth control, divorce and even abortion.

We are witnessing an interconnected degeneracy, with deadly sins linked across a continuum that defies Left/Right politics, while containing elements of both. The breakdown of the family is more than a religious issue as Republicans claim, it is also an economic one. The destruction of our quality of life and culture is more than an environmental or health care issue as Democrats claim, it is a spiritual one, based in alienation from the Word of God and having lost the fear of God, most noticeably manifested in the destruction of the family as represented by the denigration of Biblical principles upholding the father's headship.

The crisis we face transcends the rigged Left/Right paradigm that conservatives and liberals are mentally imprisoned within. The Bible contains economic laws that could be said to be Leftist, and parenting and sexual laws that could be described as Rightist, but ultimately Scripture transcends both of those crippled categories. All these sins are *connected* and to combat them effectively a holistic Biblical vision is needed which is not segmented by our idolatrous loyalty to different "wings" of a demonic, divide-and-conquer political charade, that in the end produces only rags.

7

Agents of the Money Power

A wicked people will never enjoy good government.
— Rev. James Murray

Usury is a grievous sin common to Republicans and Democrats which underscores the one-dimensional essence beneath the Left/Right rivalry: we can't pick and choose which mortal sins we want to campaign against and which we hope Our Father in Heaven will give us a pass on. Grievous sins are *all* soul and nation-destroying.

Until we emerge from dualist finger-pointing party politics, the judgment of God on our nation will stand. Sodomy as practiced by male Democrat homosexuals, contraception as practiced by Republican Churchianity, and a usurious economic system perpetrated by both, are all from the same Satanic root. America harbors a demonic entertainment industry, demonic militarism, demonic sodomy of the contraceptive and "gay"" variants, all stoked by a Shylock financial swindle. Those who target one or two of these devilish endeavors for extirpation while participating in the others and wondering why God doesn't bless America, are lost in the ozone. All of these wicked sins have the same root, but we are too dumbed down to recognize it. Contraception, abortion and homosexuality are, in part, derived from the corruption of a society that has legalized the crime of usury.

Most of the current schemes for "saving" the economy are opposed to how the Bible suppresses greed and regulates the economy. It is obligatory on us to restore Biblical economics if we desire to be granted the much sought after "divine blessing on America."

"Among the Hebrews, perpetual alienation of immovable goods was impossible, and the contracting of debts very difficult. Engrossing of lands was forbidden by the Jubilee law and the greedy were further restrained by the Sabbatical release." [235]

The "*greedy*." Greed: one of the seven deadly sins. (There are seven, by the way, not just one, not just "lust," as pernicious and pervasive as the sin of lust is in our time). Does the "pro-life" "Christian"/Republican base imagine that God is more angry at lust than at greed? If so, what does God think of the conservative Republican lust that excites marriage without all the children He wills to send to a married couple? Are there gradations of mortal sin, one more soul-destroying than another? (If so, then we have a new gospel).

"Oh, but the Biblical laws on usury were intended for the Israelites alone." In that case perhaps the same can be said about the Biblical laws on abortion and contraception, since Jesus uttered not a word concerning them. Do we then, proceeding from that fact, allow for childless marriages? No, rather, we take the *whole* of the Biblical laws into account.

The Republican party base will brook no compromise with abortion but shakes hands with Shylock, under a rationale created by the Prince of Darkness to palliate the crime of usury. They succumb to modern philosophy (2 Tim. 4:3) on usury, but reject it on abortion. Sorry folks, but schizophrenia will not succeed as a core principle of a purported Christian politics. To speak with authority it is necessary that one not be mad, and Republican conservatives are far gone in madness as they pour forth wrath in the eyes of liberals for their sins of abortion-enablement and homosexual culture while regarding not the beam of sins, like usury, in their own eyes.

---

235 Benjamin N. Nelson, *The Idea of Usury*, p. 121.

TV talk-show host Glenn Beck gave the keynote address at a Conservative Political Action Conference in Washington D.C. In the course of his clownish, rambling talk to the dumbed-down audience, Mr. Beck announced that the most scurrilous and destructive villain in the entire history of these United States are the "progressives." Beck claims to be a Jeffersonian, but he's attacking progressives – the American leaders who clashed most fiercely with the Money Power and the military-industrial complex. Mr. Beck has urged parishioners to leave churches that promote "social justice" or "economic justice," saying these are "code words" for Communism. Actually, in almost all cases these supposed "code words" refer to *renewing the ancient Christian fight against the mortal sin of usury.*

In the 1930s, Fr. Charles E. Coughlin's anti-war, anti-usury organization was called The National Union for Social Justice. In the eyes of a predatory capitalist like Beck, the fight against usury is a manifestation of Communist extremism, in which case the most eminent representatives of Western Civilization from Shakespeare (*The Merchant of Venice*) to Charles Dickens (*Bleak House*) were Communists. This is malarkey from a mouthpiece for mammon who is not fit to shine the shoes of Coughlin and other progressives such as William H. "Alfalfa Bill" Murray, Charles A. Lindbergh Sr., Louis McFadden; Burton K. Wheeler, Jeannette Rankin of Montana, and Ezra Pound's colleague, Idaho's own William Borah. All of these eminent American legislators – and many more – fought the Money Power and the military-industrial complex.

Our great-grandparents would never have been seduced by so obvious an agent of the plutocracy as Mr. Beck. They favored *free enterprise* but opposed *predatory Capitalism.* Today, does anyone know the difference? Free enterprise operates under the limits of

Biblical law, and recognizes a moral compass infinitely higher than the profit motive. Mr. Beck conceals the fact that his "free-market capitalist" gospel of greed is every bit as inimical to the Gospel of Jesus Christ as Soviet Communism. Predatory Capitalism is one side of a two-headed materialist ideology. Communism represents the other side. The same *materialism* informs both.

Ludwig von Mises: Jesus Christ is "the evil seed"

The most radical economic theoreticians of capitalism, from Jeremy Bentham to Ludwig von Mises and Ayn Rand, are extremely antagonistic to Christianity and *literally hate* the teachings of Jesus Christ. Von Mises, patriarch of "Austrian School economics" whose only god is greed, is perhaps the most revered and influential of all "free market capitalists," across the spectrum of the Right wing. In chapter 29 of his book, *Socialism: An Economic and Sociological Analysis,* Ludwig von Mises wrote:

"Jesus' words are full of resentment against the rich, and the Apostles are no meeker in this respect. The Rich Man is condemned because he is rich, the Beggar praised because he is poor. The only reason why Jesus does not declare war against the rich and preach revenge on them is that God has said: 'Revenge is mine.' In God's Kingdom the poor shall be rich, but the rich shall be made to suffer. Later revisers have tried to soften the words of Christ against the rich, of which the most complete and powerful version is found in the Gospel of Luke, but there is quite enough left to support those who incite the world to hatred of the rich, revenge, murder and arson. Up to the time of modern Socialism no movement against private property which has arisen in the Christian world has failed to seek authority in Jesus, the Apostles, and the Christian Fathers, not to mention those who, like

Tolstoy, made the Gospel resentment against the rich the very heart and soul of their teaching. This is a case in which the Redeemer's words bore evil seed."

Von Mises' indictment of Jesus Christ as progenitor of "evil seed" is purely distilled hatred which ought to disqualify him as an economist which any faithful Christian could follow. Alas, he is the doyen of the "Christian" capitalists. Von Mises states further: "A living Christianity cannot, it seems, exist side by side with Capitalism." [236]

In this he is absolutely correct! What we have today is a *dead* Churchianity that has sold-out the Gospel and cut a lucrative deal with the capitalists, while *impersonating living Christianity*. This is why Senator Bob Corker, a Tennessee Republican in the "buckle" of the "Bible belt," was the leading defender in Congress of the $10 billion a year Shylock "payday loan" industry that preys on working people with annualized interest rates of up to 400%! This grave sin should be an alarm for the Church. But the pulpits are mostly silent. "Payday lender" shylocks spent $2.1 million buying (i.e. "lobbying") senators and Congressmen in 2008. "Conservative Christian" Senator Corker has been a recipient of their tainted money; so has Senator Richard Shelby of "Christian" Alabama.

The people in the pews live in enforced ignorance of the statutes and judgements of God concerning the corrosive Capitalist avarice that rots a society from the bottom up, as ours is being rotted. The most "conservative" so-called "Christian" states in the union, such as Alabama and Tennessee, are among the most stalwart protectors of usury.

---

236 Mises' Austrian School philosophy can be traced to the Renaissance Catholic "School of Salamanca," which "paved the way for the modern subjectivist theory of value developed by the Austrian School of Economics." Jesús Huerta De Soto, *Money, Bank Credit and Economic Cycles*, p. 83.

Ayn Rand, Goddess of Usury

Ayn Rand was born Alissa Zinovievna Rosenbaum on February, 2, 1905, in St. Petersburg, Russia, of a prosperous merchant family.[237] "Rand" was the author of several books including *The Fountainhead* (which was made into a movie starring Gary Cooper), *Atlas Shrugged* and *The Virtue of Selfishness*. It is no secret that in her personal life she was known to favor degenerate sado-masochist sex acts in which the woman performs as a groveling slave of a vicious man. Rand served as the future Federal Reserve Bank Chairman Alan Greenspan's teacher and mentor. She taught the concept that "greed is good." Just as Karl Marx founded Communism, which possessed no moral constraint, the woman who called herself "Ayn Rand" founded a super-Shylock, hyper-Capitalism (dubbed "Objectivism") that also lacked any moral constraint. This thesis and antithesis, Communism and Capitalism, share a fundamental characteristic, *materialism*, which forms the synthesis of modernist determinism as it announces the inevitability of its dominion, due to the supposed evolution of history toward "advancement." This is the conceit of both "scientific socialism" and "free market capitalism." These seeming antipodes—Communism's Commissar and Capitalism's Scrooge—are actually symbiotic expressions of a *wholly material spirit,* which is sold to rootless modern people as fighting either "the bosses" or "the collectivists."

Rep. Ron Paul, Alan Greenspan, Glenn Beck and Paul Ryan all extol Rand, who viewed charity to the poor with more jaundice than Ebenezer Scrooge. Rand, who was the author of *The Virtue of Selfishness,* cannot comprehend charity to anyone, except perhaps one's own inner circle, and then only as a personal

---

237 Cf. Anne C. Heller, *Ayn Rand and the World She Made* (Doubleday, 2009).

choice, not a duty. The Christian virtue of doing for others and for the less fortunate is regarded by Rand as a violation of the will and ego of the Atlas man, the money maker supreme. This skinflint, dog-eat-dog barbarism is what Von Mises, Ayn Rand and their Republican cheerleaders are all about.

What is the outcome of their usurious society? Rand described the results candidly: "There is no such thing as 'a right to a job'—there is only the right of free trade, that is: a man's right to take a job if another man chooses to hire him. There is no 'right to a home,' only the right of free trade: the right to build a home or to buy it. There are no 'rights to a 'fair' wage or a 'fair price' if no one chooses to pay it, to hire a man or to buy his product." (Rand, *Man's Rights,* 1963).

What happens to the New Testament's poor man Lazarus, in a land ruled by Ayn Rand's Capitalism? Under Rand, Lazarus would not have a scrap of food off the rich man's table. He would die, as did the Biblical Lazarus in Luke 16, in privation and agony. Rand can approve of this because in her world, exactly as in the Soviet empire of Lenin and Trotsky, there is no god except the material world itself. Like the Communists, the Capitalist Rand refuses to acknowledge the Scriptural truth that every property-owner is God's tenant and *owes* charity to the poor, and thus is impelled by an informed conscience to voluntarily share one's wealth in some measure (Isaiah 58:7; Nehemiah 5:1-19). Instead, Ayn Rand promotes the option of depraved indifference to the poor. [238]

We would not be expending five words on this debased loanshark, who was so far gone that she shamelessly trumpeted her "virtue" of selfishness to

---

238 "...not only the theft of others' goods, but also the failure to share one's own goods with others is theft and swindle and fraud..." —St. John Chrysostom, *Second Sermon on Lazarus and the Rich Man.*

the world, were it not for the astonishing datum that Ayn Rand is a guiding light to many who claim the mantle of the "Christian Right" in the early 21st century. Rand's ideological perversion is the driving force behind NAFTA, the WTO, "free trade," many Internet technology capitalists, and many preachers of Churchianity, along with Right wing "Constitutionalists" who don't know or simply don't care that the Christian and classic "paleo" Conservatives rightly viewed Rand as an evil force almost from the beginning of her celebrity – the personification of the terminal usurer – usury taken to its farthest and most degenerate extreme as palpable darkness out of the bottomless pit. In 1957 William F. Buckley's *National Review* denounced the "wickedness of *Atlas Shrugged*." In the words of the magazine's critique of her bestseller, *Atlas Shrugged*:

"It is...in the book's last line, that a character traces in the air, 'over the desolate earth,' the Sign of the Dollar, in lieu of the Sign of the Cross...that Dollar Sign is not merely provocative...it is meant to seal the fact that mankind is ready to submit abjectly to an elite of technocrats, and their accessories, in a New Order, enlightened and instructed by Miss Rand's ideas that the good life is one which 'has resolved personal worth into exchange value,' 'has left no other nexus between man and man than naked self-interest, than callous 'cash payment.' The author is explicit, in fact deafening, about these prerequisites....But the words quoted above are those of Karl Marx. He, too, admired 'naked self-interest' (in its time and place), and for much of the same reasons as Miss Rand: because, he believed, it cleared away the cobwebs of religion and led to prodigies of industrial and cognate accomplishment.

"...Henceforth man's fate...is up to him. And to him alone. His happiness, in strict materialist terms, lies with his own workaday hands and ingenious brain. His happiness becomes, in Miss Rand's words, 'the moral purpose of his life.' Here occurs a little rub whose effects are just as observable in a free enterprise system, which is in practice materialist (whatever else it claims or supposes itself to be), as they would be under an atheist Socialism, if one were ever to deliver that material abundance that all promise....For, if man's 'heroism' (some will prefer to say: 'human dignity') no longer derives from God...then Man becomes merely the most consuming of animals, with glut as the condition of his happiness. And this, of course, suits the author's economics and the politics that must arise from them...

"Something of this implication is fixed in the book's dictatorial tone, which is much its most striking feature. Out of a lifetime of reading, I can recall no other book in which a tone of overriding arrogance was so implacably sustained. Its shrillness is without reprieve. Its dogmatism is without appeal...The same inflexibly self-righteous stance results, too...in odd extravagances of inflection and gesture — that Dollar Sign, for example. At first, we try to tell ourselves that these are just lapses, that this mind has, somehow, mislaid the discriminating knack that most of us pray will warn us in time of the differences between what is effective and firm, and what is wildly grotesque and excessive. Soon we suspect something worse. We suspect that this mind finds, precisely in extravagance, some exalting merit; feels a surging release of power and passion precisely in smashing up the house..." [239]

---

239 Whittaker Chambers, "Big Sister is Watching You," *National Review,* December 28, 1957.

Paul Ryan's Speech to the Atlas Society

In 2005 Roman Catholic Republican Rep. Paul Ryan delivered a speech at The Atlas Society's "Celebration of Ayn Rand" gala, where he extolled Rand, and in particular her book, *Atlas Shrugged*:

"I just want to speak to you a little bit about Ayn Rand and what she meant to me in my life and (in) the fight we're engaged here in Congress. I grew up on Ayn Rand, that's what I tell people...you know everybody does their soul-searching, and trying to find out who they are and what they believe, and you learn about yourself....I grew up reading Ayn Rand and it taught me quite a bit about who I am and what my value systems are, and what my beliefs are. It's inspired me so much that it's required reading in my office for all my interns and my staff. We start with *Atlas Shrugged*. People tell me I need to start with *The Fountainhead* (Rand's other novel), then go to *Atlas Shrugged*. There's a big debate about that. We go to *Fountainhead*, but then we move on, and we require (Ludwig von) Mises and (Friedrich) Hayek as well.

"...And when you look at the twentieth-century experiment with collectivism—that Ayn Rand, more than anybody else, did such a good job of articulating the pitfalls of statism and collectivism—you can't find another thinker or writer who did a better job of describing and laying out the moral case for capitalism than Ayn Rand.

"...It's so important that we go back to our roots to look at Ayn Rand's vision, her writings, to see what our girding, under-grounding (sic) principles are. I always go back to, you know, Francisco d'Anconia's speech (at Bill Taggart's wedding) on money, when I think about monetary policy. And then I go to the 64-page John Galt (the hero of *Atlas Shrugged*) speech, you know, on the radio at the end, and go back to a lot of other things that she did, to try and make sure that

I can check my premises so that I know that what I'm believing and doing and advancing are square with the key principles of individualism…

"Is this an easy fight? Absolutely not…But if we're going to actually win this we need to make sure that we're solid on premises, that our principles are well-defended, and if we want to go and articulately defend these principles and what they mean to our society, what they mean for the trends that we set internationally, we have to go back to Ayn Rand. Because there is no better place to find the moral case for capitalism and individualism than through Ayn Rand's writings and works."

In an Aug. 20, 2012 column, Catholic Archbishop Samuel J. Aquila of Denver, Colorado wrote, "...claims that Paul Ryan's (budget) plan run deeply counter to Catholic social teaching are unfounded and unreasonable."

In the summer of 2012, when he was named Mitt Romney's Republican vice-presidential running mate, it appears that it was decided that Mr. Ryan's adulation of Rand might harm the duo's election chances, and Ryan subsequently distanced himself from his Russian-American guru. The *New York Times* mocked his hypocrisy after he used St. Thomas Aquinas as a cloak for his usury-based budget: "...when his embrace of Rand drew fire from Catholic leaders, Mr. Ryan reversed course with a speed that would make his running mate, Mitt Romney, proud. 'Don't give me Ayn Rand,' he told *National Review* earlier this year. 'Give me Thomas Aquinas.' He claimed that his austere budget was motivated by the Catholic principle of subsidiarity...Mr. Ryan has attempted a pirouette, but it is too late: driven by the fever of the Tea Party and drawing upon a wellspring of enthusiasm for Rand, politicians like Mr. Ryan have set the philosophy of *Atlas Shrugged* at the core of modern Republicanism..." [240]

Despite its center-Left political orientation, the *New York Times* has a lingering affection for Rand and sought to rehabilitate her reputation from a presumed taint resulting from her following among "Christian" social-conservatives, who the executives at the *Times* abhor: "...modern conservatives ignore the fundamental principles that animated Rand: personal as well as economic freedom. Her philosophy sprang from her deep belief in the autonomy and independence of each individual. This meant that individuals could not depend on government for retirement savings or medical care. But it also meant that individuals must be free from government interference in their personal lives. Years before Roe v. Wade, Rand called abortion 'a moral right which should be left to the sole discretion of the woman involved.' ...These aspects of Rand do not fit with a political view that weds fiscal and social conservatism. Mr. Ryan's selection as Mr. Romney's running mate is the kind of stinging rebuke of the welfare state that Rand hoped to see during her lifetime. But...(a)s a woman in a man's world, a Jewish atheist [241] in a country dominated by Christianity, and a refugee from a totalitarian state, Rand knew it was not enough to

---

240 Stanford University Prof. Jennifer Burns, "Atlas Spurned," *New York Times*, Aug. 14, 2012.

241 Rand's disciple, atheist Alan Greenspan, before he became the chairman of the Federal Reserve Bank, mysteriously swore his first oath of office (as head of the Office of Budget Management), on a copy of the Talmud, rather than the Bible, as Rand looked on approvingly. Since the Talmud is a religious tome, how do we account for this behavior on the part of atheists?

promote individual freedom in the economic realm alone." [242]

Janet Maslin writing in the *New York Times,* Oct 21, 2009: "...Rand's popularity has endured, not only among college students...but also by entrepreneurs. From the young Ted Turner, who rented billboards to promote the 'Who is John Galt?' slogan from *Atlas Shrugged*, to the founders of Craigslist and Wikipedia..."

Adam Kirsch, *New York Times,* Oct. 29, 2009: "At 'tea parties' and other conservative protests, alongside the Obama-as-Joker signs, you will find placards reading 'Atlas Shrugs' and 'Ayn Rand Was Right.' Not long after the inauguration (of Obama), as right-wing pundits like Glenn Beck were invoking Rand and issuing warnings of incipient socialism, Representative John Campbell, Republican of California, told a reporter that the prospect of rising taxes and government regulation meant 'people are starting to feel like we're living through the scenario that happened in *Atlas Shrugged.*'

"...in a poll in the early '90s, sponsored by the Library of Congress and the Book of the Month Club, 'Americans named *Atlas Shrugged* the book that had most influenced their lives,' second only to the Bible...'

"In 1949, Rand was living with her husband...Frank O'Connor, in Southern California...Then she got a fan letter from a 19-year-old college freshman named Nathan Blumenthal and invited him to visit. Rand...quickly fell in love with this confused boy, whom she decided was the 'intellectual heir' she had been waiting for....When Blumenthal, who changed his name to Nathaniel Branden, moved to New York, Rand followed him; she inserted herself into her protégé's love life, urging him to marry his

---

242 Burns, op. cit. Ayn Rand's racist slurs against Arabs (on the nationally televised Phil Donahue program), are not mentioned by Prof. Burns in her fawning *New York Times* column.

girlfriend; then Rand began to sleep with Branden, insisting that both their spouses be kept fully apprised of what was going on...the Brandens formed the nucleus of a growing group of young Rand followers...Rand 'charmed so many young people into quoting John Galt (hero of *Atlas Shrugged*) as religiously as clergymen quote Matthew, Mark, Luke and John."

"Free market" Capitalism is among the most revolutionary of all of modernism's constituent factors, representing an enormous break with Christendom. Ersatz "Christian Conservatives" of the type who predominate now, prattle ceaselessly about getting back to the basics, educating their young people in the classics, reviving traditional liturgy and the ideology of the American Republic, and other rhetoric of this sort in vogue on the Right. This is a movement that *pretends* to want to cultivate what is most authentic about our heritage, culture and religion, while forgetting that this cannot be done while the plague of usury stalks our land.

Most of the "conservative" and "traditional" movements in our nation are so fundamentally compromised, so drowned in doublethink as to be, at their heart, a type of self-delusion for the benefit of assuaging their own profoundly troubled consciences. An honest revival of our heritage, as opposed to going through the motions, would mean that we would, each of us, become the most radical members of modern society. America is suffused with the cult of the new; with all that represents trends and innovation, and this is true even inside the churches. By "radical" we signify membership in the Christian counter-culture. In response to the world, the Gospel of Christ is necessarily counter-cultural. Long before the "60s counterculture" occurred, authentic Christians were witnesses throughout history against the corruption wrought by criminal politics, militarism and bloodshed, and the fashions both of the mind and the body as established by the trends, fads and consensus reality of the world. Acceptance of the ethical correctness of charging interest on money is a universal consensus of the modern world. It would be difficult to find a soul-damning sin more prevalent and unthinkingly accepted as the norm, as proper and morally right, than the sin of usury and all the sins of greed that attend upon it.

In north Idaho the formerly pristine Rathdrum prairie is increasingly crammed with cheap, ugly houses built five or more to an acre. Millionaires can escape this blight but the regular guy has lost the beauty of the landscape and hence, a part of his soul. No yardstick has yet been found to adequately measure the psychic and spiritual loss and disconnection which this money-mad development has perpetrated on the land, which is God's property, not man's. Man is merely the steward.

"Is it not enough for you to feed on the good pasture, that you must tread down with your feet the rest of your pasture; and to drink of clear water, that you must muddy the rest of the water with your feet? And must my sheep eat what you have trodden with your feet, and drink what you have muddied with your feet?" (Ezekiel 34: 18-19). Considerations like this are wholly alien to the economic philosophy of materialism promoted by those who adorn themselves with the Cross of Christ while embracing the Dollar Sign of Antichrist.

8

On Quality of Life
Ezra Pound, Wendell Berry, Arthur Penty, Vincent McNabb, John Ruskin

> Because your avarice afflicts the world, trampling the good and lifting the depraved: ye have made yourselves a god of gold and silver; And from the idolater how do ye differ?
>
> Dante, The Inferno (XIX)

Fecundity vs. usura

In his book *Citizenship Papers*, [243]Christian farmer-philosopher Wendell Berry of Kentucky, argues that the George W. Bush administration and its "Conservative Republican" supporters, adopted a claim to a sort of official Christianity whose religion is the "free market." In the name of Christ, Bush and his cohorts sacrificed to this religion our communities, farmers and farmlands; our self-sufficiency and our dignity as laborers, which were in days of yore endowed by the God of the Bible and the precepts of the ancient Church with the inalienable right to a living wage for their toil ,and a just price for their goods.

In his Cantos, Ezra Pound described usury as *contra naturam*, a sin against nature:

---

243 We do not endorse this book in its entirety. For example, Mr. Berry conflates Christ and Buddha with distressing insouciance. The meatiest chapters are: "Let the Farm Judge"; "A Long Job, Too Late to Quit"; and best of all, "The Total Economy."

With ursura, sin against nature,
is thy bread ever more of stale rags
is thy bread dry as paper,
with no mountain wheat, no strong flour
Usura slayeth the child in the womb
It stayeth the young man's courting
It hath brought palsey to bed, lyeth
between the young bride and her bridegroom
CONTRA NATURAM
They have brought whores for Eleusis
Corpses are set to banquet
at behest of usura.
(Canto XLV)

The masterstroke of the Cryptocracy has been to eradicate among Christians in our time passionate indignation and protest against a U.S. economic system based on usury. The modern "Christian Conservative," consumed with a crusade against homosexuals, abortion and Islam, is often blind to the insidious evil that is father to all the rest, the present usurious economic system which wars upon every working American for the benefit of those who operate and profit from such exploitative warfare.

With Ezra Pound, we observe that usury is *the cause, rather than the effect* of that which "slays the child in the womb" (abortion), "stayeth the young man's courting" (penury) and "lyeth between the young bride and her bridegroom" (contraception).[244] The

[244] Greek grammarians and Christian theologians employed *tokos*, a Greek word which signifies both begetting children *and* interest on money; implying both natural and unnatural offspring: "So an ancient grammarian derives *faenus* (interest on debt) from *fetus*, because it is *quaedam faetura pecunia parturientis* (the brood of increase)," connoting monstrous increase.

prime offenders are private banks, which are empowered to create money, or credit, out of nothing.

It is on behalf of this wicked system that, since Sept. 11, 2001, many Americans of a slave orientation are flag-waving themselves into a jingoist stupor as they celebrate and defend their own executioners and worst enemies, in a remarkable display of mass psychosis. Our people are ensnared by a profound failure of imagination, or *vision*, as the Old Testament termed it. The failure to be sufficiently radical, by dealing with effects, rather than causes, is to ensure one's own failure.

Our fellow citizens are ignorant of Christian economics and of the historic opposition of the Church to the heinous crime of usury. The history of western civilization's campaign against usury is not studied in school; it is not preached on Sunday, and is not reported in the media, thus it has lapsed into near total oblivion.

Depraved Economics Breeds Depraved Morals

Contemporary 'Conservatives' seldom make the connection between a depraved economic system and depravity of morals among a passively consumptive, dehumanized populace possessed of disposable income and unlimited wants. These "Conservatives" view Communist economics as a great evil, but never the Capitalist. But as Wendell Berry observes:

> "Communism and 'free market' Capitalism both are modern versions of oligarchy...The fraudulence of these oligarchic forms of economy is in their principle of displacing whatever goods they recognize (as well as their debts) from the present to the future...Communists and Capitalists alike have needed to replace genuine religious faith with some form of determinism, so they can say to their victims.... 'It's inevitable."

Predatory Capitalism hides the destruction it wreaks through a process of *false accounting,* substituting for the real economy of creative labor and natural production, the symbolic economy of money "which cannot symbolize or account for anything but itself. And so we have before us the spectacle of unprecedented 'prosperity' and 'economic growth' in a land of degraded farms, failing families and perishing communities."

The Wal-Mart behemoth, in search of ever more bloated profits, is free to devastate communities, and eradicate ("compete against") small, local, Mom-and-Pop enterprises, and this corrosive greed is saluted by preachers, pastors and patriots as "the American Way" which ought to be exported to usury-free Islamic lands as the wondrous gift of America, because after all, "God loves America."

In this respect, "Christian" Capitalism is far more hypocritical than Communism, for the Communists did not blasphemously invoke God as a cover for their crimes, yet somehow "Conservatives" in America feel impelled to drag God into their dog-eat-dog corporate system and invoke His mantle as justification for the unbridled money-worship that is turning towns once full of neighborhoods, into suburbs crammed with soulless housing developments, ripping communities that are indispensable to the spiritual well-being of a nation to pieces, and creating the symptoms of rootlessness and alienation which manifest in our young people as drug addiction, suicide, squalor and perversion, and in our elderly as extraordinary isolation and loneliness. An example of how the soul of Americans is being rotted by this system is recounted by Wendell Berry:

"I remember speaking with the owner of a small, independent drugstore who told me that he had seen his customers drifting away to the chain stores, but he said they remained *his* faithful customers when they needed medicine late at night. That is to say, they were members of 'the market economy' when they were looking for a bargain, but they returned to membership in the local community when they needed a neighbor — a fickleness that obviously cannot be kept up indefinitely."

Loyalty to one's home-place, the obligation to protect the neighborhood and the community as a locus of ennobling and humanizing values and folkways worthy in themselves, apart from any immediate gain on the profit-ledger, is derided by the globalists as "protectionism," as if the preservation of the neighborhood where the Christ-centered practice of neighborliness is made possible, is some kind of sinful subversion. Berry:

"A corporation, essentially, is a pile of money to which a number of persons have sold their moral allegiance. Unlike a person, a corporation does not age...it does not come to see the future as the lifetime of the children and grandchildren of anybody in particular. It goes about its business with the single purpose of becoming a bigger pile of money. The stockholders are essentially usurers, people who 'let their money work for them,' expecting high pay in return for causing others to work for low pay. The World Trade Organization enlarges the old idea of the corporation-as-person by giving the global corporate economy the status of a super-government with the power to overrule nations. I don't mean to say, of course, that all corporate executives and stockholders are bad people. I am only saying that all of them are very seriously implicated in a bad economy."

To write of usury as a cancer eating out the bowels of our civilization as an underlying *cause* of the *symptoms* of decay, will strike some Americans as utterly bizarre as the babbling of a Martian, because no prominent Christian leader has railed against this scourge since the days of C.H. Douglas in Canada and Dorothy Day in the U.S.A.

"The usurers of Pound's *Canto*...owe their identities to C.H. Douglas' historical analysis, but we can trace their configurations...to *Inferno* XIV, where usurers squat 'like dogs in summer that ply, now snout, now paw, when they are bitten by fleas or gnats or flies.' In the end, we must acknowledge that Dante combined with Douglas in Pound's mind to make usury not just a contemporary problem, but the *Cantos*' most important emblem of the fall of the 'green world' of natural bounty. The Cantos condemn *usura,* the 'obsession of wealth defined in terms of money,' not just because it interferes with an artist's creation ('Came not by usura Angelico'), but because it perverts the bounty and sustenance of God's art, which is nature." [245]

"Conservatives" proclaim their allegiance to a financial system that squats like a vulture upon the smoking ruins of the Christian commonweal. Their decayed memories are empty of the ancient knowledge that Christendom did not regard interest banking as reaping ethical or legitimate earnings. Rather, the Church rightly viewed gain from interest as *unearned* profit, i.e. *theft.* Contemporary "Conservatives" have conserved none of this once sacred wisdom — they are wreckers, not conservatives. Rather, they treacherously certify the mythical Christian character of the wreckage that constitutes the buccaneers' status quo. The word "Conservative" has devolved into

---

[245] Ronald Bush, *The Genesis of Ezra Pound's Cantos* (Princeton University Press, 1989).

Newspeak, a debased form of communication which makes it "impossible to mean what we say."

All of the politicians who become "immortal statesmen" in the eyes of the media, Ronald Reagan being the most recent example, have achieved this lofty status by certifying the need for constant change. The rootless cosmopolitanism that was once characteristic only of gypsies and nomads has now become the celebrated ethos of "Christian America."

America was not founded on the metropolitan model, however, but upon the vision of agrarianism, which was itself an American interpretation of an old Biblical value. Berry gives an account of his life as a young student in Italy, in the region of Tuscany. He observed the way the land there was cultivated:

"It was a way of farming that was lovingly adapted to its place. It was highly diversified. It wasted nothing. It was scaled to permit close attention to details. It was beautiful. I began to understand that probably the supreme works of art in Tuscany were its agricultural landscapes. This daily work of art was very old. The terraced slopes and small valleys had been farmed in essentially the same way by essentially the same people for centuries. Through all that time, these people had performed a continuous act of fidelity to the land. They had maintained their work and their faithfulness through hardships of every kind."

"We will discover that...our destruction of nature is not just bad stewardship, or stupid economics, or a betrayal of family responsibility; it is...horrid blasphemy. It is flinging God's gifts into His face, as if they were of no worth beyond that assigned to them by our destruction of them. To Dante, 'despising Nature and her goodness' was a violence against God. We have no entitlement from the Bible to exterminate or permanently destroy or hold in contempt anything on the earth or in the heavens above it or in the waters beneath it. We have the right to refuse the gifts of nature but not to ruin or waste them. We have the right to use what we need but no more, which is why the Bible forbids usury and great accumulations of property.

"...When humans presume to originate value, they make value that is first abstract and then false, tyrannical and destructive of real value. Money value, for instance, can be said to be true only when it justly and stably represents the value of necessary goods, such as clothing, food and shelter...Humans can originate value money in the abstract, but only by inflation and usury, which falsify the value of necessary things and damage their natural and human sources. Inflation and usury and the damages that follow can be understood, perhaps, as retributions for the presumption that humans can make value.

"...if Christianity is going to survive as more than a respecter and comforter of profitable iniquities, then Christians, regardless of their organizations, are going to have to interest themselves in economy — which is to say, in nature and in work. They are going to have to give workable answers to those who say we cannot live without this economy that is destroying us and our world..." [246]

The memory and affections of the American people have been alienated from the land. The land is no longer a work of agrarian art for them, but an empty quarter that should be "developed." The deep disorder and psychic malaise afflicting America, which emerged into the open at Abu Ghraib prison in Iraq, where helpless Arab captives were made to strip naked, pantomime perverted sex acts and perform these acts

---

[246] Berry, *The Art of the Commonplace: The Agrarian Essays,* pp. 225, 308-309.

for recordings on home video, is not just a matter of the failure of American schools or parental upbringing in the home. Increasingly, American youth inhabit the landscape of nowhere; a cash-register geography that consists of the same string of fast-food joints and chain stores from Hoboken to Houston. In these canyons of sterility, displacement, rootlessness and deracination are pandemic. No Communist or Muslim raped America in this way. Her agrarian principles, her Biblical vision of the land as a sacred trust, were torn away and dumped into the refuse bin of history by the usury of the banks, the respectable Chamber of Commerce and the revered Fortune 500, amid the sybaritic complacency, conformity and Scripture-twisting of our "ministers of the gospel."

Rev. Fr. Vincent McNabb

Fr. McNabb (1868-1943) was an example of the spirit of Aquinas, very much alive in a Catholic priest in the early twentieth century, despite the modernism and heresy burgeoning from within the hierarchy of his own Church. He celebrated the small, independent farms, hand-crafts, local produce, weaving and rural path of the English and Irish yeomanry, as an aid to salubrious, Christ-like living and holiness. We have found Fr. McNabb's pro-life, anti-Mammon current in many Catholics. It is as though God has miraculously preserved the spirit of the Gospel — even the spirit of St. Anthony of Padua at the funeral of the usurer — in at least a sizable minority of contemporary Catholics, despite unconscionable betrayals of Luke 6:34-35 by their shepherds.

Decades ago the majority of the Catholics we encountered — whether they were welders, farmers and carpenters, or businessmen and industrialists — seemed to harbor a suspicion of wealth, a real concern for the poor, and a spirit of generosity. It has only been since the 1990s that we have noticed a creeping, acquisitive attitude in younger Catholic activists enamored of Mises, Rand and libertarianism, and proud of their Me generation's greed-is-good cupidity; a pride which carries with it a certain shamelessness.

If we were asked to distill the faith and mission of the early Puritans to a single essence, we would say that it was a burning desire to order the world according to Biblical standards, beginning with those passages in the Old Testament which contain the eternal law of God, rather than the ceremonial rules. Specifically, we would cite the Mosaic Law, and with regard to combatting the greatest evil of all, the early Puritans found the remedy for it in the divine economics of the Pentateuch. We have lost our way today because we do not proceed from first principles. We do not look to the fundamentals. We have a pathological need for complexity, for making matters more complicated than they need to be. In the all-important realm of choosing to obey God's plan for money and finance, rather than falling for man's rebellious refusal of the divine order, which has resulted in convoluted and competing economic systems which that rebellion has generated, Fr. Vincent McNabb, the crusading Catholic economist, like the early Puritans, stood with Moses:

"There is a likelihood that the Bible, which, as a book of dogma and morals, has largely lost its hold upon modern minds, may be able to recover its hold as a book of economics. Nor is this to be wondered at; unless, indeed, men fail to realize that those dogmas and ethics which yield no fruit of sound economics can hardly be accepted as themselves sound. St. Thomas Aquinas in the thirteenth century was among the first to recognize in the Mosaic code of laws a collection of economic principles, which was of first importance to the Europe of his day. His work in summarizing and, if we may be allowed the phrase, in codifying the Mosaic laws has made his *Summa Theologica* one of the indispensable introductions to scientific economics." [247]

What McNabb was saying is: *to Moses through Aquinas*. The most direct route is by way of St. Thomas's nonpareil masterwork, the *Summa*. [248] The destination is reached when we become obedient to God's law; when the mortal sin of charging interest on loans of money is condemned and everywhere exposed and avoided, something which Fr. McNabb, burdened by the sophistry of the popes of usury, could not accomplish. Nonetheless, we cannot withhold our admiration for him when he writes of that lay saint, the poverty-stricken poet of the streets, Francis Thompson; humbly confessing his sin of neglect toward Francis, and recounting how Thompson's life embodied Christ-like virtues: "It was the boldness of Francis Thompson in an age of agnosticism and mammon to offer the incense of poetry to the true God.[249] The spirit of the "*Il Poverello,*" and Anthony of Padua seems to have never completely abandoned the Catholic people. Pre-Vatican II Roman Catholic culture in Ireland, Britain and the United States hammered mammonism relentlessly in sermons and books. This was a cultural signifier among the Catholic layfolk and their priests.

---

247 *Church and the Land*, p. 73. McNabb didn't believe the Puritans knew the way to Moses. Reading Milton's *Paradise Lost* made him detest them: "the God-hound of Milton is yearning to devour," while in Catholicism, "the Hound of Heaven is yearning to embrace the soul whom it pursues." Among the dozens of signal Puritan texts which refute this familiar canard are: Jeremiah Burroughs, *Moses' Self-Denial* (Reformation Heritage 2010); also *Rare Jewel of Christian Contentment* (Banner of Truth, 1964); Jonathan Edwards, *Charity and Its Fruits* (Banner of Truth, 2005).

248 *The Summa Theologica of St. Thomas Aquinas*, trans. Fathers of the English Dominican Province (Christian Classics, 1981), five volumes, 3020 pages. *Nota bene*: the medieval scholasticism of Aquinas should not be confused with "Late Scholasticism," a degenerate Renaissance movement typified by the Salamanca School of Luis de Molina, S.J., Martin de Azpilcueta, and others.

249 McNabb, *Francis Thompson and Other Essays*, p. 16.

Protestants on the other hand, indoctrinated to believe that their church was birthed by grizzled men whose eyes twinkled with dollar signs and whose hands were stained with gold dust, has sometimes not benefited from a sense of itself as having reproved the vice of greed with the same fervor and dedication with which it pursued its protest against the corruption of Rome, and its horror of the ancient Catholic Mass. [250]

Arthur Penty & the Medieval Guild Alternative

British philosopher Arthur Penty was a Christian economist, part of the "Distributist" school which opposes Capitalism in part because they believed its debt-dependent, "monopoly-driven" finance is an enemy of Christianity and man's "peace of soul." But whereas Wendell Berry is a classical liberal in the old Victorian sense, Penty's worldview, like that of John Ruskin, is deeply grounded in the medieval model and "the re-establishment of the Guild system" which "was the centerpiece of Arthur Penty's Distributist vision of a reformation of human economy and society." By the Guild system is meant the institution of a system of just and fixed prices maintained by the master craftsmen of the Guild itself (not bureaucrats), coupled with the insistence on the payment of a living wage.

---

250 One of Calvin's most revolutionary conceits was his conviction that not just the Catholic Mass as it existed in the 16th century, but the Mass at any time in the history of the Church when the Eucharist was held to be the literal flesh and blood of Christ, was "a most wicked infamy and unbearable blasphemy." Consequently, for a thousand years and more, the Fathers, saints and councils had been guilty of "blasphemy," and it took a French lawyer to set them straight. This is a type of spiritual Bolshevism, instantly decreeing that the past of the patriarchs is now criminal and subject to immediate abolition. It led Protestants to imagine it was their duty to imprison and kill all those like the Irish who clung to the Mass of the ancient Church. Moreover, Calvin expressed no similar level of thundering vitriol and five-alarm anathema for the *Talmudic blasphemy* that justified the murder of Jesus Christ (cf. BT Sanhedrin 43a; also Sanhedrin 107b and BT Gittin 57a).

"...economic liberty would be achieved precisely by the suppression of the capitalists' 'right' to set prices according to 'market forces.' In the fixing of prices at a just rate, you would have the entrance of moral considerations into the economic calculus ... the intrinsic value of the work of a man would be considered, rather than just questions of 'profitability.'"[251] Penty expanded on this:

"Unregulated currency gradually disintegrated the civilizations of Greece and Rome, and mankind had to wait until the Middle Ages before a solution was forthcoming, when it was provided by the Guilds in the light of the teaching of Christianity...What then was the solution provided by the Guilds? It was to stabilize currency by the institution of a Just and Fixed Price...They taught that to buy a thing for less or to sell a thing for more than its real value was in itself unallowable and unjust, and therefore sinful...

"This doctrine — that wares should be sold at a Just Price — together with another — that the taking of interest was sinful — was insisted upon by the Church, and obedience enforced from the pulpit, in the confessional and in the ecclesiastical courts," as well by the Guilds themselves, "whereby alone the reputation of the Guild for honorable dealing and sound workmanship can be carried on from generation to generation." Profiteering was punished by fines and in repeat offenses, by expulsion from the Guild, whereby a "man lost the privilege of following his trade or craft in his native city." Penty further observes: "...when in the thirteenth century the validity of the Just Price came to challenged by the lawyers, who maintained the right of every man to make the best bargain he could for himself, the moral sanction on

---

251 Peter Chojnowski, *The Gauntlet: A Challenge to the Myth of Progress* by Arthur J. Penty (an anthology of writings from 1917, 1922, 1923, 1932 & 1941).

which the maintenance of the Just Price ultimately rested, was undermined...”

Penty and his colleagues offered insight into how Capitalism uses debt to “anesthetize the populace” through the availability of “easy credit, which ultimately is not ‘easy’ at all on the borrower...Since we seem to be able to get all the things that we want, the reality of real money being increasingly unavailable to the average man is lost in the delusional state of the consumerist utopia. Only when the ‘benefit’ of usurious credit is cut off do we realize the full extent of the problem and the debt-slaves begin to rise up.”

Penty shows how the human spirit is impoverished by predatory Capitalism, striking at the heart of the contemporary debate over the loss of character in our leaders and youth. Fans of the current American system-of-things want to solve this dilemma by slapping externals and bromides onto our young people, who are urged to “discipline themselves, seek moral guidance, develop self-control.” To this is added a lament over single-parent households, feminism and the decline of the family. Yet all of these symptoms are traceable to the usury system of economics that is immune to criticism in these circles, being in these people’s minds, an axiom of American and Christian liberty.

The critical failure of vision is to be found in the inability to see “free market” Capitalism as *a revolutionary departure* from western civilization and Christian ethics. As Penty writes, “Aristotle and Aquinas each desired to restrict foreign trade within the narrowest limits, because of the economic and moral disorders which they recognized followed in their wake...It is only when a people live a local life, are rooted in local traditions, that they develop character...”

Underneath this departure from immemorial tradition is, according to Penty, the charlatans' mind control mantras of "progress" and "futurism":

"The charlatan, by appealing to the future while denying the past, discounts beforehand any possible criticism of his position, and cajoles the public into acquiescing in things they know to be wrong. Worst of all, belief in progress has silenced intelligent discussion of social and economic questions with the slogan, 'We can't go back,' unmindful of the fact that history abounds in such returns...Theories of Social Evolution provide a pseudo-scientific sanction to the idea of Progress."

Penty, like Pound, invokes the spiritual dimension of beauty and Art in traducing the severe decline in the ennoblement of man that is brought about by the Capitalist system. For example, he solves the riddle of how the process of "dumbing down to the lowest common denominator" that bedevils our culture across the board, from education to media, came to be:

"...the Qualitative Standard of the art inevitably conflicts with the Quantitative Standard of industrialism. It comes about this way. If you produce in (massive) quantities, you must, if you are to sell your products, take the world as you find it. From this it follows that you exclude everything that is above average....But to exclude everything that is above average is to exclude the best men and things. And this, in the long run, is fatal to society, for unless average men are in contact with persons and things higher than themselves, they tend, progressively, to degenerate. Society loses its salt by being deprived of true leadership, and because of this, the theory of averages in industry, as in politics, leads ever to a lower level...Well has it been said that our high standard of living is not really a high standard of living at all, but a high standard of wasting." [252]

Alas, Penty's admirable articulation of wisdom such as this, is disfigured in certain respects. In a brief digression into the jingoism of the wars of religion, he accepts at face value the poorly researched claims of Hilaire Belloc and other defenders of the star-chamber, "divine right" rule of the Anglican King Charles I. He reanimates stereotypes about the Puritans being "invariably" miserly Capitalists. He revives the canard that the Old Testament teaches that the virtuous man becomes materially prosperous; that the Puritans are "inhuman and anti-asethetic" and the "spirit behind industrialism." These reckless generalizations are grossly unfair, particularly in light of his own failure, common to many Catholic social justice and "distributist" activists, to offer one word of lament or warning concerning the popes who enabled usury. Penty's book is also peppered with troubling statements equating freedom of speech with "Liberalism," insinuating support for the abridgment of free speech and the use of force against "heretics." Penty's insights into modern commerce and the medieval system of social justice are sufficiently thought-provoking to merit consideration in spite of his errors.

---

252 Penty attributes the root of the dissolution of the Guilds to the revival of the laws of the Roman empire within medieval England: "...it is true to say that the ultimate cause of their (the Guilds) decline is to be traced to the revival of Roman law. The Guilds went down not because they were unfitted by their nature to grapple with the problems of a wider social intercourse, as historians have too hastily assumed, but because the moral sanctions on which they rested had been completely undermined by the revival of a system of law that gave legal sanction to usury and permitted speculation in prices."

John Ruskin

John Ruskin (1819-1900), of Scottish descent, was a product of a strict evangelical Protestant upbringing in England. An economic thinker as well as an aesthete, he combined extraordinary insight into medieval Catholic Gothic architecture, with fidelity to medieval Catholic economic teaching. Ruskin was Slade Professor of Fine Art at Oxford University and the bane of Victorian-era usurers. His many studies of art include *The Seven Lamps of Architecture*, and *The Stones of Venice*. His essay in volume two of the latter work, "The Nature of the Gothic," is suffused with exquisite discernment of the Christian spirit of the architecture of the Middle Ages.

In the 1870s Ruskin began to address a series of public letters to the English working class. One of these made its way into the literary magazine, *Contemporary Review,* in the December, 1879 issue. Ruskin's missive read in part: "I have never yet heard so much as *one* (preacher) heartily proclaiming against all those 'deceivers with vain words' that no 'covetous person, which is an idolater, hath *any* inheritance in the Kingdom of Christ and God;' and on myself personally and publicly challenging the Bishops of England generally, and by name the Bishop of Manchester, to say whether usury was, or was not, according to the will of God. I have received no answer from any one of them."

The Anglican Bishop of Manchester, Dr. James Fraser, sent a reply which was published two months later, along with Ruskin's rejoinder.[253] Bishop Fraser wrote, "...in the old law there is no denunciation of usury in general...It seems to me plain also that our Blessed Lord's precept about 'lending, hoping for nothing again' (Luke vi. 35)...was simply intended to

---

253 "Usury: A Reply and a Rejoinder," *Contemporary Review*, February, 1880, pp. 314-339.

govern a Christian man's conduct to the poor and needy...and cannot, without a violent twist, be construed into a general law determining forever and in all cases the legitimate use of capital."

In the words of a Ruskin biographer, Edward Cook, Ruskin's rejoinder "proceeds with ruthless exactitude" in "the condemnation of 'usury' by the text of the Bible and by the authority of learned divines." He begins his rejoinder to the bishop by quoting a prayer recited in the Church of England:

"Have mercy upon all Jews, Turks, infidels, and heretics, and so fetch them home, blessed Lord, to Thy flock, that they may be saved among the remnant of the true Israelites."

Ruskin then asks, "Who *are* the true Israelites, my Lord of Manchester? ...Have they any underhanded dealings with the liable-to-be-damned false Israelites: Rothschilds and the like?

"...What I mean by that word (usury), my Lord...(is) what David and his Son (Jesus) meant by it. I have prayed your Lordship to tell your flock, in the name of the Church which dictates the songs of the one, and professes to interpret to them the command of the other. And although I can easily conceive that a Bishop at the court of the Third Richard might have paused in reply to a too curious layman's question of what was meant by "murder,"[254] and can also conceive a Bishop at the court of the Second Charles hesitating as to the significance of the word Adultery[255]...at no time, nor under any conditions, can I conceive any question existing as to the meaning of the words...*foenus, usura*, or usury: and I trust that your Lordship will at once

---

254 The last of England's Plantagenet monarchs, King Richard III (1452-1485), was suspected of the murder of his two young nephews and his own wife.

255 England's Anglo-Catholic King Charles II (1630-1685) was a notorious philanderer and the keeper of numerous mistresses; Nell Gwyn being the best known.

acquit me of wishing to attach any other significance to the word than that which it was to the full intended to convey on every occasion of its use by Moses, by David, by Christ, and by the Doctors of the Christian Church...Usury in any degree is asserted by the Doctors of the early Church to be sinful, just as theft and adultery are asserted to be sinful, though neither may have been accompanied with violence; and although the theft may have been on the most splendid scale, and the fornication of the most courtly refinement...."

"Thy True Heritage"

It may seem like the height of naiveté and pipe-dreaming in this "money-get mechanic age," as playwright Ben Jonson presaged our modern era, to do battle against a seemingly Universal Shylock System. Yet that system, in planetary terms, is not as all-encompassing as the Federal Reserve Bank and the International Monetary Fund would wish; several hundred million Muslims have not yet succumbed to it, and it is also in broad disrepute in Latin America.

Here in the United States, Shylock's prize cheap labor colony, the battle for the good and the true, and what the Old Testament terms "the old paths," is more than a matter of economics. How we order commerce and trade is but a reflection of the spiritual consciousness we choose to project and by which we envision the world. The whole point of berating mammon worship is to give testimony to a higher power. Contrary to the delusions of the age, we do not preserve our families or our nation by money and materiel, but by a transcendent and indestructible love that no power on earth can take from us.

"What thou lov'st well shall not be reft from thee/ What thou lov'st well is thy true heritage." (Ezra Pound).

9

"Jewish" Usury

If but a probable suspicion arose
of a man to occupy that filthy trade [256]
He was taken for a devil in the likeness of a man.
But good Lord, how is the world changed?

That which infidels cannot abide, Gospellers allow,
That which Jews take only of strangers
and will not take of their countrymen for shame,
That do Christians take of their dear friends
and think for so doing they deserve great thanks.

Thomas Rogers
Good Lord, how is the world changed? [257]

The erudite Puritan compiler of the customs of Shakespearean England, Philip Stubbes, wrote, "...he that kills a man, rids him of his pains at once, but he that takes usury is long in butchering his patient, suffering him little by little to anguish and sucking out his heart blood...a usurer is worse than a Jew, for they to this day will not take any usury of their brethren, according to the law of God." [258]

---

256 Filthy trade: usury.

257 Quoted by William Cunningham, *The Growth of English Industry and Commerce*, vol. 1, p. 76. Thomas Rogers (ca. 1555-1616), was an Anglican theologian and the translator of both *The Imitation of Christ,* and Philipp Caesar's *A General Discourse Against the Damnable Sect of Usurers*.

258 Philip Stubbes, *Anatomy of Abuses* (London, 1583), chapter eight.

Rogers and Stubbes were not alone in breaking with our modern observers of the history of usury who regard it as having been largely a case of "Jews" preying on Christians. The idea that Christian usurers were worse than "Jews," was widespread in the Middle Ages and the Renaissance; a sentiment that is mostly lost to history now. St. Bernard of Clairvaux asserted that some Christian moneylenders acted "worse than any Jew."[259] Even though it is little remarked upon or studied, St. Bernard's sentiment was not uncommon among Christian leaders of his or subsequent eras. [260]

We could not write of usury in Christendom without touching upon the "Jewish" role, of course. In most modern books on the subject, this "Jewish" role occupies the whole or the better part of the entire study. For us it is the reverse. Our concentration is on bringing into focus the largely neglected chronicle of non-Judaic usury in Christendom, which has generally escaped scrutiny. In the history of ideas, the ideology responsible for gentile usury has successfully eluded study, and therefore it has also escaped responsibility for the legacy of its sins and crimes.

There is no doubt however, that Christendom was much occupied with the Judaic variety:

"The term 'usurer,' meaning either 'illicit moneylender' or simply 'moneylender,' was considered practically synonymous with the term 'Jew.' Many

---

[259] *The Letters of St. Bernard of Clairvaux* (London, 1953), trans. Bruno James, no. 391.

[260] Cf. for example Sebastian Brant in his 1493 work, *The Ship of Fools* where he writes of "Christian" usurers worse than Jews; contrast McTeague's insanely covetous gentile wife with the Judaic miser in *McTeague* by Frank Norris, or Oliver's half-brother Monks who is shown to be worse than Fagin in *Oliver Twist*. Liam O'Flaherty wrote: "In every little town in Ireland you will find a man like Ramon Mor, a grabber, who makes his money by worse usury than Shylock ever practiced." (*The House of Gold*, p. 18).

thirteenth-century discussions of usury perpetuated these impressions: Robert de Courson, for example, stated in the section of his *Summa* dealing with usury that 'Jews have nothing except what they have gained through usury.'

"This sentence is repeated verbatim in the contemporary *Summa* for confessors by the English cleric Thomas of Chobham (formerly a colleague of Courson at the University of Paris), and probably reflects widespread popular conceptions in England and on the Continent...by the early thirteenth century lending at interest had indeed become an important factor in Jewish economic life...Similarly, the term 'usurer' was used virtually interchangeably with 'Jew' in secular texts, and regulation of usury generally figures prominently in sections of both secular and ecclesiastical legislation assigned to Jewish issues. The Fourth Lateran Council's legislation concerning usury, for example, occurs in the context of the canons dealing with the Jews. The employment of images of Jews to illustrate textual references to usurers in the *Bible moralisée* mirrors this tendency to equate the terms.

"However, the concept 'Jew' was not only employed by Christian theologians as a synonym for 'usurer'; it also frequently functioned as a synecdoche (a figure in which a less inclusive term is used for a more inclusive term), as 'Jews came to stand for the entire practice of moneylending and its negative economic effects as a whole. Bernard of Clairvaux used the term *judaizare* to mean any form of moneylending, and the Council of Paris (1213) called financial institutions 'synagogues for the wicked." [261]

[261] Sara Lipton, op. cit., pp. 33-34.

"Judaizers" and "Judaizing"

While Judaic usury was considered particularly malevolent, in that it was perhaps, more often than not, used as a weapon of warfare by people outside the Christian ethos and distinctly hostile to it, there has been an attempt to paint the Christian campaign against usury as predominantly a racist ("anti-semitic") act, with canon law and secular legislation targeting usury among gentiles mostly an afterthought, or a by-product of "biased" agitation aimed primarily at Judaic usury. This hypothesis rests on the supposition that a hidden agenda was at work and that usury was not the principal offense. Rather, the actual transgression supposedly consisted in being of Judaic descent. Gavin I. Langmuir writing in his *Toward a Definition of Antisemitism*,[262] states, "Although there is no doubt that Jewish moneylending began to arouse hostility in northern Europe by the middle of the twelfth century, it was their Jewishness rather than their 'usury' that made their lending seem particularly bad." Mr. Langmuir's allegation is an extreme distortion. As we have seen, prior to the Renaissance, usury by *anyone* was a grievous transgression on the basis of the inherent moral turpitude present within the act itself. The claim that usurers were pursued mainly based on "anti-semitic" criteria is not sustained by the documentary record. Such a perception presupposes that gentile usurers were left unmolested to ply their trade. Actually, the reverse was true. In many cases usury was permitted to Judaic persons, in part because they were unbaptized and therefore outside the jurisdiction of

---

262 University of California Press, 1996, p. 368.

Church discipline,[263] as well as due to the chicanery and criminal politics of certain "Christian" rulers who sought usurious financing and went beyond the Christian community to obtain it.

These monarchs and aristocrats, even before 1500, permitted some degree of license for Judaic usury, partly to finance their own various enterprises and wars, (or with a view to taxing Judaic usury and gaining revenue from it), while mostly forbidding the gentile version, except in certain city-states of Italy such as Venice and Florence which gave birth to gentile usury. "In 1396, the Florentine commune instructed the priors to invite the Jews to lend in the city, but the proposal was not implemented...In 1430, there was another fruitless attempt to invite the Jews into Florence; only with the rise of the Medici, at the end of 1437, did Jewish money-lenders begin to operate in Florence...money-lending in Florence itself, unlike in the surrounding territory,[264] was practiced only by Christians as there were no Jews living in Florence (in the fourteenth and early fifteen centuries)."[265] Another factor to ponder is the degree to which "Christian" usurers helped to make an issue out of Judaic usury as a smokescreen to draw attention from their own usury. This ploy has cachet even today when Christian discussion of usury is misdirected by associations in the public mind with the "Jewish Shylock," since so little is known about the gentile Shylock, with the exception of another

---

[263] On ecclesiastical jurisdiction, cf. Thomas Pink's paper, "What is the Catholic Doctrine of Religious Liberty?;" Conference on Natural Law, Cambridge University Center for Research in the Arts, Sciences and Humanities, Sept. 10, 2009.

[264] "Surrounding territory" – the outlying towns in the Florentine state as well as beyond it; cities such as Siena, Padua, Perugia, Pisa and Lucca. From 1382 to 1397 Judaics obtained the right to conduct their business and reside in Venice.

[265] Nirit Ben-Aryeh Debby, op. cit., p. 179.

stereotype, the Puritan/Calvinist who is inevitably portrayed as both a usurer and a "Judaizer." [266]

In truth, interest on money obtained de facto permissibility in the West, due to a gradual relaxation of usury law enforcement by the Catholic Church, sparked by toleration for usury on the part of radical, but eventually mainstream, Roman Catholic theology that gained the attention of early Protestant thinkers and leaders. The perspective on the roots of usury in western Christendom has been misdirected by a focus that has been almost exclusively on the "Jews" and their supposed subversive agents, "the Protestants."

Judaic financiers who came to be allied with gentile banking houses, gained firm purchase in the West as a result of a symbiotic partnership of mutual

---

[266] "Judaizer" is sometimes absurdly applied to Martin Luther, the author of the incendiary volume, *Von den Juden und ihren Lügen* ("On the Jews and their Lies"). Peter Milward in *Shakespeare the Papist,* argues that Shylock in *The Merchant of Venice,* though presented "on the level of the story" as a Jew, was intended to be understood as a Puritan, in line with the Elizabethan public's "ideas about the Puritans." Actually, the view of Puritans as synonymous with usurers was a recusant Catholic one, shared by Shakespeare's alleged spiritual guide, Jesuit Father Robert Southwell. That Shakespeare may have been a crypto-Catholic and accepted the conflation of Puritans and usurers, does not signify that the Elizabethan masses accepted it. Theatre-goers would have been more jaundiced toward Puritans, given Puritan polemics against cross-dressing actors and play-acting in general. To accept that the English would have shared Southwell's identification of Puritans as notorious money-lenders, one would have to be nearly completely ignorant of the extent to which the Puritans publicly agitated against usury in pamphlets and pulpits, associating it with the "pope's rags." Fr. Southwell's prejudice toward Puritans (understandable in that he was a hunted fugitive), was a product of his less than objective perspective. While Shakespeare may have been under the Jesuit's influence, that possibility does not serve to confirm Southwell's stereotype of Puritans as loan sharks. Moreover, Shakespeare's Roman Catholic father was himself a usurer. Perhaps Shylock should have been named John: "In 1570 one John Shakespeare of Stratford was fined 40 shillings for charging an astonishing £20 interest for a one month £80 loan..." —Charles Edelman, "Which is the Jew that Shakespeare Knew?" in *Shakespeare Survey 52: Shakespeare and the Globe*, p. 103.

profit to both. This was due to the avarice of both, with some Judaic persons operating within and against Christendom by using a modern capitalist praxis unrestrained by considerations of ethics. In the rabbinic world, usury had always been recognized as a tool of warfare against the *goyim*. Talmudic *halakha* encourages the taking of interest from Christians and gentiles: "Christianity: Since that faith involves acceptance of other gods, almost all authority permit loans at interest...It is preferable to loan money at interest to a gentile..." [267]

The gentile banking dynasties would not have been in a position to form alliances with Judaic financiers and slowly dissolve the stigma on usurious finance, were it not for the relaxation of usury laws that formerly had restrained this transgression in Christendom. In other words, while the Money Power benefited enormously from the liberalization of usury prohibitions in Europe and America, the liberalization itself was primarily the fault of gentiles, not Judaics. Therefore, to direct blame for the dissolution of Christian usury doctrine mainly toward "Judaizing" is a sly way of exculpating the gentile malefactors responsible for permitting the crime of usury. Consequently, in this regard, the "Judaizing" caricature has served to conceal the identity of the advocates of usury and impede the process whereby we discover how usury came to be legal and "moral" in Christendom. [268] The stratagem has consisted in

---

[267] Rabbi Ezra Basri, *Ethics of Business and Finance and Charity According to Jewish Law*, vol. 1, chapter 16, "Loans at Interest to Gentiles, Apostates, and the Like." This is a modern book published in 1987 and authored by the Chief Justice of the District Court of Jerusalem.

[268] The term "Judaizing" is regarded by the politically correct standards of our times as a racial slur, and never an objective, unbiased description of historical movements and trends. Fathers of the Church such as St. John Chyrsostom used the term scripturally and without racial prejudice.

throwing investigators off the track by tossing responsibility for the momentous change with regard to usury in Christendom entirely in the lap of Judaics and those Protestants stigmatized as Judaizers. The documentary record testifies to the contrary.

Misdirection from the Right

One major source of this misdirection is Werner Sombart (1863-1941), who, after Max Weber, was the most influential German economist in the period between the two world wars. In his 1911 book *Die Juden und das Wirtschaftsleben*, which was translated into English as *The Jews and Modern Capitalism*, Sombart taught that the Old Testament was the source of the capitalist predation perpetrated by the "Jews," to whom he ascribed the development in Europe of free trade and *laissez-faire* capitalism.[269] The strict observance of Sunday as a day of rest from commerce and labor in England, the study of Hebrew and the Hebrew Old Testament, the naming of Scottish children with Old Testament patronymics, all were cited by Sombart as evidence of the nefarious rabbinic dominion over Puritanism. He writes: "Only recently Max Weber demonstrated the connection between Puritanism and Capitalism. In fact, Max Weber's researches are responsible for this book. For any one who followed them could not but ask himself whether all that Weber ascribes to Puritanism might not with equal justice be referred to Judaism, and probably in greater degree; nay, it might well be suggested that that which is called Puritanism is in reality Judaism... there is an almost unique identity of view between Judaism and Puritanism...Puritanism *is* Judaism." [270]

---

269 Sombart, *The Jews and Modern Capitalism*, (The Free Press, 1951), p. 248.

270 Ibid., pp.191-192; 248-249.

While Weber held the Old Testament responsible for the ascendance of *predatory capitalism in the West*, German New Age philosophers in Adolf Hitler's early circle, such as Dietrich Eckart, indicted the Old Testament as the evil inspiration for the *Communist revolution in Russia*, as the title of Eckart's influential 1925 pamphlet indicates: *Der Bolschewismus von Moses bis Lenin* ("Bolshevism from Moses to Lenin"). While it is true that twentieth century German nationalists distrusted the papacy and thought of it as an anti-Teutonic force in history, Catholicism was viewed as less toxic than Calvinism, because Catholics were thought to be in some degree hostile to, or at the least, less guided by, the Old Testament.

Right wing animus toward the Old Testament intensifies among those who subscribe to the thesis of Douglas Reed (1895-1976), former foreign correspondent of the London *Times,* in his book *The Controversy of Zion.*[271] Mr. Reed identified nearly every form of evil committed by Zionism or Orthodox Judaism with either the doctrines of the Old Testament or the Talmud. In blending the two, it never occurred to him (or to Sombart), that the Talmud represents, as Jesus stated in Matthew 15 and Mark 7 concerning its oral form, the *nullification of the Old Testament.* Jesus and the apostles quoted the Old Testament a total of approximately 287 times. The attack on the Old Testament is the Marcion heresy, and it constitutes an attack on the very doctrine of Jesus, who taught from the Old Testament repeatedly.

Furthermore, from Belloc to Sombart, it seems that no paleo-Right-winger can pass by the figure of Oliver Cromwell without transforming him into the *representative Puritan of the ages*, using irresponsible generalizations that would be risible, if they did not so seriously delude and mislead concerning the Puritan

---

[271] Durban, South Africa: Dolphin Press, 1978.

movement. Take for instance Sombart's statement that "the Jews in England in the 17th century were held in very high esteem by the Puritans." [272]

What "Jews in England"? Sombart himself admits that three years after Cromwell's death, "in 1661 there were only 35 Jewish families in London." [273]

Sombart also writes, "Cromwell himself dreamed of a reconciliation between the Old and New Testaments..." We've got news for Professor Weber: the reconciliation already happened. It's called Christianity.

The effect of Sombart's mythomania has been to draw attention away from the instrumental role which the Renaissance Vatican acted in the ascendance of the Money Power, as well as the power of Neoplatonist occultists who arose, not surprisingly, in those areas of Italy and Germany where Catholic usury was most virulent. With these factors in the rise of mammonism in the Church concealed, the Puritans take center stage in the Right's fractured history of religion's impact on British and European economics from the fifteenth to the seventeenth century.

The Puritans represented an enormous range of diverse views concerning Judaism, including large pockets of hostility and resistance, centered on the Puritan conviction that rabbinic Judaism nullified the Old Testament. This was the firm belief of the Puritan leader who Sombart, Belloc and other mythologizers ignore, William Prynne (1601-1669), member of Parliament, author of more than sixty books and pamphlets, and the principal organizer of the Puritan parliament's stubborn obstruction of Cromwell's mercenary plan to allow Judaic immigration to England. The gaping hole in paleo-Right-wing biographies of Cromwell is the historical fact that the

---

272 Sombart, op. cit., p. 249.

273 Ibid., p. 185.

Puritan Parliament resoundingly rebuffed his proposal, and Cromwell lost prestige and influence among the English Puritans for having sought to advance his scheme. This weakening of support was a contributing factor in the dissolution of his regime.

Yes, of course, there were Puritan exegetes enamored of Rabbi Moses Maimonides, just as there were Medici-sponsored Florentine Neoplatonists enamored of Kabbalist rabbis. Would Catholics like to have Sombart and Belloc's tactics turned on them, and have saints such as Joseph of Cupertino, John Bosco and Thérese of Lisieux, all slimed with accusations of occult Neoplatonism because of the beliefs of an elite Vatican cabal? If those accusations would be a gross injustice, how then does the philo-Judaism of one faction of Puritanism taint all or even most Puritans? In hundreds of Puritan pamphlets and sermons there are denunciations of rabbinic tradition. There are learned Puritan books wholly excoriating the rabbis for adulterating the Old Testament with Talmudic traditions. [274] Because there was no pope in Calvinism (Calvin was only the "pope" of Geneva, and that's not entirely fair, since he did not ever enjoy absolute rule there), the matter of Puritan attitudes toward Judaism was never definitively resolved, and remains to this day a serious debate in the remnants of the Puritan Church extant.

What we are encountering with these half-truth caricatures of Puritans, is in some cases abysmal ignorance, [275] and in others intellectual dishonesty

---

[274] Cf. for instance, *A Short Demurrer to the Jews' Long Discontinued Remitter into England* (London: Edward Thomas, 1656).

[275] Marilynne Robinson observes that the modern consensus on the Puritans "is a great example of our collective eagerness to disparage without knowledge or information about the thing disparaged, when the reward is the pleasure of sharing an attitude one knows is socially approved" (*The Death of Adam*, p. 153).

from partisans who disseminate demonstrable falsehoods, and turn history into a *maison enchantée,* where the inhabitants have no true understanding of how the Money Power came to rule them, because the history is condensed into an almost exclusively Puritan-Protestant scapegoat narrative, which is swallowed by the naive, and gulped by bigots who search history not to discover knowledge and truth, but to find arguments that will confirm their prejudices and monomania. In so far as that habit of mind has been associated with religion, it has contributed to the agnosticism of our time.

Catholics and independents of good will and fair mind ought to pause long enough to thoughtfully consider whether the elisions of this scapegoat process serve the cause of Christ's truth, and whether they empower us with the knowledge we need to decode the criminal politics of the past, the better to navigate the civic and ecclesiastical crime syndicates of the present. The Right wing libels noted above have occluded our vision with a myopia that conceals the trail to those money-intoxicated churchmen who first sold our birthright to the usurers, in exchange for a golden repast whose sumptuous fare is as inexhaustible as the compound interest that is its source. The anti-Puritan libelers pay little or no attention to the modernizing Catholic nominalism that emerged in the fifteenth century, and provided a philosophical rationale for the gradual erosion of the war against Mammon.

Where do we find in the pages of Sombart, Chesterton or Belloc an exposé of nominalist intrigue?

"...economic ideas of the mercantilists fostering the growth of market capitalism moved from public tracts to public policy and became institutionalized in new economic arrangements only in those regions where nominalistic epistemologies took root and weakened the constraints of scholasticism. Where mercantilists' nominalist thinking supported the relaxation of regulations, the increases in monetary supply influenced the transition from medieval organization of finance, industry, and trade to capitalistic forms. Mercantilists sought to affect public policy without explicit recourse to arguments derived logically from bodies of doctrine. They attempted to describe how economic relations should be ordered without applying abstract rules of distributive and commutative justice that were thought, by theologians at least, to be infused with real significance for the cosmos and the individual's economy of salvation. The sharp line that scholastic thinkers inclined to realism drew between licit and illicit behavior was blurred by the introduction among mercantilists inclined toward nominalism, of an intermediate group of morally neutral actions, including the pursuance of self-interest in the economic sphere. Self-interest, perceived by the scholastics in religious and classical ethical terms of avarice and greed, was transvaluated by the mercantilists into a cause of civil happiness." [276]

Renaissance Catholic Nominalism seriously eroded the Thomistic principle of real value, and opened the way for the metaphysical fraud behind the unnatural act of breeding money from money. This perversion occurred decades before the birth of John Calvin. Those who seek to have us commence our study of interest on money with "Calvin and the Jews" are shielding perpetrators of usury from scrutiny and exposure.

Cui bono?

---

[276] Hillel Levine, p. 91. Levine sees nominalism metastasizing from Renaissance Catholicism into "Protestant chiliasm."

Medieval Catholic scholasticism, as Prof. Christopher A. Franks[277] and others have shown, inspired the promulgation and enforcement of laws against usury with a new literalness. This move was consonant with the historic identification of the Church as *the final arbiter of the real*, both in the sense of the "Real Presence of Christ" in the Eucharist, and the real presence of value as represented by God-given resources and labor. Nominalism transformed money from a medium of exchange to a "value" in itself. This philosophic counterfeit typified the emergence of a Renaissance philosophy wherein image prevailed over reality, and from hence forward, in spite of public exhortations harkening to Catholic verities of the past intended mainly for consumption by the masses, the abandonment of real value proceeded inside Catholic hierarchical circles with the march of usury toleration and legalization; commensurate with the opening to a Neoplatonism that viewed rabbinic Judaism as a repository of an esoteric "wisdom" which complimented and propelled the evolutionary development of Catholic doctrine. Is it a coincidence that as interest on Fugger loans in Germany and *monte pietatis* interest on "loans to the poor" in Italy were condoned or approved by the Church, Roman Catholicism began to lose its authority as final arbiter of the real? The move away from that authority reached its omega point in 1965 – less than a half century after the promulgation of the 1917 Code of Canon Law which contained the most complete and unambiguous legalization of interest on money in the history of the Church. It was in 1965 that the Second Vatican Council issued the declaration *Dignitatis Humanae*, which represented as astonishing a

---

277 *He Became Poor: The Poverty of Christ and Aquinas's Economic Teachings,* op. cit.

departure from medieval Catholic dogma as Canon 1543 of the 1917 Code. [278]

Modernism's false accounting of the Catholic faith had its earliest root not in Rousseau or Kant, as the habitués of the playpen school of infantile history are forever talking about, but in fifteenth century Catholic nominalism's recalculation of net losses and gains, with new bookkeeping methods under rules divorced from the accounting of real value, in favor of bills of exchange based not on agriculture or industry, but the artifice of usurious generation. The growth of the cheat that is market capitalism was fueled by the growth of the illusions put forth by Catholic nominalism. How can this ominous fact be blamed mainly on "the Jews" or "the Puritans"?

It cannot even be said that Catholicism itself can be faulted, if we take the view that the True Church was captured by anti-Catholic heretic-usurpers who fabricated a Renaissance institution which cast off the substance of the ancient Catholic ecclesia that had existed, as the sworn enemy of the Money Power, from Apostolic times through the Middle Ages. Whether or not one accepts this conspiracy theory, the fact is that nominalism was a spiritual virus, a bacterial decay organism which grew from the manure of Fugger gold. What shameful trait is revealed in those who struggle to find in this Catholic drama a Judaic hand, or a

---

[278] On June 30, 2012, Pope Benedict XVI wrote with his own hand a letter to the Superior General of the Society of St. Pius X (SSPX). It was signed personally by the pope: "I confirm to you in fact [that], in order [for you] to be truly reintegrated into the Church it is necessary to truly accept the Second Vatican Council and the post-conciliar Magisterium." In other words, the members of the SSPX, and any other person that seeks to be recognized as Catholic by Rome, must accept the truthfulness and validity of *Dignitatis Humanae,* and all other constitutions, decrees and declarations of Vatican II, which, the pope says, are part of the Magisterium of the Church since the council. [For testimony concerning the provenance of this letter cf. http://rorate-caeli.blogspot.com/2012/09/important-with-popes-own-signature.html]

Calvinist finger? Is it so impossible for the gentile heirs of the Catholic progenitors of usury to take responsibility and sincerely utter the words, "*Mea maxima culpa,*" and then proceed to an investigative reckoning with history, free of sectarian bias? Until we stop trying to read into the chronicle of the past only that which confirms our pre-conceived beliefs, while suppressing whatever frightens us with a truth we dare not countenance, we cannot be the people God has destined us to be.

Primacy of Gentile Usury in Economic History

We have presented in these pages evidence of a substantial corpus of theological and penal impediments to usury in Christendom, from its founding through the year 1500. These were by no means limited to, or specifically crafted for, Judaic persons.[279] How could it be otherwise? Usury was defined *de fide* as destructive of the spiritual welfare and eternal destiny of humanity as a whole, and this was never denied by the true Church, which viewed interest on money as a moral contagion which gives rise to other grave evils, and to the abasement of the nation at large.

After the expulsion of Judaics from England by King Edward I in 1290, there was no relaxation or abridgment of the legal and ecclesiastical proscriptions against usury. Interest on money bore the same iniquitous stigma in post-Expulsion England as it always had, although undoubtedly the association, in the popular mind, between usury and Judaizing remained strong. To the medieval mind, a Judaic

---

279 "The State thus followed up the Church condemnation of usury by confiscating the property of those who died in that 'sin' (usury). In this regard equal measure was dealt out to both Jew and Christian, and if a Jew's property fell into the King's hand at his death that would be no more than would happen if a Christian were a usurer." — Joseph Jacobs, *The Jews of Angevin England: Documents and Records*, p. 49-51.

nation that institutionalized in its religion the execration of Jesus Christ was viewed as more prone to engage in sinister practices, including taking interest on loans of money. Christians perceived that usury was alien to the Gospel and therefore alien to sincere followers of Jesus, making a Christian who was a usurer a perverse and unnatural creature; whereas usury, being unscrupulous, was viewed as normative for "the Jew," who was thought to have few scruples, beginning with the fact that he did not scruple to follow Christ.

Until the late eighteenth century, Judaism existed almost exclusively as Orthodox Judaism— a Talmudic, not a Biblical religion. In violation of the Word of God, the Mishnah and its innumerable successor texts created loopholes, often times ingenious, for charging interest on loans to *fellow Judaic persons*, not just against pagan aliens and nations with which they were at war, as the Scripture allows. We have for example the Pharisee Hillel's abrogation (*prozbul*) in Mishnah Shebit 10:3 of the Mosaic institution for the forgiveness of debt (Deuteronomy 15: 1-2).

Shmuel Safrai points out (in *The Literature of the Sages*, Part One, p. 164), that in the Gittin Tractate, the Babylonian Talmud nullifies the Biblical teaching concerning usury and money-lending: "Hillel decreed the *prozbul* for the betterment of the world. The prozbul is a legal fiction which allows debts to be collected after the Sabbatical year and it was Hillel's intention thereby to overcome the fear that money-lenders had of losing their money."

To free God's people from perpetual indebtedness, the Old Testament mandated that as part of the sabbatical (seventh) year of release (*shemitta*), outstanding loans made to fellow Israelites must be annulled (Deuteronomy 15:1-2; Nehemiah 10:31). Hillel's *prozbul* created a loophole which handed supervision of the loan to the *beit din* (rabbinic court), thereby allowing the creditor to collect his debt even after the sabbatical year. Hillel's abrogation of the Mosaic institution for the forgiveness of debts is an instructive example of the Pharisaic nullification of God's law. We note that the deceitful commentary on Deut. 15:1-3 in the "English Standard Version" *ESV Study Bible* [280] supports the Pharisee Hillel's position: "All debts between Israelites are to be canceled or merely deferred for one year." *There is no Biblical basis for this claim of debts being "deferred."* The *ESV Study Bible* is paying heed to the rabbinic Mishnah over the Word of God in the Old Testament; a betrayal typical of modern Churchianity.

In this study we have found that guilt for the actions of revolutionary traitors – the rendering, as legal and moral, of financial transactions consisting of interest on money – falls squarely on the shoulders of Catholic popes, cardinals, bishops, theologians and monarchs, and Protestant bishops, presbyters, preachers and monarchs.

The opprobrious phrase, "Judaizing Protestants," wielded in connection with usury, is a function of ignorance and selective indignation: ignorance of the enduring legacy of the heretical papal permission for usury, and selective indignation toward Protestant variants of ideas and beliefs pioneered by Catholics.

We have heard and read of Catholics sneering at what they revile as "the miserly usury and Judaizing of the city of Amsterdam," with reference to that Protestant citadel from the seventeenth century onward. These same self-righteous critics are silent however, concerning the usury of the city of Florence, which preceded the decay in Amsterdam *by two hundred years*.

Judaic moneylenders were sometimes used as an alibi for gentile usury: "Cosimo's own ambassador to

---

280 Crossway Bibles, 2007, p. 354.

Pope Julius III had heard the pontiff say that he tolerated this rate of interest (ten to twelve percent), the Pisans told the duke, because only in this way could the even higher interest rates of the Jews be avoided."[281]

In our reading of eminent Christian observers of usury in history such as G.K. Chesterton, we are struck by the extent to which they convey a distinct impression of a proprietary relationship between "Jews" and the practice of usury. Whether deliberate or unconscious, this emphasis causes the record of gentile usury and its infiltration of the Church to vanish by the wayside. Chesterton's essay, "The Problem of Zionism,"[282] in which he gives an account of usury, is well-crafted and in some sections, sagacious. But his concentration is almost entirely on Judaic rather than gentile usury. The latter barely exists in his universe. Here is Chesterton, an illustrious savant of the West, ignoring a vital factor in the history of how the Money Power ascended to dominion over our civilization.

One of the heretofore hidden routes which gentile usurers accessed on their path to power was the exploitation of the fear of Judaic usurers. They stampeded Christendom from the frying pan of rabbinic usury into the fire of gentile usury, and people were supposed to be elated that they were being burned by their fellow Christians rather than "those awful Jews." The failure to exhume and investigate this swindle and all its networks and personalities, has cost us dearly, and profited the Money Power incalculably.

Like Dante Alighieri, Girolamo Savonarola turned his attention to the struggle against interest on loans

---

281 Menning, op. cit. p. 238.

282 Collected in the 1920 anthology, *The New Jerusalem* (London: Thomas Nelson).

of money. But unlike Dante, he centered his campaign on Judaic lenders. In the name of fighting "the Jews" his colleague, Marco di Latteo Strozzi, pushed for a *monte di pieta* "charity bank" that would facilitate the commission of mortal sin by charging "moderate" interest, thereby supposedly foiling the Judaic usurers who charged a high rate of interest. The fact that interest whether high or low was a mortal sin, got lost in the hysteria over the Judaics. Partly through that hysteria, interest gained a foothold in Christendom.

In 1494 a book was circulated by an ally of the Strozzi family in Florence. It was titled *Tabula della salute.* It contained examples of huge profits reaped by high-interest Judaic loans. One chapter was titled, "Of the Good and Utility of Creating a Holy *Monte di Pieta.*" It urged the people to put their money in the hands of the administrators of the "benevolent" *monte*, not in the clutches of the "malicious Jews." It insinuated a good and bad category of interest on money that still afflicts our thinking nowadays.

The Catholic administrators of the *Monte di Pieta* were also usurers. This could not be admitted, however. A farcical denial was put into place that went to elaborate lengths of semantic subtlety to conceal the truth. Operating according to the guidelines of the purported Jew-hater Strozzi, "...the *monte* was above all to avoid any taint of usury. Yet in the exercise of charity, it was both necessary and permissible to expect some small return on loans...To redeem the pledge, the borrower had to pay a fee small enough not to burden the borrower, but large enough to keep the *monte di pieta* in the black; the Jews had, after all, charged much higher rates for their usurious loans."[283]

A test of the lucidity of visionaries and prophets lies in whether they can see past this cunning dodge and

---

283 Menning, op. cit., p. 48.

indict the usurious "Christians" who were attempting to distract attention away from themselves, in order to pin it exclusively on the "Jews." Or, to absolve their usury by pointing to the claim that it represented a form of rescue from Judaic power and oppression. The problem with this type of thinking was that it was blatantly unscriptural. Usury was not to be charged to a fellow believer according to the Old Testament, and was not to be imposed on anyone whomever, according to the New Testament (Luke 6:34-35).

Dante was *not* seduced by the gentile usurer's scapegoating feint. Ezra Pound, having drunk deeply from Dante's fountain, immunized himself against the forces that would attempt to create a trademark out of the image of the Judaic-as-usurer, sending the record of gentile usury and the treachery inside the Church which brought it about, down the memory hole. Chesterton and many of his generation (Belloc, Sayers), were myopic in this respect. They furthered retrograde myths of a near Judaic monopoly on usury, and the nearly exclusive association of the money-lender with "the children of Israel," as Dorothy L. Sayers styled them in one of her Lord Peter Wimsey mystery novels.

Many individuals, especially Catholics, who, in the twenty-first century are seeking to make sense of the consumer greed and mercantile madness that has seized hold of our society, have been influenced by Chesterton, Belloc and the others of their erudite and highly cultured generation, and are therefore misdirected away from exploring the record of Renaissance Catholic usury and treachery. Many such people are in a hypnotic state, distributing papal encyclicals and urging others to convert to post-Renaissance papist Rome as a means of fighting for "social justice." In their minds, usury comes from "out there" – the alien Judaic and Protestant worlds. These Catholics, many of them of undoubted good will and pure hearts, have been hoodwinked by the suppression of the authentic history of their own Church, and are living a lie as result; which is one reason why their various Distributist, Chesterton/Belloc think tanks and fraternities have been so impotent. Thomistic scholasticism is concerned with proceeding from first principles. Catholics who aspire to the intellectual standard of Aquinas ought to proceed first from the historical fact that since the Renaissance, the popes of Rome have radically departed from the Catholic Faith of their Fathers, and either enabled usury or tolerated it, by letting stand their predecessors' heretical moves in favor of it.

The field of study becomes hopelessly muddled when it is mainly the Rothschilds who are made infamous as archetypes of financial comspiracy and manipulation, while the Medici and the Fuggers are mentioned in passing, when mentioned at all. Certainly Rothschild banking deserves and has earned notoriety and opprobrium. Yet hundreds of years before Amschel Moses Rothschild was peddling cloth in the ghetto of Frankfurt, the banking house of Fugger was buying theologians and importuning them into rendering the Fugger's thieving usury, respectable. The fact that the name Rothschild is notorious in Right wing and populist circles, and the Fuggers and their successors are a mere footnote in the annals of financial chicanery, is not an accident. In some cases, gentile usurers urged Catholic sermons and campaigns against Judaic usurers in order to clear the field of their business rivals. We are reminded, in this vein, of the case of the manipulation by the Milanese Catholic usurer Tomaso Grassi, of St. Bernard of Siena. In other cases, gentile moneylenders disguised themselves as 'Jews' to evade the usury prohibition. [284]

---

[284] Lester K. Little, *Religious Poverty and the Profit Economy in Medieval Europe*, p. 175.

There is a species of Right-wing conspiracy researcher who believe that subversion emanates mainly from the Left, and who do not question or investigate the shadow forces when they are hidden behind movements on the Right that rail against "Jewish usury and the Rothschilds." They don't see how, by maneuvering Pavlovian responses to obsessions with these themes and personalities, they are being misled by pied pipers with hidden agendas, and distracted from perceiving the whole of the network of evil. When the Right wing has focused on usury it has been almost exclusively on Judaic usurers; the gentile ones are an afterthought. Yet, sin is sin no matter who commits it. The evil is there, the damage is done. In establishing its networks centuries ago, the Money Power created a huge web of usury finance, deploying agents into all wings of the political spectrum, Left and Right. Their Right wing agents misdirected campaigners against usury into an obsession mainly with the Judaic, and later, Protestant brand. But the devil works both sides of the aisle, Right and Left.

The situation of Florence on the eve of the Renaissance is a laboratory for observing how gentile money-lenders used Judaic shylocks as bogeymen in order to hype the supposed necessity of allowing interest on money so as to build a "gentler, more compassionate," non-Judaic system of banking, in the name of compassion for poor Christians. It is much more than merely an irony that when the gentile usury banks grew exceedingly large with the passage of time, they merged with the Judaic banks to form the modern, hydra-headed international system of finance that oppresses the entire world.

The habits of mind that have seduced us, or which have been imposed on us, must be discarded. There must be a reckoning with the legacy of Roman Catholic and Protestant usury, without which there can be no future reform. The Money Power could not have reached its zenith through Judaic usury alone. It has achieved most of its power by cozening Christians and gentiles, but this fact does not fit classic conspiracy theory, repeated as a truism in dozens of volumes purporting to decode the "secrets of money," but which mainly help to ensure that we never grasp the hidden history of how the Money Power came to ascendance in Christendom.

10

Epilogue

"The love of money is the root of all evils."
1 Timothy 6:10

Most modern people would find any equivalence between our contemporary banking system and sorcery to be laughable. In a modern world of illusion where a twilight zone terrain between hallucination and perception is termed "virtual reality," the ability to discern the difference between appearance and substance is increasingly atrophied. The essence of magic is to deceive people into believing that illusion is reality; as David Hawkes terms it, "to attribute determining power to representation" — to mistake the sign of the thing for the thing itself:

"When the goldsmiths of sixteenth-century London realized that the paper certificates they issued, which represented the gold that had been deposited with them, possessed exactly the same practical power as the gold itself, financial value took on a life of its own. When they understood that they could issue notes for ten times the value of the gold in their possession, and that these notes would retain their value and potency, financial signs revealed their own nature and potency, financial signs revealed their own nature as pure representation. These signs achieved independence from what they represented.

"...The 'hot money' of recent decades is barely connected to the world of tangible things at all, but it is immensely potent, easily capable of transforming the material conditions of the objective world, and can be moved across the world at a click of a (computer) mouse. The fact that it is not 'real' in a material sense is an asset rather than a hindrance to its power...The mind was usury's initial battleground, for usury describes a mental process, not a material one...In what we call 'economics,' theories and practices that were once the preserve of the sorcerer and the alchemist achieved respectability, then eminence, and then total predominance..." [285]

"...the (western) monetary system in its historical development...is a direct psychological derivative from the gold-idol worship of barbarism..." [286]

It has been alleged that Pope Leo XIII condemned usury on May 15, 1891 in the encyclical *Rerum Novarum*: "Rapacious usury has increased the evil which, more than once condemned by the Church, is nevertheless, under a different form but in the same way, practiced by avaricious and grasping men."

Rapacious usury; hence it follows that there must be non-rapacious usury, as well. And what is to be done about this "*rapacious* usury"? Nothing. This was more hypocritical papal rhetoric which served to conceal the Catholic policy since Pius VIII of leaving usurers "undisturbed."

The Fribourg Union

In the 1880s an influential group of prestigious Catholic laymen in Europe sought to unite to lobby Pope Leo XIII to formally condemn interest on money. Count Blöme was an Austrian-Catholic diplomat, statesman and advocate for social justice, who sought the abolition of usury through the restoration of traditional Catholic medieval dogma forbidding

---

[285] Hawkes, op. cit. pp. 7-9.

[286] Jeffrey Mark, *The Modern Idolatry*, p. 11.

interest on loans. "In 1884 Count de La Tour du Pin, in behalf of the French Social Catholic group, proposed to Counts Blöme and Kuefstein — two Austrian leaders — that an international federation of social-minded Catholics be formed...A group of leaders met together in Cardinal Mermillod's library at *Fribourg* and formed an organization, the Catholic Union of Fribourg for economic and social studies. The Fribourg Union, as a result of its conferences, succeeded in agreeing upon a joint statement of the Social Catholic position, and in February, 1888, Cardinal Mermillod presented the members of the Union to Leo XIII, handing him a memorial explaining their views..." [287]

"The Fribourg Union...submitted the fruits of their studies to Rome where, without doubt, they were utilized in the preparation of Leo XIII's historic encyclical, the *Rerum Novarum*. The membership of the Fribourg Union included statesmen, jurists, economists and theologians. The three founders of the Union were the Austrians, Counts Blöme and Kuefstein, and the Frenchman, La Tour du Pin...The active patron of the Union was Cardinal Mermillod, Blöme was president...The procedure of the Union was to draw up memoranda or theses on particular subjects and, after adoption, send them to Rome. In 1887 there was adopted a statement on capitalism and credit. It declared that the prevailing system of credit was what constituted the system called capitalism, and this system was based on transactions bearing the marks of usury...The consequences of this system are that the worker is separated from the material means of production to be brought into contact again only by means of the credit system in which everything is capitalized. The credit system causes an excessive concentration of economic power and wealth...

---

287 Parker Thomas Moon, *The Labor Problem and the Social Catholic Movement in France*, p. 139.

"It would appear that Blöme and perhaps some other members of the Fribourg Union, were disappointed that Leo XIII did not go further than he actually did in the condemnation of usury.

"...(in) an address on the *Rerum Novarum* which Blöme made at the final meeting of Fribourg Union...held five months after the issuance of the Encyclical...Blöme...put the question whether the Encyclical had dealt in principle with the whole of the social problem and its solution. The enumeration of the causes of social disorder was comprehensive, but the indication of remedies was less complete. Blöme's summary of what the *Rerum Novarum* says and what it leaves unsaid is as follows...'the Encyclical is limited to the observation of rapacious usury, often condemned by the Church, is still practiced under various disguises. We have long thought this the fundamental question demanding our attention. We believe it must be the chief problem for our future studies. For my own part, I am convinced that unless we reform credit all other reforms will fail in the long run to save us from ruin." [288]

"*...all other reforms will fail.*" The passage of time has proved Count Blöme's prophecy true.

"...'the Encyclical is limited to the observation of rapacious usury..."

This is the way of the pontiffs since the Renaissance. They make quite a show of being "against usury," and their "opposition" takes the form of various empty rhetorical flourishes and admonitions, even as the Vatican Bank profits from usury, and the 1917 Code of Canon Law gave

---

288 Henry Somerville, *Studies in the Catholic Social Movement*, pp. 84-87.

permission for interest rates permitted by the civil law (otherwise undefined, other than that the rate is supposed to be a less than an "excessive" one; again, undefined). The resulting confusion generated by the disparity between what the popes mouth with their words, and the mortal sin and Money Power they enable or tolerate by their actions, has led to full participation in loans at interest on the part of Catholic capitalists in good standing with the Church, who are under no obligation to confess their involvement in order to be received into the Church, or admitted to reception of the Eucharist. It has led to the creation and operation of an international usury operation in Vatican City under direct papal auspices, a bank with the pious Latin name of *Istituto per le Opere di Religione* ("Institute for Works of Religion"). This is now the "work of religion": making money from interest on loans of money.

Thomas Storck claims to be a conservative Catholic opponent of usury and yet he writes, "...no one can be criticized for taking moderate interest...it does seem possible to roughly distinguish a just rate of interest..."[289]

This double-mind is rife within contemporary Catholic circles, where, it is our sad duty to state, self-deluded "conservatives" and "traditionalists" allow themselves to be blinded by piety and papalolatry into engaging in the fool's errand of distinguishing moderate levels of mortal sin from excessive mortal sin, while boasting of the noble economic teaching of the Church, which they contrast to ill effect with Protestant doctrines.

---

289 *Communio: International Catholic Review* (no. 36, Fall 2009).

Roman Catholic capitalist Thomas E. Woods Jr. does not pretend, as these "conservative" and "traditional" Catholics do, that the Church has not repudiated magisterial dogma against interest on money. He quotes approvingly from the writing of Catholic scholar Patrick M. O'Neil in *Faith and Reason*:

"The error concerning the charging of interest is an example of correct moral principles (against economic exploitation and so forth) mistakenly applied on account of inadequacies of early economic theory. When better economic theory became available (along with lessons of practical experience), the Church could change its position...Changes under these circumstances do not threaten the claims of the Magisterium of the Church in any way. The discovery that the charging of interest does not (necessarily) involve exploitation, but represents instead legitimate payment for the time-value of money and for the risk factors endured by the lender, denies the antecedent of the hypothetical." [290]

Mr. Woods' concludes his quotation from Mr. O'Neil with the following observation: "For this reason, combined with explicit Vatican statements over the past two centuries, no Catholic need trouble his conscience over the ordinary transactions involving the charging and earning of interest in which he engages over the course of his economic affairs."

---

290 O'Neil, "A Response to John T. Noonan Jr., Concerning the Development of Catholic Moral Doctrine," *Faith & Reason*, (Spring/ Summer 1996). Mr. Noonan's original article, "Development in Moral Doctrine" was published in *Theological Studies* no. 54 (1993).

The Sin of Rebellion

In so far as he is referring to man's law as formulated by the usurpers who have occupied the Catholic Church from the Renaissance onward, Woods speaks truly. By the man-made laws of the Renaissance Catholic Church and succeeding generations of popes and councils, no one who receives interest on loans of money "need trouble his conscience."

If one believes that the popes of the Church of Rome since the Renaissance are indeed pontiffs of the Catholic Church of all time, and not manifest heretics, then according to the Catholic theology of papal sovereignty, this would signify that they can indeed alter the law of God. If this is true, how does the Church of Rome differ from the synagogue? Has the Roman Church the power to suspend God's laws against idolatry? Against adultery? If not, how does it have the power to suspend God's laws against interest on money? If idolatry and adultery will always be mortal sins, how is interest on money not a mortal sin?

The Word of God concerning interest on loans of money, the words from the very lips of Jesus Christ concerning loans, their confirmation by the apostles, fathers, popes, councils and theologians comprising the Magisterium, for a millennium-and-a-half, are now, by the light of modernist revelation, "mistaken," "inadequate" and subject to "changes" based on "circumstances" and "discoveries."

To say this about dogma, about that which is received from the Holy Spirit, is to destroy the sacred Deposit of Faith by rendering it subject to revision. What we have seen evolve by papal directive since the Renaissance is not only the ascendance of Mammon, but the ascendance of the theology which permits man to revise God, and it is not only the popes who bear guilt for this abomination. When John Calvin, the premier "Reformed Bible Christian," decided he had the right to qualify and revise the words of Jesus Christ in Luke 6:34-35 and nullify, with his five percent interest, the Word of God in Exodus, Leviticus, Deuteronomy, Nehemiah, Proverbs and Ezekiel, he too became guilty of placing his own prideful human mind above the All-Knowing God.

In the West this rebellion has a formal theological basis: the rabbinic hubris that man has the right to amend the revelation of God (Babylonian Talmud: Mo'ed Kattan 16b; Bava Metzia 59b; Berakhot 7a). This megalomaniacal pride is mirrored in Roman Catholic humanism, Neoplatonism, phenomenology and the hermeneutic of continuity; as well as, on the Protestant side, an exegesis of interpretive nullification as seen in the teaching on interest on money of such giants of the Protestant Reformation in England and America as Richard Baxter and Samuel Willard.

Once the right to tamper with the Word of God has been established, our consciences and Christendom itself are henceforth ordered by the ever-shifting sands of man's egotistical imaginings, and by situation ethics intended to fit the occasion of our human wants and desires, in place of God's Will. Here is the sin of rebellion (I Samuel 15:23).

From the nullification of the mortal sin of interest on money we proceed to the weakening of every other truth.

Our human nature being what it is, we would rather consult any palliative, bromide or band-aid and exhaust ourselves in meetings, synods, symposia and theological and philosophical tempests and disputes, than face up to the reality of this one stark and overwhelming fact concerning the *root of all evil,* whose symptoms we congratulate ourselves on being so feverishly engaged in fighting.

The inspired Word of God states without any ambiguity, that the love of money is the root of evil. On the basis of this Biblical doctrine, throughout western Christian civilization for more than one thousand years, usurers were declared to be *hostis humani generis* — the enemy of all mankind.

If it is accurate to say that "when better economic theory became available" the Church rightly nullified the mortal sin of interest on money, it follows inexorably that when "better" human reproductive theory became available contraception was, de facto, no longer a mortal sin (as is the case in too many confessionals in the West where priests declare it to be venial, or no sin at all). And when "better" liturgical theory became available, the unambiguous Sacrifice of the Mass was ruled to be no longer the "ordinary form" of the liturgy.

When "better" understanding of rabbinic Judaism was discovered after the "Holocaust," then the ancient Biblical, apostolic and patristic truth that Pharisaic-Talmudic Judaism is the enemy of God, became obsolete, and was replaced by Pope John Paul II's *Shoah* theology, which has, in turn, been affirmed and extended by Benedict XVI.

When "better scientific knowledge" was discovered, then Darwinian evolution replaced the book of Genesis, and the first ten chapters of the first book of the Pentateuch are now said to be merely allegorical.

The love of money is the root of all evil in the theological sense that this ardor for gain through the acceptance of interest on money, initiates the opening of the floodgates of revolutionary overthrow of numerous other defined dogmas of the Faith.

The love of money is the root of evil in the secular realm in that it makes possible abnormal monstrosities such as cloning, genetic modification of crops and the combining of human and animal genes in one living organism. Whoever endeavors to reign in these horrors encounters the love of money obstructing the way.

"The Light of the World We Live In"

In 2012 Sister Pat Farrel was president of the Leadership Conference for Women Religious, which in that year was said to represent an estimated 80% of women religious in the U.S. In challenging Catholic dogma on contraception and homosexuality she utilized, (in the second sentence of her statement below), the Church of Rome's own rationale for nullifying the dogma on interest on money:

"We have been, in good faith, raising concerns about some of the church's teachings on sexuality. The problem being that the teaching and interpretation of the faith can't remain static and really needs to be reformulated, rethought in light of the world we live in. And new questions and new realities need to be addressed as they arise." [291]

The "*light of the world we live in.*" What other rationale can there be for the overthrow by Rome of the light of the Gospel concerning interest on money? As Sister Pat is seeking a new understanding of contraception and homosexuality, the Money Power obtained, by the light of the world (II Cor. 4:4), as embraced by the papacy from 1515 onward, a new understanding of usury. A Faith that has not "remained static," has rendered Christians who take interest on debt, sinless. Therefore, by the same "light of the world" are also justified other radical alterations

---

[291] La Stampa, July 19, 2012 http://vaticaninsider.lastampa.it/en/homepage/world-news/detail/articolo/stati-uniti-united-states-estados-unidos-16910/

of the sacred dogma of the Faith. Those "conservatives" and "traditionalists" who scapegoat Sister Pat as "rebellious" are infected with a double-mind (James 1:8), that cannot see that she is only conforming to the epistemology of the Church since the Renaissance.

Observe that the usury promoters such as Mr. Woods and Mr. O'Neil will assent to the correctness of other forms of struggle against "economic exploitation," as long as that struggle is not "mistakenly applied" to a ban on interest on money. They know that as long as they have usury in their financial toolkit, then capitalist institutions cannot be fundamentally challenged. Catholics and Christians generally who engage in social justice organizing and educational efforts, working to stop "exploitative" interest on loans, and performing corporal works of mercy on behalf of the poor, homeless, disabled, the ill, the incarcerated, widows, orphans, and the elderly, are all to be commended for their Christ-like assistance to "the least of His brethren." Yet, as they undertake these works of mercy they should harbor no illusions: their assistance represents the palliation of a usurious world of murderous greed and the idolization of profit. The ruinous results of disobedience to the law of God cannot be corrected by treating symptoms. The corporal works of mercy must be performed, but nothing approaching a Christian commonweal can be built when Mammon reigns freely over the West.

Our Age of Money Power has led to the hardening of the hearts of the rich, who for centuries had been looked upon with suspicion and pity as barely able to save their souls, but in our time are flattered and fawned upon as pillars of a "Christian" society and culture ruled by the wealth amassed from interest on loans — in other words from a sin that damns the soul to eternal perdition. The alliance of the Church with the Money Power has confused, demoralized and alienated millions of people. "The name of God is blasphemed among the gentiles because of you" (Romans 2:24).

The Breeding of Money: Hell on Earth

The curses that are upon us, from the destruction of human scale, poison-free agriculture, to the reign of the machines and robots which is on the near horizon of a programmed "Skynet" future, to the very occlusion of human perception by "virtual reality," all start with the love of money, as embraced by the Church in its quasi, de facto, semi-clandestine and then later — open legalization — of interest; an abominable crime for 1500 years — the mortal sin that was, and now is not.

We are not surprised by twenty-first century "test-tube" conception that permits women to have children without the physical presence of a man, or legal permission for marriage in America for men who insert their genital organs in each other's rectums and, if they promise to do this only to each other for the rest of their lives, demand that the government recognize it as the holy sacrament of matrimony. The reversal of everything begins with the permission for the breeding of money.

Both St. Basil the Great (*Homily on Luke*) and St. Ambrose (*De Tobia admonitio*) perceived that by interest on money, "gold was made to breed gold." It was prophesied of old that when this unnatural act became the norm, the doors of hell would be opened to vomit forth their monstrosities and depravities on earth. David Pogue's nationally televised "NOVA" science program on the PBS network, presented to the American people a mindless and merry panegyric to a perversion that beggars description — a "transgenic" goat whose DNA had been crossed by scientists with the genes of a spider, in order to produce a profusion of spider-silk material for profitable marketing as having a tensile strength greater than steel or Kevlar. [292] This horror from a real-life Island of Dr. Moreau, was triumphantly shown to the American people in a nationwide broadcast seen by millions, as glorious progress, with the added advantage of being profitable.

Yet this is all a lie. No one profits in the sense that Our Lord used the word [293] from this type of horrific perversion, this last-gasp of our own putrification.

Usury, the *sine qua non* of the monstrous, is also a lie, in that it denies what it is and what it produces. More than a house of gold, it is a house of mendacity, crowned on its dung heap of riches by our self-deceit.

> "Almost everyone today would condemn excessive or overtly exploitative usury, but few people, even on the political Left, would endorse a blanket condemnation of usury in principle...Our society lacks an ethical critique of usury as such...two vital moral insights possessed by sixteenth and seventeenth century English people (are) lost to us...that usury was the reproduction of autonomous representation. They understood that money is a sign, and they objected on ethical grounds to the idea that signs could 'breed'...Financial value was recognized as the alienated form of human life as a whole, and this was the second source of the virtually universal opinion that usury was evil. It was evil in a metaphysical sense; it was the logical, practical, and manifest antithesis of human life itself. It is hard to overstate the importance that attached to this issue as a result. The people of Renaissance England believed that if it was allowed to do so, usury would bring about the triumph of atheism, the reign of Satan and the death of the human soul."
>
> —David Hawkes

---

292 The spider silk protein is excreted in the milk of the part spider goat. The protein liquid from the spider-goat's milk is then injected into an alcohol bath, which causes the liquid protein to solidify into a strand of actual spider silk. Two or three meters of silk can be obtained from a quart of this creature's milk. Cf. http://www.pbs.org/wgbh/nova/tech/making-stuff.html#making-stuff-stronger (scroll to "Randy Lewis"). Mr. Pogue's program was nationally broadcast on PBS television on Jan. 19, 2011 and repeated on Sept. 19, 2012.

293 Matthew 16:26.

11

Appendix I

Saint Anthony of Padua
The Miracle of the Usurer's Heart

"Where your treasure is, there will your heart be also."
—Matthew 6:21

Tullio Lombardo, *The Miracle of the Usurer's Heart* (1520)

For a decade Anthony preached in northern Italy and southern France; at times he taught theology as well. Stories are told of immense crowds that assembled for his sermons, of the many who came several hours early to be sure of getting good places, and of the need of protecting him from souvenir-seekers. His greatest triumph came during the Lenten season of 1231, with his preaching campaigns against civil strife, against usury, and in favor of including the lower classes in the processes of communal politics...Gregory IX saw fit to make (him) a saint within less than a year after his death." [294]

It is not an easy matter to find a full account of St. Anthony's "Miracle of the Usurer's Heart," since it is a huge embarrassment to "Christian" usurers and a devastating rebuke to the contemporary Church which permits their trade. Consequently, in Orwellian fashion, the miracle has been classed as too parochial and dated and has been renamed. When it is presented to the public it is no longer a parable about a money-lender who grew wealthy from charging interest on debt. It has been rewritten as "The Miracle of the *Miser's* Heart," and the dead man's sin is no longer specifically usury, but the more generic theme of parsimony. By means of this con, the people do not learn of the degree of hostility which medieval Catholic culture – and one of the most esteemed of all saints of the Church – harbored for the sin of charging interest on loans of money.

As we have noted in our section on Father McNabb, long after the Renaissance, Catholic culture at the folk level persisted in execrating usury. St. Anthony's electrifying example of righteous wrath against the den of thieves who sought a place in the Church in spite of their intractable addiction to money breeding, resonated among the lay people down through the centuries, commemorated in magnificent art works by Francesco Pesellino, Domenico Campagnola and Tullio Lombardo, and contributing to a living culture of revulsion toward the sin of usury for millions of Catholics for hundreds of years, even while their cardinals and popes trafficked in and profited from

294 Lester K. Little, op. cit., p. 186.

partnering with capitalism's immensely powerful banking houses.

What the old Church had believed and taught left deep traces in the cultural memory of the Catholic people for many centuries during the time that usury was being rehabilitated from on high. This holy memory persisted long after the theology itself had decayed. Lowly parish priests and peasants preserved indignation over income derived from interest into the nineteenth and even the twentieth century. Many were outraged to discover, in the 1800s, that when impenitent usurers complained to the Catholic hierarchy about priests who refused to grant them absolution in the confessional, the hierarchy stood with the unrepentant sinners against the confessors.

St. Anthony's miracle, which imparts a stern and somber moral lesson, was part of a corpus of literature in circulation among the people, concerning accounts of usurers in purgatory or hell. In one popular tale, the usurer's fiery torment is meted out in terms of the quantity of money he received: it equals the quantity of firewood sent to hell to burn him. In 1219 Caesarius of Heisterbach (1180-1240), a German monk of the Cistercian order, began to compile a series of similar exempla, the *Dialogus Miraculorum*, centered on horror stories concerning the dreadful fate that awaited usurers and other transgressors, in the afterlife. [295] Another such literary work of this genre was *Der Renner,* compiled by Hugo von Trimberg (ca. 1230-1313), rector of St. Gangolfstift School near Bamberg. Its thematic scope consisted of a schema of the seven cardinal sins, structured on a critique of a medieval society ruled by usurers. Nascent capitalism was shown to be a work of the devil, and the typical portrayal of the fate of the unscrupulous wealthy in

---

[295] Caesarius of Heisterbach, *The Dialogue on Miracles,* trans. H. von E. Scott and C. Swinton Bland, two volumes (London: Routledge, 1929).

eternity, was not pretty. These writings were not simply the equivalent of lurid pulp novels. Trimberg, for instance, marshaled not only fables and folklore but scripture, and homilies from classical and medieval preachers, all of which served to help keep alive the spirit of the ancient doctrine of justly revered, true popes, such as the fifth century St. Leo I, as expressed in his proverb, "*Fenus pecuniae, funus est animae*" ("Usurious profit from money is the death of the soul").

Jacques Le Goff recounts a popular medieval story which presents sophisticated Thomistic/Aristotelean insights, followed by an allegorical twist-ending, regarding the doom awaiting the usurer:

"Usurers sin against nature by seeking to breed money from money, like a male horse from a male horse, or a male mule from a male mule. What is more, usurers are thieves because they sell time, which does not belong to them, and to sell something that is not your own against the wishes of the owner, is theft. Further, as all they sell is waiting for money, that is, time, they are selling days and nights. But day is the time of light and night is the time of repose. It would not be just, therefore, for the usurers to have eternal light and eternal repose." [296]

Jacques de Vitry (1160-1240), was an important Augustinian preacher both in his native France and Palestine, where he was chaplain to the armies of the Fifth Crusade, 1218-1221. Afterward he served as Gregory IX's papal legate to the Low Countries. De Vitry compiled his sermons, representing a wealth of edifying parables, as models for other preachers. These were widely circulated as the *Sermones vulgares*. Twelve of these (numbers 167-179), pertain to the damnation of usurers. In one such exemplum, a usurer is so grasping that after his death he is buried with a

---

[296] *Money and the Middle Ages*, p. 64.

third of his property. As a result, a demon comes and fills the mouth of the usurer's corpse with red-hot coins, as a foreshadowing of the eternal retribution that awaits his soul. [297]

Not every parable endeavored to frighten people out of usury. In one sermon from his vast 14th century encyclopedic resource for preachers, the *Summa praedicantium*,[298] John Bromyard, Dominican professor of theology at Cambridge University, related a homily in which embarrassment was used to convey a moral lesson: "A certain preacher, knowing that many usurers were in his congregation, asked if there were any present in the church that Sunday morning. No one answered. He then inquired if there were any sewer cleaners present. One man rose dutifully and humbly admitted that this was indeed his profession. "Observe," replied the preacher, "how usury is the filthiest of all trades, for another filthy trade is admitted by its worker and he is not ashamed, while the usurers in this congregation dare not publicly reveal themselves."

The Miracle at the Funeral of the Usurer

"Among the many vices infesting Florence, usury was the one against which St. Anthony of Padua waged the greatest war. He exhorted his hearers to conquer the lust for wealth which brought them within the clutches of the pitiless money-lenders; he advised

---

297 Thomas F. Crane, *The Exempla or Illustrative Stories from the Sermones vulgares of Jacques de Vitry*, p. 72.

298 Originally published in the 1300s, the copy we consulted was printed in Venice, 1586. Sixteen stories in volume two alone concern usury. In spite of the folkloric nature of some of these, it is Biblical and patristic authorities that form the grist of Bromyard's moralizing mill. Bromyard was not so much the author as the editor, however, since he was the inheritor of "the gathered fruits of Mendicant preaching throughout the 14th century and indeed even earlier...the bulk of (his) material has been drawn from 13th century sources." (G.R. Owst, p. 224).

them to be content with such things as they had; to live rather in poverty than in debt; and on the other hand, he preached against usurers and their cold-blooded cruelty, like one consumed with divine fire. St. Anthony compared those who reaped interest on money to '*reptilia, quorum non est numerous*,' and to vultures. Some of his words may apply to the twenty-first as well as to the thirteenth century: 'How many rich men of our day are clad in purple — that is, in stuffs dyed with the sweat and blood of the poor, because the clothes they wear are woven out of theft, larceny, usury and illegitimate gain?...The garment dyed with the blood of the poor shall be the prey of eternal flames.'

"The usurer,' he says elsewhere, 'is worse than Judas. That traitor, having sold the Blood of his Divine Master, brought back to the priests and princes the thirty pieces he had received, but the usurer guards and keeps his unjust gains.'

"St. Bonaventure himself relates an occurrence which took place in that city (Florence), and of which St. Anthony availed himself in a sermon, to illustrate how severely God punishes that vice. A rich usurer died, and while the saint was in prayer God revealed to him that this man's soul was in hell on account of his unjust dealings with others. An immense crowd of people had gone to hear the saint preach at the funeral of the usurer. St. Anthony took as his text, 'Where your treasure is, there will your heart be also' (Matthew 6:21). He began by pointing out the heinousness of the sin of usury, declaring that usurers in their thirst for gold were the enemies of mankind, desiring nothing so much as war, famine, pestilence and so forth, so as to enrich themselves at the expense of others, and satisfy their craving for those riches in which their happiness alone consisted. Then, speaking with still greater emphasis, he exclaimed: 'They are also the enemies of their own souls, for it is indeed rare for a usurer to become holy.' Adding: 'This is precisely what has happened to the one to whom these last honors are being paid,' and pointing to the catafalque before him, he continued: 'To prove the truth of my assertion you need only go and look at the chest of money, which, for the short time he lived on earth, was the joy and god of his heart, and you will find there his own heart lying under his gold. For the Son of God Himself has declared, 'Where thy treasure is there also is thy heart.'

"At this announcement the family of the deceased and the people in attendance remained at first perfectly dumbfounded, after which crowds of them rushed to the family home in order to ascertain for themselves the truth of the assertion, insisting on the money chest being opened, and there, to their great astonishment, they found the usurer's heart, lying under the gold. Not yet fully convinced of the truth, the man's family approached a surgeon and returned with him to the church where the corpse was lying. The surgeon opened the dead usurer's chest cavity and on inspection it was found that the body contained no heart.

"Filled with indignation against the unrepentant usurer who had not made restitution by returning his ill-gotten gains to his victims, the people present declared that his body should not be buried in consecrated ground. Removing it from the catafalque, they dragged it out of the city and threw it on a dung heap, where dead dogs and the remains of other beasts were abandoned. [299]

---

[299] Cf. Catherine Mary Antony Woodcock, *Saint Anthony of Padua The Miracle Worker*, pp. 81-82; Joseph A. Keller, *Anecdotes Proving the Miraculous Power of St. Anthony*; and Raphael M. Huber, *St. Anthony of Padua, Doctor of the Church Universal: A Critical Study of the Life, Sanctity, Learning and Miracles of the Saint of Padua and Lisbon* (Milwaukee: Bruce Publishing, 1948).

12

Appendix II

Bishop Jewel Smites Usury

John Jewel

Bishop Jewel was born at Bowden farm, May 24, 1522, in north Devonshire, England, one of ten children of "yeoman stock." He began his studies at Merton College, Oxford University, at the age of thirteen in 1535. In 1539 he continued at Oxford's Corpus Christi College, obtaining his BA in 1540 at age 18. In 1544 he received his MA degree and was named Professor of Humanities, Greek and Rhetoric at Oxford. In the wake of the ascension of Queen Mary Tudor he went into voluntary continental exile in 1554, eventually settling in the city of Zurich. After Mary's death he returned to England in March, 1559. He was named Anglican bishop of Salisbury on Jan. 21, 1560 and held the office until his death on Sept. 23, 1571. He is buried in Salisbury Cathedral. His chief theological work is the *Apologia ecclesiae Anglicanae* (1562). Richard Hooker, in *Of The Laws of Ecclesiastical Polity*, eulogized Jewel as the "worthiest divine that Christendom has bred for some hundreds of years."

A Sermon on Usury [300]

John Jewel
Anglican Bishop of Salisbury, England

"That no man oppress or defraud his brother in any matter; for the Lord is an avenger of all things; as we have also told you beforetime and testified."
I Thessalonians 4:6

Let no man defraud his brother, neither by false weight, nor by false measure, nor by lying words. Let your measure and weights and words be true: let your gains be just and true, that God may bless them. His blessing will make you rich; and whatsoever he blesses not, shall waste and consume, and do you no good. Do unto others as you would they should do unto you. This is true dealing and upright.

If you speak more than is true, if you take more than your wares are worth, your conscience knows it is

300 This sermon, together with other homilies by Bishop Jewel, was first published in 1583 under the title, "An Exposition Upon the Two Epistles of Saint Paul to the Thessalonians." It was reprinted in 1584, 1594, 1609, 1611, 1811 and 1847. Our text is derived from *The Works of John Jewel: The Second Portion* (Parker Society, Cambridge University Press, 1847), pp. 850-861.

Jewel appointed John Garbrand, fellow of New College, Oxford and afterward prebendary of Sarum, as his literary executor. According to Garbrand's preface to the first edition, Jewel's sermon was "delivered unto the people of his charge" in "the cathedral church of Sarum." Garbrand writes that "many of his hearers thought it worthy to be made common and besought him (Jewel) earnestly, even as since his blessed departure out of this life they have often required me to publish the same." Garbrand further states concerning the bishop's expositions on Thessalonians, "In this discourse...are there two matters, the one of usury, the other of antichrist, that is, of the bane and poison of the commonwealth and of the infection and decay of the church, wherein he bestowed more pains to open them and make them manifest, that all men might know and abhor them, and beware of them. What has been wrought by these two mischiefs...the utter destruction of the souls and bodies of many thousands of subjects of this realm within these late years..."

none of thine. God will destroy all the workers of iniquity. He that delights in sin hates his own soul. The mouth that is accustomed to lie slays the soul.

Defraud not your brother: he is your brother, whether he be rich or poor: he is your brother, and the son of God. Will you do wrong to your brother? Will you oppress the son of God, even in the sight of God? God is his Father: He will not leave it unpunished.

If he be simple and unskilful, abuse not his simplicity. God is the God of righteousness. Deal justly, that your own conscience accuses you not. Teach not your sons nor your servants to deceive others, and to gain by wickedness. After they have learned from you to deceive others, they will deceive you also. Job prayed daily for his children. Be careful that your children and employees deceive no man, nor hurt any. Their sins shall be laid to your charge. Why ask God to feed you, and give you your daily bread; and wait not upon his will, but feed upon the bread of iniquity? This meat will not nourish thee, this wealth will not stand by thee; for God will not prosper it. The wise man says: "The bread of deceit is sweet to a man; but afterward his mouth shall be filled with gravel." Ill-gotten goods have an ill end. God has said by the prophet Aggeus: "Ye have sown much, but you have brought in little: ye brought it home; and I did blow upon it." We have examples hereof daily. We have seen great heaps of wealth suddenly blown away, and consumed to nothing; great houses decayed, and the hope of the wicked quite overthrown.

Here will I speak somewhat of the unhappy trade of usury, because therein stands the most miserable and shameful deceiving of the brethren. I will not speak all that may be said; for it would be too long and overwearisome. I will have regard of that which shall be agreeable, and profitable, and worthy for you to hear. And that you may the better consider hereof, and see the whole matter of usury, I will show you, first, what usury is; then, from whence it is derived, and what are the causes of usury; thirdly, what comes of it, what hurt it works to the commonwealth; and I will lay forth such reasons as may make any good man abhor it; then I will declare what the holy fathers, and the apostles, and martyrs, and Christ, and God himself have thought and spoken of usury.

Many simple men know not what is usury, nor never heard of the name of it. The world were happy if no man knew it: for evil things do less harm when they be most unknown. Pestilences and plagues are not known but with great misery. But that you may learn to know it, and the more to abhor it, this it is. Usury is a kind of lending of money, or com, or oil, or wine, or of any other thing, wherein, upon covenant and bargain, we receive again the whole principal which we delivered, and somewhat more for the use and occupying of the same: as, if I lend 100 pounds, and for it covenant to receive 105 pounds, or any other sum greater than was the sum which I did lend. This is that which we call usury: such a kind of bargaining as no good man or godly man ever used: such a kind of bargaining as all men that ever feared God's judgment have always abhorred and condemned.

It is filthy gains, and a work of darkness. It is a monster in nature, the overthrow of mighty kingdoms, the destruction of flourishing states, the decay of wealthy cities, the plagues of the world, and the misery of the people. It is theft, it is the murdering of our brethren, it is the curse of God and the curse of the people. This is usury. By these signs and tokens you may know it; for wheresoever it reigns, all those mischiefs ensue. But how and how many ways it may be wrought, I will not declare. It were horrible to hear; and I come now to reprove usury, and not to teach it.

Let us see then what is the cause hereof, from whence it grows, who is the mother, the nurse, or the breeder of usury. For it grows not everywhere, nor among all men. Many hate it and detest it, and had rather die than live of such spoil. It is not of God; for God straitly forbids it. Neither is it found among the children of God; for love seeks not her own profit, but to do good to her neighbor.

Whence then springs usury? Whence theft, murder, adultery, the plagues and destruction of the people, do spring? All these are the works of the devil and the works of the flesh. Christ tells the Pharisees: "You are of your father the devil, and the lusts of your father you do." Even so may it truly be said to the usurer: Thou art of thy father the devil, and the lust of thy father thou wilt do; and therefore thou hast pleasure in his works.

The devil entered into the heart of Judas, and put in him this greediness and covetousness of gain, for which he was content to sell his Master. Judas' heart was the shop: the devil was the foreman to work in it. St Paul said: "They that will be rich fall into temptation and snares, and into many foolish and noisome lusts, which drown men in perdition and destruction. For the desire of money is the root of evil." And St. John says: "Whosoever commits sin is of the devil." Thus we see that the devil is the planter and the father of usury.

Covetousness, desire of money, insatiable greediness, deceitfulness, unmercifulness, injury, oppression, extortion, contempt of God, hatred to the brethren, and hatred of all men, are the nurses and breeders of usury. It springs from Satan, and grows, and is watered, and is fed and nourished by these cruel and damnable monsters.

Let us see further what are the fruits which come of usury. For perhaps it does some good, and you may think that many are the better for it. These therefore are the fruits. It dissolves the knot and fellowship of mankind. It hardens men's hearts. It makes men unnatural, and bereaves them of charity and love to their dearest friends. It breeds misery, and provokes the wrath of God from heaven. It consumes rich men, it eats up the poor, it makes bankrupts, and undoes many households. The poor occupiers are driven to flee, their wives are left alone, their children are helpless, and driven to beg their bread, through the unmerciful dealing of the covetous usurer.

When David lays out the wickedness of the country where he was persecuted, he said of them: *Non defecit usura et dolus in plateis eorum*: "Usury and deceit departs not from their streets." One seeks to spoil and eat up another. These are the commodities and the fruits of usury. Such is usury in the midst of a city, and such good it works as fire does when it is set to the roof of a house; or as the plague does when it is taken to the midst of the body, and touches the heart.

We have heard whence usury springs, and what hurt it does. Which whosoever considers may find cause enough to loathe it and forsake it. Someone asked of Cato, "What is it to commit usury?"

'What is it" replied Cato, "to kill a man? He that is a usurer is a murderer." The same Cato said: "Our fathers punished a thief with payment of the double of that he had taken; but the usurer was always condemned to pay four times the value." They were wise men. They thought that a usurer was much worse than a thief.

For a thief is driven by extremity and need; the usurer is rich, and has no need. The thief steals in corners and in places where he may be unknown; the usurer openly and boldly at all times and in any place. The thief, to relieve his wife and children; the usurer, to spoil his neighbor and to undo his wife and children. The thief steals from the rich, which have enough; the usurer from the poor, that have nothing. The thief flees, and will be seen no more; the usurer stands by it, continues, and steals still: day and night, sleeping and waking, he always steals. The thief repents of his deed, he knows he has done wrong, and is sorry for it; the usurer thinks it is his own, that it is well gotten, and never repents nor sorrows, hut defends and maintains his sin impudently. The thief, if he escape, many times becomes profitable to his country, and applies himself conscientiously in some trade of life; the usurer leaves his merchandise, forsakes his husbandry, gives himself to nothing whereby his country may have benefit. The thief is satisfied at length; the usurer never has enough. The belly of the wicked will never be filled. As the sea is never filled with water, though all the streams of the world run into it; so the greediness of a usurer is never satisfied, though he gain never so unreasonably. The sea is profitable; the usurer is hurtful and dangerous. By the sea we may pass, and come safely to the haven; but no man passes by usury without loss or shipwreck.

Now hear what the godly and learned fathers of the church have thought of usury. No doubt they were godly men, and wrote hereof as God had inspired them, and as others before them had done. Augustine said: *Quid dicam de usuris, quas ipsae leges*[301]: "What shall I speak of usury, whereof the laws and judges require that restitution be made? Is he more cruel which steals some thing away from the rich man, or he that kills a poor man with usury?" Mark this: a usurer, said Augustine, is cruel. Why? He kills. Whom? The poor man, whom in charity he is bound to relieve.

Ambrose hereof saith: "*Usuras solvit, qui victu indiget: an quicquam gravius?*[302]" "He that lacks wherewith to keep life pays you usury. What heavier

---

301 *Quid dicam de usuris, quas ipsae leges et judices reddi jubent? An crudelior est, qui subtrahit aliquid vel eripit diviti, quam qui trucidat pauperem fenore?*

302 *Usuras solvit, qui victu indiget: an quicquam gravius? Ille medicamentum quaerit, vos offertis venenum: panem implorat, gladium porrigitis: libertatem obsecrat, servitutem irrogatis.*

case may there be? He seeks to be healed; and you poison him: he asks you for bread; and you give him a knife: he desires you to set him at liberty; and you bring him to further bondage."

And again: "You, usurer, grow wealthy by other men's heaviness: you make gains of their tears and weeping: you are fed with their hunger: you coin your money of the skins of those men whom you destroy: how think you to yourself to be rich, and yet beg alms of him that is poor?" [303]

And the same father said further: "*Ab hoc usuram exige, quem non sit crimen occidere.*" "Whomsoever it is lawful to kill, thou mayest lend him thy money to usury." He that takes usury kills without a sword. These be holy fathers, and worthy of credit: they show us that usury is as bad as to kill and murder a man willfully.

Chrysostom likewise: "*In his sensibilibus pecuniis prohibuit ne quis usuram acciperet,* etc.": "God hath forbidden that man shall take usury in this sensible or common money. Why? Because either of them is much hindered. He that owes the money is made poorer, and he that lends it by this kind of enriching himself increases the number of his sins."

Again Chrysostom said: "*Sicut enim fermentum modicum, quod mittitur in multam farinam, totam conspersionem corrumpit...*" [304] "Even as a little leaven leavens the whole lump of dough, even so usury, when it comes into any man's house, draws all his substance, and changes it into debt."

---

[303] *De serumnis ditaris, de lacrymis lucrum quaeris, de fame aliena pasceris, de exuvis spoliatorum hominum cudis argentum; et judicas te divitem, qui stipem poscis a paupere?*

[304] *"Sicut enim fermentum modicum, quod mittitur in multam farinam, totam conspersionem corrumpit et trahitillam, et facit illam totam fermentum: sic quum usura in domum alicujus intraverit, totam substantiam ejus ad se trahit, et convertit in debitum."*

He that is a usurer wishes that all others may lack, and come to him and borrow of him, that all others may lose, so that he may have gain. Therefore our old forefathers so much abhorred this trade, that they thought a usurer unworthy to live in the company of Christian men: they did excommunicate him. They did not suffer a usurer to be a witness in matters of law. They suffered him not to make a Testament and to bestow his goods by a Will. When a usurer died, they would not suffer him to be buried in places appointed for the burial of Christians; so highly did they mislike this unmerciful spoiling and deceiving our brethren.

But what speak I of the ancient fathers of the church? There was never any religion, nor sect, nor state, nor degree, nor profession of men, but they have disliked it. Philosophers, Greeks, Latins, lawyers, divines, catholics, heretics, all tongues and nations have ever thought a usurer as dangerous as a thief. The very sense of nature proves it to be so. If the stones could speak, they would say as much.

Therefore our Savior said: "Do good, and lend, looking for nothing again." He did say not, Lend, and look not for your principal again: but, Look for no gain thereby, look not to receive more than thine own for the use and occupying of it. Defraud not another: you would not another should defraud you. Oppress him not, have pity on his wife and children: you would not have your wife and children undone. In Leviticus (25: 34-36) God said: "If one of thy brethren be impoverished and fallen in decay then thou shalt help him...thou shalt take no usury of him nor vantage; but thou shalt fear thy God, that thy brother may live with thee." [305]

God said, thou shalt take no usury. And he has power and authority to command. And in Exodus

---

305 Leviticus 25:37 "Thou shalt not lend him they money for usury, nor lend him thy food at a profit."

(22:25): "If thou lend money to any of my people that is poor by thee, thou shalt not be to him as an usurer, neither shalt thou lay upon him usury." Shew them mercy for my sake: they are my people. I can enrich him, I can impoverish thee. I set up and throw down whom I will. When thy neighbour needeth thy help, and seeketh comfort at thy hands, afflict him not as an enemy, oppress him not like a tyrant."

Ezekiel the prophet set down the wrath of God against usurers: "He that hath given forth his money upon usury, or hath taken increase, shall he live? he shall not live,' saith the Lord." (Ezekiel 18:12-13). He shall perish in his own sin: his blood shall be upon his head. Therefore when he reckons the offenses of Jerusalem, and declares the heavy plagues that are prepared against that wicked city, he said: "Thou hast taken usury and increase, and thou hast defrauded thy neighbors by extortion, and hast forgotten me, saith the Lord God. Behold, therefore, I have smitten mine hands upon the covetousness that thou hast used." You have done injury to my people, that you might make your own gain. Your wrongs and oppressions done by usury rise up into heaven; therefore I will gather you, and blow the fire of my wrath upon you, says the Lord.

Thus has God spoken, even the Lord of heaven and earth, which can scatter your gold in the wind, and blow it to nothing. Thus he speaks to you that hear and read his word, who know that his will is that you should not lend your money to usury. You do oppress, says he. Whom? Your brother, for whom Christ vouchsafed to shed his blood. And what brother? Him that was poor, which came to you for need, to seek your help. How? Wickedly, closely, falsely, craftily, deceitfully, like an hypocrite, under color to do him good. Wherewith? With your money, your gold and silver, which God has given you to relieve the poor and needy withal.

God has said you shall not take usury; and what are you, that despises the voice of the Lord? Whose words will you hear, that will not hear the word of God? Remember the words: you cannot forget them. Thou shalt not take usury of thy brother: he is poor and fallen in decay: thou shalt not be an usurer unto him: thou shalt not oppress him with usury. For it is cruelty and abomination in the sight of God; therefore will God pour out his wrath, and consume the usurer: he shall not enter into the tabernacle of the Highest, he shall have no part in the kingdom of Christ and of God, but shall be cast into the outer darkness.

But some will say, all kinds of usury are not forbidden: there may be cases where usury may stand with reason and equity. And herein they say so much as by wit may be devised to paint out a foul and ugly idol, and to shadow themselves in manifest and open wickedness. Whatsoever God says, yet this or this kind of usury, say they, which is done in this or this sort, is not forbidden. It profits the commonwealth, it relieves great numbers. The poor should otherwise perish: no man would lend to them.

By like good reason there are some that defend theft and murder. They say there may be some case where it is lawful to kill or to steal; for God willed the Hebrews to rob the Egyptians, and Abraham to kill his own son Isaac. In these cases their robbery and the killing of his son were lawful. So say they. Even so by like reason do some of our countrymen maintain concubines, courtesans, and brothel-houses, and stand in defense of open stews.[306] They are (say they) for the benefit of the country: they keep men from more dangerous inconvenience: take them away, it will be worse. Although God says, "There shall be no whore of the daughters of Israel, neither shall there be a whore-

306 "Open stews": bathhouses used for immoral purposes i.e. houses of prostitution or a quarter which houses them.

keeper of the sons of Israel;" yet these men say all manner of whoredom is not forbidden. In these and these cases it is not amiss to allow it.

God said to Saul: "Go and strike Amalek, and destroy ye all that pertains to them, and have no compassion on them; but slay both man and woman, both infant and suckling, both ox and sheep, both camel and ass." So strait and precise was God's commandment. Marches forth Saul and sets upon his enemies; God assisted him, and gave him the victory. When he took Agag prisoner, and saw him to be a goodly tall gentleman, he had pity on him, and saved him alive. And the best and fairest of the sheep, and oxen, and other cattle, he did not destroy, although he knew well that God had commanded him to kill man and beast, every one without exception. Then came Samuel unto him, and said: "O why hast thou not done as thou were commanded?" Here let us mark the wicked answer of Saul in defense of his willful disobedience. "It would have been a great pity to have slain Agag, so comely and tall a gentleman. I have taken him and kept him prisoner. And, if I should have destroyed this goodly cattle, they had come to nothing. It was better to save them for the victualing of my soldiers; and the fairest of them may be offered in sacrifice."

So brake he the commandment of God under pretense of doing honor to God. But Samuel said: "Hath the Lord as great pleasure in burnt offerings and sacrifices as when the voice of the Lord is obeyed? Behold, to obey is better than sacrifice." And to disobey his holy will is to renounce and forsake him.

So may we say to the usurer: you have devised cases and colors to hide your shame; but what regard has God to your cases? What cares he for your reasons? The Lord would have more pleasure, if when you hear his voice you would obey him. For what is your device against the counsel and ordinance of God? What bold presumption is it for a mortal man to control the commandments of the immortal God, and to weigh his heavenly wisdom in the balance of human foolishness?

When God says you shall not take usury, what creature of God are you, which can take usury? When God makes it unlawful, who are you, O man, that makes it lawful?[307] This is a token of a desperate mind. It is found true in you, what Paul said: "The love of money is the root of all evil." You are so given over unto wicked mammon, that you care not to do the will of God.

Willfulness and presumption are tokens that such men are impudent and past shame. He that offends of simplicity may find mercy: but they which of pride and boldness go against the known truth, and do that thing which they know to be ill, and devise shifts to color that which all reason and learning of God and men, and nature itself have condemned, they are fallen into temptation and snares, and into foolish lusts which do drown them in destruction.

God is the Lord. We are but servants: he has made us, and not we ourselves: we are but as clay in his hands: we cannot repeal the law that God has established: we must obey it. We may not do the things that seem good in our own eyes, they may deceive us; but we must do whatsoever God bids us to do, and forsake to do those things which he forbids.

Thus much for an entry to those which can bring so good reasons for so ill a matter.

Many defend their usury by that liberty which they think they have to use their goods in such sort as seems best to themselves, and is most to their own advantage.

---

307 "When God saith thou shalt not take usury, what creature of God art thou, which canst take usury? When God maketh it unlawful, what art thou, O man, that sayest it is lawful?"

May I not, say they, do with my own goods what I will? This would they not say, if they were of him which hath said by his holy apostle: "Let every man, as he hath received the gift, so minister the same one to another as good disposers of the manifold grace of God" (I Peter 4:10). It is the law of nature, that no man abuse the things that are his to the hurt and hindrance of another. May a man take his own dagger, and therewith commit murder? Or may a man take of his own fire, and therewith burn his neighbor's house? He that said, “Thou shalt not kill,” has also said: “Thou shalt not steal: thou shalt not commit usury: thou shalt not defraud thy brother in bargaining." He is not unrighteous, that he will judge the murderer, and will not condemn the usurer. In that day the usurer shall know whose money it was wherewith he defrauded his brother. His money shall not help him: he shall no shift to convey himself from the wrath of God: he and his money shall perish together.

But the usurer will say: “The poor man came to me: I was not in haste to seek him. He moaned his case to me. I took pity on him and lent him money. Since then he and all his have been the better.”

Here you shall see the great kindness and pitiful heart of this rich usurer. He draws his purse, gives out his goods, and helps the poor; and the poor are much eased by him. But, alas! What help is this? Even such as he finds, that in the midst of his fit of an ague drinks a great draught of cold water. No doubt he is refreshed and cooled, and for that present time much the better. But after a while, when his heaves renew, the heat increases: his heart pants, his pulse beats, his mouth is dry, his tongue burns: he is more terribly tormented than ever before. So fares it with him that borrows money upon usury. He looks in his hand, and sees somewhat: it is not his own; yet he is refreshed therewith, and much eased. The year passes, the day of payment draws on, the creditor calls for money: then the heats and fits and agonies begin to grow. Then must pot and pan trudge to redeem his body. Then he feels more cruel torments than ever before.

Thus does the gentle usurer help to relieve the poor in time of his necessity: as if a man would cure a sore finger by cutting off the arm; or as if he would cure the blemish of the eyesight by the pulling out the eyes; or as if he would quench thirst by giving poison to drink; or as if, to save one from drowning in a boisterous tempest, he would cast him over the boat into the sea.

The scorpion embraces a man sweetly with its legs, but in the meanwhile strikes him deadly with his tail: his face looks amiable; his tail poisons. So a usurer looks fair, and gives good words; but at the end he undoeth.

Who is stung by an adder, [308] perceives no hurt, but feels a gentle beating of his veins with some delight, whereat he rejoices. After this he falls into a slumber: then the poison works, overcomes him, and kills him. Even so he that borrows upon usury finds himself wonderfully amended, and rejoices; but he is stung, and has a deadly stroke. The poison will grow over him: he shall die in a slumber, and be undone before he is aware, So necessary is a usurer to relieve the poor and needy, as rust is to help iron, and as the moth is to help a garment: it eats him through from one side to other.

Therefore said Ambrose: "*Talia sunt vestra, divites, beneficia. Minus datis, et plus exigitis. Talis humanitas, ut spolietis etiam dum subvenitis*": Such are the benefits that you rich men bestow; you give out little, and require much again. Such is your kindness, that you undo them whom ye help."

And thus much of the ease that poor men find in borrowing upon usury. They are bitten, and stung, and eaten up and devoured by it. Most men confess

---

308 A venomous snake.

that this kind of usury is forbidden, because it relieves not, but spoils and consumes. May God take the liking of it out of all men's hearts! Then shall they be the better able to judge of the other sorts, which they yet think allowable.

What if one rich man lends money to another? What if a merchant takes money to usury of a merchant, and both be the better, and both be gainers? Here is no sting nor biting. What shall we think of this? What if a thief or a pirate take usury of a pirate or a thief, and both be partakers of the gain, and be both of them helped? Let no man mislike the comparison. For, as I said before, a pirate or a thief is not so injurious as a usurer.

Here, say you, he that lends is a gainer, and he that borrows is a gainer. It does good unto both. If both be gainers, who is the loser? For usury never passes without working loss. Take this a rule: there is never usury without loss.

Here I pray you to lend me your minds, and consider what I say. A merchant takes up of his neighbor a hundred pounds,[309] and most answer again a hundred and ten pounds. He bestows it all in corn, and buys with his hundred pounds a hundred quarters of corn. He sends it to the market: the people have need of it, and buy it. If he sold it for eight groats a bushel, he mightt make up his hundred pounds, and be a gainer. But unless he comes up with a hundred and ten pounds to discharge his usury, he must needs be a loser and undone. But undone he will not be: he will rather undo many others. 'Therefore he sets the price at three shillings the bushel, and so makes his money, and pays the usurer, and saves himself, and is no loser. Who then pays the ten pounds? Who is the loser? Any man may see. The poor people who buy the corn. They find it and feel it in every morsel they eat. Thus,

---

309 A hundred pounds was a large sum in 1583.

if the merchant borrower be not hindered by the usurer, yet the people who buy his wares are plagued. Thus it is no hard matter to find that, howsoever usury us used, it is always dangerous and beguiles the people, and is therefore the destruction and overthrow of the commonwealth.

But, says he, why should I not make money to yield me gains, as well as my wares? I lend my shop for a year, or two, or three, so many pieces of velvet, satins, taffeta, grograin, camlet, hollands etc. And for the use he shall pay me by the year forty pounds, and in the end restore me my shop, so many pieces of velvet, etc., so long, so broad, of the same making, so good, so fine, as were the other. This, says he, is lawful; therefore the other is lawful.

No, his is not lawful. It is not lawful set out your shop: it is usury, it is forbidden. But he that takes the shop shall be a gainer: who shall be the loser then? They that buy the wares must needs buy at the higher price. We may not allow one ill thing by the allowance of another. He should rather say: Usury taken upon wares is not lawful; therefore usury for bare money is less lawful. Jerome upon Ezekiel says, "*Putant quidam usuram tantum esse in pecunia; quod proevidens scriptura divina omni rei aufert superabundantiam, ut plus non accipias quam dedisti*": "Some think there is no usury but in money. This did the holy Scripture foresee, and therefore takes away the increase or gains in any manner of thing, and requires that you receive no more than you delivered."

An occupier waxes old, his occupying is done. He has in stock two hundred pounds: he comes to a young man, wise, of good credit, and of honest dealing, and says: I give thee this money freely: it shall be thine forever, upon this condition, that you give me twenty marks by the year during my lifetime. This may be done. It is no usury. Why? It is a plain gift with a condition. The principal is gone from me forever: I have no right unto it: it is none of mine. If I die tomorrow before I receive any penny, my executors cannot claim anything. But in usury it is otherwise: the usurer requires his whole sum again, and somewhat more for the use and occupying. Therefore the (two hundred pounds) is a gift, and not usury.

Again, I lend my neighbor twenty pounds until a day. He has it freely and friendly without any usury. Yet I say to him: Neighbor, you must needs keep day; for the next day after I must discharge a pain, I stand bound for payment. I have no more but this which you borrow. If I miss, I forfeit five pounds. I pray you be careful for it. The day comes, my neighbor comes not: I lack my money, and, because I lack it, I lose five pounds. He comes afterward and offers me my own money.

Then say I: Neighbor, I have lost five pounds by your negligence and slackness: I hope you will not suffer me to be a loser for my gentleness. This is interest, it is no usury. Here, by the way, you may learn wherefore it is called interest, because he may say, "*Interfuit mea habuisse*," "It behoved me, it stood me upon to have it," and now by your default I sustain loss.

It is good to know the one from the other. This kind of dealing is interest, and not usury.

In usury I seek to be a gainer: in interest I seek only to be no loser: gain or profit I seek none. And hereof I may lawfully seek to be answered: it stands with equity and conscience and good reason. This is interest, and no usury, that a man who requires no gain should seek to save himself harmless.

Bear patiently with me if I be long. My desire is that you should understand this whole matter, and be able to know one thing from another; that so no man may excuse his usury by the name of interest; and others be not offended, nor reckon all men to be usurers which lend forth their money, or anyways dispose of their stock.

A poor orphan left in his cradle has a hundred pounds' stock. This stock may be put out to usury: and the usury is allowed. This is a deed of charity; it is no usury, as shall appear. For, if the hundred pounds should lie still without increase, and be bestowed from year to year to the use of the child, the whole stock would be spent before the child should come to maturity. But if the stock be put to occupying, and into an honest man's hands, something will grow to the relief of the orphan, and yet his stock remain whole. This is charity, to relieve the infant that cannot relieve himself.

The like (case) is in using the stock of a man that has not his wits, and is not able to dispose of his goods. Or if a merchant, by sickness, or disability, or any other hindrance, be not able to follow his business, he desires another to use and occupy for him, and to do with his stock as it were his own, only to maintain him with the increase thereof. This is not usury. Why? Because he that takes the stock of the orphan, or of the madman, or of the diseased merchant, is not bound to answer all adventures (hazards) and casualties that happen. As, if to like use I take a stock in cattle, and they die without my default, or a stock in money or wares, and the wares are burned by fire, or the money stolen without my default, I am not bound to answer for the principal: therefore it is no usury.

But he that takes money to usury, whether he gain or lose, or whatsoever happens to him, he must answer for the whole stock he borrowed. And this is it that is the undoing of many, and makes them bankrupts. But this happens not in this case. He that occupies the orphan's money or stock is charged only to use it as his own, and no otherwise. If it perish or decay or miscarry without his default, he is not bound to answer it. Therefore, as I said, it is no usury.

Yet say they further for defense of usury: It is suffered in other countries; in France, Spain, Italy, Rome, etc. the laws permit it. And what law does suffer it? I believe, not the law of God; for that law straitly forbids it. But what speak I of the law of God? The civil law condemns usury, the canon law condemns it, the temporal law condemns it, and the law of nature condemns it. And how is that sufferable by any law, that by so many laws is condemned? Or how is he worthy to live among men, that despises the authority of so many laws? Or what will you judge of that man that will be tempered and ordered by no law; neither by civil, nor by canon, nor by temporal, nor by law of nature, nor by law of men, nor by law of God? I say not – how may, we think him to be a man of God? – but, how may we think such a one to be a man? For it is the part and duty of a man to be ruled by law and reason.

But (it is argued) usury is everywhere, and therefore to be suffered. Too true, that it is common every where. Would God it were false! It undoeth all the world. So the devil is everywhere, and suffered, so are the brothels suffered in France, Spain, Italy, Lombardy, Naples, Venice, and in Rome. Rome is called the holy city: the most holy has his seat there, and yet suffers the stews in Rome. So were the Canaanites among the people of God, and suffered. But they were as goads in their sides and as thorns in their eyes. As these were suffered, and as the stews are suffered, and as the devil is suffered, so and no otherwise are usurers. Such good, and no better, do they. For they are the children of the devil: their houses be the shops wherein the devil does his work of mischief. They be Canaanites and enemies of God's people. They be goads in our sides and sharp thorns and prickles in our eyes. God grant that the law may espy them, and the people abhor them, and they may repent and loathe their wickedness!

Some other are bold to take authority for usury from Christ himself. He said: "The kingdom of heaven is as a man that, going into a strange country, called his servants, and delivered to them his goods; and unto one he gave five talents, and to another two, and to another one; and said unto them, 'Occupy until I come.' The first did so, the second accordingly. They increased his stock, and are commended for their usury. The third wrapped his talent in a napkin and kept it together. His master returned, and chid him, and said: "Wherefore gavest not thou my money into the bank, that at my coming I might have required it with vantage?" [310] Therefore usury is allowed by the mouth of Christ. The first two are commended, not for any thing else but for the gain they made by usury, the third is rated and rebuked, not for theft nor adultery, but because he laid not out his stock to usury.

What? And is usury allowed? And allowed by the witness of Christ? How can that be? For Christ, as we heard before, does plainly forbid it. How is it then? What is the meaning of this parable? This it is: when Christ delivered his gospel unto his disciples, he gave them charge to be diligent, and to multiply and increase the number of them that should believe. To this purpose he said, be as careful in this business for

---

310 This may be Bishop Jewel's own translation of what amounts to a summation of Luke 19:11-13; 15-22. We have checked New Testament English versions extant in his lifetime [Tyndale (1525); Great Bible (1539); Geneva Bible (1560) and the Bishop's Bible (1568)] and did not find a text exactly as he has quoted it. A literal translation from the Greek reads: "A certain well-born man went into a place afar, to receive for himself a kingdom and to return. And having called ten of his servants he gave to them ten *minas* and said to them, Be engaged in matters until I return...And it came to pass in his returning back, having received the kingdom, that he spoke to the ones to whom he gave the money, that he should know what business each did..." 19:22-23: "...O wicked servant...why did you not give my money unto the money-lenders' table, with interest, and I having come, would have exacted it?" (*The Apostolic Bible Polyglot* [Newport, Oregon: Apostolic Press, 1996]).

the glory of God and the salvation of your brethren, as worldly-wise men show themselves in seeking wicked mammon. Behold the usurers: they occupy their stock, and make it grow, and so of five pounds make ten, and of ten make twenty pounds, and so they become rich. So deal you in the gifts and knowledge that God hath bestowed on you, give them to the exchangers, put them out to usury, increase the Lord's stock. If they be diligent and faithful in the things of this world, how much more ought you to be so in heavenly things! This therefore is the meaning: covetous men and the children of this world be wise in their generation; you are the children of light, be you also wise, and do you so likewise in your office and service as you see them do. So he saith, "Behold the fowls of heaven," "learn how the lilies of the field grow." What of this? The lilies are but grass, the fowls of the air are but birds. The mercy of God in his providence and care, wherein he gives us all things needful, is made plain by example of these, and thereby our distrust and overmuch carefulness reproved. So does Christ speak this parable of the usurer, that, as he is diligent in doing ill, so we should be diligent [311] and ready to do well.

But shall usury therefore be lawful, because Christ draws a comparison or makes an example by a usurer? If it were so, we should do many things otherwise than well. For in the scriptures we are oftentimes required to take example of those things which are ill. In the sixteenth chapter of Luke, Christ bids his disciples take example of the unfaithful steward, to be provident and careful as he was. Does he therefore commend the falsehood of the steward? Shall falsehood therefore be

---

311 Jewel in his original text used the word *painful,* which in his time, in this context, denoted "diligent, assiduous, careful" *(Oxford English Dictionary)*. *Bede's History* (T. Stapleton, 1565): "...in consideration of their virtuous sermons and painful preaching." This usage is now very rare.

lawful? St Paul said, "The day of the Lord shall come in even as a thief in the night." Is theft therefore lawful? St James said, "The devils believe and tremble": take example of the devils. They believe, but their bare, vain, and dead faith, in which they can do no good, cannot serve them. Even so your faith shall not save you, if it be dead and void of all good works.

God himself, to reprove the unthankfulness and forgetfulness of his people, which did so often forsake him and followed Baal and Astaroth, said in this manner unto them: "What nation did ever forsake their gods?" Does he in this speech approve that the idols of the heathen are gods? or, because God takes example of idolatry, shall idolatry therefore be lawful? He bids his servants to be as faithful and willing and ready to serve him, the God of heaven and earth, as the gentiles were in service of their idols, the works of their own hands. As God did will the Israelites to take example of the idolaters, and as Christ bids us take example of the false steward, and as James of the devils; so is this parable an example of that which is commendable, that is, the diligence of the servants. Usury is no more allowed by this than idolatry and falsehood and the devil is by the other.

Some will say, I have no trade to live by. I must give my money to usury, or else I must beg. This is it that I spake of: this shows that despair and mistrust in the providence of God is the mother of usury. If this were cause why he should be a usurer, if this be well spoken for defense of his wickedness; why may not the thief, or the bawd, or the enchanter, by like answer, excuse themselves, and stand in defense of their doings? Augustine therefore said, "*Audent etiam foeneratores dicere, Non habeo aliud unde vivam. Hoc mihi et latro diceret, deprehensus in fauce; hoc et effractor diceret, deprehensus circa parietem alienum; hoc mihi et leno diceret, emens puellas ad prostitutionem; hoc et maleficus incantans mala, et vendens nequitiam suam:*

quid-quid tale prohibere conaremur, responderent omnes, quia non haberent unde viverent, quia inde se pascerent; quasi etc. unde vitam transigant, et inde, etc."

"The usurers are bold to say they have no other trade whereby to live. So will the thief tell me, when I take him in his theft. So will he say that breaks into other men's houses. So will the bawd say that buys young maidens to use them to filthiness. So will the wicked enchanter that sells his sin. If we reprove any of these, they will answer that this is their maintenance, and that they have no any other way to earn a living."

But Augustine stated: "*Quasi non hoc ipsum in illis maxime puniendum est, quia artem nequitiae delegerunt unde viverent, et inde se volunt pascere, unde offendant eum a quo omnes pascuntur*": "As if they were not therefore most worthy to be punished, because they have chosen a trade of wickedness to live by, and will maintain themselves by that thing wherewith they displease Him by whom all are maintained." How much better would it be with them, if they did serve God truly in such place and calling wherein they might most set forth his glory, and do such things as should be profitable to themselves and others!

The servant of God knows there is no want to those that fear Him. He knows the Lord has care over him, and therefore casts his care upon the Lord. He says as the prophet: "The Lord is my shepherd; I shall want nothing." And, "The Lord is the defender of my life; of whom then shall I be afraid? I trusted in thee, 0 Lord, and said, Thou art my God. My times are in thy hand."

Thus much I thought expedient to speak of the loathsome and foul trade of usury. I know not what fruit will grow thereby, and what it will work in your hearts. If it please God, it may do that good that I wish. I have done my duty: I call God for a record unto my soul, I have not deceived you. I have spoken unto you the truth.

If I be deceived in this matter, O God, thou hast deceived me. Thy word is plain. You say, "Thou shalt take no usury": you say, He that takes increase shall not live. What am I, that I should hide the words of my God, or keep them back from the hearing of His people? The learned old fathers have taught us it is no more lawful to take usury of our brother than it is to kill our brother. They that be of God hear this, and consider it, and have a care that they displease him not.

But the wicked, who are not the least moved, and care not what God says, but cast His word behind them; which have eyes, and see not, and ears, yet hear not; because they are filthy, they shall be filthy still. Their greedy desire shall increase to their confusion; and, as their money increases, so shall they increase the heaps of their sins. Pardon me if I have been long or vehement. Of those that are usurers I ask no pardon.

I hear that there are certain in this city, which wallow wretchedly in this filthiness without repentance. I give them warning in the hearing of you all, and in the presence of God, that they forsake that cruel and detestable sin. If otherwise they continue therein, I will open their shame and denounce excommunication against them, and publish their names in this place before you all; that you may know them, and abhor them as the plagues and monsters of the world; that, if they be past all fear of God, they may yet repent and amend for worldly shame.

Tell me, you wretched wight [312] of the world, you unkind creature, who are past all sense and feeling of God, who know the will of God, and do the contrary,

---

[312] A "wight" is supernatural creature — and in the sense intended by Bishop Jewel — of a malignant nature.

how dare you come into the church? It is the church of that God which has said, "Thou shalt take no usury;" and you know He has said it: how dare you read or hear the word of God? It is the word of that God who condemns usury; and you know he condemns it. How dare you come into the company of your brethren? Usury is the plague and destruction and undoing of your brethren; and this you know. How dare you look upon your children? You make the wrath of God fall down from heaven upon them: your iniquity shall be punished in them to the third and fourth generation. This you know.

How dare you look up into heaven? You have no dwelling there: you shall have no place in the tabernacle of the Highest. This you know.

Because you rob the poor, deceive the simple, and eat up the widows' houses; therefore shall your children be naked and beg their bread; therefore shall you and your riches perish together.

But Christ says: "The hour shall come, and now is, when the dead shall hear the voice of the Son of God, and they that hear it shall live." Zacheus was a receiver of tribute, and was rich when he received Jesus to abide in his house: "He stood forth, and said unto the Lord, Behold, Lord, the half of my goods I give to the poor; and if I have taken from any man by forged cavillation,[313] I restore him fourfold. Then Jesus said unto him, This day salvation is come into this house; forasmuch as he also is become the son of Abraham."

God may make His word work in the hearts of usurers, that they may also receive Jesus, and forsake usury, and restore fourfold if they have deceived any, and so may also receive salvation. Let us increase in

---

313 Cavillation: taking advantage of technical flaws, so as to defraud; hence, chicanery, trickery, sophistry (*Oxford English Dictionary*).

that usury which is to the glory of God. He hath given us knowledge and many excellent graces. Let us put them forth, let us occupy that talent which he hath left us. He will return: the day of his coming is at hand. He will require his talents: we must answer them. Let us restore them with increase, that our service may be allowed, and we received into his tabernacle.

13

Timeline of Papal Usury

May 4, 1515

Lateran Council V, Session X

Leo X

Bulla Concilii in decima sessione super materia Montis Pietatis.

It is believed that in 1462 the first *Monte di Pietà* was permitted, at Perugia, that permitted lending money to the poor against pledged property. Unlike

earlier endeavors which had relied exclusively on donations to raise the capital for these "charity bank" loans, the Franciscan founders charged a "moderate" interest rate "to defray administrative expenses." Bitter opposition was aroused, both from Judaic money lenders defending their monopoly, as well as from the Dominicans who held that the Church's strict laws against usury were being contravened. The dispute raged for fifty years and was brought to the Lateran Council V, where Pope Leo X officially promulgated, for the first time in the history of the Roman Catholic Church, the lawfulness of interest-bearing loans, for charitable purposes. He ordered the excommunication of all those who publicly expressed doubts concerning his judgment. From 1515 onward, the interest-bearing, *Monte di Pietà* "charity" banks became a papally-chartered, permanent institution.

Nov. 1, 1745

Encyclical *Vix Pervenit*

Benedict XIV

In *Vix Pervenit* Benedict XIV expanded Leo X's promulgation of the lawfulness of charging interest for philanthropic ends, to include the lawfulness of interest on investment credit capital. While *Vix Pervenit* is often cited, by the semi-literate, as a reaffirmation of the magisterial pre-Renaissance dogma on usury, such claims represent an intellectually lazy failure to note and comprehend the *Vix Pervenit*'s "fine print." After many anti-usury rhetorical flourishes throughout the document, the technique of the devolutionary degradation of God's law through gradualism was deployed with the following subtle papal statement:

"We do not deny that at times together with the loan contract certain other titles — which are not intrinsic to the contract — may run parallel with it. From these other titles, entirely just and legitimate reasons arise to demand something over and above the amount due on the contract."

A modernist Catholic theologian saw the pope's declaration for what it was: "Benedict XIV's encyclical, *Vix Pervenit*, in 1745...refrained from condemning interest received from investments (loans) in productive property...this is good logic and common sense." This theologian stated further concerning papal liberalization of usury law: "If it is right for the stockholder of a railway to receive dividends, it is equally right for the bondholder to receive interest. If it is right for a merchant to take from the gross returns of his business a sum sufficient to cover interest on his capital, it is equally right for the man from whom he has borrowed money for the enterprise to exact interest...*the church was right to adjust slowly to the logic of capitalism...*"

The Catholic capitalist-theologian offering this encomium was the Right Rev. Msgr. John A. Ryan (1869-1945) of the Catholic University of America, a distributist who campaigned against low wages. [314] He differed from other distributists in refusing to hide behind a subterfuge, having the candor to acknowledge the papal gradualism ("slow adjustment") that changed the dogma on the charging of interest. Msgr. Ryan failed however, to make the fundamental connection between the social injustice he witnessed and vigorously protested in early 20th century America, and the prevalence in America of interest on money. In his book *Distributive Justice*, Msgr. Ryan argued that landowners and capitalists had an equal right to take rent and interest, respectively, but that tenants and employees had a stronger right to a decent livelihood and living wage. [315] Here is the all-too-common blindness of a "social justice" economist who will not proceed from first principles. The nation that

---

[314] Gary Dorrien, *Social Ethics in the Making*, p. 198 (emphasis supplied).

[315] Cf. pp. 71-73 and 345-346.

violates the Word of God concerning the taking of interest on money will not have "distributive" or any other kind of justice, or structural reform of the system of oppression, which interest on money *ipso facto* engenders. Modernists deny this core truth. Consequently, whatever remedy they propose in order to heal a diseased commonweal infected with interest on money, whether "Distributism" or any other "ism," is destined to fail.

August 18, 1830

***Resp. Pii VIII ad episc. Rhedonensem datum in audientia* (Denziger-Bannwart, nos. 1609 and 1610).**

Pius VIII

This papal ruling directed the absolution of those Catholics who persist in accepting interest on loans of money at the rate set by the government. This statement by the pope directed both the Holy Office and the Penitentiary (charged with oversight of priests who hear the auricular confessions of Catholics who confess their sins), that the confessor must absolve a lender who intends to continue to accept interest that does not exceed the legal rate of interest of the nation where the confession is being heard. The sum effect of this papal directive was that those who take interest on money according to the rate permitted by law "must not be disturbed."

Subsequent 19th century Holy Office and Penitentiary rulings proceeding from this papal precedent released Catholic usurers from the obligation to confess taking revenue from interest on money at the rate considered legal by the state.

May 19, 1918

1917 Code of Canon Law [316]

Benedict XV

'If a fungible thing is given to another so that it becomes his, and later it must be restored in the same sort, no profit can be made by reason of the contract; but in the loan of a fungible thing, it is not by itself illicit to reap a legal profit, unless it can be shown to be immoderate of itself, and even greater profit (can be made) if there is a just and proportionate title so supporting." [317]

This Code of Canon law was promulgated on Pentecost, May 27, 1917 and for that reason it is titled with that date. However, Pope Benedict XV stipulated that it would not have "force of law" until Pentecost of the following year (May 19, 1918). It is sometimes referred to as the "Pio-Benedictine" Code because it was inaugurated, and its

---

[316] *"Codex Iuris Canonici, Pii X Pontificis Maximi iussu digestus, Benedicti Papae XV auctoritate promulgatus* (Typis Polyglottis Vaticanis, 1917)."

[317] *1917 Pio-Benedictine Code of Law*, p. 516. Emphasis supplied.

compilation was initially directed, by Pope St. Pius ("Pio") X, who did not live to see its completion. [318]

No pontiff following Leo X in 1515 has proclaimed or promulgated any document or ruling to impede the heretical allowances for the mortal sin of usury of their predecessors even when, under certain circumstances, interest on money became no longer a sin after 1830, and even after interest on money, under certain circumstances, was promulgated by canonical right in 1917. There has either been, on the part of the other popes from the Renaissance onward, silent acquiescence and toleration, or active collusion, though the latter is almost always accompanied by flowery avowals of economic justice in the most minute details, and eloquently worded appeals for an end to the oppression of workers and the excesses of capitalism. In that sense, *all the popes* since the sixteenth century pontificate of Leo X have been popes of usury.

The two papal statements in the modern era preceding the Second Vatican Council which are most often proudly cited by Roman Catholics as supporting lofty Christian social justice principles, Leo XIII's *Rerum Novarum* and Pius XI's *Quadragesimo Anno,* offer nothing that addresses the mortal sin of interest, except to evade the responsibility to teach the truth that was always taught, before the *il fumo di Satana* (smoke of Satan) entered the Church. [319]

---

[318] The actual work on the 1917 Code was conducted principally by Cardinal Pietro Gasparri (1852-1934). We have not seen records of correspondence or discussions by Pius X or Benedict XV with Gasparri concerning canon 1543. Assuming these records exist in the Vatican archives, or of the late cardinal, an analysis of the papal thinking behind canon 1543 would be of considerable value in the history of the development of the legalization of usury by the Church of Rome in the 20th century.

[319] *"Da qualche fessura sia entrato il fumo di Satana nel tempio di Dio."* –Pope Paul VI, elocution of June 29, 1972; an extraordinary and unprecedented revelation.

Rather, they supported the system of interest on money with ambiguous rhetoric and circumlocution. Leo XIII, *Rerum Novarum,* May 15, 1891: "God has left the limits of private possessions to be fixed by the industry of men and institutions of peoples."

While usury raged during the Great Depression and the people of the world who respected the Catholic Church turned to the pope for restoration of the ancient Christian truths, and an end to the plague of usury, they received from Pius XI, on May 15, 1931, the following:

"Those who are engaged in producing goods, therefore, are not forbidden to increase their fortune in a just and lawful manner; for it is only fair that he who renders service to the community and makes it richer should also, through the increased wealth of the community, be made richer himself according to his position, provided that all these things be sought with due respect for the laws of God and without impairing the rights of others and that they be employed in accordance with faith and right reason. If these principles are observed by everyone, everywhere, and always, not only the production and acquisition of goods but also the use of wealth, which now is seen to be so often contrary to right order, will be brought back soon within the bounds of equity and just distribution."

The preceding vague permission for riches procured with "faith, right reason, the laws of God, the rights of others..." substitutes for a simple reaffirmation of the formula of the eternal dogma that for five centuries has cried out to be professed anew from the Chair of Peter. Something like the following proposed formula, *if* issued by the pope *ex cathedra,* would strike a devastating blow to the Money Power: We declare that all interest on loans of money without exception constitute a grave transgression against the eternal Law of God, for which the penalty is eternal punishment after death. All who teach or insinuate to the faithful that the charging of interest on loans of money is moral and not sinful, are heretics.

It has been nearly 500 years since Leo X's promulgation of his modernizing bull on interest, and in that passage of time not one pope can be said to have found it in his conscience to publicly affirm *and enable* in substance, anything approaching the preceding model formula.[320] Whatever their other merits, these popes have all heretically permitted the Church's gradual adjustment to the "logic" of the damning sin of usury-based capitalism. Those who speak of the heresy of modernism within the papacy ought to turn their clocks back 500 years, to its inception point.

Mortal Sin Mandated by the 1983 Code

The 1983 Code of Canon Law promulgated by John Paul II, which is still in force as of this writing, *commands* the commission of mortal sin. Canon 1294: "Stocks, bonds, certificates of deposit or money involved in prudent loans may belong to a juridic person as part of its stable patrimony, if they belong to special funds or endowments." Canon 1305: "...goods are to be invested cautiously and profitably..."[321]

"According to the 1983 Code of Canon Law, it is even required of church administrators that they invest for profit funds not needed to pay expenses."[322]

---

320 An affirmation alone, is not sufficient. The Council of Trent issued a dogmatic affirmation but it was not implemented, except for a few token instances that amounted almost to a charade. See p. 388.

321 James A. Cordiden, ed., *The Code of Canon Law* (1985), pp. 883; 887.

322 *Modern Catholic Encyclopedia* (Liturgical Press, 1994) p. 884.

14

The Dogma of the Council of Trent

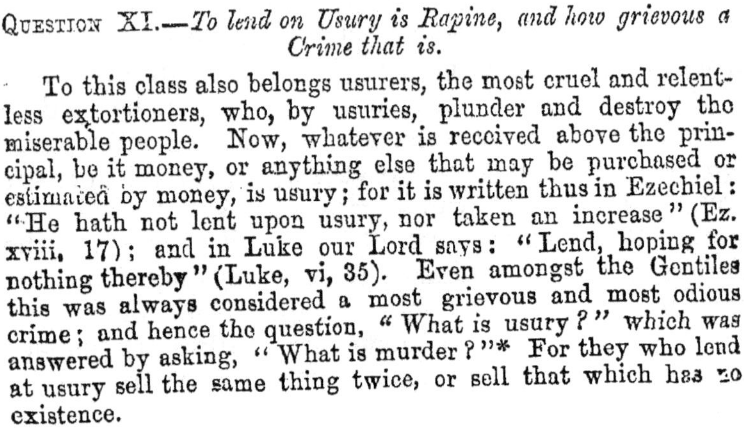
Question XI.—*To lend on Usury is Rapine, and how grievous a Crime that is.*

To this class also belongs usurers, the most cruel and relentless extortioners, who, by usuries, plunder and destroy the miserable people. Now, whatever is received above the principal, be it money, or anything else that may be purchased or estimated by money, is usury; for it is written thus in Ezechiel: "He hath not lent upon usury, nor taken an increase" (Ez. xviii, 17); and in Luke our Lord says: "Lend, hoping for nothing thereby" (Luke, vi, 35). Even amongst the Gentiles this was always considered a most grievous and most odious crime; and hence the question, "What is usury?" which was answered by asking, "What is murder?"* For they who lend at usury sell the same thing twice, or sell that which has no existence.

Photographically reproduced from *The Catechism of the Council of Trent Translated into English.* [323]

This reaffirmation of the divine truth should have served as the final judgment on usury of the Roman Catholic Church. In almost every other respect, all that was promulgated at the Council of Trent (1545-1563) was regarded as definitive, fixed dogma. Alas, the divine teaching on usury declared at Trent was subject to practical evasion in several ways, some devious and others blatant. The blatant case is the interest-bearing *monte pietatis* banks: they were not interdicted or overturned after the Council of Trent. The devious cases involve the numerous ingenious devices used by Catholic banks in Europe for the concealment of interest on money. These were not

---

323 Trans. Jeremiah Donovan (Dublin: J. Duffy & Co., 1910); Part III, "Of the Precepts of God Contained in the Decalogue," Chapter VIII, "Thou shalt not steal," pp. 383-384.

noticeably interdicted or disturbed in the wake of the Council. These devices, in addition to the *montes*, included: the *depositum confessatum*, and the *discrezione* on time deposits, among many other sophistries. If we judge by Our Lord's criterion, "By their fruits ye shall know them," the anathema against usury as declared by the Council of Trent was theatrical, intended mainly for dramatic effect in the Counter-Reformation's ideological war, as a means for branding Protestants as usurers, and Catholics as God's loyal campaigners against usury. If Trent's declaration on usury had been something more than a ploy to gain propaganda advantage, Catholic usury would have been fought tooth and nail in its wake. Nothing like that transpired, except where local Catholic authorities took the declaration on usury at face value and attempted to proceed against usurers.[324] The development of the theology of Catholic usury at the command levels of the hierarchy, was not impeded by the Council of Trent. After Trent, interest on money grew in latitude and acceptance, as the authoritative *Moral Theology* of Rev. Dr. Heribert Jone, O.F.M. Cap., J.C.D., which was printed eighteen times in separate German and English editions, demonstrates.[325] "Traditional Catholic" publisher Thomas Nelson reprinted *Moral Theology* in 1993, and

---

[324] This was mostly at the parish level. The exception was France at the diocesan level, under the Gallican Bishop Bossuet (1627-1704). He published a treatise claiming that the Church had never deviated from the ancient stand against usury. To prove his point, he proceeded against usurers in his diocese, aided in part by the unique character of seventeenth century French aristocratic culture, which was adverse toward commercial enterprise.

[325] Westminster, Maryland: The Newman Press, 1962.

wrote in his preface: "May this book circulate far and wide and do all the good it is capable of doing. Especially, may priests everywhere once more consult it in their pastoral work, digest its contents and come to revere and love the divinely inspired morality of the Catholic faith, as yet one more gem of evidence pointing to the divine origin of our holy religion."

From *Moral Theology*: "For extrinsic reasons, however, which nowadays are always verified, in case money is lent, a just rate of interest may be charged. In general one may be guided by the rate of interest established either by law or custom" (p. 195).

Dante's linkage of usury and sodomy is confirmed when we learn that the *Moral Theology* manual's permission for interest on loans of money is matched by its permission for sodomizing one's Catholic wife: "...it is neither sodomy nor a grave sin if intercourse is begun in a rectal manner with the intention of consummating it naturally, or if some sodomitical action is posited without danger of pollution..." (p. 539).

Christians must clean house and demand that the unassailable, non-negotiable, unchanging, unerring Magisterial dogma on usury, which was declared again at Trent, be restored, and the rogue theories of the popes of usury, which have enabled the modernist-mutation of Christian morals, be reversed.

It may be that Divine Providence ensured that the declaration on usury was included as part of the Council of Trent, so that in the coming struggle to restore all things in Christ, there could be no argument over how usury is defined: "*whatever is received above the principal*;" and what type of mortal sin it constitutes: "*a most grievous and odious crime*."

15

Glossary of Terms

***Commenda* contract**: A form of medieval Roman Catholic free enterprise that arose in the 10th century "to pool capital and to bring together investors and managers." It entailed an ethical and moral non-usurious business partnership based on shares in an enterprise.

Damnum emergens: A financial loss incurred by the creditor during the time his money was loaned out, rather than being put into some other investment. As a result of *damnum emergens* it was theorized that the lender was "entitled" to be paid interest. This could be legitimate, viz. when a simple loan without usury went unpaid and the debtor owed the creditor the amount loaned; or it could become a loophole-exception to the moral law against usury from which permission for charging interest on money was derived. John Duns Scotus and Thomas Aquinas opposed *damnum emergens* exceptions, ruling that the lender should have foreseen the consequences of making the loan. See *interesse*.

Fenerari: usury; to charge interest on a loan.

Fenerator: a usurer

Fenus: (also: *faenus*; *foenus sortis*): interest paid on a loan. Derived from the word fetus, in the sense that interest produces offspring, is *quaedam faetura pecunia parturientis* (the brood of increase); the "embyron" of riches.

Florin: a gold coin.

Foenus foeneris: compound interest.

Fructus: income from property; from the root word "fruits."

Fixed value of fungibles: a bushel of corn is always worth a bushel of corn, not two bushels of corn. A fungible is never worth more than itself. In contracting for more than the principal lent, the creditor subverts intrinsic value.

Fungibles (artificial): paper money; digital representations on a computer screen.

Fungibles (natural): grain, wine, oil, gold and silver.

Imprestitum: compulsory loan to the city-state of Venice (Italy) by a citizen thereof.

Interesse: (Medieval Latin; cf. Matthew Paris): "Refers to the compensation which, under Roman law, was due by the debtor who had made default" (*Oxford English Dictionary*). This compensation was more than the recovery of the actual amount owed, since another factor was considered in estimating the damages accruing from the default on a loan: the loss experienced by the lender in not having his money returned in the time allotted and agreed to beforehand. Usury advocates were keen to expand the concept of *interesse* – compensation for failing to repay the principal on a loan – into a condonation of interest, through the concept of *lucrum cessans.*

Interest: Money paid for the use of money lent. Usury.

Lombard: a peripatetic banker-usurer of any Christian nationality; though originally a reference to a native of Lombardy in northern Italy.

Lucrum cessans: (Lost potential); the loss of a profit which a lender might otherwise have gained from his money if he had not loaned it to a debtor. Under *lucrum cessans* a charge for a loan of money was justified as "damages," on the basis that the creditor had reserved his money for the debtor instead of putting it into some other investment; the precedent cited was *interesse*.

An example of the condonation of interest created by twisting the meaning of *interesse* as applied to *lucrum cessans,* was furnished by the canon lawyer Hostiensis: "...if some merchant, who is accustomed to pursue trade and the commerce of the fairs and there profit much, has, out of charity to me, who needs it badly, lent money with which he would have done business, I remain obliged from this to his *interesse*, provided that nothing is done in fraud of usury...and provided that said merchant will not have been accustomed to give his money in such a way to usury." [326]

---

[326] Joel Kaye, *Economy and Nature in the Fourteenth Century*, p. 84.

This is a redefinition of the ancient understanding of "*interesse*," which had always been defined strictly as a penalty on the debtor for non-payment of the principal. The lawyers used *lucrum cessans* to gradually develop a theory which would evolve to the point where the lender is "entitled" to a payment from the borrower, in addition to the principal, on the far-fetched notion, that the extra payment was not interest, but compensation to the lender for making a loan when he might otherwise have invested his funds in a business enterprise of another, more lucrative sort.

In the fifteenth and sixteenth century usury toleration and legalization did not simply sprout from nowhere. Even in the Middle Ages crafty lawyers were sowing antecedents like *lucrum cessans* which came to be embraced in future, degenerate ages, as one of the exceptions out of which charging interest on money would was justified. The sophistry of calling interest on a loan "compensation" for having made a loan, was detected by the vigilant Pope Innocent IV, and a host of theologians and canonists including Gregory of Rimini and Johannes Calderinus, who rejected the *lucrum cessans* arguments, terming them a "highway to usury." St. Thomas Aquinas "denied the lender's right to demand compensation for *possible* lost profit, since doing so involved selling what had only been *probable*, rather than real existence. He wrote, 'one should not sell something which one has not yet got and which one may be prevented in many ways from getting." [327]

Medium of exchange: Without usury, money can only serve its natural function, as a medium of exchange; never as an end – rented or sold in itself. As a medium, money has no separate value except for its use to facilitate exchange. The usurer who charges for the use of money is selling something that has no existence apart from the exchange.

Monte* or *Montes: The word *mons*, even in ancient Latin, was used to signify a great quantity, or heap with reference to money, while the juridic term for a monetary fund was *massa*. Long before the creation of the *monte di pieta* ("mountain of compassion" according to the *Oxford Encyclopedia of Economic History,* volume 4, pp. 1-2), the word *mons* (in Italian *monte*) was used to designate collected funds destined to various ends. Thus the "public debt" of the city-state of Venice was called *Mons* or *Imprestita*, and

---

[327] Ibid., 85-86.

similar *montes* were created by Genoa and Florence. Stock companies were called *montes* and the same was true of the banks of exchange or credit that were in the hands of the so-called Lombards. As these banks often lent money on objects delivered to them in pawn, the charitable institutions which were created for transactions of that class also took the name of *mons*. The term *pietatis* was added to advertise the claim that these establishments were beneficent and not speculative. [328]

Mutuum: A simple loan of a fungible such as money (capital) which the debtor repays as the exact sum loaned.

Prestanza: A compulsory loan made to the government of the city-state of Florence (Italy) by a citizen thereof. Citizens were paid interest on these loans. Ridolfi: "When the commune of Florence needs money it imposes on its citizens obligations that are commonly called *prestanze*." In this case, not much of a semantic evasion was employed: the interest-bearing loans were justified by Satan's oldest shibboleth, "from necessity." Florentines such as Guido de Belloreguardo, Prior-General of the Augustinian order in 1371, protested the rationalization and insisted that citizens could not be forced to partake of the sin of usury by means of the *prestanza*.

Usury (medieval Latin: *usuria*): The practice of lending money at interest.

---

328 The legend that Saint Anthony of Padua founded a *mons pietatis* has no basis in fact. Medieval Catholic institutions had loaned money to the poor without interest, under various names including *monte pietatis*. These early associations were funded by generous Catholic philanthropists, and are not be confused with the later and more numerous by far, usurious Renaissance *monte pietatis* institutions.

16

Bibliography

Addis, William E., and Arnold, Thomas, *The Catholic Dictionary* (1896).

Alonso-Lasheras, Diego, *Luis de Molina's De Iustitia et iure* (Brill, 2011).

Andrewes, Lancelot, *Concerning Usuries: a Theological Computation made in the Public Theological School of Cambridge* (London: Felix Kyngston, 1629).

Anyanwu, Akannamdi Gerard Stephen, *The Christological Anthropology in St. Hilary of Poitiers' Tractates on the Psalms*. (Rome: Ponficia Studiorum Universitas Salesiana, 1983).

Aristotle, *The Politics of Aristotle*, trans. Ernest Baker (Oxford: Clarendon Press, 1948).

Armstrong, Lawrin David, "Review of Eric Kerridge 'Usury, Interest and the Reformation," in *Journal of Early Modern History* (2004), no. 8.

Armstrong, Lawrin David, *Usury and Public Debt in Early Renaissance Florence* (Pontifical Institute of Mediaeval Studies, 2003).

Aquinas, Thomas, *The Summa Theologica of St. Thomas Aquinas*, trans. Fathers of the English Dominican Province (Christian Classics, 1981).

Ayres, Clarence Edwin, *The Theory of Economic Progress: A Study of the Fundamentals of Economic Development and Cultural Change* (North Carolina University Press, 1955).

Azpilcueta, Martin, "Commentary on the Resolution of Money," in *Sourcebook in Late-Scholastic Monetary Theory* (Lexington Books, 2007).

Bacon, Francis, "Of Usury," *The Essays or Councils, Civil and Moral, of Francis Bacon* (London, 1625).

Bagehot, Walter, *Lombard Street: A Description of the Money Market* (New York: Scribner's, 1873).

Bainton, Roland H., *Here I Stand: A Life of Martin Luther* (New York: 1950).

Baldwin, John W., *The Medieval Theories of the Just Price: Romanists, Canonists and Theologians in the Twelfth and Thirteenth Centuries* (American Philosophical Society, 1959).

Barlow, Frank, *Edward the Confessor* (University of California Press, 1984).

Barnes, Albert, *Barnes' Notes on the New Testament* (Grand Rapids: Kregel Publications, 1962).

Barnum, Priscilla Heath, *Dives and Pauper* (Oxford University Press, 2004), vol. II.

Barty-King, Hugh, *The Worst Poverty: A History of Debt and Debtors* (Alan Sutton, 1991).

Basri, Rabbi Ezra, *Ethics of Business and Finance and Charity According to Jewish Law*, (Haktav Institute, 1987), vol. 1.

Basil, St., and Schroeder, C. Paul., *On Social Justice*. (St. Vladimir's Seminary Press, 2009).

Baxter, Richard, *Christian Directory* (London, 1838), v. 1.

Beldo, Francisco, "*Etica de la creacíon de creditos según la doctrina de Molina, Lesio y Lugo*" in *Pensamiento*, no. 19, (Society of Jesus Espana, 1963).

Biéler, Andre, *La pensée économique et sociale de Calvin* (Geneva, Switzerland: Librairie de l'université, 1959).

Belloc, Hilaire, *Charles I, King of England* (J.B. Lippincott, 1933).

Bellenger, Dominic Aidan, and Fletcher, Stella, *Princes of the Church: A History of the English Cardinals* (Gloucertshire, UK: Sutton, 2001).

Bellitto, Christopher M., *The General Councils: A History of the Twenty-One Church Councils* (Paulist Press, 2002).

Benedict XIV, Pope, V*ix Pervenit* (Rome, 1745).

Benedict XV, Pope, *The 1917 or Pio-Benedictine Code of Canon Law,* Edward N. Peters, trans. (Ignatius Press, 2001).

Bériou, Nicole, and Chiffoleau, Jacques, *Economie et religion: L'expérience des ordres mendiants* (Lyon, 2009).

Berry, Jason, *Render Under Rome: The Secret Life of Money in the Catholic Church* (New York: Crown Publishing Group, 2011).

Berry, Wendell, *Citizenship Papers* (Washington, D.C.: Shoemaker & Hoard, 2003).

Berry, Wendell *The Art of the Commonplace: The Agrarian Essays,* (Counterpoint, 2003).

Blackstone, Sir William, *Commentaries on the Laws of England: Book the Second* (Clarendon Press, 1775).

Blaxton, John, *The English Usurer, Or, Usury Condemned* (London, 1634).

Bolles, John Augustus, *Treatise on Usury and Usury Laws* (Boston: 1837).

Bolton, Robert, *A Short and Private Discourse* (1637).

Bossuet, Jacques-Benigne, "*Traité sur l'Usure*" in *Works* (Versailles, 1817), v. 30.

Bradley, James E., *Religion, Revolution and English Radicalism* (Cambridge University, 2002).

Bremer, Francis J., *John Winthrop: America's Forgotten Founding Father (Oxford University Press, 2003).*

Brendler, G., *Martin Luther: Theology and Revolution* (New York, 1991).

Brett, R. Dallas, *Usury in Britain* (London: St. Botolph Publishing, 1946).

Bromyard, John, *Summa praedicantium*, two volumes (Venice, 1586).

Brown, Raymond, *The Anchor Bible Commentary: The Gospel According to John I-XII* (Doubleday, 1966).

Buckland, W.W., *A Text-Book of Roman Law from Augustus to Justinian* (Cambridge University Press, 1963).

Burn, Richard (translator), *Ecclesiastical Law in Four Volumes* (London: A. Strahan, 1797).

Burns, Jennifer, *Goddess of the Market: Ayn Rand and the American Right* (Oxford University, 2011).

Caesar, Philip ("Philippus"), *A General Discourse Against the Damnable Sect of Usurers* (London, 1578).

Caesarius of Heisterbach, *The Dialogue on Miracles*, trans. H. von E. Scott and C. Swinton Bland, two volumes (London: Routledge, 1929).

Calvin, John, *Calvin's Ecclesiastical Advice,* trans. Mary Beaty and Benjamin W. Farley (Westminster, 1991).

Carandé, Ramon, *Carlos V y sus banqueros* (Barcelona, 2000).

Carleton, William, *The Black Prophet* (London, 1847).

Carreró, Rafael, *Carlos V y uno de sus banqueros: Jacob Fugger* (Madrid, 1993).

Chambers, Whittaker, "Big Sister is Watching You," *National Review,* December 28, 1957.

Chesteron, G.K., "The Problem of Zionism" in *The New Jerusalem* (London: Thomas Nelson, 1920).

Cheyette, Bryan, *Between Race and Culture* (Stanford University, 1996).

Cipolla, Carlo M., *The Monetary Policy of Fourteenth Century Florence* (University of California, 1982).

Clark, G. N., *The Wealth of England from 1496 to 1760* (London: Oxford University, 1946).

Cookson, William, *A Guide to the Cantos of Ezra Pound* (New York: Persea Books, 1985).

Coquillette, D., "The Mystery of the New Fashioned Goldsmiths: From Usury to the Bank of England (1622-1694)," in *The Growth of the Bank as Institution and the Development of Money-Business Law* (Berlin: Comparative Studies in Continental and Anglo-Saxon Legal History, 1993), vol. 12.

Coriden, James A., ed., *The Code of Canon Law* (Canon Law Society of America, 1985).

Cotton, John, "John Cotton on Usury," *William and Mary Quarterly*, 3rd series 47 (1990) p. 548-565.

Coughlin, Rev. Fr. Charles E., *Money! Questions and Answers* (Royal Oak, Michigan: National Union for Social Justice, 1936).

Crompton, Louis, *Homosexuality and Civilization* (Harvard University, 2003).

Cunningham, William, *The Growth of English Industry and Commerce in Modern Times* (Cambridge University Press, 1892).

Cyprian, St., and Etienne Baluze, *Sancti Caecilii Cypriani Episcopi Carthaginensis Et Martyris: Opera Ad Mss. Codices Recognita & Illustrata Studio Ac Labore Stephani Baluzii Tutelensis* (Venetiis: Apud Antonium Groppum & Granciscum Pitterium, in Via Marcatoria Sub Signo Fortunae Generoase).

Dante Alighieri, *The Comedy of Dante Alighieri The Florentine: Cantica I, Hell,* trans. Dorothy L. Sayers (Penguin Books, 1959).

Dante Alighieri, *The Divine Comedy of Dante Alighieri, Volume 1: Inferno*, trans. Robert M. Durling (Oxford University Press, 1996).

Davanzati, Bernardo, *A Discourse Upon Coins* (London, 1696).

Debby, Nirit Ben-Aryeh, *Renaissance Florence in the Rhetoric of Two Popular Preachers* (Turnhout, Belgium: Brepols Publishing, 2001).

Dempsey, Bernard W., *Interest and Usury* (Washington, D.C: American Council on Public Affairs, 1943).

DeRoover, Raymond, "Scholastic Economics: Survival and Lasting Influence from the Sixteenth Century to Adam Smith," in Julius Kirshner, *Business, Banking, and Economic Thought in Late Medieval and Early Modern Europe* (University of Chicago Press, 1974).

DeRoover, Raymond, *The Rise and Decline of the Medici Bank* (W.W. Norton, 1966).

Desai, Meghnad, "Money and Usury in the Economics of Ezra Pound" in *Money and Markets: A Doctrinal Approach* (Routledge, 2007).

De Soto, Jesús Huerto, *Money, Bank Credit and Economic Cycles* (Mises Institute, 2009).

De Vitry, Jacques, *The exempla or illustrative stories from the sermones vulgares of Jacques de Vitry*, ed. Thomas Frederick Crane (London: Folklore Society, 1890).

Dew, Thomas Roderick, *Essay on the Interest of Money and the Policy of Law Against Usury* (Virginia, 1834).

Divine, Thomas F. *Interest: An Historical & Analytical Study in Economics & Modern Ethics* (Milwaukee: Marquette University Press, 1959).

Donovan, Jeremiah, *Catechism of the Council of Trent Translated into English* (Dublin: James Duffy, 1910).

Doob, Leonard W., *Ezra Pound Speaking: Radio Speeches of World War II* (Greenwood Press, 1978).

Dorrien, Gary, *Social Ethics in the Making* (John Wiley, 2009).

Douglas, C.H., *Social Credit* (New York: W.W. Norton & Co. 1933).

Downame, George, *Lectures on the XV Psalme Read in the Cathedral Church of S. Paule, in London : Wherein besides Many Other Very Profitable and Necessarie Matters, the Question of Usurie Is Plainly and Fully Decided* (London: Adam Islip for Cuthbert Burbie, 1604).

Edelman, Charles, "Which is the Jew that Shakespeare Knew?" *Shakespeare Survey 52: Shakespeare and the Globe* (Cambridge University Press, 2003).

Edwards, John, *Theologia Reformata* (London, 1713); two volumes.

Elton, Geoffrey R. and Pettegree, Andrew, *Reformation Europe 1517-1559* (Wiley-Blackwell, 1999).

Farrow, Thomas. *The Money-lender Unmasked* (London: Roxburghe, 1895).

Fanfani, Amintore, *Catholicism, Protestantism and Capitalism* (Sheed and Ward, 1935).

Fenton, Roger. *A Treatise of Usurie Divided into Three Bookes: The First Defineth What Is Usurie. The Second Determineth That to Be Unlawfull. The Third Removeth Such Motives as Persuade Men in This Age That It May Be Lawfull* (London, 1612).

Fenton, Roger, and Filmer, Robert, *The Usury Debate in the Seventeenth Century: Three Arguments* (Arno Press, 1972).

Ferguson, Niall, *The Ascent of Money: A Financial History of the World* (London, 2008).

Finkelstein, Andrea, *The Grammar of Profit: The Price Revolution in Intellectual Context* (Brill, 2006).

Franks, Christopher A., *He Became Poor: The Poverty of Christ and Aquinas's Economic Teachings* (Erdmans, 2009).

Gelpi, Rosa-Maria, and Julien-Labruyére, Francois, *The History of Consumer Credit* (St. Martin's Press, 2000).

Gerard of Sienna, *Tractatus de usuris et de praescriptionibus* (Cesena, 1630).

Glaeser, Edward, "Neither a Borrower nor a Lender Be: An Economic Analysis of Interest Restrictions and Usury Laws," *Journal of Law and Economics* (1998), 41:1.

Glare, P.G.W., *Oxford Latin Dictionary* (Oxford University Press, 2006).

Glazier, Michael, ed., *The Modern Catholic Encyclopedia* (Liturgical Press, 1994).

Grady, Hugh, "Timon of Athens: The Dialectic of Usury, Nihilism and Art," *A Companion to Shakespeare's Works* (Blackwell, 2005), v. 1.

Grabill, Stephen J., *Sourcebook in Late Scholastic Monetary Theory* (Plymouth, England: Lexington Books, 2007).

Graeber, David. *Debt: The First 5,000 Years*. (Brooklyn, New York: Melville House, 2011).

Gratian, Johannes, *Concordia Discordantium Canonum* (*"Decretals,"* ca. 1140).

Gregory of Nyssa and Friedrich Dübner, *Homélie Contre Les Usuriers* (Paris: Lecoffre, 1885).

Greenhill, William, *An Exposition of Ezekiel*, 2nd ed. (Edinburgh, Scotland: James Nichol, 1863).

Grice-Hutchinson, Marjorie, *The School of Salamanca: Readings in Spanish Monetary Theory, 1544-1605* (Clarendon Press, 1952).

Häberlein, Mark, *The Fuggers of Augsburg: Pursuing Wealth and Honor in Renaissance Germany* (University of Virginia Press, 2012).

Harris, Jonathan Gil, *Sick Economies* (University of Pennsylvania, 2004).

Hayek, F.A., "English Monetary Policy and the Bullion Debate," in *The Collected Works* (University of Chicago Press, 1989), v. 3.

Heimert, Allan, ed., *The Puritans in America: A Narrative Anthology* (Harvard University Press, 1985).

Heller, Anne C., *Ayn Rand and the World She Made* (Doubleday, 2009).

Helmholz, Richard H., "Usury and the Medieval Church Courts," in *Speculum*, no. 61 (1986).

Herbermann, Charles George (ed.), *The Catholic Encyclopedia: An International Work of Reference on the Constitution, Doctrine, Discipline, and History of the Catholic Church* (New York: The Encyclopedia Press, 1913), volume x.

Heywood, William, *The "ensamples" of Fra Filippo: A study of mediaeval Siena* (Siena, Italy: Enrico Torrini, 1901).

Hickman, Miranda B., *One Must Not Go Altogether With the Tide: The Letters of Ezra Pound and Stanley Nott* (McGill-Queen's University Press, 2011).

Holmer, Joan Ozark, "Miles Mosse's The Arraignment and Conviction of Usurie (1595): A New Source for the Merchant of Venice," *Shakespeare Studies* 21: 11-54 (1993).

Holzapfel, P. Heribert 0. F. M., *Die Anfänge der Montes Pietatis* (Munich, 1903).

Homer, Sidney, *A History of Interest Rates* (Rutgers University Press, 1963).

Hugo von Trimberg, *Der Renner von Hugo von Trimberg*, ed. Gunther Schweikle, (Berlin: de Gruyter, 1970-1971).

Ingram, Jill Phillips, *Idioms of Self-Interest: Credit, Identity and Property in English Renaissance Literature* (Routledge, 2006).

Jacobs, Joseph, *The Jews of Angevin England: Documents and Records* (London, 1893).

Jarrett, Bede, *Social Theories in the Middle Ages* (Routledge, 1968).

Johnson, E.A.J., *American Economic Thought in the Seventeenth Century* (Russell and Russell, 1961).

Jone, Heribert, *Moral Theology,* Urban Adelman, trans., (Westminster, Maryland: The Newman Press, 1962).

Jones, Norman, *God and the Moneylenders* (Basil Blackwell, 1989).

Jonsen, Albert R., and Toulmin, Stephen, *The Abuse of Casuistry: A History of Moral Reasoning* (University of California Press, 1988).

Kaplan, M. Lindsay (ed.), *The Merchant of Venice: Texts and Contexts* (Bedford/St. Martin's, 2002).

Kastan, David Scott, *King Henry IV Part 1 (Arden Shakespeare: Third Series, Part 1,* London, 2002).

Kaye, Joel, *Economy and Nature in the Fourteenth Century* (Cambridge University Press, 1998).

Kearns, George, *Ezra Pound, the Cantos* (Cambridge Univ. Press, 1989).

Keller, Joseph Anton, *Anecdotes proving the miraculous power of St. Anthony* (New York: Benziger, 1899.)

Kenner, Hugh, *The Pound Era* (University of California, 1971).

Kermode, Lloyd Edward, *Three Renaissance Usury Plays (*Manchester University Press, 2009)

Kirshner, Julius, "From Usury to Public Finance," *Studies in Mediaeval and Renaissance History* 9 (1972).

Kirshner, Julius, "Reading Bernardino's Sermon on the Public Debt," in *Atti del Simposio internazionale Cateriniano-Bernardiniano* (Siena: Accademia Senese degli Intronati, 1982).

Knox, Thomas R. "Thomas Spence: The Trumpet Of Jubilee," (*Past and Present* 76:1, 1977).

Kuran, Timur, *Islam and Mammon* (Princeton University Press, 2004).

Langholm, O. I., *Economics in the Medieval Schools* (E.J. Brill, 1992).

Lansing, Richard, *The Dante Encyclopedia* (Routledge, 2000).

Le Bras. G., "La doctrine ecclesiastique de l'usure á l'epoque classique" in *Dictionnaire de théologie catholique*, 15, 2 (1950).

Lecky, William Edward Hartpole, *History of the Rise and Influence of the Spirit of Rationalism in Europe* (London: Longmans, Green, 1887-1890), two volumes.

Lefévre, Georges, *Le Traité 'De Usura,' de Robert de Courcon* (l'Université de Lille, 1902).

Le Goff, Jacques, "The Usurer and Purgatory" in *The Dawn of Modern Banking* (Yale University Press, 1979).

Le Goff, Jacques, *Money and the Middle Ages* (Polity Press, 2012).

Leo X, Pope, *Bulla concilii in decima sessione super materia Montis Pietatis* (Rome, 1515).

Lever, Thomas, *Sermons 1550*, Edward Arber, ed. (Westminster: Constable, 1901).

Levillain, Philippe. *The Papacy: An Encyclopedia* (New York: Routledge, 2002).

Levine, Hillel, *Economic Origins of Antisemitism* (Yale University Press, 1991).

Liebermann, F. *Über Die Leges Edwardi Confessoris.* (Halle A.S., M. Niemeyer, 1896).

Lipton, Sara, *Images of Intolerance: The Representation of Jews and Judaism in the Bible Moralisée* (University of California, 1999).

Little, Lester K., *Religious Poverty and the Profit Economy in Medieval Europe* (Cornell University Press, 1983).

Lohse, Bernhard, *Martin Luther's Theology in Historical and Systematic Development* (Fortress Press, 1999).

Lopez, Robert Sabatino, *Medieval Trade in the Mediterranean World* (Columbia University Press, 2001).

Lortz, Joseph, *The Reformation in Germany* (New York: Herder and Herder, 1968), two volumes.

Lowrie, Ernest Benson, *The Shape of the Puritan Mind: The Thought of Samuel Willard* (Yale University, 1974).

Luther, Martin, "Trade and Usury," in *Luther's Works*, (Muhlenberg Press, 1962), vol. 45.

Malynes, Gerard, *Saint George for England, Allegorically Described* (London, 1601).

Marino, John A., and Kuehn, Thomas, *A Renaissance of Conflicts* (Toronto: Centre for Renaissance and Reformation Studies, 2004).

Mark, Jeffrey, *The Modern Idolatry: Being an Analysis of Usury and the Pathology of Debt* (London: Chatto & Windus, 1934).

Marsh, Alec. *Money and Modernity: Pound, Williams, and the Spirit of Jefferso*n (Tuscaloosa: University of Alabama, 1998).

Maurin, Peter, *Easy Essays* (Wipf & Stock, 2010).

McLaughlin, T.P., "The Teaching of the Canonists on Usury," *Mediaeval Studies*, vol. 2. no. 2 (Pontifical Institute of Mediaeval Studies, 1940).

McNabb, Vincent, *Francis Thompson and Other Essays* (Pepler & Sewell: Saint Dominic's Press, 1935).

McNabb, Vincent, *Old Principles and the New Order* (Sheed and Ward, 1942).

McNabb, Vincent, *The Church and the Land* (Norfolk, Virginia: IHS Press, 2003).

Menning, Carol B., *Charity and State in Late Renaissance Italy* (Cornell University Press, 1993).

Michell, John, *Eccentric Lives and Peculiar Notions* (San Diego: Harcourt Brace Jovanovich, 1984).

Mielants, Eric H., *The Origins of Capitalism and the Rise of the West* (Temple University Press, 2007).

Mill, John Stuart, *Principles of Political Economy with some of their Applications to Social Philosophy* (London: Longmans, Green and Co., 1909).

Miller, Perry, and Johnson, Thomas H., *The Puritans*, vol. 1 (Harper and Row, 1963).

Milton, J.R., "John Locke and the Nominalist Tradition" in *John Locke* (New York: Walter de Gruyter, 1981).

Milward, Peter, *Shakespeare the Papist* (Sapientia Press, 2005).

Molina, Luis, "Treatise on Money," in *Sourcebook in Late-Scholastic Monetary Theory* (Lexington Books, 2007).

Mollat, Michel, *The Poor in the Middle Ages*, trans. Arthur Goldhammer (Yale University Press, 1986).

Montanari, Geminiano, *La moneta in Scrittori classica italiani di economia politica* (Milan, 1804), v. 3.

Moon, Parker Thomas, *The Labor Problem and the Social Catholic Movement in France* (New York: Macmillan, 1921).

Mooney, S. C., *Usury, Destroyer of Nations* (Warsaw, Ohio: Theopolis, 1988).

Mormando, Franco, *The Preacher's Demons: Bernardino of Siena and the The Social Underworld of Early Renaissance Italy* (University of Chicago Press, 1999).

Moser, Thomas, *The Canon in the History of Economics* (Routledge, 2000).

Mueller, Reinhold, *Money and Banking in Medieval and Renaissance Venice, vol. 2: The Venetian Money Market, Banks, Panics and the Public Debt, 1200-1500* (John Hopkins University Press, 1997).

Munro, John, "Usury, Calvinism and Credit in Protestant England," in *Religione e istituzioni nell'economia europea: 1000-1800* (Firenze University Press, 2012).

Murray, James, *Sermons to Asses*. (London: Printed for J. Johnson; T. Cadell and W. Charnley, at Newcastle, 1768).

Nashe, Thomas, *Christ's Tears Over Jerusalem* (London: James Roberts, 1593).

Nelson, Benjamin N., *The Idea of Usury* (Princeton University Press, 1949).

New Catholic Encyclopedia (Catholic University of America, 1967).

Newhauser, Richard, *The Early History of Greed: The Sin of Avarice in Early Medieval Thought and Literature* (Cambridge University Press, 2000).

NIV Holy Bible: New International Version (Zondervan, 1984).

Noonan, John T. Jr., "Development in Moral Doctrine," in *The Context of Casuistry* (Georgetown University, 1995).

Noonan, John T. Jr., *The Scholastic Analysis of Usury* (Harvard University Press, 1957).

North, Gary, *An Introduction to Christian Economics* (Nutley, N.J., Craig, 1973).

Oberman, Heiko, *Masters of the Reformation: The Emergence of a New Intellectual Climate in Europe* (Cambridge University Press, 1991).

O'Brien, George *An Essay on Mediaeval Economic Teaching* (Longmans, Green, 1920.)

O'Callaghan, Jeremiah, and Coppinger, W., *Usury, Funds, and Banks* (Burlington, 1834).

O'Flaherty, Liam, *The House of Gold* (London: Cape, 1929).

Owst, G.R., *Literature and Pulpit in Medieval England* (Basil Blackwell, 1966).

Ozment, Steven, *The Serpent and the Lamb* (Yale University, 2011).

Palgrave, R.H.I., *Dictionary of Political Economy* (London: MacMillan, 1915).

Parks, Tim, *Medici Money: Banking, Metaphysics, and Art in Fifteenth-Century Florence* (W.W. Norton, 2005).

Partee, Charles, *The Theology of John Calvin* (Westminster John Knox Press, 2008).

Paulin, Michael, and J. R. Greene, *The Ballad of Daniel Shays* (Athol, Mass: Transcript, 1986).

Pearson, John B., *On the Theories on Usury Adopted or Enforced by the Ecclesiastical and Secular Authorities in Europe During the Period 1100-1400 A.D.* (Cambridge: Deighton, Bell and Co., 1876).

Pellicani, Luciano, *The Genesis of Capitalism and the Origins of Modernity* (Telos Press, 1994).

Penty, Arthur, J., *The Gauntlet: A Challenge to the Myth of Progress* (IHS Press, 2003).

Perkins, John, *Confessions of an Economic Hit Man* (San Francisco: Berrett-Koehler Publishers, 2004).

Peters, Edward N., ed., *The 1917 Pio-Benedictine Code of Canon Law* (San Francisco: Ignatius Press, 2001).

Pirckheimer, Willibald, and Cotta, Joannes Franciscus Lembergius, *Eccius Dedolatus; a Reformation Satire* (Lexington: University of Kentucky, 1971).

Pius VIII, Pope, *Resp. Pii VIII ad episc. Rhedonensem datum in audientia,*(Denziger-Bannwart, 1830), no. 1609 and no. 1610.

Pius X, Pope, and Benedict XV, Pope, *Codex Iuris Canonici* (P.J. Kennedy and Sons, 1918).

Pound, Ezra, *The Cantos Of Ezra Pound* (New Directions, 1996).

Pound, Ezra, and Borah William, *The Correspondence of Ezra Pound and Senator William Borah,* ed. Sarah C. Holmes (University of Illinois, 2001).

Porder, Richard, *A Sermon of God's Feareful Threatnings for Idolatrye, Mixing of Religion, Retayning of Idolatrous Remnaunts, and Other Wickednesse: With a Treatise Against Usurie* (Henry Denham, 1570).

Pullan, Brian, *Rich and Poor in Renaissance Venice: The Social Institution of a Catholic State* (Oxford, 1971).

Prien, Hans-Jürgen, *Luther's Wirtschaftsethik* (Göttingen: 1992).

Prynne, William, *A Breviate of the Life of William Laud, Archbishop of Canterbury* (London, 1644).

Prynne, William, *A Short Demurrer to the Jews Long Discontinued Remitter into England* (London, 1656).

Prynne, William, *The Sovereign Power of Parliaments and Kingdoms* (London: Michael Sparke, 1643).

Rand, Ayn. *Atlas Shrugged* (Random House, 1957).

Rand, Ayn, *Capitalism: The Unknown Ideal* (Signet, 1967).

Rand, Ayn, *The Virtue of Selfishness* (Signet, 1964).

Rand, Howard B., *Digest of the Divine Law* (Destiny Publishers, 1982).

Rao, John, *Black Legends and the Light of the World* (Forest Lake, Minnesota: Remnant Press, 2011).

Raw, Charles. *The Moneychangers: How the Vatican Bank Enabled Roberto Calvi to Steal 250 Million for the Heads of the P2 Masonic Lodge* (London: Harvill, 1992).

Richards, R.D., *The Early History of Banking in England* (London, 1929).

Ritter, Gerhard, *Luther: His Life and Work* (New York: Harper and Row, 1963).

Roberts, Phyllis Barzillay, *Studies in the Sermons of Stephen Langton* (1968).

Rocke Michael, *Forbidden Friendships: Homosexuality and Male Culture in Florence* (Oxford University Press, 1996).

Rothbard, Murray N., *Economic Thought Before Adam Smith: An Austrian Perspective in the History of Economic Thought* (Edward Elgar, 1995).

Rushdoony, Rousas John, and North, Gary, *The Institutes of Biblical Law* (Presbyterian and Reformed Publications), 1973.

Ruskin, John, *Bibliotheca Patorum: Vol I, The Economist of Xenophon* (London, 1876).

Ruskin, John, *The Works of John Ruskin: Volume II, Munera Pulveris (*George Allen, 1880).

Ruskin, John, *Unto this Last and Other Writings* (Penguin Books, 1997).

Ruud, Jay, *Critical Companion to Dante: A Literary Reference to His Life and Work* (Facts on File 2008) .

Ryan, Franklin W., *Usury and Usury Laws* (Houghton Mifflin, 1924).

Ryan, John A., *Distributive Justice* (New York: Macmillan, 1916).

Ryan, John A., *Economic Justice* (Westminster John Knox Press, 1996).

Reyerson, Kathryn, *Business, Banking and Finance in Medieval Montpellier* (Pontifical Institute of Mediaeval Studies, 1985).

Salmon, George, *The Infallibility of the Church* (London: John Murray, 1914).

Schlecht, Joseph, "Dr. Johann Eck's Anfänge," in *Historisches Jahrbuch der Görresgesellschaft* 36 (1915).

Schneid, J., "Dr. Johann Eck und das kirchliche Zinsverbot in *Historischpolitische Blätter für das katholische Deutschland,* 108 (1891).

Scrivener, Michael, *Seditious Allegories* (Pennsylvania State University, 2001).

Searls, Paul, *Two Vermonts,* (University of New Hampshire Press, 2006).

Smith, Henry, *Examination of Usury in two sermons* (1591).

Soddy, Frederick, *Money versus Man* (E.P. Dutton, 1933).

Soddy, Frederick, *Wealth, Virtual Wealth and Debt: The Solution of the Economic Paradox* (George Allen & Unwin, 1926).

Sombart, Werner, *Die Juden und das Wirtschaftsleben* (Leipzig: Duncker & Humblot, 1911).

Somerville, Henry, *Studies in the Catholic Social Movement* (London: Burns Oates & Washbourne, 1933).

Speltz, George H., *The Importance of Rural Life According the Philosophy of St. Thomas Aquinas* (Wipf and Stock, 2003).

Spuford, P., *Money and Its Use in Medieval Europe* (Cambridge University Press, 1989).

Storck, Thomas, "Is Usury Still a Sin"?, *Communio: International Catholic Review* (no. 36, Fall 2009).

Strauss, Gerald, *Manifestations of Discontent in Germany on the Eve of the Reformation* (Indiana University Press, 1971).

Stubbes, Philip, *Anatomy of Abuses* (London, 1583).

Summenhart, Conrad, and Jakob Wimpheling, *Conradi Summenhart Commentaria in Summam Physice Alberti Magni, in Conradum Summenhardum Theologum Secularem Alberti Magni Interpretem Exasthycon Jacobi Wymphelingi* (Hagenau: Henricus Gran, 1507).

Swabey, Rev. Henry S., "The Church of England and Usury," Ezra Pound Collection, Harry Ransom Humanities Research Center, University of Texas at Austin.

Tawney, R.H., *Religion and the Rise of Capitalism* (New York: Mentor, 1954).

Terrell, Carroll F., *A Companion to The Cantos of Ezra Pound* (University of California Press, 1993).

Tertullian, *Adversus Marcionem* (Oxford: Clarendon, 1972).

Turner, Roger. *The Usurers Plea Answered in a Sermon Preached at Southampton* (London: Robert Bostocke, 1634).

Valeri, Mark, *Heavenly Merchandize: How Religion Shaped Commerce in Puritan America* (Princeton University Press, 2010).

Van de Wiel, Constant, *History of Canon Law* (Louvain: Peeters Press, 1991).

Van der Kemp, Johannes, *The Christian Entirely the Property of Christ in Life and Death: Exhibited in Fifty-Three Sermons on the Heidelbergh Catechism* (New Brunswick, N.J., 1810).

Van Dyken, Seymour, *Samuel Willard* (Eerdmans, 1972).

Von Mises, Ludwig, *Human Action: A Treatise on Economics* (Irvington-on-Hudson: Foundation for Economic Education, 1996).

Von Mises, Ludwig, *Socialism: An Economic and Sociological Analysis* (New Haven: Yale University Press, 1951).

Wadsworth, Benjamin, *The Saint's Prayer to Escape Temptations* (1715).

Weber, Max, *The Protestant Ethic and the Spirit of Capitalism* (New York: Scribner, 1930).

White, Andrew Dickson, *A History of the Warfare of Science with Theology in Christendom* (London: MacMillan, 1896).

Willan, Philip. *The Last Supper: The Mafia, the Masons and the Killing of Roberto Calvi*. (London: Robinson, 2007).

Willard, Samuel, *A Compleat Body of Divinity in Two Hundred and Fifty Expository Lectures on the Assembly's Shorter Catechism* (Boston, 1726).

Willison, John. *An Example of Plain Catechising upon the Assembly's Shorter Catechism (*Edinburgh: Thomas Lumisden and John Robertson, 1737).

Winroth, Anders, *The Making of Gratian's Decretum* (Cambridge University Press, 2007).

Wither, George. *Abuses Stript, and Whipt (*London: Francis Burton, 1613).

Wood, Diana, *Medieval Economic Thought* (Cambridge University Press, 2002).

Woodcock, Catherine Mary Antony, *Saint Anthony of Padua The Miracle Worker* (Longmans, Green, 1911).

Wood, Neal, *Foundations of Political Economy: Some Early Tudor Views on State and Society* (University of California Press, 1994).

Woods, Thomas E. Jr., *The Church and the Market: A Catholic Defense of a Free Economy* (Lexington Books, 2005).

Wright, Robert E., *Hamilton Unbound: Finance and the Creation of the American Republic* (Greenwood Press, 2002).

Zucker, L. M., and Ambrose, Saint, *De Tobia.* (Washington D.C: Catholic University of America, 1933).

CPSIA information can be obtained
at www.ICGtesting.com
Printed in the USA
[illegible]SHW010341060121
[illegible]ES
9 780970 378491